*The American
Immigration Collection*

Norwegian Migration to America 1825-1860

THEODORE C. BLEGEN

Arno Press and The New York Times

NEW YORK 1969

NORWEGIAN MIGRATION
TO AMERICA
1825-1860

NORWEGIAN MIGRATION
TO AMERICA

1825-1860

BY

THEODORE C. BLEGEN

*Associate Professor of History in the University of Minnesota
and Assistant Superintendent of the Minnesota Historical Society*

Northfield, Minnesota
The Norwegian-American Historical Association
1931

PREFACE

SINCE the days of Puritan and Cavalier, children of the Old World have thronged to the shores of the New seeking well-being and happiness. As nation-builders they have been focal points for the interplay of two creative forces in our national life — the European heritage and the American environment.

Among environmental influences the westward-moving frontier, which marked the advance of the army of settlers, has attracted the particular attention of historians. The transit of people and of culture from Europe to America, however, is still to a considerable extent unexploited as an historical theme. Perhaps preoccupation with the current problems involved has delayed the objective study of immigration as a constant factor in our history; possibly the coming of the Europeans has seemed prosaic compared with the transcontinental march.

That the two movements are interrelated even the casual observer is aware. We must turn to fiction, however, rather than to history, for an adequate treatment of the interrelations between them; and it is worth noting that the power of such a novel as *Giants in the Earth* lies not so much in its portrayal of the external scene as in its understanding of the psychological realities underlying the struggle of the immigrants to subdue the prairie that stretched away toward the western rim.

Many of the possibilities of American immigration as a field for historical research have been recognized by scholars. Historians, plowing and cultivating it, are aware of its extent and are alive to the fact that much work remains to be done. The advance of its cultivation is evidenced in a yearly product of special studies; and the

challenge of the task of collecting and editing pertinent
documents is being met with vigor. The importance of
the subject for an understanding of some of the realities
of civilization in America seems to be recognized; and research in it is integrated with a significant trend in our
historiography, that of exploring cultural backgrounds
and writing the history of American life.

This book deals with one portion of the field of nineteenth century immigration to the New World. It traces
the history of the migration of Norwegians to America
from 1825, when the movement was inaugurated by the
coming of a little sloop bearing the first load of immigrants from Norway in the nineteenth century, down to
the eve of the American Civil War. In dealing with this
germinal period in the development of a great movement,
I have not permitted myself to forget that the emigrant
and the immigrant were one person, notwithstanding the
fact that he pressed forward on the highway to transition. This book is written from the point of view that
European backgrounds, the transit of people from one
country to another, and the processes of adjustment of
the individual to his new surroundings are parts of one
story, international in scope and rooted deeply in the social,
economic, and political life of the modern world. A
chapter in the history of Europe merges with one in the
making of America. In exploiting this view I have drawn
upon widely scattered materials both in the United States
and in Norway.

Much attention is devoted to backgrounds. In this
connection it may be noted that a little understood but
very important aspect of American immigration is that of
its repercussions in Europe. While the emigrants were
drawn westward by the magnet of cheap land, a steady
current of ideas and influences washed back upon the Old

World.   As one runs through newspapers and books published in Norway after 1825 and pores over hundreds of
immigrant letters, one senses the fact that a potent influence was defining and enlarging the concepts that Norwegians entertained of America.   In the light of the
sources I have tried to present a picture of this influence
at work.   The process seems to me to have been in the
nature of a new discovery of America, a discovery that
was brought home to the consciousness of the humblest
farmer and of the commonest laborer.

How thoroughly America gripped the consciousness of
the people of Norway is, I think, illustrated by several
types of material used in the preparation of this book,
perhaps especially the emigrant ballads and songs, to which
I devote a separate chapter.   These novel sources also help
one to understand something of the pervasive human
interest and deep human significance that the story of
the migration of Europeans to America possesses.   And
the immigrant letters, " America letters," as they were
called everywhere in Norway, make one's understanding
of the human side of the story more intimate.   They are
" documents that betray the spirit, hopes, and aspirations
of the humble folk who tilled the soil, felled the forest,
and tended the loom."   Such personal records swing wide
the door to the realization that immigrants are people, not
lines in a graph or figures in a table.

I hope to bring out later a book carrying the history of
Norwegian migration to America forward from 1860 to
1924, and I am reserving for that volume a general account of the emigrant traffic and of the conditions of the
emigrant's journey, together with the related topic of
American-Norwegian trade relations.   The Civil War
period and the great exodus that followed it, the movement at high tide, and the spread of Norwegian settle-

ment in the United States and Canada are among other themes to which space will be devoted. In dealing with the later aspects of the subject attention will be given to the movement for the restriction of emigration and for inner colonization in Norway, and certain significant cultural movements and forces among the Norwegians in the United States will be discussed. A general bibliography of printed and manuscript materials will be included.

A fellowship from the John Simon Guggenheim Foundation of New York, which permitted me to spend the year 1928–29 in Norway studying the movement at its source, made possible the special emphasis in the present volume upon the European aspects of the migration. Sir Karl Knudsen of London provided a fund with which to meet the expenses of transcribing or photostating records found in Norway and thus facilitated the making of a large collection of documentary material. In order to forward the publication of the book by the Norwegian-American Historical Association a generous friend of that organization donated the sum of two thousand dollars. To the John Simon Guggenheim Foundation, to Sir Karl, and to the anonymous donor I desire to give my cordial thanks.

Thanks are due also to officials of the University library at Olso for their unfailing courtesy in making available for my use that institution's rich resources of newspapers, pamphlets, and other printed materials; and to officials of the *Riksarkiv,* or Royal Archives, of the *Historiografisk Samling,* and of the *Statsarkiv,* or State Archives, and of various other local depositories in Norway for invaluable help in the search for sources.[1] I am under obligation

---

[1] In footnote references to materials found in the *Riksarkiv,* I have employed the arbitrary symbol R. A., Oslo, and in referring to the *Statsarkiv* I have used the symbol S. A., followed by the name of the city of their location.

to Mr. Arne Kildal, Professor Oscar Albert Johnsen, and Professor Oluf Kolsrud for many courtesies during my stay in Oslo. I wish also to acknowledge the friendly interest that Mr. Laurits Swenson, then the United States minister to Norway, took in my work. Miss Rachel Syrrist of the staff of the Oslo university library served as my assistant in the work of making transcripts of hundreds of newspaper items and other sources. I am grateful to Mr. Andreas Bryne of Stavanger for his kindnesses to me when I explored the rich treasures of manuscript materials in the possession of the Society of Friends in that charming old city of southwestern Norway. One of the cherished rewards of a scholar is the good will that he meets in his wanderings and delvings, and I must confess that I have pleasant recollections of aid freely given to me on both sides of the Atlantic in libraries, archives, and other institutions by individuals too numerous to be mentioned here by name. This book had its inception in a dissertation presented at the University of Minnesota in 1925 for the degree of doctor of philosophy and I desire to record here my deep appreciation of the encouragement and counsel received from my former teacher and adviser, now my colleague, Dr. Solon J. Buck. In general I have retained the plan of the dissertation, but I have rewritten the volume in the light of my researches abroad and I have added some six or seven new chapters.

Many writers have delved in the Norwegian-American field since the late sixties, when Svein Nilssen, a genuine pioneer of culture, journeyed about the Norwegian communities of the Middle West interviewing settlers and recording their accounts of immigration and of pioneering. All students in the field are under obligation to that indefatigable collector, who possessed a keen sense of the value of primary historical material. I have attempted to make a first-hand examination of primary sources found on both sides of the Atlantic. The task necessarily involved a patient search for and sifting of materials and it has naturally brought to light considerable material that has not hitherto been used. The cultivation of the field by Nilssen and more recent writers, however, has made this primary investigation much more fruitful than it otherwise could have been. My specific indebtedness to others I have taken pains to make clear in the annotations accompanying the text of this account, but I desire here to mention especially my sense of obligation to Professor Rasmus B. Anderson and Dr. George T. Flom for the valuable pioneering work they have done in the field of Norwegian immigration. New points of view and useful suggestions have come to me as a result of the studies made by my colleague, Dr. George M. Stephenson, in the field of American immigration. I am grateful to Professor O. E. Rölvaag for the interest with which he has followed my studies. Mr. Lyder L. Unstad kindly read a portion of chapter 15 and suggested a number of changes that I subsequently made. Mrs. Elizabeth H. Buck and Miss Bertha L. Heilbron read the manuscript of the book and gave me the benefit of detailed criticisms, and Mrs. Buck and Miss Gladys Heimes aided me in seeing the book through the press. In the making of the index I have had the aid of Miss Heilbron and of Mrs. Helen Katz.

In some of the chapters I have drawn freely upon articles or introductions to documents that I have contributed to the *Mississippi Valley Historical Review*, *Minnesota History*, the *Wisconsin Magazine of History*, and *Nordmands-forbundet*, and to certain publications of the Norwegian-American Historical Association and of *Det Norske Videnskaps-Akademi* in Oslo. For permission to do this I am grateful to the editors of the periodicals and to the organizations mentioned.

If my obligations to my wife, Clara Woodward Blegen, are acknowledged last, it is only because they are the deepest of all, since in large tasks and small, from the beginning to the end of the project, she has helped me.

THEODORE C. BLEGEN

UNIVERSITY OF MINNESOTA
    MINNEAPOLIS

CONTENTS

ILLUSTRATIONS AND MAPS

NORWEGIAN MIGRATION
TO AMERICA
1825-1860

I. INTRODUCTION

HE who would understand the vast outpouring of emigrants from Norway to the United States in the nineteenth century must ever bear in mind the fact that tales of a boundless expanse of inexpensive, fertile land in the American West captivated the imaginations of people whose livelihood was won in the face of a nature both stern and niggardly. "It is by dogged, persistent, indomitable toil and endurance, backed up in some cases by irrepressible daring," wrote William Archer in 1885, "that the Norwegian peasant and fisher-folk — three-fourths of the population — carry on with any show of success their struggle against iron nature." [1] The scenery of Norway delights the eye of the traveler and the sombre beauty of its mountains, fjords, and valleys has inspired many makers of music and writers of poetry; but to the humble husbandman confronted with the task of winning a livelihood, the land, save perhaps in the broadest valleys of the south and the southeast, has been a stern taskmaster. "Nature is no spendthrift in any part of the Scandinavian peninsula; small economies are the alphabet of her teaching and her lessons once learned are rarely forgotten," writes Dr. Kendric C. Babcock. "Her children of the North, therefore, down to the stolidest laborer, mountaineer, and fisherman, are generally industrious and frugal, and when they migrate to the American West, to enter upon the work of pioneering, with its stern requirements of endurance, patience, persistent endeavor, and thrift, they start out in the new life with decided temperamental advantages over most other immigrants, and even over most native-born Americans." [2]

[1] "Norway Today," in *Fortnightly Review*, 44: 415 (September, 1885).
[2] *The Scandinavian Element in the United States*, 17 (University of Illinois,

1

From its southern part, which has a width of two hundred and sixty miles, Norway sprawls irregularly eleven hundred miles to the north. Its full western shore line, traced in all the intricate windings of fjords and bays, has a length nearly equal to half the distance around the globe. On the east a stretch of plateau intervenes between the Norwegians and their neighbors. " The general conformation of the Scandinavian peninsula," writes Beckett, " may be compared with a gigantic wave of rock flowing in from the east and breaking into the ocean on the west. This great plateau is intersected by those lengthy indentations of the coast — the fjords — literally sea-flooded valleys, forming the distinctive characteristic of coast scenery, and constituting one of the most interesting and beautiful land formations on the earth. To the east and south the plateau is cut by long and wide valleys with less steep sides than the chasm-like fissures on the west side." [3]

Three-fourths of all the land in Norway can not be cultivated, and of the remaining one-fourth by far the greater portion is forested. In fact, not more than from three to four per cent of all the land comprised within the total area of 124,495 square miles is tillable, and even of this the larger part is meadow land.[4] Not a few

Studies in the Social Sciences, vol. 3, no. 3, Urbana, 1914). Andreas Ueland, a Norwegian immigrant, contends that the native American's two hundred years of experience in America, coupled with the initial language handicap of the Scandinavian, gave the American a decided advantage over the latter " as to fitness for the new country." *Recollections of an Immigrant*, 47–49 (New York, 1929).

[3] Samuel J. Beckett, *The Fjords and Folk of Norway*, 2 (London, 1915). A. M. Hansen discusses the geographical situation and topography of the country in *Norway: Official Publication for the Paris Exhibition 1900*, 1–34 (Kristiania, 1900). A monumental work dealing with the various *amter* is Amund Helland, *Norges Land og Folk Topografisk-statistisk Beskrevet*, in many volumes; and a very useful geography is Hans Reusch, *Norges Geografi*: I. *Naturen og Folket* (Kristiania, 1915) and II. *Bygder og Byer* (Kristiania, 1917). Each section of this work contains bibliographical suggestions and there is a more general bibliography, 1: 193–195.

[4] See G. Tandberg's chapter on " Agriculture," in *Norway: Official Publication*, 307. Bare mountains comprise 59.2 per cent of Norway's land area; woodland,

of the Norwegians who concerned themselves with the emigration question about the middle of the nineteenth century argued that the solution of the farmer's problem was not emigration but agricultural education and reform.

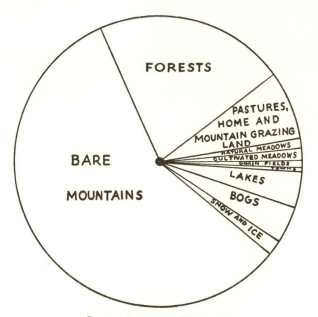

LAND AREAS IN NORWAY

There was a substantial element of truth in the contention, but the fact can not be gainsaid that fertile land, available for agricultural production, was scarce in Norway — and the fact was of greater consequence in the earlier nineteenth century than after the rise of industrialism had made less difficult the support of an increasing population. One must not ignore the shortcomings in the European situation, but it must be emphasized that Norwegian farmers were constantly being lured away by the almost Utopian magnificence of the wide-stretching lands

forests, etc., 21.0; pastures, etc., 7.6; natural meadows, 1.0; cultivated meadows, 1.2; grain fields, 0.7; towns, 0.1; lakes, 3.8; bogs, 3.7; snow and ice, 1.6.

to the west. Some writers on emigration lay great stress upon the gulf that existed between the pictures of America that were formed in the minds of prospective emigrants and the grim experience that so often fell to the lot of the pioneer settler in the West. Various forces unquestionably contributed to the creation of unduly high expectations on the part of many emigrants, but the fact must not be overlooked that the American public domain, with its broad acres, was a reality. The land was there, open, fertile, cheap, inviting — a magnet drawing both native Americans and immigrants westward with irresistible force.

Restricted though the Norwegian agricultural lands were, the overwhelming majority of the people derived their livelihood from them in the earlier part of the century. The town population in 1801 comprised only 86,000 in a total of 883,440. In 1865 two-thirds of the population gained their living from agriculture, cattle-raising, and lumbering. The leading cereal crop raised by Norwegian farmers about the middle of the nineteenth century was oats, with barley and mangcorn — the latter a mixture of barley and oats — next. Wheat was grown, but only on a very small scale. A considerable acreage was devoted to potatoes, though a marked decline in potato raising occurred after 1850.[5] In Norway, as elsewhere, the nineteenth century witnessed great economic changes, and it is not surprising to learn that the percentage of the population engaged in agriculture and allied pursuits was reduced from 66.6 in 1865 to 58.7 in 1875 and to 48.65 in 1891. Meanwhile the portion of the total population engaged in industries and mining increased from 15.4 per cent in 1865 to 19.39 per cent in 1876 and to 23.04 per cent in 1891. Contrary to popular impressions the portion of the population working in fisheries has been com-

[5] O. J. Broch, *Kongeriget Norge og det Norske Folk*, appendix, p. 37 (Kristiania, 1876).

paratively small: 5.1 per cent in 1865; 5.46 per cent in 1876; and 8.58 per cent in 1891. Trade, transportation, and navigation have engaged a somewhat larger proportion: 9.6 per cent in 1865; 13.63 per cent in 1876; and 15.37 per cent in 1891. The element of the population in the professions and "intellectual work" was 3.3 per cent in 1865 and 4.36 per cent in 1891.[6]

A convenient point at which to examine the rural population groupings is the year 1845.[7] The total population was then 1,328,471. There were 77,780 independent land holders, most of them presumably family heads. These freeholders made up the *bonde* element — perhaps the most powerful and influential element in the population of nineteenth- and twentieth-century Norway. The designation of peasants as applied to this class is misleading. Norway never had a feudal system, and the *bønder* had behind them ancient traditions not only of independence but also of vigorous self-assertion.[8] These freeholders in fact constituted a rural aristocracy, which through centuries had been the very heart of the national culture. They were proud of their traditions, but their position carried with it no necessary implication of wealth. In truth, the economic position of the *bønder* has been difficult. Many, pressed to the wall by adverse conditions, have sold their ancient farms and emigrated to America. And in many other cases younger sons, barred by the practical workings of the odel system of land tenure from having a share in the ancestral estates, have sought their fortunes in the West. One result of the odel system has been the holding of estates through many generations by one line in direct descent. It is not uncommon in the

---

[6] *Bidrag til en norsk Befolkningsstatistik*, 109–113 (Det Statistiske Centralbureau, *Norges Officielle Statistik*, new series, C. no. 1).

[7] *Bidrag til en norsk Befolkningsstatistik*, 102 ff.

[8] A scholarly study of the *bønder* is Oscar Albert Johnsen, *Norges Bønder: Utsyn over den Norske Bondestands Historie* (Kristiania, 1919). On the old culture of the *bønder* see K. Visted, *Vor Gamle Bondekultur* (Kristiania, 1908).

Norwegian valleys to find farms that have remained in
the possession of one family, handed down from father
to son, generation after generation, since the fifteenth or
sixteenth century. Some understanding of the feeling
about land ownership bred by such traditions may be
had by noting the view of a Norwegian immigrant who
explains that all the sons in his father's family, though
only a few of them became farmers, insisted upon owning farm lands in America, " largely for reasons of sentiment, in harmony with the old conception of land
ownership." The essence of this conception was that
" land possessed a certain dignity and worth, aside from
its purely commercial value. It was the pride of the old
chieftains; it insured economic well-being and personal
independence; it gave stability and permanence to the
family in whose possession it remained from century to
century." [9]   It is not to be wondered at that the
bondestand made itself a power in the affairs of modern
Norway. After the establishment of constitutional
government in that country in 1814, the *bønder,* becoming increasingly class-conscious, entered upon a protracted
but successful contest with the privileged official class
and the clergy for leadership in the state. The " rural
population," as Hardy says, " survived centuries of foreign domination, until in the nineteenth century it came
once more into its own as the heart and kernel of Norwegian democracy." [10]   Various aspects and implications
of the battle of the *bønder* are considered in later chapters
of the present work; it remains to be noted here that
from the *bondestand* have come a large number of the
political leaders, writers, poets, musicians, and professional
men of modern Norway; and that the same class has

[9] Knut Gjerset, " A Norwegian-American Landnamsman: Ole S. Gjerset," in
Studies and Records, 3: 94 (Norwegian-American Historical Association, Northfield,
Minnesota, 1928).

[10] G. Gathorne Hardy, *Norway,* 241 (New York, 1925).

contributed liberally, in various fields, to leadership among the Norwegians transplanted to America.

The rural population of Norway in 1845 included, in addition to the *bønder,* 58,049 *husmænd,* 25,047 renters, 47,000 laborers, and 146,000 servants. The *husmænd* and laborers, mainly family heads, have been estimated to represent elements of respectively 300,000 and 230,000 people.[11] Most interesting of these classes from the point of view of emigration were the *husmænd,* or cotters. These people, most of whom were to be found in the eastern parts of Norway, ordinarily leased small pieces of land to work for themselves, and were required, usually under written contracts, to give a specified amount of service to their landlords, the *bønder.* Small lots of land, with cottages and other buildings, usually some distance behind the central buildings of the *gaard,* were reserved for the use of *husmænd.* It is clear that heavy demands were made upon the cotters. In 1850 they were asking that their required services be restricted to five days a week and the working day to eleven hours. One writer states that practically the only free time the *husmænd* had for work on their own plots of ground was on Sundays. The value of services beyond the stipulated arrangements might be placed as high as twelve pennies a day in summer, less than half that in winter. Professor Koht writes that the *husmænd* were personally free — that is, they were not bound to the soil — but that in effect they were economic serfs. "It was only on rare occasions," he continues, "that any of them were able to win their way out of poverty."[12] Hardy characterizes the *husmand* historically as the liberated thrall.[13] Both

---

[11] Halvdan Koht, *Marcus Thrane,* 1; Jacob Friis, *Marcus Thrane,* 10. Both of these works were published at Oslo in 1917.

[12] Koht, *Thrane,* 2; Friis, *Thrane,* 12. The best study of the *husmand* system is S. Skappel, *Om Husmandsvæsenet i Norge: Dets Oprindelse og Utvikling* (Kristiania, 1922).

[13] *Norway,* 250.

politically and socially the class was on a lower plane than that of the *bonde*. It lacked the suffrage, since its members could not meet the property qualification. The *husmænd* were on the increase in the period when the emigration movement was rising, an increase that went from 48,571 in 1825 to 65,060 in 1855, the latter being the highest point in the history of the class. In a later chapter the movement for reform with reference to the cotters and its connections with emigration are considered in some detail. Poverty coupled with stern demands upon the time and service of the cotters tended in many cases to embitter their attitude toward the *bønder*, whose relationship to the lesser class had had a patriarchal flavor in an earlier day.[14]

A considerable number of pensioners, who had surrendered their property to their heirs upon condition of receiving annual allowances and living quarters, are represented in the population of 1845 — 46,512 of them.[15] The dower house, it may be added, is a familiar feature in the usual cluster of buildings at the center of a Norwegian *gaard*. Samuel Laing in his journal from the thirties prints a translation of an advertisement in a Christiania newspaper offering a Norwegian *gaard* for sale at a price of four thousand dollars. This presents some interesting concrete detail concerning buildings, equipment, and other aspects of a typical *gaard*: [16]

---

[14] Johnsen, *Norges Bønder*, 382. The figures given for 1825 and 1865 represent the *husmænd* alone; they do not take families into account. An interesting Norwegian-American novel by Hans Foss, *Husmands-Gutten: En Fortælling fra Sigdal* (The Cotter's Boy: A Tale from Sigdal), pictures the social gulf between the *bonde* and the *husmand*.

[15] *Bidrag til en norsk Befolkningsstatistik*, 102 ff.

[16] *Journal of a Residence in Norway during the Years 1834, 1835, and 1836*, 300 (London, 1837). Laing gives a careful description of a Norwegian log house and adds, "I give this minute description because one hears so much of the log huts of America, and this is probably their mother country" (p. 30). *Cf.* H. D. Inglis, *A Personal Narrative of a Journey through Norway, Part of Sweden, and the Islands and States of Denmark*, 45 (London, 1835).

A two-story dwelling-house, with seven apartments, of which two
are painted. A large kitchen, hall and room for hanging clothes, and
two cellars. There is a side building of one story, containing servants'
room, brewing kitchen, calender room, chaise-house, and wood-house.
A two-story house on pillars with a pantry, and a store-room. The
farm buildings consist of a threshing barn, and barns for hay, straw,
and chaff; a stable for five horses; a cattle house for eight cows, with
divisions for calves and sheep. There is a good kitchen garden, and a
good fishery; and also a considerable wood, supplying timber for house-
building, for fences, and for fuel, besides the right of cutting wood in
the common forest. The scater (sæter) or hill pasture is only half a
mile (that is, three and a half English miles) from the farm. The
arable land extends to the sowing of eight barrels of grain and twenty-
five or thirty of potatoes (the barrel is half a quarter), besides the
land for hay; and the farm can keep within itself, summer and winter,
two horses, eight cows, and forty sheep and goats. There is also a
houseman's farm and houses. It keeps two cows, six sheep, and has
arable land to the sowing of one and a half barrels of grain and six
barrels of potatoes. The property adjoins a good high road, is within
four miles (eight and twenty English miles) of Christiania.

It is difficult to exaggerate the isolation of many of the
Norwegian communities in the earlier part of the nineteenth century. One consequence of this isolation, the
geographical basis for which is apparent from an examination of a relief map of the country, has been the
development, with the march of centuries, of notable
differences among the various groups of the population.
These show themselves strikingly in the dialects and customs that obtain among the people of the various districts,
or *bygder*. Today the railroad and the automobile, supplementing earlier modes of transportation, promote a
lively communication among the districts. With the
advance of mobility, there is a tendency for some of the
more obvious peculiarities to disappear. It must be
remembered, however, that before 1854 there were no
railroads in Norway and that communication between
bygder was in many cases extraordinarily difficult. When
road conditions were favorable in the middle forties a
journey with wagon or carriage and horses from Kristiania

to Bergen or Trondhjem might be made in as short a
time as eight days, provided one traveled steadily ten
hours a day; but if the roads were in bad condition the
trip might require two weeks or more. That the earlier
emigration was so distinctly of the group type is in part
a result of the difficulty of travel — not only in Norway,
but also on the ocean and in the American interior —
before invention, enterprise, and organization paved the
way for a greater mobility. An immigrant commentary
upon the differentiating characteristics of the *bygd* has
been the organization in the United States of approximately fifty societies, the members of each of which are
bound together by their common origin in one Norwegian
district. Each *bygdelag* cherishes the folk tales and songs,
the special flavor of speech, and the local history and
traditions that form the substance of its own backgrounds.[17] Thus are the differences, for example, between
the inhabitants of Hardanger, in western Norway, and
those of Telemarken, in south central Norway, consciously marked among people derived from these regions.
And the characteristics of a given community in Norway in some cases have been transferred, through group
settlement, to communities in the American West.

If dialectal and other specific differences among the
smaller districts are important, so also are certain general
divergences in customs and types of people that are disclosed upon a comparison of the " Westland " and the
" Eastland." The people along the west coast are under
the influence of a grim nature, dwell " in the cold shadow
of high mountains," and are isolated to a greater degree
than those living in the east. " He who wishes to see
this ice and stone nature of western Norway embodied
in one great picture," declares Agnes M. Wergeland,

---

[17] For information about the Norwegian-American *bygdelag* movement see *Skandinaven Almanak og Kalender*, 1930, pp. 67 ff.

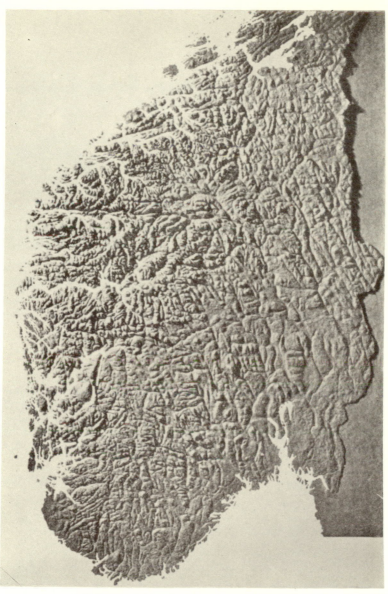

A RELIEF MAP OF SOUTHERN NORWAY
[From Hans Reusch, *Norges Geografi*, 1: 31]

" must read Ibsen's *Brand,* the most tremendous and most one-sided expression of this nature " in Norwegian literature. Writing of the period before modern means of transportation and communication tended to lessen divergences, she says, " The whole West was long bound . . . by traditions and had a decidedly old-fashioned character. The houses were many and small, low and dark. Little was seen of modern improvement. The agricultural implements were more fit for a museum than for a farmer; and the conveyances — the cart, the carjol, or the sled in winter — were the terror of more than one traveler." The " Westland " has indeed its summer and its brighter moods, but it offers a sharp contrast to the " Eastland," with its " broad, expansive valleys that end in broad rivers " and in general its sunny nature. Dr. Wergeland believes that " the spiritual power of the West is greater " than that of the East, and that many of the best men of Norway have come from the mountains and the coasts, " the true home of the Vikings," whose surroundings materially aided in giving them " their courage, able to battle with the unknown, their deep earnestness, their imaginative freshness, their salty humor." [18] It is not without interest in connection with this characterization to recall the fact that modern Norwegian emigration began from the southwestern coast region.

No one familiar with the geography of Norway will suppose that its population is evenly distributed or that it has been so at any time in the past. The coasts and the regions about the fjords have claimed the greatest portion of the population relatively — about two-thirds of the total. Approximately a fourth have inhabited the

[18] Agnes M. Wergeland, *Leaders in Norway and Other Essays,* 23–27 (Menasha, Wisconsin, 1916). A popular description of conditions in Norway in 1845 is in Immanuel Ross, *I Norge 1845* (Kristiania, 1899); on difficulties of travel see ch. 2.

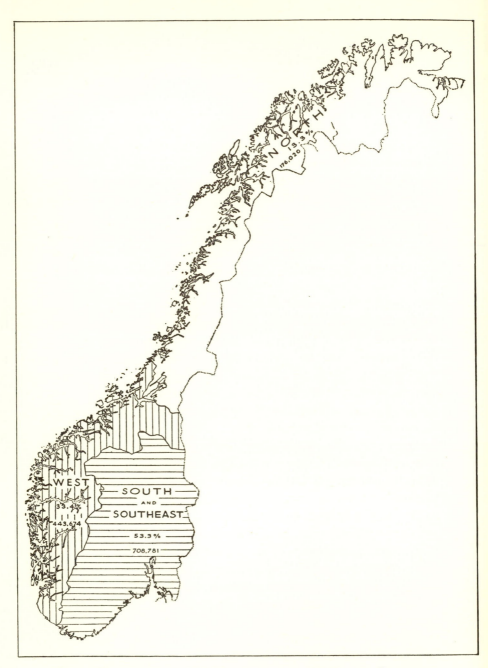

WEST
33.4%
443,674

SOUTH
AND
SOUTHEAST
53.3%
708,781

NORTH
13.3%
176,020

THE NORWEGIAN POPULATION IN 1845 BY SECTIONS

interior lowland districts; and about a tenth the mountain districts. Since the mountains " descend precipitously to the sea toward the west," whereas the incline toward the southeast is more gentle, with long valleys and rivers, and broader and flatter areas toward the extreme southeast, it is natural to assume that the center of population would be in the southeast. This in fact is the case. Here on the beautiful Oslo fjord — a long, twisted finger of the sea where once the Vikings steered their craft — is the capital of the nation, and in the counties in this section in 1845 were to be found 53.3 per cent of the total population, or 708,781 out of 1,328,471. The western counties from Stavanger on the southwest to South Trondhjem on the north, counted 443,674 people, or 33.3 per cent of the total. The shape of Norway is not unlike that of a huge club with a large blunt head and a long, crooked handle. The head, which comprises the two sections named, had in 1845 more than four-fifths of the total population — 86.6 per cent. The handle, stretching through six degrees of latitude, counted 176,020, or 13.3 per cent. This handle extends some three hundred miles into the arctic zone, and about one-third of the country " is the domain of the midnight sun and the winter darkness." Even in southern Norway, however, the summer nights are bright and the winter days short. Great extremes of temperature there are, to be sure, and many of the inland valleys have severe winters. On the whole, however, the portion of Norway from which the migration has been heaviest — the South and the West — has a climate comparable with that of the upper Mississippi Valley, with cooler summers and somewhat milder winters. The " influence of the Gulf Stream can be traced all over the country," observes Steen. " It is in the power of this mighty current to heat the strata of air above it, and it thus becomes one of the chief agencies to which Norway owes her conditions as a civilized

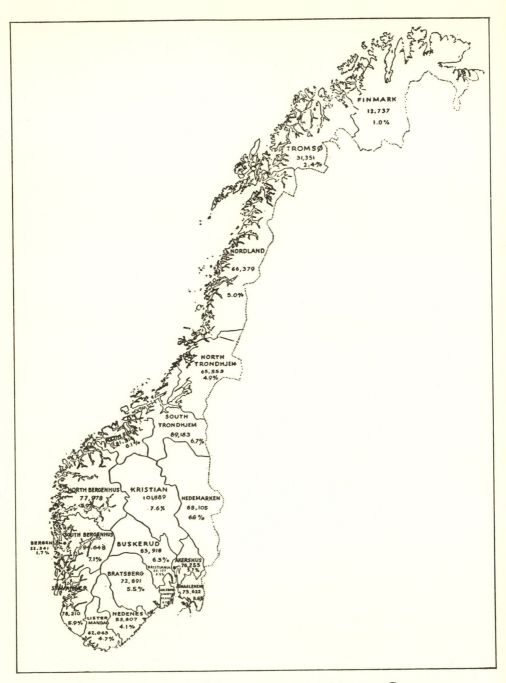

FINMARK
12,737
1.0%

TROMSØ
31,351
2.4%

NORDLAND
66,379

5.0%

NORTH
TRONDHJEM
65,553
4.9%

SOUTH
TRONDHJEM
89,183   6.7%

NORTH BERGENHUS   KRISTIAN   HEDEMARKEN
77,978   101,889   88,105
6.1%   7.6%   6.6%

SOUTH BERGENHUS   BUSKERUD
BERGEN   94,648   83,918   AKERSHUS
22,341   7.1%   6.3%   76,255
1.7%   KRISTIANIA   5.7%
23,177
BRATSBERG   SMAALENENE
72,891   73,622
5.5%   5.6%
STAVANGER   JARLSBERG
LAURVIK
78,210   NEDENES
5.9%   LISTER   53,807
MANDAL   4.1%
62,043
4.7%

THE NORWEGIAN POPULATION IN 1845 BY COUNTIES

inhabited country to her very farthest bounds on the shores of the polar sea." [19]

The nineteenth century was emphatically a period of political awakening and reform in Norway, and the *bønder* played a conspicuous part in this renaissance. When the members of the most important political body in Norwegian history were chosen,— the Eidsvold Assembly of 1814, — the process began with a church service in each parish, after which the people solemnly promised to maintain Norwegian independence. Thereupon two electors, one of whom was to be a *bonde*, were chosen. All the electors in each *amt* then assembled and chose three delegates to Eidsvold — and one of these had to be a *bonde*. Two great questions faced the Eidsvold Assembly: Should Norway be independent? Should Norway lay the foundations of constitutional liberty? Reversing the order of events in the American Revolution, the Norwegians first established their constitution. They wanted power to lodge in the hands of the people, whether the country was to be united with Sweden or not. That the year 1814 is a notable turning point in Norwegian history is owing primarily to the fact that, although the power of the allies forced Norway to accept the Swedish Union, the constitution was saved. Time was to bring national independence, but meanwhile a government of the people was set in operation. The taxing and law-making powers were lodged with the people and were to be exercised through their representatives, who were to employ the parliamentary form of government under a limited hereditary monarchy. The judiciary was to be separate from the executive and legislative branches of the government. Freedom of the press was guaranteed and hereditary privileges were abolished. Some illiberal features there were in the constitution. Jews

[19] Axel Steen, " Climate," in *Norway: Official Publication*, 57; Broch, *Kongeriget Norge*, appendix, 3–4; G. H. Gottenborg, " Befolkningsstatistikkens betydning i ældre og nyere tid," in *Nordmands-forbundet*, 6: 638–639.

were excluded from the country — a provision that was removed in the fifties after a determined agitation for racial tolerance. Religious freedom was not made complete; essential reforms on this score were won in the early forties. Manhood suffrage was not established; the times were not yet ripe for so sweeping an advance toward complete democracy. The Norwegians declared their independence, but the allies quickly forced them to accept the union foreshadowed by the Treaty of Kiel. Twenty-three years after the winning of the constitution the Norwegians passed a local self-government measure which has been characterized as " a bulwark of democratic liberty second in importance only to the constitution itself." The larger movement in which this reform marks an advance is described in the study of emigration causes in the present volume; suffice it, here, therefore, to point out that the Norwegian immigrants to the United States had breathed the air of struggle for and appreciation of self-government. This fact, coupled with a native independence and a sense of democracy bred by traditions and surroundings, and the Scandinavian adaptability, may help to explain the readiness with which, once the barriers of language had been overcome, they adjusted themselves to and participated in self-government under American institutions. The political progress of Norway was accompanied by, if not an expression of, a great nationalistic awakening, which voiced itself vigorously in literature, music, the arts, and other aspects of the life of the people. This nationalism, which found new values in the culture that had been preserved by the *bønder* through centuries of foreign domination and which fanned into flame the genius of poets and artists, undoubtedly left its deep marks upon the spirit of the Norwegian immigrants of the nineteenth century.[20]

[20] A condensed account of the Norwegian events of 1814, with bibliographical suggestions, is in Knut Gjerset, *History of the Norwegian People*, 2: 406–446. The

The vast majority of the Norwegian people, as is well known, are Lutherans, adherents of the Norwegian Lutheran State Church. " The Evangelical-Lutheran religion shall remain the public religion of the State," runs the second clause of the constitution of 1814. " The inhabitants professing it shall be required to bring their children up in the same. Jesuits shall not be tolerated." The nation was practically one hundred per cent Lutheran. How slowly dissent developed in the nineteenth century may be indicated by pointing out that as late as 1875, in a population of 1,818,853, there were only 7,180 people who did not formally belong to the state church. Only one dissenting sect had more than a thousand adherents — the Methodists, with 2,775; and the main period of Methodist increase had been in the ten preceding years, for in 1865 there were only 987.[21] In view of this general situation it is a curious fact that the beginnings of the nineteenth century emigration originated with a small Quaker community in southwestern Norway. The number of dissenters in the realm is hardly a safe clue, however, to the real situation in the church. In fact, the most important religious development in Norway in the nineteenth century was a movement led by Hans Nielsen Hauge (1771–1824), who set afoot within the state church a great pietistic revival after 1796. This influential movement, some aspects of which are considered in a later chapter,[22] had far-reaching ramifications in Norwegian life, not only along religious, but also along economic and political lines, and its marks appear to be

Norwegian constitution is printed (in English) in *Norway: Official Publication*, i–xvii. George M. Stephenson suggests that the Norwegians have exhibited greater solidarity in America than the Swedes and he attributes this to the fact that the Norwegians left their native country when it was experiencing a renaissance of national feeling, whereas the Swedes left at a time when national feeling in Sweden was at a low ebb. " The Mind of the Scandinavian Immigrant," in *Studies and Records*, 4: 63 ff.

[21] *Bidrag til en norsk Befolkningsstatistik*, 177.

[22] See *post*, ch. 7.

THE COURSE OF NORWEGIAN EMIGRATION, 1836–1928

[Statistics in *Utvandringsstatistikk*, 100–103; a chart in the possession of Den Norske Amerikalinie, Oslo]

stamped upon the Norwegian element in the United States today.

There was a not unimportant roundabout filtering of individuals — many of them sailors — from Norway to America in the seventeenth and eighteenth centuries,[28] yet Norwegian immigration as a related movement is practically confined to the period since about 1825, when a train of circumstances was set in motion that ultimately caused the name and the story of the United States to spread to every hamlet and to every country district in Norway. Viewed in its larger setting, as a part of the enormous tide of immigration to the United States in the nineteenth century, the stream of immigration from Norway has not been strikingly large. Viewed as an emigration from a single European country, however, the movement ranks among the most thorough-going of its kind in modern history. It must be remembered that the population of Norway was under a million at the beginning of the nineteenth century — 883,038 in 1801, to be exact. By 1825 it had reached a total of 1,051,318; twenty years later, 1,328,471; in 1865 it numbered 1,701,756; by 1895 the total was 2,097,328; and it rounded the century to 2,309,860 in 1905. The emigration from Norway in the period from 1836 to 1900 passed the half-million mark, and by 1915 the figure had mounted to 754,561 — which exceeds four-fifths of the entire population of Norway at the beginning of the nineteenth century. Only twelve hundred people emigrated in the latter half of the thirties. A rapid rise followed, with five thousand from 1841 to 1845 and twelve thousand in the next five years. The high-water

[28] The standard authority in the earlier portion of this field is John O. Evjen, *Scandinavian Immigrants in New York, 1630–1674* (Minneapolis, 1917). Dr. Evjen, in this scholarly book, produces evidence that at least a hundred and eighty-eight Scandinavians came to New York before 1700, of whom fifty-seven were Norwegians.

mark in the period before the American Civil War came in the fifties, with 20,270 emigrants in the first half of the decade and 15,800 in the last — a total of 36,070. Notwithstanding abnormal conditions in America under the stress of the Civil War, no less than 23,550 emigrants left Norway in the five years up to 1865. The era of mass emigration was evidently at hand, for in the next half decade more than three times as many, or 74,403, joined in the movement. The seventies witnessed a Norwegian exodus of some eighty-five thousand, 45,142 leaving in the first half of the decade and 40,244 in the second. And then came the years of the great tide, with 105,704 emigrants in the first half of the eighties and 80,665 in the second. The next two five-year periods reveal successive declines, with 60,497 and 33,366; but after the turn of the century the swing is again upward, with 103,195 from 1901 to 1905, followed by 87,663 in the next five years. The half-decade merging with the World War years saw a drop in the figures to 44,552. Norwegian emigration was less than one person per one thousand population up to the middle forties, and did not reach three in any five-year period before 1865. The half decade following the Civil War brought the level to nearly nine emigrants per one thousand population, and in the peak years of 1881–85 it rose to 11.05. Such figures are useful in gauging the average; but one needs to remember that there was no even distribution of this level, for some communities were swept more violently than others by the so-called " emigration fever." [24]

[24] Perhaps the most valuable compendium of statistical information relating to Norwegian emigration is a volume entitled *Utvandringsstatistikk* issued in 1921 by " Departementet for Sociale Saker " *(Norges Officielle Statistikk.* vii. 25. 121 p.). See especially chs. 4, 5, and the statistical tables, pp. 100 ff. A chapter by G. Amnéus on population is in *Norway: Official Publication.* An article of somewhat broader interest than its title suggests is G. H. Gottenborg, " Hjemvendte Norsk-Amerikanere, deres livsforhold i Amerika og i Norge efter hjemkomsten," in *Nordmands-forbundet,* 4: 232.

In Norway the actual increase of population was about identical with its natural increase before the decade of the forties, for neither emigration nor immigration substantially affected the situation. The rise of emigration, however, produced a striking change, the trend of which may be understood by distinguishing three periods before 1890. That from 1856 to 1865 represents the emigration after its tentative beginnings. An intermediate period follows — from 1866 to 1875 — in which emigration reaches the first of its two peaks in the last half of the century. The years from 1876 to 1900 represent the height of the movement, with the climax from 1880 to 1885. In the first of these periods, the actual increase of the Norwegian population was 89 per cent of its natural increase. In the intermediate it was 51 per cent, and in the third it dropped to 46 per cent. Thus in the last of the three periods Norway retained less than half of its natural population increase. The nineteenth century is a period in which Norway witnessed much shifting of population coincident not only with emigration but also with a rapid urban development. As has been noted, in 1801, of a total population in Norway of 883,440, not less than 796,840 lived in rural districts, and only 86,600 were town-dwellers. In 1860 the number of people living in the country was 1,361,472, in comparison with 247,181 in the towns, the total population being 1,608,653; and by 1900 the town population was 627,650 and the rural, 1,608,653. In 1860 the town population constituted 15.37 per cent of the total; in 1900, 28.02 per cent. The preponderantly rural origin of Norwegian emigration in the early period is brought out in later chapters, but a few illustrations may not be amiss at this point. From 1846 to 1855, for example, the actual population increase of the rural districts of Norway was 126,862, a natural increase of 173,415 having been offset by an emigration loss of 46,453; from 1866 to 1875 the

actual increase was 40,365, a natural increase of 180,057
having countered a loss by emigration of 139,692; and
in 1876–85 the actual increase was 67,962 — the difference between a natural increase of 209,160 and an emigration loss of 141,198.   In the three periods indicated the
towns of the kingdom had actual increases of population
considerably in excess of the natural increases.   Thus in
1846–55 a population inflow of 15,912, added to a natural
increase of 18,702, made a total town gain of 34,614; and
in 1866–75 an inflow of 31,406 with a natural increase
of 39,897 added 71,303 to the towns; and even in 1876–85
the natural increase — 65,580 — was supplemented by an
inflow, though the latter was only 6,997.[25]

At its peak the Norwegian emigration was exceeded in
percentage of total population only by that from Ireland
among all the European countries.   In the years from
1881 to 1885 the Irish emigration totaled, per one thousand of population, 15.83, whereas the Norwegian totaled
11.05.   The German was 3.82 and the English 5.71.   In
general Norway appears to have had, next to Ireland, the
greatest emigration of the nineteenth century in proportion to its population.   Emigration from the western
Scandinavian kingdom, it may be added, was uniformly
heavier in proportion to population than that from
Sweden throughout the entire period up to 1915.   In
1851–55, when the emigration per one thousand inhabitants for Norway was 2.81, that for Sweden was 0.63;
in 1866–70 the proportions were 8.64 and 3.87; and in
1881–85 they were 11.05 and 6.41.   The closest approach
of the two countries was made in the later eighties and in
the nineties, but even in those years the Norwegian emigration was relatively heavier than the Swedish.[26]

[25] *Folkemængdens Bevægelse 1866–1885,* 17–19, 39 (*Norges Officielle Statistik,*
third series, no. 106); *Norway: Official Publication,* 90, 104, 107; Broch, *Kongeriget
Norge,* appendix, 3–4.

[26] *Folkemængdens Bevægelse 1866–1885,* 117; *Utvandringsstatistikk,* ch. 4.

In discussing the earlier Norwegian emigration, one is dealing mainly with emigration to the United States. A survey made in connection with a Norwegian statistical report indicates that from 1850 to 1880 the number of Norwegian-born living in various European countries outside of Norway increased from 4,000 to 12,687, with Sweden, Denmark, England, and Germany, in the order named, having the bulk of them. In the same period the number of Norwegian-born in Australia rose from 10 to 2,030, and in Canada from a handful to 830. In South and Central America, Asia, and Africa small numbers of Norwegian-born were to be found.[27] The number of Norwegian-born in the United States in 1850, according to the census of that year, was 12,678. The predominance of the Norwegians in the Scandinavian element then in the United States is indicated by the fact that there were only 1,838 Danes and 3,559 Swedes, the total Scandinavian-born population being 18,075. By 1870 the number of Scandinavians in the American population had risen to 241,669, with the Norwegian-born numbering 114,243, the Swedes 97,328, and the Danes 30,098. Twenty years later the Scandinavians in the United States were approaching the million mark, with 933,349. By this time the Swedish immigration had greatly outgrown the Norwegian in bulk, though not in proportion to the old-country population, and the fact is reflected in the figures, for the Swedish-born numbered 478,041, as compared with 322,665 Norwegians, and 132,543 Danes.[28]

[27] " Opgaver og Beregninger over Antallet af Norskfødte bosatte i Udlandet 1850–1880," in *Folkemængdens Bevægelse 1866–1885*, 222–223.

[28] The United States figures showing the number of Scandinavian-born people for the census years from 1850 to 1890 are conveniently and accurately tabulated in O. N. Nelson, *History of the Scandinavians in the United States*, 256–260 (Minneapolis, 1904 ed.).

II. THE GENESIS OF THE MOVEMENT

THE beginnings of Norwegian immigration to the United States in the nineteenth century present the outward aspects of a simple story. A half hundred Norwegians who have learned something about America purchase a sloop of less than fifty tons, set sail on a summer's day in 1825 from a harbor on the southwestern coast of Norway, and, after being tossed about on the sea for some fourteen weeks, reach the gateway of the Promised Land — the vanguard of a host of more than three-quarters of a million immigrants from the western half of the Scandinavian peninsula.

Like most historical events, however, this migration loses its simple character as one probes into its background, for several puzzling questions emerge. The first has to do with the achievements and historical significance of an individual, Cleng Peerson by name. Some have designated this man as the " father of Norwegian immigration to the United States," the " advance agent " of the immigrants of 1825, the pathfinder for Norwegian settlement in the West, and the most influential leader of the entire movement in its earlier stages.[1] Others, however, have pictured him as a mere vagabond, whose influence was on the whole insignificant, who had comparatively little

[1] Svein Nilssen, " De skandinaviske Setlementer i Amerika," in *Billed-Magazin*, 1: 102–104; Rasmus B. Anderson, *The First Chapter of Norwegian Immigration (1821–1840): Its Causes and Results* (Madison, Wisconsin, 1904); Anderson, *Cleng Peerson og Sluppen Restaurationen* (Chicago, 1925); Anderson, " Kleng Peerson, The Father of Norwegian Immigration to America," in *American-Scandinavian Review*, 8: 502–509; H. R. Holand, *De Norske Settlementers Historie*, 33–46, 95–99 (Ephraim, Wisconsin, 1909); Knud Langeland, *Nordmændene i Amerika; Nogle Optegnelser om de Norskes Udvandring til Amerika*, 10–20 (Chicago, 1889); and E. O. Mørstad, *Elling Eielsen og den Evangelisk-lutherske Kirke i Amerika*, 76 et seq. (Minneapolis, 1917).

to do with the coming of the Norwegians in 1825, in short, whose general importance has been much exaggerated.[2] The second question has to do with the relative importance of religious and economic or other factors in bringing about the first important group emigration from Norway to America. Some writers have likened the pioneers of 1825 to the Pilgrim fathers, who, escaping from persecution in the Old World, sought religious and social freedom in the New.[3] Others have asserted not only that the economic motive was the dominant one, but that religious persecution had virtually nothing to do with the matter.[4] Yet a third problem has been discussed — that of the significance of the immigration of 1825 with respect to the whole movement of Norwegian immigration. Some writers have declared that the somewhat dramatic migration of 1825 was a mere episode without noticeable effect upon the larger movement, which took its rise about 1836.[5] Others, however, have attempted to trace a direct and important connection between the earlier and later emigrations.[6] Much light has been thrown upon these problems and various related minor questions by recent investigations; only through their solution can the genesis of the movement of Norwegian immigration be fully understood.[7]

[2] O. N. Nelson, *History of the Scandinavians, and Successful Scandinavians in the United States*, 1: 125–134P (Minneapolis, 1904); Thrond Bothne, in H. G. Heggtveit, *Illustreret Kirkehistorie*, 821–829 (Chicago, 1898); and J. B. Wist, *Den Norske Indvandring til 1850 og Skandinaverne i Amerikas Politik*, 13–17 (n.p., 1889).

[3] A vigorous statement of this view is presented in Anderson, *Norwegian Immigration*, 54–131, 217–218.

[4] Nelson, *Scandinavians in the United States*, 1: 125–134P.

[5] Nelson, *Scandinavians in the United States*, 1:125–134P; Bothne, in Heggtveit, *Illustreret Kirkehistorie*, 821–829; Wist, *Den Norske Indvandring til 1850*, 16–17.

[6] *E.g.*, Anderson, *Norwegian Immigration*, 77–198; Nilssen, in *Billed-Magazin*, 1: 18–19; Langeland, *Nordmændene i Amerika*, 16 ff.

[7] See Gunnar J. Malmin, " Norsk Landnam i U. S.," in *Decorah-Posten*, November 14, 21, 28, December 5, 12, 1924. Mr. Malmin's articles and documents comprise perhaps the most important contribution made in recent years to the history

The problem of Cleng Peerson is complicated by the fact that he was a man of curious and eccentric personality.[8] "Much has been written about this pathfinder in the West," writes Dr. Flom, "and romance and legend already adorn his memory."[9] He was born in 1783 on a farm called "Hesthammer," in Tysvær parish, Skjold district, Stavanger *Amt*, a short distance north of the city of Stavanger, Norway.[10] His name appears originally to have been Kleng (or Klein) Pedersen Hesthammer, but in his later years he seems to have called himself Cleng Peerson.[11] He is rumored to have traveled considerably as a young man, particularly in England, France, and Germany.[12] He was definitely out of sympathy with the Norwegian state church as early as 1818, for in that year a clergyman, after visiting Finnøy parish, reported that Peerson, who had then lived for some years in the annex-parish of Talgøe, had influenced others to refrain from church attendance and participation in the Lord's supper.

of Norwegian immigration. See also the valuable studies by Henry J. Cadbury, "The Norwegian Quakers of 1825," in *Studies and Records*, 1: 60–94; "De første norske Kvækere i Amerika," in *Decorah-Posten*, November 20, 1925; and "De første Kvækere i Stavanger, *ibid.*, May 21, 28, June 4, 11, 1926. The work of Andreas Seierstad (see *post*, note 17) is of special importance on the Norwegian side.

[8] See the writer's article, "Cleng Peerson and Norwegian Immigration," in *Mississippi Valley Historical Review*, 7: 303–331 (March, 1921).

[9] George T. Flom, *A History of Norwegian Immigration to the United States from the Earliest Beginning down to the Year 1848*, 48 (Iowa City, Iowa, 1909).

[10] Peerson was confirmed at Tysvær in 1800; the event is recorded in a church book entry for November 1 of that year; the age given is 17½. This places Peerson's birth in the spring of 1783, not 1782, the traditional date. Fr. Scheel, "Kleng Persson og Restauration," in *Nordmands-forbundet*, 16: 327 (1923). On Peerson's tombstone at Norse, Texas, the date of his birth is recorded as May 17, 1782. On the *gaard* "Hesthammer," see O. Rygh, *Gaardnavne i Stavanger Amt. Udgivne med tilføiede Forklaringer af Magnus Olsen*, 91, 427, 446.

[11] See, for example, a letter by Peerson in *Democraten* (Racine, Wisconsin), September 7, 1850. A printed letter of April 28, 1843, bears the signature "Cling Peerson." *Bergens Stiftstidende*, April 30, 1843. In 1851 the form "Cleng Pedersen" was used. *Morgenbladet*, June 18, 1852. The confirmation record of 1800 has the name "Klein Pedersen Hesthammer." Scheel, in *Normands-forbundet*, 16: 327. The tombstone in Norse, Texas, has "Cleng Peerson."

[12] Nilssen, in *Billed-Magazin*, 1: 104.

He was reported to have gone to Denmark.[13]   Not until 1821, when Peerson was a man of thirty-eight years, did he become associated with the Norwegian immigration movement.   In the summer of that year, in company with Knud Olsen Eide, said to have been from the island of Fogn, Peerson journeyed from Stavanger to New York by way of Göteborg.[14]   There has been some disagreement among historians as to the purpose of this trip. According to one account Peerson had married a wealthy and elderly widow with whom he became involved in such serious domestic difficulty that he deserted her and made his way, first to Göteborg, where he heard a great deal about America, and then to New York.[15]   According to another version of the matter, Peerson and Eide were sent to the United States in 1821 as the agents of a group of Quakers in Stavanger who desired to find a place of refuge where they might worship God without suffering any restrictions or persecution at the hands of state officials.[16]

One of the leaders of this society of Quakers was a carpenter, Lars Larsen (Geilene), who was born at Stavanger on September 24, 1787.   This man, who became the leader of the immigrants of 1825, had served on a merchant vessel in the war of 1807 and had been taken prisoner by the English.   With many other Norwegians and Danes he was held in England until after the Treaty of Kiel in 1814.   Among the prisoners were Elias Tastad

[13] " Visitasprotokol for Stavanger Provsti, 26 Oct. 1818, Visitas i Finnøy Kirke hos Sogneprest Jacob Hansen, holdt af Provst H. E. Støren," quoted by Malmin, in Decorah-Posten, November 21, 1924.   The record seems to be susceptible of the interpretation that Peerson had been expelled.

[14] Nilssen, in Billed-Magazin, 1: 104.   Peerson later said that he arrived in the United States in August, 1821.   Morgenbladet, June 18, 1852.

[15] See Ansten Nattestad's account of Peerson as quoted by Nilssen, in Billed-Magazin, 1: 102–103.

[16] This view, set forth in 1869 by Elling Eielsen in an interview with Nilssen, reported in Billed-Magazin, 1: 104, is accepted by Anderson, Mørstad, and others; and is rejected by Nelson, Bothne, and Wist.   See ante, notes 1 and 2.

and Enoch Jacobsen, also of Stavanger. While on prison ships near Chatham they were repeatedly visited by Quakers, who distributed religious tracts among them and evidenced a characteristic Quaker interest in their welfare. Here, amid the scoffings of comrade prisoners, a small group were won over to the beliefs of the Friends. " In the latter part of our captivity," wrote Tastad, " we were about thirty persons, Danes and Norwegians, who professed with Friends. We held our meetings for worship thrice in the week; but there was seldom any instrumental ministry among us." He listed by name twenty-four persons, including Lars Larsen, who found themselves thus in sympathy with the Friends.[17]

The release of the prisoners and their return to their native land resulted in the planting of Quakerism in Norwegian soil. As early as 1816 a little society was active in Christiania, with Enoch Jacobsen as the leader. Meanwhile a small group had formed a Quaker nucleus in Stavanger. Tastad mentions four who returned to that city: Lars Larsen, Ole Franck, Even Samuelsen, and himself. Larsen, however, had remained in England for a year after his release, in the employ of Margaret Allen, the mother of William Allen, a Quaker missionary who had visited the prisoners at Chatham. It may be noted that Jacobsen had also tarried a year in England: thus Quaker leaders at both Stavanger and Christiania had prolonged their contact with English Quakers. Tastad recorded the humble beginnings at Stavanger: " On our return we were as poor and strange servants; yet we came to live so near one another that we kept up our meetings for worship, two or three times in the week, constantly; when a few others sometimes came and sat with us, either

[17] George Richardson, *The Rise and Progress of the Society of Friends in Norway,* ix–xii, 1–9 (London, 1849). The best modern account of the Norwegian Quakers is that by Andreas Seierstad, *Kyrkjelegt Reformarbeid i Norig i Nittande Hundreaaret,* 1: 219–335 (Bergen, 1923).

in a loft or in a chamber." The path chosen by these pious followers of the doctrine of the inner light was not easy: "We were then as a strange and despised people to the great professors; but the Lord preserved us in our testimonies, through many and various trials and afflictions, which we then had to endure for the truth's sake. Our sufferings were principally caused by the clergy, who stirred up the magistrates to persecution." [18]

Quakerism in Norway received a considerable impetus through the visit in 1818 of Stephen Grellet and William Allen to that country. Grellet, a French Roman-Catholic émigré who had fled to America in 1795, had lived in the United States for twelve years. While in America he had been converted to Quakerism; thereafter he devoted his life largely to " gospel labors "; and he, like Allen, was among those who visited and influenced the Norwegian prisoners at Chatham. The two missionaries aided the Quaker groups in Christiania and Stavanger in putting their religious services on an official footing through the organization of " two months' meetings." They were present at the meeting in Stavanger on August 29, 1818, when eight individuals, four men and four women, organized the society. Tastad was chosen clerk, and Larsen and Metta Truls Datter (Hille) were made overseers. The society was very small in official membership, but there is evidence from the beginning of a much wider interest in its doctrines than the membership itself suggests. For example, Allen remarks that fifty persons were present at a morning meeting and about two hundred at an afternoon session attended by himself and Grellet. And the latter states that only eight out of nearly thirty persons considered themselves ready in 1818 for official membership. [19]

---

[18] Richardson, *Friends in Norway*, 16, 22.

[19] Grellet, *Memoirs of the Life and Gospel Labors of Stephen Grellet*, 360–366 (Philadelphia, 1862); *Life of William Allen with Selections from his Correspondence,*

English interest in the Norwegian Quakers was evidenced in numerous ways during the next few decades, notably in efforts to aid the Norwegian Friends to win entire freedom from persecution. And an English Quaker, George Richardson, brought out in 1849 a valuable little book telling of *The Rise and Progress of the Society of Friends in Norway.* Connections were also kept up through correspondence and visits. Thus Thomas Shillitoe, another English missionary, visited Norway late in 1821 and remained in the vicinity of Stavanger about a month.[20]

Meanwhile the Quakers were coming into conflict with officials of state and church.[21] Their beliefs and practices subjected them to a series of annoying difficulties. Compared with religious persecution of earlier times, these " afflictions " may have been minor, but they nevertheless constituted persecution, real and burdensome. The Quakers met their difficulties with dignity and courage; their stout opposition to their persecutors and their spirited defense of the right to freedom of belief, coupled with the vigorous support that English Quakers gave them, played an important part in Norway's advance to enlightened religious toleration. In the first four decades of the nineteenth century dissent and separatism were harshly dealt with by the government and the established Lutheran church of Norway. Hans Nielsen Hauge, the great leader of the religious revival within the state church, — a movement of laymen that had its springs

1: 361–370. " Protocol eller Udkast Bog for Wennernes Tomaanes-Forsamling i Stavanger. Begyndet Aar 1818," entry for 29th of 8th month, 1818. This important manuscript record is in the archives of the Society of Friends, Stavanger. Through the courtesy of Mr. Andreas Bryne the writer was permitted to make a transcript of the entries from 1818 to 1838.

[20] *Journal of the Life, Labors, and Travels of Thomas Shillitoe,* 1: chs. 18–20 (London, 1839).

[21] A succinct account of the Quaker difficulties appears in Seierstad, *Kyrkjelegt Reformarbeid,* 1: 219 ff.; and many pertinent manuscript records are in R. A., Oslo: Kirkedepartement, 3die Aflevering.

in a pietistic protest against the prevalent rationalism of the clergy, — was imprisoned from 1804 to 1814. His followers were recruited chiefly from the country people; they were not separatists, but their relations with the state church and with the government were strained; and the death of Hauge in 1824, which was regarded as a direct result of his imprisonment, doubtless intensified the feeling of mutual distrust.[22] Both Quakers and Haugeans were conscious of the fact that they had much in common. " It was as Haugeans," writes Cadbury, " that the revival of spiritual life came to the prisoners at London before they made connections with the Friends." [23] The most important thing that the two groups had in common was their earnest piety, their insistence upon the necessity of an awakened spiritual life, their distrust of formalism. The Quakers went further than the Haugeans: Shillitoe tells of a conversation with Hauge in which he felt moved to take the broken evangelist severely to task for his moderation with reference to the state church.[24] But the psychology of the two groups was much alike. The gifted artist Tidemand in one of his masterpieces has portrayed a gathering of Haugeans. After studying the records of the Stavanger Quakers one views the painting with the feeling that it would serve almost equally well as a portrayal of them. It is probably true, as a scholar has suggested, that Haugean and Quaker influences coalesced at Stavanger, that both streams of influence were present in the immigrant group of 1825.[25]

The Quakers were subject in far greater degree than the Haugeans to interference by church and secular officials. The marriage of Knud Halvorsen and Anne

[22] Anton C. Bang, *Hans Nielsen Hauge og hans Samtid*, 369, 483–488, and *passim* (Christiania, 1874). *Cf.* Seierstad, *Kyrkjelegt Reformarbeid*, 1: 167–197.

[23] Cadbury, in *Studies and Records*, 1: 80.

[24] Shillitoe, *Journal*, 321–323.

[25] Cadbury, in *Studies and Records*, 1: 80. The Tidemand painting is in the National Art Gallery, Oslo.

Olsdatter in Christiania in 1816 by Quaker ritual at once brought the problem of the Quakers to public attention. Christian Krogh of the church department, much more tolerant than the local clergymen, perceived the need of a general arrangement with reference to the Quakers and proposed to the king the appointment of a commission to investigate and to formulate a law. On the commission, among others, was one J. Thrane, who, according to a Norwegian historian, had learned the value of religious toleration in America and while serving as the American vice-consul in Norway. Meanwhile, however, Halvorsen informed the commission that so long as the Friends could not feel secure in Norway they would go to a land of religious liberty, and some of them did leave for England. English Quakers, it should be added, addressed a petition to the commission in 1817 and one to the king in 1818 putting the case for the toleration of the Quakers. The commission as early as 1817 worked out a report advocating the limitation of Quakers to a group of specified towns. In each town a commission was to be appointed before which all who wished to leave the state church and join the Quakers should appear and explain their reasons. They would then be freed from the obligations of oaths and of taxes for the clergy, church, and the military; and also be permitted to follow their own customs as to baptism, marriage, burial, and various other matters. In order that no one would be tempted to become a Quaker to escape military service, the commission proposed that no one should be recognized as a Quaker until he was twenty-five years of age. Proselyting was to be prohibited under penalty of deportation, but Quakers would be permitted to testify their faith at their meetings in their own way. When the church minister, Treschow, revised the proposal he reduced the number of towns listed, striking out among others Stavanger, perhaps in ignorance of the fact that there were Quakers there. The proposal went before the Storthing and, though still further revised in a conservative direction, was lost in the Odelsthing by three votes. Under a royal resolution of 1819 Halvorsen got the right to dwell in the land; but in the spring of 1821 a child of his died and he buried it in unconsecrated ground. For his action he was brought before a court and fined ten specie dollars and costs.[26]

The Christiania complications were a foretaste of what was to occur at Stavanger. When Allen visited Norway and Sweden in 1818 he used all his influence to lighten the burdens of the Quakers, through conferences with local officials in Stavanger, for example, and in an audience with the king at Stockholm.[27] But difficulties soon arose. " I may say that there are no laws yet made in favour of Friends; so that those who stand firm to their principles, act contrary to the laws of the country," wrote a Norwegian Friend in 1818. " Friends must be resigned to take the consequences." [28] In 1819 Elias Tastad was married to Guri Ols Datter Raasedahl and the next year Ole Pedersen Franck was married to Mallene Asbjørns Datter Waaga according to Quaker forms.[29] In 1820 Bishop Sørenssen took note of these events and of the fact that Quaker children went unbaptized, but he carried the matter no further than a complaint.[30] But more serious matters developed in the summer of 1821, when twin daughters of Tastad died and he, having been denied the privilege of burying them in consecrated ground without the Lutheran ceremonies, buried them in unconsecrated

[26] Seierstad, *Kyrkjelegt Reformarbeid*, 1: 221–229.

[27] *Life of William Allen*, 1: 361–370.

[28] Richardson, *Friends in Norway*, 23, quoting a letter by Enoch Jacobsen.

[29] The marriage contracts are recorded in " Prottocol eller Udkast Bog for Wennernes Tomaanes-Forsamling i Stavanger," entries for 27th, 5th month, 1819, and 5th day, 6th month, 1820. *Cf.* Tastad's list of Stavanger Quaker marriages, births, and deaths, March, 1822, in R. A., Oslo: Kirkedepartement, 3die Aflevering, 27.

[30] Seierstad, *Kyrkjelegt Reformarbeid*, 1: 230.

ground; and again the next spring when Ole Franck died and was buried by Tastad in the same ground. For the first offense Tastad was sentenced to pay five dollars a day until he should remove the bodies to consecrated burial ground. The Stavanger sheriff was unwilling to execute the judgment; and on an appeal from William Allen to the king, in which it was testified that the Stavanger Quakers were officially members of the Society of Friends, Tastad was granted a royal release. Meanwhile the church department, influenced by the intercession of Shillitoe, decided to apply to the Stavanger Quakers the procedure followed in part in the earlier case of Halvorsen. They were to furnish evidence from a recognized Quaker society that they really were Quakers, to petition for the right to remain in the land, and to report regularly all births, marriages, deaths, and other items that ordinarily came under the supervision of the church. On these conditions they were to be tolerated, but the tolerance was very limited indeed. In 1822 Bishop Sørenssen in a letter to the dean of Stavanger explained that the Quakers must not only have official certificate of membership and make a formal petition, but also be made to understand that the petition would not be granted "unless they bind themselves not to make proselytes, and from admitting new members, as also to pay taxes and duties as other subjects or bergers of the state." [31]

On October 2, 1823, the Stavanger Quakers, ten in number, dispatched their petition — drafted by Tastad — to the government, asking to be allowed to continue their religious practices. The Stavanger sheriff, Krog, in a supplementary statement of December 4, urged that the petition be granted. He gave assurance that the Quakers were diligent and respectable, and he added a

---

[31] Richardson, *Friends in Norway*, 36–37; Seierstad, *Kyrkjelegt Reformarbeid*, 1: 230 ff.; "Prottocol eller Udkast Bog for Wennernes Tomaanes-Forsamling i Stavanger," entries 5th day, 6th month, 1821, and 5th day, 3d month, 1822.

very significant statement: "A refusal to allow them to practice their religious customs would presumably not change their convictions, but the result would probably be that they would emigrate." [32] There was delay in granting the petition; a second was sent in the spring of 1825, this one without the name of Lars Larsen, soon to emigrate; not until nearly a year thereafter was the request granted. [33]

Quaker difficulties continued. Case after case, having to do with such matters as oaths, baptism and confirmation of children, burials, and military service, arose to harass the Friends. The history of these difficulties has been told in detail by a Norwegian historian; suffice it to note here that further geographical restrictions were placed upon Quakerism in 1830. The movement for legal reform in the direction of religious freedom began to gain force in the late thirties, but as late as 1845 a group of Friends in England felt constrained to petition the Norwegian Storthing in behalf of the Norwegian Quakers, asking that the following five privileges might be granted their "oppressed brethren": (1) legal security "in the undisturbed exercise of public worship, according to their conscience"; (2) the validity in law of Quaker marriages; (3) exemption from compulsion in the matter of baptism and other rites from which they dissent; (4) the legalization of the Quaker affirmation as a substitute for the oath; and (5) relief "from the harassing and oppressive proceedings to which they are now subjected in reference to ecclesiastical demands, and rates for the support of the schools." [34] Some writers, from one motive

[32] R. A., Oslo: Kirkedept., 3die Aflevering, 27.

[33] Seierstad, *Kyrkjelegt Reformarbeid*, 1: 233, 236; and Cadbury, in *Studies and Records*, 2: 83–84.

[34] Seierstad gives an account of the later period in *Kyrkjelegt Reformarbeid*, 1: 234–335. A copy of the English petition is in R. A., Oslo: Kirkedept., 3die Aflevering, 27; and a printed version is in Richardson, *Friends in Norway*, 128–131. It should be added that the petition did not reach its destination until after the church committee had completed its report on the proposed toleration act of 1845.

or another, have sought to minimize the persecution that the Quakers suffered; but the record offers a convincing historical answer. A law granting substantial freedom of worship, so far as Christian sects were concerned, was put on the statute books in 1845; but back of this lie some thirty years of complications for the state and persecution for the Quakers.[35]

Cleng Peerson remained in the United States from 1821 to 1824. The most definite bit of information about his activities during this period is contained in an American newspaper article published shortly after the arrival of the immigrants of 1825.[36] According to this news item, two men originally were sent to the United States as agents of the Stavanger group. A sum of money was raised with which to defray the traveling expenses of these men, but, the newspaper article implies, this fund was placed temporarily in the hands of a business man and was lost when his business failed. Thus it came about that the agents, handicapped by lack of money, " found themselves in a strange land, among a people of different laws, customs, and language, with all of which they were unacquainted." They were determined, however, to accomplish the objects for which they had been sent to America and they therefore proceeded with their investigation although it was necessary for them to work in order to meet the expenses which their mission entailed. One of the two, it is stated, was taken ill and soon thereafter died, despite the solicitous

Two other significant documents are an open letter by George Richardson dated April 25, 1841, pleading with Norwegians not to persecute the Quakers, in *Stavanger Amtstidende og Adresseavis* for August 12, 1841; and an open letter to Norwegian judges and ministers by Elias Tastad, in *Christianssandsposten* for March 29, 1844. Attention may be directed here also to an interesting Quaker work, John F. Hanson, *Light and Shade from the Land of the Midnight Sun* (Oskaloosa, Iowa, 1903).

[35] That the "dissenter law" came as early as it did and was as liberal as it was may be attributed in large part to the pressure by Norwegian Quakers from below and by English Quakers from above, according to Seierstad, *Kyrkjelegt Reformarbeid*, 335.

[36] *New York American*, October 22, 1825, from the *Baltimore American*; the article is reprinted in Anderson, *Norwegian Immigration*, 73–75.

care of the other. "After the decease of his friend," the account continues, " the survivor left as he was solitary and alone, proceeded on foot to examine the country, the character of the different soils, our mode of agriculture, engaging without hesitation at any kind of employment to meet the current expenses of the day, by which means he obtained a knowledge of our customs, laws, language, and agriculture." The article states that the agent in his search scoured " the vast regions of the west," but there is no indication of how far west he went. It is asserted that he kept a daily journal " which in due time he transmitted to the company, by whom he was sent to make the examination." The reports transmitted by the agent were so favorable, the article continues, " that the little colony have at length arrived here to settle amongst us, and to assume the character of American citizens."

This circumstantial account may be unreliable in precise details, but its nature and the time and circumstances of its publication scarcely leave room for doubt that in essentials it tells the truth. Indeed, it is possible that its source, if not Cleng Peerson himself, was a member of the immigrant party. Who else could have furnished such information to an American newspaper in 1825? From another source it is now possible to prove that Peerson, during his first sojourn in the United States, went as far west as the western part of New York.[37] Yet another piece of evidence exists that is confirmatory in essentials of the newspaper article in question. Elling Eielsen, a famous Norwegian pioneer preacher in the western settlements who was conversant with the situation of dissenters and Haugeans in Norway, — he himself was a zealous disciple of Hauge, — declared in 1869 that Peerson and Eide were Quakers sent by the Friends of Stavanger in 1821 to investigate conditions in America. Their expenses,

[37] See *post*, p. 39.

he asserted, were paid by the Stavanger Quakers and possibly in part by English Quakers. Eielsen found the explanation of the mission in the spirit of religious intolerance which prevailed in Norway during the first part of the nineteenth century.[38] No evidence has been found to prove that Peerson and Eide were Quakers; there is nothing in the Quaker archives at Stavanger to indicate that they were official agents of the Society of Friends; but that their trip was a preliminary investigation undertaken for a group of persons in the Stavanger region whose leader was Lars Larsen, one of the two leaders of the Stavanger Quakers, does not appear to be open to question.

In 1824 Peerson returned to Norway and reported to his friends on the conditions and prospects for immigrants in the United States. In the summer of that year, if not before, a group of Norwegians in and about the city of Stavanger definitely determined to emigrate. It has been commonly supposed that Peerson remained in Norway until 1825 and then crossed to New York by way of Göteborg. That he was not a member of the " sloop party " — the immigrant group of 1825 — and that he met the immigrants when they arrived in New York are two facts that have long been known. The truth of the matter is that Peerson returned to America in 1824, not in 1825. His stay in Norway in 1824 was but a " flying visit," wrote Ole Rynning in 1838.[39] And in a newspaper article published in Stavanger early in 1843, in which the story of the " sloopers " is reviewed, it is stated that Peerson " returned in 1824, and was the first man to inform the people here about conditions over there, and then hurried back the same year." [40] The reasons for his hasty return to America are made evident in a letter

[38] Nilssen, in *Billed-Magazin*, 1: 104.

[39] *Ole Rynning's True Account of America*, 34.

[40] *Stavanger Amtstidende og Adresseavis*, January 5, 8, 1843. The article is signed " —d." The value of this evidence is lessened by the fact that in the same article uncertainty is shown as to just when the " sloopers " left Norway

written by Peerson on December 20, 1824, from New York.[41]

In this letter Peerson informed his " father, brother, sister, brother-in-law, and friends " that after a journey of six weeks he had arrived at New York, where he was cordially received by his friends. With Andrew Stangeland, his companion on this trip, he remained in New York City for five days and then left by steamer for Albany. Thereafter the two worked their way to Troy, " Salina Salt Works," and Farmington, where Peerson had friends — evidence that he had visited western New York before.[42] Leaving his comrade, Peerson walked to Geneva to purchase land from the " land commissioner " at that city both for himself and for his friends at home. " The land commissioner," he wrote, " is very friendly and has offered to aid us as much as he can. We arrived at an agreement in regard to six pieces of land which I have selected, and this agreement will remain effective for us until next fall." Peerson does not name the land agent, but he was, in all probability, Joseph Fellows, the agent of the Pultney Land Office, which had control of a large amount of land in western New York. Fellows, a Quaker, figures prominently in the story of the 1825 immigrants after their arrival in New York.[43]

and the year 1824 is mentioned. The language used about Peerson definitely indicates a short stay, however.

[41] Thormod Madland to Mauritz Halvarsen, June 28, 1825. Minnesota Historical Society Mss. This letter, written by Madland at Stavanger before he sailed for America on the " Restauration," incorporates a letter written by Cleng Peerson from New York on December 20, 1824. For the text, an English translation, and a discussion of its genuineness see appendix.

[42] Farmington is in Ontario County, New York, a short distance from Geneva. It was a Quaker community, most of the township having been bought by a society of Quakers in 1789. C. F. Milliken, A History of Ontario County, New York, and Its People, 1:321 (New York, 1911). "The majority of the early settlers and nearly all the pioneers of Farmington were Friends." George S. Conover, ed., and Lewis C. Aldrich, compiler, History of Ontario County, New York, 392 (Syracuse, 1893).

[43] Fellows became a sub-agent of the Pultney lands in 1810 and later was made general agent in charge of the Geneva office. History of the Pioneer Settlement of Phelps and Gorham's Purchase, 281 (Rochester, 1851).

Peerson wrote that he had under construction a house
which he expected to complete by New Year's day. This
house, he said, was, " on the site selected for you whose
arrival I am awaiting," but in the spring he intended to
build on his own land. He already owned, in addition
to five acres of land that he intended to clear in time for
the spring planting, a cow — for which he had paid ten
dollars — and some sheep. " I have informed you of the
prices of all things in Knud Eie's letter," he adds. His
letter expressed great eagerness for the arrival of his sister
and other friends, whom he planned to meet in New
York. The Friends in Macedon had promised to care for
his sister and others until cabins with sufficient room to
house the party should be built.[44] He encouraged the
prospective immigrants to have faith in the promises that
he had made to them and to put their trust fully in Providence. " You must not allow yourselves to be frightened
away by talk," he wrote. " I spoke with many persons
in New York in regard to selling the vessel. You will
certainly be able to sell a small vessel, but a large one is
against the law of the land. Therefore do whatever seems
best to you. Young persons can easily cross to London
and from there to New York for thirty dollars. My
friends in New York have promised to do all in their
power to sell the vessel as advantageously as possible. On
the other hand, if you could invest your money in Swedish
iron and hire a vessel, that would accomplish the same
end." He asked the prospective immigrants to acquaint
him with their plans in good season and closed by exhort-
ing them to deal with one another in a brotherly spirit
and to heed the call and the admonitions of the Almighty.

This interesting letter proves that Cleng Peerson was
indeed the " advance agent " of the immigrants of 1825,

[44] Macedon is a short distance north of Farmington, in Wayne County. Peerson
does not state precisely where his land was, but he mentions buying a stove and
various accessory articles in Rochester. This would suggest that it was in the
region tributary to that town.

that he vigorously supported the enterprise and encouraged its promoters, that he arranged the purchase of land for his friends, that he was attempting to arrange for the sale of their vessel should they purchase one for the journey, that he had received coöperation and promises of aid from friends in New York City and in western New York, and that he had made active preparations for housing the immigrants when they should arrive. It is clear that Peerson's name is entitled to stand at the head of the list of Norwegian immigrant leaders of the nineteenth century. It may be of interest to add that Peerson was credited by an immigrant letter of 1838 with having had in mind the establishment of a communistic community. Its writer declared that Peerson's " object was then [*in 1825*], as it is now, to unite all the Norwegians in one community, which would own all its property in common." [45]

By midsummer of 1825 the group in the Stavanger district, encouraged by the optimism of Peerson's reports, was ready to set out. [46] Larsen, by virtue of his ability to speak some English and of his personal character, was the leader. He and his associates decided, perhaps as a result of Peerson's advice, to purchase a small vessel for the journey. The sum of eighteen hundred specie dollars was raised, an amount equivalent to about $1,370, and a sloop of 18½ commercial lasts (about 39 tons) — the " Restauration " — was bought, the ownership being vested in Johannes Stene, one of the prospective emigrants. A cargo consisting mainly of rod iron was either bought or received on consignment from several Stavanger

[45] This letter from Illinois dated January 28, 1838, perhaps written by Ole Rynning, is published in *Det udflyttede Norge*, 6–8 (Kristiania, 1884). It is of interest, in this connection, to note that many years later, in 1847, Peerson joined the famous communistic Bishop Hill colony in Illinois. Blegen, in *Mississippi Valley Historical Review*, 7: 323.

[46] An early account of the voyage is that in *Ole Rynning's True Account of America*, 34–36, 71–74 (1926 ed.). See also Nilssen, in *Billed-Magazin*, 1: 71; Langeland, *Nordmændene i Amerika*, 10–13; and Anderson, *Norwegian Immigration*, chs. 3–5.

firms for sale in New York.[47]   And on July 5, 1825, the
" Restauration," with a party comprising fifty-two persons, including a crew of seven, set sail from Stavanger
harbor for New York.[48]   The composition of the group
offers a foretaste of the character of Norwegian immigration generally during the nineteenth century.   There appear to have been ten married couples, two from Stavanger and the rest from outlying districts, with Tysvær
particularly well represented.   These families comprised
in all forty persons, including Margaret Allen Larsen, who
was born before the voyage came to an end, the daughter
of Lars Larsen and his wife.   One couple had five children; one four; three three; two one; and three none.
There was one unmarried woman, Sara Larsen, a sister of
Lars Larsen.   The rest of the group were single men of
varying ages, including a very young member of the crew,
Jacob Anderson Slogvig, age fifteen.   The captain was
Lars Olsen Helland of Stavanger; and the mate, Peder
Eriksen Meeland.[49]

Before following the " sloopers " on their journey westward it is necessary to consider the possible connections
of their emigration with the story of Quaker persecution
chronicled above.   A contemporary newspaper report,
dated at Stavanger, July 7, 1825, refers to the emigrants

[47] The ship's papers, submitted by Captain Helland to Consul Gahn and by him
transmitted to the Norwegian Finance Department, are in R. A., Oslo: F. D.,
Journalsaker 456/1826 F, accompanying a letter of November 29, 1826, by C. H.
Valeur, to whom they were entrusted by the consul. These papers give the sloop's
size, specify the items in its cargo, list the crew, name Stene as the official owner,
and include sundry other items of information. The writer has transcripts and
photostatic copies of these documents. The purchase price of the ship is mentioned in Ole Rynning's True Account of America, 72. The sloop drew 7½ feet
of water; its pilot was Siwert Bech. " Lods Protocol," 1825, in Stavanger Lods
Oldermandskab. Cf. Malmin, in Decorah-Posten, November 21, 1924. The material
in the Stavanger " Toldprotocol " for 1825 relating to the " Restauration " is incorporated in the sloop's papers, referred to above. A commercial last was equivalent
to 2.08 registered tons; hence the sloop's tonnage was 38.48. The length was
probably about 54 feet. Scheel, in Normands-forbundet, 16: 324–325.

[48] See post, Appendix, no. 2.

[49] See post, Appendix, no. 3.

thus: "They are said to belong to a religious society which has won a considerable number of members here in this vicinity during the last few years." [50] This is clearly an allusion to the Quakers, and it was so interpreted by the church department of the Norwegian government, which on July 29 called upon Bishop Munch of Christiansand for a report on the emigration. It desired to know especially whether or not any Quakers remained in the vicinity. Munch on August 27 replied that fifty-one persons were reported to have sailed, but that only Simon Lihme with his wife and children, and the smith, Torwad Holde, with his wife, were from the city of Stavanger. The rest were from outlying districts. He reports further, on the basis of a statement of Elias Tastad, that only one individual belonging to the Quaker society in Stavanger, Lars Larsen, was among the emigrants. The society then consisted, according to this report, of twelve members, eight men and four women. [51] That Larsen was the only officially recognized member of the "sloop party" is confirmed by the "Stavanger Quaker Protocol" — for his is the only "slooper name" that appears in its pages — and by an interesting letter from England of October 28, 1825, from Joseph Allen, a brother of William Allen, to Tastad. [52] Allen acknowledges a letter written by Tastad from Stavanger on July 15, 1825, — ten days after the sloop sailed, — and something of the content of the Tastad letter is reflected by Allen. He writes:

[50] *Den Norske Rigstidende*, July 25, 1825. The item was reprinted by Seierstad, *Kyrkjelegt Reformarbeid*, 1:234, and by Malmin in *Decorah-Posten*, November 21, 1924.

[51] The department's request and Munch's reply are in R. A., Oslo: Kirkedept., Kopibøker, 1825A, 12/663; and 3die Aflevering, 27. *Cf.* Malmin, in *Decorah-Posten*, November 21, 1924. Larsen was not technically a resident of Stavanger. He lived outside the city, in Frue Sogn.

[52] Tastad Papers, in the archives of the Society of Friends, Stavanger. On the back of this four-page manuscript, the language of which is a somewhat curious Norwegian, is the notation "Oversættelse fra Engeland. W. Allen." It is to be hoped that Tastad's letter may be found in England.

In your letter of the 15th of the 7th month you report that Lars has gone to America, and I assume, since you mention no others, that he is the only one of the members who has left. I trust that he will benefit by the move. Have you heard from him since he left? It is very pleasing to hear that you have not felt yourself free to leave Stavanger, though I can fully believe the many differences [or *difficulties*] and deficiencies that the Friends have to bear. I hesitate to judge those who are determined, according to their best view, to emigrate. Experience has of course taught many that not all those provinces which are made available for new settlers have been satisfactory and that many ensnarements and lacks have had to be faced. We may therefore conclude that it is very hard to feel it to be right to embark upon so great an enterprise. It will be very pleasant to hear both about the external and the spiritual condition of yourself and the Friends at present.

That there was only one member of the " sloopers " who was officially a Quaker does not mean that there may not have been others who, though not members, were in sympathy with the Quakers. The tone of the Allen letter indicates that, though Tastad had remained at home, the idea of emigration was very decidedly present in the atmosphere about the Stavanger Quakers and that their persecution was the central difficulty. The very fact that the leader of the " sloop folk " was one of the Stavanger Quaker leaders would tend to cause the public to associate the two enterprises. But it is doubtful if both contemporary and later reports could have emphasized the Quaker factor so sharply had there not been other Quaker sympathizers in the group that followed the Quaker leader. The Norwegian newspaper report of 1825 reflected the view that the sloopers were Quakers.[53] The American newspaper item which tells of the advance work of Peerson and Eide says of the " Restauration " group: " They belong to a religion called the Saints corresponding in many points to the principles of the Friends. We understand furthermore that they have sought an asylum in this favored land from religious persecution

[53] *Ante,* n. 50.

and that they will shortly be succeeded by a much larger body of emigrants." [54]   This points sharply in the direction of the coalescence with Haugeanism already suggested.   The Norwegian historian of Quakerism in Norway believes that though Lars Larsen was the only " legitimated Quaker " of the emigration group, Ole Johnson, Cornelius Nelson Hersdal, and Daniel Stenson Rossadal were also in fact Quakers. [55]   If this is the case, seventeen of the fifty-three " sloopers " would be embraced in the Quaker group, counting wives and children — eighteen, if Larsen's sister be included.   Moreover, the individuals mentioned were among the leaders of the party.   A Stavanger newspaper article written in 1842 by a man who had apparently derived some of his information from Cleng Peerson, then visiting in Norway, declares, in discussing the causes of the 1825 emigration: " The persecution of the Quakers and compulsion in religious matters were a contributing cause.   Three *Sødskende* [*that is, a brother and two sisters, or vice versa*] and the head of a family with his whole family went without a doubt because the latter's daughter and the formers' brother, though prepared for confirmation, though they could read, and though they were well instructed in religious matters, were not allowed to be confirmed because

[54] *New York American*, October 22, 1825, from the *Baltimore American*, reprinted in Anderson, *Norwegian Immigration*, 75.

[55] Seierstad, *Kyrkjelegt Reformarbeid*, 234.   Larsen joined the Rochester Friends in 1826; Ole Johnson (Eie) the Friends at Farmington in the same year; Halvor Iverson the Rochester Friends in 1833.   For information about these and other Quaker affiliations in New York see Cadbury, " De første norske Kvækere i Amerika," in *Decorah-Posten*, November 20, 1925; the same author's article in *Studies and Records*, 1: 85–94; and John Cox, Jr., " Norwegian Quakers in Western New York," in the *Friends' Intelligencer*, 82: 829–830, 848–850 (1925).   Anderson, who knew some members of the Rossadal family, confirms Seierstad's view that they were Quakers in fact. *Decorah-Posten*, December 19, 1924.   It is said that only one " slooper," Ole Olsen Hetletvedt, was identified with Norwegian-American Lutheranism, but it is interesting to note that even he was of the Haugean persuasion. O. J. Hatlestad, *Historiske Meddelelser om den Norske Augustana Synode*, 24 (Decorah, Iowa, 1887).

they were believed to have connections with the Quaker sect." [56]   To become officially a member of the Quaker society in Stavanger in the period under consideration was a very serious step to take.   And the Stavanger society, in part on principle and in part because of the restrictions under which it was permitted to exist at all, seems to have been very conservative about admitting new members.   To cite one example: though Ole Franck was one of the four adherents to the Quaker doctrine mentioned by Tastad as having returned to Stavanger from England after 1814, his application for admittance to the Quaker society does not appear in the records until December 31, 1818.   At three successive meetings action on his application was deferred, and not until August 5, 1819, was he officially admitted. [57]   The state policy, as has been noted, was to bind the Quakers not to proselyte or to admit new members.   Under these circumstances it would be extremely unsafe historically to minimize the Quaker influence merely because there was only one official member among the emigrants on the " Restauration."   And the Norwegian government commission which investigated the emigration question in the forties conceded, in a report of December 15, 1844, that the first sprouts of the Norwegian migrations grew out of religious intolerance. [58]   The emigrants of 1825 made Quaker connections in New York City, in the purchase of land, and in western New York; and in the traditional explanations of their motives for emigrating, the Quaker situation is given much emphasis.

In the light of these facts, though it must again be made clear that no contemporary evidence indicates that

[56] *Stavanger Amtstidende og Adresseavis,* January 5, 1843.   The article is dated December, 1842.
[57] See entries in " Prottocol eller Udkast Bog for Wennernes Tomaanes Forsamling i Stavanger."
[58] " Angaaende Udvandringer til fremmede Verdensdele," in *Kongeriget Norges Ellevte Ordentlige Storthings Forhandlinger i Aaret 1845,* vol. 1, part 6, p. 25.

the emigration of 1825 was an official Quaker enterprise, it seems undeniable that the treatment of the Quakers by the Norwegian state and church was a factor in bringing about the emigration. The English attitude toward the Stavanger situation has already been illustrated in Joseph Allen's letter: Allen obviously favored a stubborn fight in Norway for toleration. George Richardson of Newcastle seems to have shared this view. Of Tastad he remarks: "Neither did he seek to avoid afflictions in bearing the cross, by going to America, as several of this little company have done." [59] Emigration has indeed been a common story in the history of the Stavanger Quakers. Four of the eight founders of 1818 — Larsen, Thomas Trulsen, Metta W. Hille, and Mallene Asbjørns Datter — later went to America. The present writer has had access to a members' register in the archives of the Friends at Stavanger: in the period from 1818 to 1873, there are 230 names listed. Of these 72, or approximately a third, are followed by notations that they have left for America. Half of the founders, a third of the members through the first half century of the existence of the society: such is the emigration record of these Quakers.[60]

Undoubtedly the economic motive played an important part in the 1825 emigration and in that of the Quakers who later left the Stavanger region. The seven war years were followed by hard times; taxes were high; there were various burdens imposed by state and church that fell heavily upon small farmers. Economic prospects were

---

[59] *Friends in Norway*, 52.

[60] The "Members' Register" is kept in a manuscript record book which contains entries of births and burials as well as a general series of entries giving information about members. The latter gives the names, date when admitted to membership, frequently the trade or profession, place of residence, and comments. Lars Larsen is noted merely as "gone to America"; Thomas Trulsen as "left the society and gone to America"; Metta W. Hille as "came back in 1852 after having spent fifteen years in America"; Mallene Asbjørns Datter as "gone to America." In later cases the dates of departure are sometimes given. The comments appear in most cases to have been entered long after the main body of the record was made.

not encouraging. This was perhaps especially applicable to farmers, but other classes were also affected.[61] Richardson writes that in 1819 " Lars Larsen came over to London, being desirous of learning the English language. He hoped to have found employment as a cabinet maker, and to have devoted his leisure hours to learning the language; but not finding proper employment readily, he was advised to return home." [62] The Quakers and Haugeans were not recruited among the well-to-do; they were in fact generally from classes that found the struggle for existence hard. The prospects for economic betterment in the United States might be expected to make an appeal to people in such circumstances. The fact remains that organized Norwegian emigration began in 1825, not in 1815 or in 1830; through all this period the economic appeal of America was a fact and conditions among Norwegian small farmers were on the whole discouraging. The genesis of the emigration can only be explained by a conjunction of circumstances that came to a head in 1825; and the religious factor is interwoven with that story. It has been suggested that Stephen Grellet first put into the minds of the Stavanger group the idea of the United States as an emigrant goal.[63] This is interesting, but it is probably merely a conjecture. It is true that little was known about America among the Norwegian common people as early as the twenties. But the land to the west was not wholly unknown to them, especially those who lived in or near centers of trade, and it is scarcely necessary to try to attribute the idea to one individual. Now and then a Norwegian ship engaged in American trade; and Norwegian newspapers occasionally printed items about America. Thus *Drammens Tidende*

[61] *Stavanger Amtstidende og Adresseavis*, January 5, 8, 1843.
[62] *Friends in Norway*, 34.
[63] B. L. Wick, " Quakerism in Norway," in *The Friend* (Philadelphia), 67: 259 (1894).

as early as 1821 published an account of the English colonization plans in the West sponsored by Morris Birkbek
and George Flower; and in 1824 the same paper brought
out a series of articles exploiting the idea that the United
States was a land " for the present and the future." [64]   It
may be added incidentally that two Norwegians of Drammen emigrated in 1825.[65]

The route followed by the " Restauration " after it put
to sea from Stavanger was circuitous.   The sloop, after
passing through the English channel, went as far south as
the harbor of Funchal in Madeira.   The story of the
adventurous voyage was long a favorite one among early
Norwegian immigrants, who particularly relished the tale
of how, as the " Restauration " neared the harbor of
Funchal, a floating cask of Madeira wine was hauled on
board.   Ole Rynning, who reports this affair in a book
printed in 1838, states that the contents of the cask were
consumed by the crew, with the result that " the ship
came drifting into the harbor like a plague ship, without
command, and without raising its flag."   The immigrants

[64] *Drammens Tidende*, August 13, 1821; October 7, 14, 21, November 1, 1824.
The Norwegian ship "George" reached Charleston, S. C., on October 26, 1824,
from Rotterdam, and took on a cargo of cotton, rice, and tobacco. Consular report
of January 21, 1825, in R. A., Oslo: F. D., Journalsaker, F, 1825/114.

[65] An immigrant letter writer of 1838 says, "I have recently met two Drammen
men who have been in America for thirteen years. Their names are Peder B. Smith
and Hans E. Hjorth." He adds that they were established near Monticello, White
County, Indiana; had land; and also owned a sawmill which netted them good
profits. Smith had said that he had only eighteen dollars in his pocket when he
first came to America. A letter from Illinois dated January 28, 1838, in *Det
udflyttede Norge*, 6–8. Rynning, perhaps the author of the letter here cited, refers
to these Norwegians in his *True Account of America* (1926 ed.), 78, as the owners
of 1,100 acres of land. Probably through a printer's mistake the amount is given
as 11 acres in the printed version of the letter. The identification of these two men
apparently solves the interesting little problem mentioned by Anderson, *Norwegian
Immigration*, 368. Another emigrant of 1825 was Gunder Anderson Hellerig of
Stavanger *Amt*. He had been sentenced, for some offense, to four days' imprisonment on bread and water, but Foged Bredrup, in a letter of September 6, 1825,
states he had left for America by way of Hamburg. S. A., Bergen: Stavanger Amt,
Journalsager, 1825, packet 501–1300.

narrowly escaped being greeted by cannon.[66]   No mishap
resulted, however, and the party remained at Madeira from
August 1 to 7.[67]   " The captain and passengers of the
sloop Restoration from Norway," ran a later notice in
a New York newspaper, " desire in this public manner,
to express their grateful thanks to John H. March, Esq.,
American consul at the island of Madeira, for his humane
and generous relief, when compelled to touch at that place
for refreshment after a long and perilous voyage, and to
the inhabitants of that island for the kind and hospitable
manner in which they entertained destitute strangers." [68]

After this pleasant stop the voyage was continued, and
on October 9, more than three months after leaving
Stavanger, the sloop arrived at New York.   The coming
of this first group of Norwegian immigrants attracted
considerable attention.   " The appearance of such a party
of strangers, coming from so distant a country and in a
vessel of a size apparently ill calculated for a voyage across
the Atlantic," according to a New York newspaper,
" could not but excite an unusual degree of interest."
The account, which bears the title " A Novel Sight," [69]
went on to describe the group:

[66] *Ole Rynning's True Account of America,* 72.   Rynning also tells of a stop
at an English port, where the " sloopers " sold whisky, not knowing of local regulations that made such sale illegal.   They put to sea again, he says, " in greatest
haste."   It is possible that the circuitous route followed by Captain Helland was
not the result of mischance.   He was at any rate equipped with a signal for use
in communication with Swedish ships in waters off the African coast.   This may
have been merely a conventional precaution.   Statement of Løwold, June 16, 1825,
published in *Norgesposten,* October 8, 1925.   On the other hand the consul in
New York (see *post,* n. 72) complained that the vessel lacked, among other things,
an " Algierian " pass for protection against Barbary pirates.

[67] The following shipping notice is printed in *Morgenbladet,* September 29, 1825:
" Arrived from Stavanger.   To Madeira the 1st of August and sailed from there
for New York on the 7th, same month."   The name of the ship is not mentioned.
The " Restauration's " ship papers were indorsed by the Swedish-Norwegian consul
at Madeira on August 6.   R. A., Oslo: F. D., Journalsager 456/1826 F.

[68] *New York Daily Advertiser,* October 15, 1825, reprinted in Anderson, *Norwegian Immigration,* 72.

[69] *New York Daily Advertiser,* October 12, 1825, reprinted in Anderson, *Norwegian Immigration,* 70–71.   A notice of the arrival, in the *New York Commercial
Advertiser,* October 10, 1825, is reprinted in *ibid.,* 70.

An enterprise like this argues a good deal of boldness in the master of the vessel as well as an adventurous spirit in the passengers, most of whom belong to families from the vicinity of a little town at the southwestern extremity of Norway, near Cape Stavanger. Those who came from the farms are dressed in coarse cloths of domestic manufacture, of a fashion different from the American, but those who inhabit the town wear calicos, ginghams and gay shawls, imported, we presume, from England. The vessel is built on the model common to fishing boats on that coast, with a single mast and topsail, sloop-rigged.

Cleng Peerson met the immigrants at New York as he had promised and the connections that he had already made in that city stood the party in good stead. Most of the immigrants were extremely poor, and for them the problem of proceeding to the interior and getting established before the winter season came on was a difficult one. Assistance was secured from the Quakers and others in New York whose attention was called to the needs of the party. The sale of the sloop must have proved a great disappointment to its owners, for it brought them no more than four hundred dollars — less than one-third of its cost.[70] Under the circumstances, however, they were fortunate in realizing even this small amount, for they narrowly escaped losing the " Restauration " through confiscation as a result of their violation of an American federal act of 1819 which permitted only two passengers to each five tons of the tonnage of a trans-Atlantic vessel.[71] Under the act the forty-five passengers of the " Restauration " — not including the crew of seven — should have had the accommodation of a ship of 112½ tons. If the child born during the voyage were counted in deciding the question, the minimum legal tonnage should have been 115 tons. In fact, as has been noted, the tonnage was under 40, though newspaper reports put it at 45. Customs officers at first generously reckoned the tonnage as 55; later it was pushed up to 60 and a fraction, but even this was far short of the legal tonnage. Officials

---

[70] Ole Rynning's True Account of America, 73.
[71] United States, Statutes at Large, 3: 488.

manifested a generous desire to overlook the unwitting offense of the immigrants and the case also aroused a friendly
public interest; the collector of customs offered to draw
up a statement to be transmitted to the secretary of the
treasury asking that the sloop be restored to its owners.
The Norwegian-Swedish consul reported the affair fully
to the Norwegian government on October 15, 1825; and
on November 24 he sent a supplementary report announcing that the government had released the sloop and had
excused the immigrants from all costs and obligations in
connection with the confiscation. The consul was much
disturbed over certain inadequacies in the ship's papers,
but since the " sloopers " had been legally " passed " by the
Norwegian authorities at Stavanger, he believed they were
entitled to his good will and aid. He mentioned incidentally
that public sympathy for the immigrants had been expressed in considerable gifts both of money and of clothes
to enable them to proceed on their journey.[72] Of the confiscation Ole Rynning remarks:

> Now I cannot say with certainty whether the government volun-
> tarily dropped the matter in consideration of the ignorance and child-
> like conduct of our good countrymen, or whether the Quakers had
> already at this time interposed for them; all I am sure of is that the
> skipper was released and the ship and its cargo were returned to their
> owners.[73]

A contemporary newspaper article states that the Norwegians were " all bound to Ontario County, where an
agent, who came over some time since, purchased a tract

---

[72] Henry Gahn to the Finance, Trade, and Tariff Department, October 15,
November 24, 1825, in R. A., Oslo: F. D., Journalsaker, F, 1825/487; and 1826/33.
At the end of his letter of November 24, Gahn remarks that he is inclosing a letter
for Elias Eliasen Tastad from one of the " Restauration " passengers and asks the
government to send it on. Would that the government had confiscated this letter
in the interest of future historians! The writer has been unable to find it among
the Tastad Papers in Stavanger. Items about the arrival of the " Restauration,"
its confiscation, and subsequent release appear in *Den Norske Rigstidende*, December
1, 1825; January 23, 1826.

[73] *Ole Rynning's True Account of America*, 73.

of land." [74]   A possible explanation of this statement is
the fact that the Pultney land office was at Geneva, in
Ontario County, though the company also controlled
lands in Orleans County.   At any rate, the majority of
the immigrants went to Orleans County and took land in
Murray Township, some thirty-five miles northwest of
the city of Rochester.   Fellows, the Pultney land agent,
met the party in New York, doubtless by previous arrangement with Peerson, and is said to have given considerable assistance to the " sloop folk." [75]   They left New
York some ten days after their arrival and on October
22 passed Albany on their way to their destination.
" They appear to be quite pleased with what they see in
this country, if we may judge from their good-humored
countenances," wrote the *Albany Patriot*.   " Success attend their efforts in this asylum of the oppressed." [76]

The immigrants reached their destination about the beginning of November.   The Erie Canal was open and the
westward movement was going forward vigorously.   The
western part of New York was being very rapidly settled
at the time.   The city of Rochester, for example, nearly
doubled its population in 1825. [77]   The land to which
Joseph Fellows piloted the company was on the shores of
Lake Ontario in the northern half of Murray Township.
This part later became Kendall Township and the colony
therefore has been known generally as the " Kendall settlement."   The agent charged the Norwegians five dollars
an acre for their land and sold to each adult of the party
of settlers a tract of forty acres.   As the immigrants were

[74] *New York Daily Advertiser*, October 12, 1825, in Anderson, *Norwegian Immigration*, 70.

[75] Anderson, *Norwegian Immigration*, 64, 77.

[76] Copied in the *New York Evening Post*, October 24, 1825, and reprinted in
Anderson, *op. cit.*, 70.

[77] " Rochester is celebrated all over the union as presenting one of the most
striking instances of rapid increase in size and population, of which the country
affords an example." Basil Hall, *Travels in North America*, 1: 153.

very nearly without means, Fellows agreed to a plan
whereby payment was to be made in ten annual installments. That better land could be secured at lower prices
much farther west was probably then unknown to these
pioneers. Nor could they have foreseen that the bulk
of the immigrants who were to follow would go to the
upper Mississippi Valley. Not all the members of the
original party went to the Kendall settlement. Several
remained in New York and at least two settled in
Rochester. The leader, Lars Larsen, probably went to the
Kendall settlement first, but he was a carpenter, not a
farmer. He soon removed to Rochester, where he was
destined to play an important rôle as an adviser to thousands of later immigrants who passed through that city
on their way to the West. It is said that a group of
twenty-four of the Kendall settlers constructed a comparatively small log house which served as their shelter
during the winter months. Employment secured from
American neighbors helped to ease the economic difficulties of the first few months.[78]

In December, 1825, Henry Gahn reported to the Norwegian government that he had heard a rumor that the
immigrants were dissatisfied with their expedition, that
they had not realized the advantages which they had believed would inevitably result from the enterprise.[79] " We
were all poor, and none of us could speak English," wrote
one of the immigrants later. " When we arrived in Kendall the most of us became sick and discouraged. The
timber was heavy and it took a long time before we could

---

[78] Ole Rynning's True Account of America, 73–74; Nilssen, in Billed-Magazin,
1: 72. Rynning states that the two who settled in Rochester — he names only
one, Larsen — were Quakers. Cadbury correctly assumes (Studies and Records,
1: 94) that one was Ole Johnson (Eie). For verification of the truth of this
assumption, see post, p. 108, n. 48.

[79] Henry Gahn to the Norwegian government, December 16, 1825, in R. A.,
Oslo: F. D., Journalsaker, F, 1826/33.

raise enough to support us." [80]   Of the settlement Rynning wrote in 1838: " The land was thickly overgrown with woods and difficult to clear.   Consequently, during the first four or five years conditions were very hard for these people.   They often suffered great need and wished themselves back in Norway; but they saw no possibility of getting there without giving up the last mite of their property, and they would not return as beggars.   Well-to-do neighbors assisted them, however, and by their own industry they at last got their land in such condition that they could earn a living from it, and live better than in their own native land." [81]   Peerson appears to have acted as a kind of self-appointed agent of the settlers in securing aid from American neighbors; there is evidence that his methods were criticized by his countrymen; but an immigrant letter-writer of 1838 remarks of him: " Meanwhile Cleng Peerson was always active.   Heavy work was never to his taste, but on the other hand he never attempted to enrich himself; he worked for all and benefited all, though often in so indirect a way that few or none thanked him for his efforts." [82]   A curious reference to the Kendall settlement occurs in a Norwegian pamphlet of 1839, written by Peter Testman, who may have derived his information from Peerson.   He writes that the settlers at Kendall " suffered exceedingly from sickness, especially in the beginning, and this set them back considerably in their external circumstances.   It is true that after one man had taken it upon himself to seek aid for them they received not a little help from the Americans residing in the vicinity, but a large portion of their gifts unfortunately went up in flames when a fire broke out in the

[80] A letter from H. Hervig originally printed in *Fædrelandet og Emigranten* (La Crosse, Wisconsin), February 9, 1871; reprinted in Anderson, *Norwegian Immigration*, 79–80.

[81] *Rynning's True Account of America*, 73–74.

[82] Illinois letter of January 28, 1838, in *Det udflyttede Norge*, 6–8.

house in which they were kept. The little aid which was again given them was far from sufficient to relieve the great distress, and they had to contend with straitened circumstances for a long time before their condition was somewhat bettered. In recent times property there, as well as in every place where population increases, has risen considerably in price." [83]

Thus, despite difficulties of language, sickness, poverty, and pioneering, the first Norwegian settlement established in the United States in the nineteenth century took root. The importance of the migration of 1825 with reference to the movement as a whole can be understood only by following the rising stream of immigration after 1825. It is sufficient to note here that a beginning had been made and thus connections had been established between the Norwegian community in and about Stavanger and a settlement in the United States. The other two problems suggested at the beginning of this account may be definitely answered in the light of the evidence brought forward. The figure of Cleng Peerson stands forth as the promoter of the migration of 1825. It is certain that this pathfinder — his later achievements remain to be narrated — was, as some writers have maintained, the " father of Norwegian immigration to the United States." It would doubtless be a mistake to attribute too much significance to one individual in connection with the larger movement of Norweg n immigration, a movement involving hundreds of tnousands of people. The point is simply that the leadership of Peerson does figure prominently in the migration of 1825. It is certain also that however important the economic needs of the Stavanger emigrants of 1825 were as a motivating factor, the treatment accorded the Quakers by the Norwegian government and by the established church played a significant part in the initiation of modern Norwegian immigration.

[83] *Peter Testman's Account of His Experiences in North America, 49.*

III. THE BEGINNINGS OF WESTERN SETTLEMENT

THERE is no record of a group emigration from Norway between 1825 and 1836. This fact evidences the lack of general preparation for a considerable Norwegian emigration movement in the twenties and early thirties. Most of the rural communities in Norway were extremely isolated in the early part of the nineteenth century. Much as people may have felt the pressure of economic or other burdens, they knew little about the United States and its possibilities for the European immigrant. Save for stray newspaper items — and this was a period of few newspapers, most of them with little space for items other than official announcements and advertisements [1] — there was an almost total lack of printed information in the Norwegian language concerning America. The departure of the Stavanger emigrants in 1825, though news of it crept into the leading newspaper at Christiania, probably caused few ripples of interest outside of Stavanger *Amt*. And even there, it must be remembered, emigration had been in no sense general. It was an expression of the discontent of a little minority that was, in part at least, marked off from the general community by its spirit of nonconformity. Emigrants are always nonconformists in some sense; some were in the religious as well as the economic or social sense. Furthermore, it was natural even for those who, as relatives or neighbors or sympathizers, were especially interested in the fortunes of the " sloop folk " to wait for definite news about the outcome of the experiment before embarking upon a similar venture.

[1] *Norske Aviser 1763–1920: Fortegnelse over Aviser som findes i Universitetsbiblioteket og andre Samlinger* (Kristiania, 1924); S. C. Hammer, "Den Periodiske Presse i Norge: Historisk Oversigt," in *Norges Næringsliv*, 4: 1–16 (1911).

Direct regular communication between the Norwegian ports and New York or other American ports was not available. Consequently, in the absence of groups of emigrants large enough to charter or buy vessels for the voyage, it was necessary for individual emigrants to go by indirect routes. Occasionally Swedish ships carrying cargoes of iron sailed from Göteborg for American ports, and many Norwegian emigrants between 1825 and 1850 made Göteborg their first objective. Once arrived at that port they waited, sometimes for weeks, for a ship on which they could get passage. They might cross to Hamburg, an important point of departure for German emigrants, and wait for an opportunity to take one of the ships leaving that port for America. Yet another possibility was Havre, and considerable numbers of Norwegian immigrants went to the United States by way of France in the thirties and forties. Peerson in 1824 called attention to the possibility of going to England and there getting passage for New York, but evidence that many Norwegians followed this route in the early period is lacking.[2]

In the American immigration statistics for the years from 1820 to 1868 Norwegian and Swedish immigrants are grouped together.[3] For the years following the Norwegian immigration of 1825, therefore, the American

[2] The earliest example that the writer has yet found of the use of the Hamburg route by a Norwegian is in 1825. See *ante*, ch. 2, n. 65. On June 30, 1843, the Swedish-Norwegian consul at Havre reported that during the year 841 Norwegian emigrants had arrived at that port on their way to America. Report of Ch. Broström, in Social Dept., Lovkontor, Oslo: Utv., Kong. Prop. 1845, folder 2. For Peerson's advice, see Madland to Halvarsen, June 28, 1825, in appendix.

[3] *Statistical Review of Immigration 1820–1900* in *Senate Documents*, 61 Congress, 3 session, vol. 20, no. 756, p. 14–29 (Washington, 1911 — serial 5878). This statistical review, prepared for the Dillingham Report by the chief statistician of the Immigration Commission, is a convenient and reliable summary of American immigration statistics for the period indicated. It should be noted that the figures for the year 1868 cover only the six months ending June 30. Table 9 tabulates the arrivals from 1820 to 1910 by country of origin. Beginning with 1869 the Norwegian arrivals are listed separately.

records are of little help in determining the number of immigrants from Norway. The figures that are available, moreover, are woefully inaccurate. For the eleven years from 1820 to 1830 inclusive, 94 Norwegian and Swedish immigrants arrived in the United States, according to American statistics.[4] It is noteworthy, however, that only 4 are listed for 1825, the year in which the " Restauration " brought to New York 53 persons, including the crew of 7. The figures indicate, notwithstanding their inaccuracy, that a few Scandinavians were arriving each year. According to the same American records, 415 immigrants from the two countries came in the years from 1831 to 1835; but only 57 are listed for 1836, the year when two Norwegian ships landed 167 immigrants and there was some indirect Norwegian emigration by way of Göteborg. For that year the official Norwegian statistics, which are unreliable for the earlier years because they give only round numbers, indicate an emigration of 200.[5] It is evident that for the first period of Norwegian immigration the American records of arrivals cannot be used with any assurance of even approximate accuracy.[6]

During the period from 1825 to 1833 the Norwegian settlers at and near Kendall triumphed over their initial difficulties and, according to Rynning, became so well established that their economic situation was a distinct improvement over what it had been in Norway. " As a result of their letters," wrote Rynning, " more Norwegian peasants were now encouraged to try their fortunes in America; but they went only singly, and

[4] *Statistical Review*, 14–17 (serial 5878).

[5] *Statistical Review*, 17–19 (serial 5878); Cadbury, " Four Immigrant Shiploads of 1836 and 1837," in *Studies and Records*, 2: 22–37; *Utvandringsstatistikk (Statistique de l'émigration)*, 101 (Departementet for Sociale Saker, *Norges Offisielle Statistikk*, series 7, no. 25 — Kristiania, 1921).

[6] Babcock and Nelson arrive at a similar conclusion. See the table of statistics in Babcock, *Scandinavian Element*, 206–209, and Nelson, *Scandinavians in the United States*, 243–264d.

commonly took the route by way of Göteborg, Sweden, where there is often a chance to get passage for America." [7] Now and then Norwegians returned to their native land from the West; thus two went back in the spring of 1828.[8] One of the "sloop folk," Ole Johnson (Eie), returned to Stavanger, was married there on July 24, 1828, to a member of the Quaker society, and very soon thereafter again departed for America.[9] Specific cases of individual emigrant ventures are Christian Olson and Gudmund Sandsberg in 1829; Knud Anderson Slogvig, a Quaker who was to become prominent as an emigrant leader, Rasmus Christensen, and Mikkel Halvorsen with his wife and child in 1830; Knut Evenson, Ingebrigt Larson Narvig, and Gjert G. Hovland in 1831; and Johan Nordboe in 1832.[10] Most of these were from southwestern Norway in the Stavanger region; but it is of interest to note that Nordboe was from eastern Norway, Ringebu in Gudbrandsdalen, and thus he was one of the earliest emigrants from a great valley that was later to contribute large numbers to the movement. Most of these emigrants, including Nordboe, went to the Kendall settlement. This colony was never large, but in 1834 it had at least fourteen families.[11]

[7] *True Account of America,* 74.

[8] On May 22, 1828, Gahn reported that he was sending a bundle of newspapers to the government "by two Norwegian countrymen who are departing from this place for their homes." R. A., Oslo: F. D., Journalsager F, 1828/240.

[9] The marriage contract of Johnson with Mallena Asbjørns Datter, the widow of Ole Frank and one of the original eight founders of the Quaker society, is recorded in "Prottocol eller Udkast Bog for Wennernes Tomaanes-Forsamling i Stavanger," following the entry for June 5, 1826. In November of the same year Johnson, his wife, and her son (Peter Olson Frank) were listed as members of the Rochester Quaker Society. Cadbury, in *Decorah-Posten,* June 4, 1926.

[10] On Slogvig, Christensen, and Frøland see S. A., Bergen: Kirkebøker, Skjold, 5, 1815–30. "This couple, whose conduct here so far as known to me has been christianlike, now intend to emigrate with their children to America in the hope of there getting better conditions than in the fatherland," wrote a Norwegian minister at Hjelmeland in a testimonial issued on June 9, 1829, to Sandsberg and his wife. Anderson, *Norwegian Immigration,* 133–134. On Narvig, a Quaker, and Nordboe, see *ibid.,* 138 ff.

[11] See *post,* n. 27.

The year 1834 marks the beginning of the break-up of the New York colony. In 1833 Cleng Peerson, who again appears in the rôle of trail blazer, set out on an exploratory journey to the West in search of suitable lands for settlement by the Norwegians. His travels took him into Ohio, across Michigan, and through northern Indiana into Illinois. It has been asserted that he walked along the shore of Lake Michigan as far north as the present site of Milwaukee. Here he met the founder of that city, the famous fur-trader Solomon Juneau, who in response to an inquiry informed him that Wisconsin land was heavily forested and entirely unsuitable for settlement. If Peerson did visit Milwaukee, he made his way back to Chicago without delay.[12] In Illinois he selected a site which determined the location of the first Norwegian settlement in the Mississippi Valley and gave great impetus to the westward migration of the Norwegians. This was in the Fox River region, in the township of Mission, near Ottawa, La Salle County, Illinois. Some years later, in describing the manner of his choice, Peerson said that while on a walking trip from Chicago he came to a hill overlooking the Fox River Valley. Almost exhausted from hunger and fatigue, he threw himself on the grass and thanked God for having directed his steps to such an attractive land. In his enthusiasm he temporarily forgot his hunger and weariness and his thoughts turned to Moses and the Promised Land.[13] After making this selection, Peerson

[12] Holand, *De Norske Settlementers Historie*, 43–44. In a letter to the writer, Mr. Holand states that the story was based upon an interview with an old settler. When Peerson left New York he is said to have been accompanied by Ingebrigt Larson Narvig and perhaps another companion. Narvig went no farther than Monroe County, Michigan. Anderson, *Norwegian Immigration*, 144 ff., sketches the later career of Narvig.

[13] Langeland, *Nordmændene i Amerika*, 18–19. The story was told to Langeland by Peerson in Norway in 1843. Langeland was a prospective emigrant and one must reckon with the possibility that Peerson may have devised the tale to picture America as favorably as possible. Langeland's simple statement of the affair seems to have given rise to numerous elaborate accounts of what is termed " Cleng Peerson's dream," some of them embroidered with artistic details.

trudged back to the Norwegian settlement in New York. In all, he is said to have walked more than two thousand miles on his pilgrimage to the West and his return to the East.

That Peerson served as the chosen representative of the Kendall settlers in this venture is not certain. But the facts indicate that his glowing reports on conditions in the West found ready acceptance among the New York colonists, for in 1834 six families moved to Illinois and there established the second Norwegian settlement in the United States — the "Fox River Settlement." [14] The period was one of rapid settlement in La Salle County and in fact throughout the valley of the Illinois River. The air was full of schemes for internal improvements. A land grant to aid the construction of a canal from Lake Michigan to the Illinois River had been made six years before Cleng Peerson visited Illinois. Work on the canal did not begin until 1836, but in the early thirties much interest was shown by settlers and speculators in La Salle County, for it was believed that the proposed canal would make a junction with the Illinois River in that county.[15] Thus the trend of settlement in northern Illinois made it entirely natural for Peerson and his followers to go to

[14] Hovland to Mæland, April 22, 1835. See *post*, n. 27.

[15] "The Illinois and Michigan canal from Chicago to the Illinois river, was to connect with the latter somewhere in La Salle County. Settlers flocked in hoping to obtain lands on or near the proposed line. When the land sales were made in 1835, however, the speculators present took the lion's share. During the following year came the greatest immigration of the period. Ground was broken for the canal, July 4, 1836, and the beginning of active operations no doubt tended to increase greatly the crowd of newcomers. . . . The arrival, at this time, of the first band of Scandinavians was an event of some importance in the settlement of this part of Illinois. . . . Soon there was to be a great throng of foreigners poured through the Chicago gateway upon the prairies." William V. Pooley, *The Settlement of Illinois from 1830–1850*, 384–385 (University of Wisconsin, *Bulletins*, no. 220, History series, vol. 1, no. 4 — Madison, 1908). See also Theodore C. Pease, *The Frontier State, 1818–1848*, chs. 9 and 21 (*Centennial History of Illinois*, vol. 2 — Springfield, 1918). Some attention is given to the effect of the canal

La Salle County when in 1834 they turned their backs upon the East. They knew of the effect which the Erie Canal had had upon settlement and land values in New York. The region in Illinois to which they went offered land at $1.25 per acre — a price considerably lower than that at which land was available in western New York. A settlement in the Fox or Illinois river valley, moreover, would afford comparatively easy access, by natural and developed routes, to markets.[16]

The advance guard of settlers in 1834 at first took claims, for not until 1835 were land sales held. But in June, 1835, land purchases by Peerson and others from Kendall were recorded. These records show that the nucleus of Norwegian settlement in Illinois and the West was in the La Salle County townships of Mission, Rutland, and Miller.[17] Those Norwegians who remained in the New York settlement were interested in the Illinois venture of their countrymen. " Six families of the Norwegians who had settled in this place sold their farms last summer and moved farther west in the country to a place which is called *Ellenaais*," wrote Gjert G. Hovland from Kendall on April 22, 1835. " We and another Norwegian family have also sold our farms and intend to journey, this May, to that state, where land can be bought at a better price, and where it is easier to get started." In the same letter he says, " The eight Norwegian families still in this neighborhood desire to sell their land as soon

upon the growth of La Salle County and the surrounding region in James W. Putnam, *The Illinois and Michigan Canal: a Study in Economic History*, ch. 4 (Chicago Historical Society, *Collections*, vol. 10 — Chicago, 1918).

[16] Pooley, *Settlement of Illinois from 1830 to 1850*, ch. 5. In this chapter there is a valuable discussion of the " Illinois and Fox River Valleys."

[17] Land records show that Cleng Peerson bought at least two hundred and forty acres of land in the settlement in June, 1835. Original land records at Ottawa, Illinois, were examined by Mr. Anderson, and are printed in his *Norwegian Immigration*, 175–176.

as they can, and to move west." [18]   Less then two months
after this letter was written Hovland's purchase of 160
acres in La Salle County was recorded.[19]   In the same
year, 1835, several other families emigrated from the older
settlement.   Among these may be mentioned Nels Nelson
Hersdal, who had a farm of a hundred acres in the New
York settlement.   In exchange for this land he secured
640 acres in La Salle County — an amount of land that
might well astound peasants in Norway, who were unac-
customed to such figures.[20]   The New York settlement
did not completely lose its identity, but when Rynning
wrote his account of conditions in America some three
years later he said of the Norwegian colony in New York:
" Only two or three families remain there now; the others
have moved farther into the country." [21]

Meanwhile information concerning America was being
transmitted to Norway in letters from immigrants who
already had had the benefit of several years' experience
in the New World.   Their written reports of personal
observation played an important part in the entire emigration movement, particularly in the period before books
and pamphlets that contained the kind of precise information wanted by the Norwegian commoners were available.   The informative value of these letters, which were
commonly called " America letters," was everywhere recognized.   In many cases they were copied and recopied,
sent among the parishes from neighbor to neighbor, carried by lay preachers from one parish to another, and

[18] Hovland to Mæland, April 22, 1835.

[19] Hovland's land purchase in Miller Township was recorded on June 17, 1835.
Anderson, *Norwegian Immigration*, 175.

[20] *Ibid.*, 102.   Evidence of the continued interest of Joseph Fellows in the Norwegian immigrants is the fact that Hersdal's purchase in Illinois was arranged
by Fellows.

[21] *True Account of America*, 78.   Rynning comments on the tendency of the
Norwegians " to seek a place where they can expect to find countrymen," but he
adds that " it is always difficult to get good unoccupied land in the vicinity of
those who immigrated one or two years earlier."

thus given a circulation that in time carried the story of the Norwegian settlements and American conditions far and wide in southern Norway. In some cases, it is said, the process went on until hundreds of copies of an original letter were in circulation. The situation resembles that among certain groups in England in the period of the Puritan emigration of the seventeenth century, when a letter from New England was " Venerated as a Sacred Script, or as the Writing of some Holy Prophet, 'twas carried many miles, where divers came to hear it." [22]

Especially important in the late thirties and early forties were the letters written by Gjert G. Hovland, who went to the Kendall settlement in 1831 and, as has been noted, removed to Illinois in 1835. Rynning mentions his letters as a factor in the dissemination of information about the United States in the diocese of Bergen.[23] Langeland, an emigrant of 1843, writes of the hundreds of copies of Hovland's letters that were in circulation, awakening " great interest among the people." [24] Specific instances may be cited of immigrants who reached their decision to emigrate as late as 1839 as a result of reading Hovland's letters.[25] The letters were also given wide newspaper pub-

[22] See the writer's pamphlet The " America Letters " (Det Norske Videnskaps-Akademi i Oslo, Avhandlinger, II Hist.-Filos. Klasse, 1928, no. 5). Unfortunately, few texts of " America letters " for the period from 1825 to 1836 are available. Now and then one finds stray allusions to such letters. For example, a letter from Ole Johnson to Elias Tastad was transmitted to the Norwegian government in 1834 by Consul Gahn to be forwarded to Tastad. R. A., Oslo: F. D., F, Journalsager, 1834/341. But this letter has not been found in the Tastad Papers at Stavanger. For the English quotation see S. E. Morison, Builders of the Bay Colony, 342 (Boston and New York, 1930).

[23] True Account of America, 74.

[24] Nordmændene i Amerika, 16 and note. Langeland characterizes Hovland as " an intelligent and liberal peasant from Hardanger " who was well known in several parishes in the Bergen diocese. His letters, in Langeland's opinion, had a " very decisive influence upon the emigration." Langeland had himself read a copy of one of them.

[25] See, for a general estimate of Hovland's importance, Billed-Magazin, 1: 74. Anderson tells of the influence of the Hovland letters in Voss: " a lay preacher had brought a copy of one of Gjert Hovland's letters to Voss, and it was the

lication from 1835 to 1843, and in some cases were used as the starting point for discussions of the entire emigration problem.[26] When in 1837 the dean of the Hardanger district, the Reverend Nils Hertzberg, reported to the local sheriff on the emigration from that area, he attributed much influence to Hovland's letters and included with his report a copy of one written from the Kendall settlement on April 22, 1835. There is evidence that late in April of that year Hovland dispatched at least three long letters to Norwegian friends, substantially identical in content. These and perhaps others were probably carried to Norway by an immigrant who returned in that year. Two of these were later given newspaper publication and a copy of the one already referred to was eventually sent to the government and is now preserved in an archival collection. In view of the undoubted vogue and influence of Hovland's views it may be of interest to analyze one of his letters in detail, that of April 22, 1835. Though it has a special importance, it may perhaps also be considered typical of numerous favorable " America letters." [27]

" Nothing has made me more happy and contented than the fact that we left Norway and journeyed to this country," writes Hovland. " We have gained more since our arrival here than I did during all the time that I lived

With it were published two other letters by Hovland written after he had removed to Illinois.

[26] See for example a letter of April 28, 1835, with a discussion of emigration, in *Den Norske Rigstidende*, May 25, 28, 1837. A Hovland letter of April 23, 1835, was brought out eight years later in *Christianssandsposten*, February 23, 1843. With it were published two other letters by Hovland written after he had removed to Illinois.

[27] The letter is addressed to Torjuls A. Mæland of Kingservig parish, Ullensvang, Hovland's brother-in-law. A transcript from the Ullensvang church archives is in the manuscript collection of the Minnesota Historical Society; the letter may also be found with Hertzberg's report of July 6, 1837, in Socialdept., Oslo: Lovkontor, Utvandringen, Kong. Prop. 1845, folder 1. Hertzberg says that the Hovland letters were brought to Norway by Knud Anderson Slogvig. He also alludes to several other letters written by Hovland. For the published letters see *ante*, n. 26.

in Norway, and I have every prospect of earning a livelihood here for myself and my family — even if my family
were larger — so long as God gives me good health." The
writer of this " America letter " does not content himself
with generalizations.   He tells of his emigration from
Norway, with full particulars about the results as measured in land and money.   With his family he sailed from
Göteborg on July 30, 1831, reached America on September 18, and on October 4 arrived at the Kendall settlement
in Orleans County.   The day after his arrival he began
to work for an American.   In December he bought fifty
acres of land.   By March, 1832, he had built a house into
which he moved with his family.   His land was wooded
and he set to work clearing it " with the greatest will and
pleasure."   In the fall of 1833, he writes, " we harvested
fifteen barrels of wheat, six barrels of Indian corn, and
fourteen barrels of potatoes."   In July, 1834, he sold his
farm of fifty acres and " by the transaction earned in cash
the sum of five hundred dollars."   He was about to leave
for Illinois, where he was to buy a quarter section of land,
and in the letter under discussion he writes about the
prospects in Illinois, pointing out that " the supply of
trees there is only sufficient to meet one's actual needs,"
and that cattle can be fed there at practically no cost.
" There is an untold amount of land which the United
States owns," he continues, " and which is reserved by
an established law at a set price for the one who buys
first from the government.   It is called public land, and
is sold for $1.25 per acre. . . . Whether native-born or
foreign, one is free to do with it whatever one pleases."
Some of Hovland's comments on general American
conditions are of interest as illustrations of the sort of
information which was considered important for the prospective emigrant.   For example, he states that his son has
been sent to an American school and already " talks English as well as the native-born."   Writing of provisions for

the care of the poor in the United States he says, " I do
not believe there can be better laws and arrangements for
the benefit and happiness of the common man in the whole
world." Hovland was impressed by certain aspects of
American democracy. He points out, for example, that
in the election of officials " the vote of the common man
carries just as much authority and influence as does that
of the rich and powerful man." In dress and in privileges,
he observes, no distinctions can be noted as between farmers and clerks. " The freedom which the one enjoys is
just as good as that of the other." The absence of passports and the liberty of everyone " to engage in whatever
business he finds most desirable, in trade or commerce, by
land or by water " are duly noted. He assures his correspondent that no duties are levied upon goods produced
in the country and marketed in the city. With reference
to the inheritance of property he remarks, — with a touch
of reminiscent bitterness, — " There is no one here who
snatches it away, like a beast of prey, wanting only to
live by the sweat of others."

The letter contains specific information on the prices
of commodities and on wages. Wheat is from three dollars to four dollars per barrel, corn from one and a half
to two dollars, oats one dollar, potatoes fifty cents.
" We purchased a cow in April of the first year that we
were here for eighteen dollars, from which we milked six
kander (Norwegian measure) a day and sometimes more."
The prices of butter, salt pork, and meat are listed. The
wages of hired men and servant girls are given. There
is also exact information as to the size of an acre and
as to land measurements generally. " This is a beautiful
and fertile country," writes Hovland. " Prosperity and
contentment are to be seen almost everywhere one goes."
But " everyone must work for his living here, and it
makes no difference whether he is of low or of high estate."

" Excellent order and good laws " exist in America,
he points out, and adds that " the country is governed by
wise authorities."   " Everyone has the freedom to practice that teaching and religion which he himself favors."
Taxes, he writes, put no heavy burdens upon the people.
" For the fifty acres which I have sold I paid annually
one dollar in taxes."   A little thrust at Norwegian officialdom appears in the following statement: " Nor are there
other useless expenditures for the support of persons —
as in many places in Europe — who are no benefit, but
much rather are of harm to the country."

In one passage of the letter Hovland writes, " It would
heartily please me if I could learn that all of you
who are in need and have little chance of gaining support
for yourselves and your families would make up your
mind to leave Norway and to come to America, for, even
if many more were to come, there would still be room
here for all."   Those who are willing and able to work
can easily secure employment, he writes, and " it is possible for all to live in comfort and without suffering want."
Those who suffer under the oppression of others and are
attempting to raise their children under straitened circumstances are urged to emigrate.   Many persons of
course lack the necessary means to make the venture and
others, according to the letter writer, lack the initiative
to move even though " they have nothing but hard bread
to satisfy their hunger. . . . It is as if they should say
that those who move to a better land, where there is
plenty, commit a wrong."   Apropos of this Hovland remarks loftily, — his phrase was much quoted by the early
immigrants, — " But I can find no place where our
Creator has forbidden one to seek one's food in an honorable manner."   He admits that he would enjoy a visit
with some of his Norwegian friends but asserts that he
does not wish to live in Norway.   " We lived there alto-

gether too long. Nor have I talked with any immigrant in this country who wished to return."

The letter is packed with homely details, but they were precisely the details the Norwegian *bønder* wanted to know. Hovland painted his picture in bright colors and perhaps caused some of his readers to anticipate an Eldorado which, to their tragic disappointment, they failed to find. But it must be noted that he wrote after four years of pioneering. Hostile newspapers, seeking to discredit the evidence in his letters, sometimes contrasted them with gloomy letters written by immigrants soon after their arrival. Hovland reflected the optimism of the American frontier, where land and liberty, which he vaunted, were undeniable realities, though the trials, both material and spiritual, which he did not appraise, were also real. It is worthy of note that after he left New York he had his full share of the trials of a pioneer, but though his letters from the later period are somewhat more conservative than those of 1835 he retains his faith in America. Of an emigrant who gave up and returned to Norway, he wrote in 1842, " He was not reared among that class of people who are equipped to meet difficulties." [28]

The people in southwestern Norway were not left to depend alone upon the written word as transmitted in letters for their knowledge of American conditions. In 1835 Knud Anderson Slogvig, who had emigrated five years earlier and had lived in the Kendall settlement until 1834, when he removed to the Fox River settlement in Illinois, returned to Norway, probably with a companion. Slogvig was not the first immigrant to return, but he was in a position to report on the ten years' progress of the New York colony and on the situation in the Mississippi Valley. It was one thing to read letters from the earlier

---

[28] Hovland to Peder J. Sætten, July 9, 1842, in *Christianssandsposten*, February 23, 1843. *Cf.* the writer's *The " America Letters,"* 8.

immigrants detailing their experiences, but it was a different matter to talk with a man who had first-hand knowledge of the settlers' experiences and fortunes. The scores of problems relating to the ocean voyage, the journey to the interior, the life of a pioneer immigrant farmer both in western New York and in Illinois could be explained to Norwegian commoners by this "America traveler" — the phrase is a common one in emigrant sources — in an authoritative way.[29] "There before them at last," writes Dr. Babcock, "was a man who had twice braved all the terrors of thousands of miles of sea and hundreds of miles of far-distant land, who had come straight and safe from that fabulous vast country, with its great broad valleys and prairies, with its strange white men, and stranger red men."[30] The news of Slogvig's return spread far beyond his home district of Skjold on the southwestern coast. "From all parts of the diocese of Bergen and from Stavanger," writes an immigrant of 1843, "people came to talk with him." Three of this man's relatives visited Slogvig in the winter of 1836 and returned to their homes suffering from an acute attack of "America fever."[31] The constant use of this term as descriptive of the frame of mind of prospective immigrants from 1836 on indicates that there was a mounting interest among Norwegians as they received more definite information about the New World.[32] Slogvig not only brought his own testimony as to the situation in America, but he also was the bearer of letters from immigrants to their relatives and friends. The sensation caused

[29] *Rynning's True Account of America*, 74; the narrative of Ole Nattestad as given by Nilssen in *Billed-Magazin*, 1: 83; Langeland, *Nordmændene i Amerika*, 17; Stavanger *Amt* report of April 20, 1837, in S. A., Bergen: Stavanger Amt Copie-Bog, 1836–37.

[30] *Scandinavian Element*, 32.

[31] Langeland, *Nordmændene i Amerika*, 17.

[32] "Slogvig's return may be said to have started the 'America-fever' in Norway, though it took some years before it reached the central and the eastern parts of the country." Flom, *Norwegian Immigration*, 63.

by the return of Slogvig and his companion is reflected in an official report made two years later by Stavanger *Amt* to the finance department, in which reference is made to the earlier emigrants. " A few of these," runs the report, " came back after a year's time, and a few were hired as seamen, but the greater part of them settled in the interior of the country as farmers. A couple of these returned in 1835 for a visit to their relatives, and they reported that it was much better to live in America, that it was possible to live in that country without much exertion and labor, that wages were higher, that it was not necessary there to eat oaten bread and other such simple foods, but that everyone could have wheat bread, rice pudding, meat, and the like, in abundance. Such a Canaan — so it was reported — naturally would be welcome to many who in these regions have a wretched enough existence." The report goes on to stress the importance of the connections with the earlier colonists. Many of the prospective emigrants who came under Slogvig's influence " also had relatives in America from the first emigration from whom they received reports that all was going well there and encouragement to emigrate to that country." [33]

The best evidence of the influence of Slogvig lies in the fact that he became the leader of a group of immigrants in 1836. Two emigrant vessels left Stavanger for New York in that year, the brigs " Norden " on May 25 with 110 passengers and " Den Norske Klippe," which was cleared on June 8, with 57 passengers.[34] In addition to these emigrants there were some who went by a sloop to Göteborg, where they got passage for New York. All

[33] Report of April 20, 1837, in S. A., Bergen: Stavanger Amt Copie-Bog, 1836–37. *Cf. Storthings Forhandlinger i Aaret 1845*, vol. 1, part 6, p. 24–25.

[34] Stavanger Customs Office, " Toldboden: Udgaaende for Aar 1836," entries 140 and 171.

told, the emigration of 1836 was in the vicinity of two hundred. A contemporary newspaper reports:

With the exception of a couple of individuals all these emigrants are farmers, most of them from Ryfylke, and proportionally many more families (parents and children) than unmarried persons. Many of the heads of families owned *gaards* or places here, but nearly all were so burdened with interest and other payments that their income did not come up to their expenses. With what they have left they hope, however, not only to place themselves in a position to earn their living in America but also to be able to leave something to their children. Most of them intend to go to Illinois, where some of the earlier emigrants from this region have settled and where they have in part already selected land for them. One woman gave birth to a child shortly before the ship left and two other births are expected during the voyage.[35]

An official report of 1837 presented an interesting analysis of the groups that went on " Norden " and " Den Norske Klippe." There were 29 families, made up of 28 married men with their wives, 1 widow, and 73 children; 27 single men and 8 single women. Two men were from Bergen; 4 families, comprising 16 persons, were from Søndre Bergenhus *Amt;* 1 man and wife, 8 single men, and 1 woman from Stavanger; 2 men and 2 women from Jedderen and Dalerne; and the rest from Ryfylke.[36]

The desire on the part of these people to better their economic circumstances was undoubtedly a prominent motive for this emigration. On May 14, 1836, Andreas Sandsberg of Hellen wrote to a brother in America:

A considerable number of people are now getting ready to go to America from this *Amt* [*Stavanger*]. Two brigs are to depart from Stavanger in about eight days from now, and will carry these people to America, and if good reports come from them, the number of emigrants will doubtless be still larger next year. A pressing and

---

[35] *Stavanger Adresseavis*, May 27, 1836. The item, dated May 27, refers to the departure of 110 persons " i Forgaars," that is, the day before yesterday. This is a reference to " Norden." The clearance (*cf.* preceding note) is dated May 25.

[36] Stavanger *Amt* report of April 30 in S. A., Bergen: Stavanger Amt, Copie-Bog, 1836–37.

general lack of money entering into every branch of industry, stops or at least hampers business and makes it difficult for many people to earn the necessaries of life. While this is the case on this side of the Atlantic there is hope of abundance on the other, and this, I take it, is the chief cause of the growing disposition to emigrate. I am very anxious to get a letter from you, in which I beg you to inform me about your own circumstances and about the condition of the country in general.[37]

In a contemporary discussion of the causes of this Norwegian emigration, a writer attributed it to the discontent especially prevalent among tillers of the soil in Stavanger *Amt* because of heavy taxes, complications in land inheritance, and more particularly burdens involved in the purchase and sale of the state's beneficed lands, alienation of which was authorized in a law of 1821. This law was believed to be in need of amendment; such beneficed lands, it was asserted, were frequently so loaded with delinquent obligations that purchase proved to be impossible for the tenant. As a result they were in some cases left uncultivated. Through a series of years taxes had been particularly heavy in Stavanger *Amt* and no relief appeared to be imminent. Farmers were therefore in a mood to listen to the favorable reports brought to them from the United States, where land taxes were comparatively light. The emigrants were characterized as careful, industrious, and sensible; and it was predicted that unless reforms in the direction of lower taxes and greater ease in the acquisition and sale of lands by farmers were effected, Norway would witness an emigration that would be proportionately larger than that from any other country save England.[38]

That the economic formula does not fully explain the migration, however, is clear from several bits of evidence.

[37] Quoted in Anderson, *Norwegian Immigration*, 135.

[38] "Hvad kan vel Grunden være til Udvandringen fra Stavanger-Amt i Norge til Nordamerica?" in *Aften-Bladet eller Nyeste Skilderie af Christiania og Stockholm*, May 28, 1836 (no. 38). England as used here is probably intended to include the British Isles.

There were undoubtedly Quaker connections in the migration of 1836 as well as in that of eleven years earlier. The leader, Slogvig, was himself a Quaker; one of the emigrants on " Norden " was Metha Trulsdatter, who was among the eight original founders of the Stavanger Society of Friends; [39] and there were probably not a few others who were in sympathy with the Quakers. *Amtmand* Aas sent a report to the justice department, on April 11, 1836, telling of the proposed emigration and inquiring whether or not official action should be taken to prevent it. " The persons who intend to undertake this emigration," he declared, " are to a large extent individuals who accept the basic principles of the Quaker sect and therefore find their consciences troubled by being subjected to the teachings and ceremonies of the Evangelical Lutheran religion, especially with reference to the baptism of children, confirmation, marriages, and burials. Some, however, do not belong to this sect or follow special teachings, but expect to find better circumstances in the new world than here." Aas also refers to " a couple " of earlier emigrants, whose return had encouraged the emigration, and he speaks of the fact that some of the prospective emigrants had relatives or friends among the settlers in America. The department in its reply took the stand that if military service obligations or other duties did not interpose and if the emigrants were properly supplied with permits issued by the local police, nothing was to be done to hinder their going.[40]

[39] Cadbury, in *Studies and Records,* 2: 27; " Prottocol eller Udkast Bog for Wennernes Tomaanes-Forsamling i Stavanger," entry for August 29, 1818. Metha Trulsdatter is identical with the Metta W. Hille mentioned in ch. 2, n. 60. See also Cadbury, in *Decorah-Posten,* June 4, 1926.

[40] The magazine article previously referred to (n. 38) scouts the view that Quaker (or Haugean) persecution was an important factor in the emigration and declares that not more than a couple of the emigrants of 1836 were in fact Quakers. Malmin prints the Aas report of April 11, 1836, and the department's reply of May 2 in *Decorah-Posten,* December 19, 1924. The originals are in R. A., Oslo: Justis-

The case of Bjørn Anderson Kvelve, one of the emigrants on " Norden," is of special interest. He was from Vigedal, north of Stavanger. This man, according to his son,[41] was responsible for the fact that the " emigrants required two vessels, instead of only one." Although not formally a Quaker, he had come under the influence of Larsen, Tastad, and other Stavanger Friends. His " life and conduct were controlled by Quaker principles," and he felt " more or less " the persecution that was visited upon dissenters. But he was more than a religious nonconformist. He was an agitator who was able to gather " a crowd around him outside of the church before service or at other public gatherings to listen to his sarcastic criticisms of Norwegian laws and of the office-holding class." When he learned of Slogvig's plans he decided to emigrate and to use his influence to persuade others to join him. It appears, further, that he had reasons of a social nature for leaving his native land, having married above his class. The marriage resulted in the social ostracism of his wife, who was the daughter of a military officer, and this fact contributed to his desire to cast his lot with the immigrants in America. With his wife and two small sons, therefore, he set off in 1836.[42]

The departure of so many emigrants must have stirred the interest of people in southwestern Norway. " This first large emigration occasioned much comment and great surprise both in the town and the rural district," declared one of the emigrants many years later. " There was no

dept., A1, Journalsaker 1836/288 and Kopibøger 1836A, 57, no. 1012. A draft of the Aas letter is in S. A., Bergen: Stavanger Amt, Copie-Bog, 1835–36. Cf. a news note in *Morgenbladet*, May 26, 1836.

[41] Professor Rasmus B. Anderson of Madison, Wisconsin.

[42] Mr. Anderson gives a detailed account of his father's emigration in *Norwegian Immigration*, 154–170. His father was from the *gaard* Kvelve; hence the surname. It is curious to note, however, that in the passenger lists of 1836 his surname appears as Eike. Cadbury, in *Studies and Records*, 2: 25; and ship list of the " Norden," dated Stavanger, June 17, 1836, in S. A., Bergen: Stavanger Amt, Eldreafd., Pakke 678.

lack of admonitions; and warnings of slavery, disease, and death found a large place in conversations with acquaintances and other countrymen before the departure."[43]

It is of interest to note that Elias Tastad had close connections not only with the emigrants of 1836 but also with Tønnes Willemsen, the captain of "Norden." A letter by Willemsen of November 18, 1836, to Tastad describes the voyage; touches on health conditions and speaks of colds incurred because the immigrants lacked sufficient clothing, though it fails to mention the deaths of a man of 20, a girl of 14, and three children, recorded in the New York manifest; mentions the friendly attitude of Americans toward Norwegian immigrants; says that so

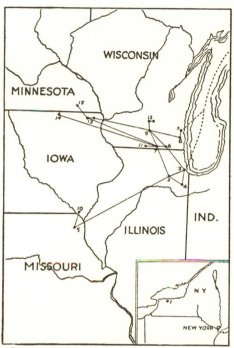

SITES OF SOME EARLY NORWEGIAN SETTLEMENTS
IN THE UNITED STATES

[From Knut Gjerset and Ludvig Hektoen in
Studies and Records, 1: 4]

1. Kendall, Orleans County, New York. 2. Fox River, La Salle County, Illinois. 3. Chicago. 4. Beaver Creek, Iroquois County, Illinois. 5. Shelby County, Missouri. 6. Jefferson Prairie, Rock County, Wisconsin. 7. Rock Prairie (Luther Valley), Rock County, Wisconsin. 8. Muskego, Wisconsin. x. Milwaukee. 9. Koshkonong, Dane County, Wisconsin. 10. Sugar Creek, Lee County, Iowa. 11. Wiota, Lafayette County, Wisconsin. 12. Spring Prairie and Bonnet Prairie, Columbia County, Wisconsin. 13. Washington Prairie, Winneshiek County, Iowa. 14. St. Ansgar, Mitchell County, Iowa. 15. Fillmore County, Minnesota.

[43] Amund Anderson Hornefjeld, a member of the group, tells the story of the emigration in *Billed-Magazin*, 1: 226.

many greetings were sent Tastad by the passengers that he is unable to write them down; and requests Tastad " again " to arrange for freight for an American voyage. It is obvious that the Stavanger Quaker leader was very much interested in the emigration.[44]

A member of the immigrant group of 1836 states that Slogvig acted as guide and interpreter for the group, but the Willemsen letter indicates that he remained temporarily in New York while the main body of immigrants started for Rochester.[45] Nor is there contemporary evidence that Cleng Peerson met the party in New York and acted as its guide to the interior.[46] A few of the immi-

[44] Tønnes Willemsen to Elias Tastad, November 18, 1836, in Tastad Papers, Quaker archives, Stavanger. Malmin prints this interesting letter in *Decorah-Posten,* December 5, 1924. Willemsen wrote from " Bremerhavn."

[45] Hornefjeld's narrative in *Billed-Magazin,* 1: 226; Willemsen to Tastad, November 18, 1836. H. J. Cadbury in " Four Norwegian Shiploads of 1836 and 1837," *Studies and Records,* 2: 20 ff., has made a useful contribution by printing the New York ship manifests of " Norden " and " Den Norske Klippe." He has also brought together much biographical information about the various members of the two parties. The two manifests are dated respectively July 20 and August 15, thus indicating the approximate time of arrival. (In *Den Norske Rigstidende* for October 30, 1836, the dates of arrival are given as July 18 and August 14.) Unfortunately the American lists contain many misspellings of names. Not a few of these Mr. Cadbury has been able to correct by comparison with other data, especially biographical notes in Anderson and Flom. It is now possible to collate both lists (in part) with Norwegian manifests drawn up before the departure of the two vessels. The present writer found such lists (unfortunately somewhat mutilated by mice or other natural enemies of historians) in S. A., Bergen: Stavanger Amt, Eldreafd., Pakke 678. To give only a few illustrations of the types of corrections that need to be made: " Saml P. Custod " of " Den Norske Klippe " should be Samuel Pedersen Thuestad; " Tormes Tollevson," Tønnes Tollefsen; " Ole T. Gismerierz," Ole Torjulfsen Gismervig; " Thorbjen T. Honde," Torbjørn Torbjørnsen Haarde; " Thorbjen N. Klonning," Torbjørn [*mutilated*] elsen Kløvning; and on " Norden," " Holger Hansen Natvig," should be Nøstvig; " Osmund Endresen Tretland," Tvetland; " Peder Ornmundsen," Omundsen; " Johannes Berecssen Hetland," middle name should be Reiersen; " Ole Tensen " should be Jensen; " Ole C. L. Lomme," Ole Truls Larsen Sømme. Such corrections show that the New York manifests need to be used with extreme care. Nevertheless they are sources of great value, and it is probable that for numerous shiploads it will be impossible to find Norwegian manifests.

[46] Langeland states that Peerson guided the party and that his descriptions of the Fox River Valley had much to do with the party's choice of that region as its destination. *Nordmændene i Amerika,* 19. In all probability the destination had

grants remained at Rochester, where the main group perhaps took counsel with Lars Larsen. The party proceeded to Chicago, where a number established themselves, forming the nucleus of Norwegian settlement in that city. The majority, however, continued to the colony near Ottawa in La Salle County, where they joined those who had come from New York in 1834 and 1835. " Most of us," writes one of the party, " secured work immediately and the wages paid us were good as measured by the standards of that time." [47]

The going of the party to the Fox River settlement resulted in an expansion of the Norwegian colony into Adams Township, north of Mission and Miller townships. Others, traveling singly or in smaller groups, made the same region their destination. Essentially the emigration of 1836 was a unit, for most of those who went by indirect routes were also from southwestern Norway and went to the Illinois country.[48] This does not take into account stray seamen, however. It should be mentioned that occasionally Norwegian trading vessels touched at American ports in the period under consideration. That there were desertions of Norwegian seamen in those ports is implied in a consular report as early as 1830, and such desertions were said to be common by 1834.[49]

been determined before the immigrants left Norway. On the ship manifest of " Den Norske Klippe " Illinois is given as the destination for all the passengers. For " Norden " it is indicated merely as the " United States," but the fact that Slogvig, the leader, was from Illinois, together with the fact that the entire emigration of 1836 was unified, makes it highly probable that Illinois was the destination. Cadbury, in *Studies and Records*, 2: 22.

[47] Hornefjeld's account in *Billed-Magazin*, 1: 226.

[48] *Ibid.*, 1: 226.

[49] An article on " De unionelle nordamerikanske Stater " appears in *Den Bergenske Merkur* for June 12, 1834. A certain Ove Thomsen had received a document, " Bemærkninger angaaende N. Amerika, især med Hensyn til Udvandrene." The author had recently been in the West Indies and South America and had met many Americans. He had the greatest praise for the United States. Passage via Copenhagen was suggested. The writer has not been able to run down the publication (or manuscript) alluded to in this report. The same newspaper (May 29, 1836) states that the " North American consul " at Bergen had been much questioned

By 1836 Norwegian settlement in the West was firmly established. The Fox River colony was thriving. Some Norwegians had settled in Chicago. The Kendall settlement had practically run its course. Letters sent from the immigrants to Norway had been influential in spreading the movement. A returned immigrant had led back to the American settlement a group of immigrants more than three times as large as the party of 1825. Though mainly from the Stavanger region, these immigrants were recruited in part farther north, touching the area tributary to Bergen.[50] The preceding narrative proves that the emigration during the period between 1825 and 1836 was related and in fact unified. The movement had broadened into a second stage, though no great intensification had yet occurred. The time was ripe for a considerable augmentation of numbers, but before any large emigration of more than local character could be expected to develop, fuller information about America and the advantages of emigration was needed in the Norwegian communities, however difficult or onerous the economic and social conditions among their inhabitants.

about America and how to get there. A manuscript list of emigrants from Sønd-hordlehn and Hardanger up to May 30, 1837, refers to thirty emigrants of 1836, twelve from Kingservig parish, two from Strandebarm, twelve from Graven, and four from Skonevig. Socialdept., Oslo: Lovkontor, Utv., Kong. Prop. 1845, folder 1.

[50] On January 1, 1828, Consul Gahn of New York reported that no Norwegian vessels had arrived at that port for several years. The schooner "Frembringeren," Skipper Balchen, brought a cargo of salt to Philadelphia from Iceland in 1828. The "Krondprindsesse Josephine" of Kristianssand arrived at New York on July 1, 1833. R. A., Oslo: F. D., F, Journalsager, 1828/92 and 384; 1833/340. Desertions of sailors are referred to in 1830–32/109; 1835/20.

IV. OLE RYNNING AND THE "AMERICA BOOK"

IN 1837 a very considerable augmentation of the Norwegian emigration movement occurred and among the emigrants of that year was one man, Ole Rynning, whose influence on the early Norwegian emigration was as great as that of Cleng Peerson and possibly greater. The significance of the migration of 1837 lies not so much in the facts that two emigrant vessels sailed for New York from Norway in that year and that some groups emigrated by indirect routes — although this swelling of the movement is important — as in the facts that it brought about the publication of a handbook of information for Norwegians on conditions in America and that it broadened the geographical scope of the movement in Norway.

It is significant of the rising interest of the *bønder* in emigration that the bishop of the diocese of Bergen, Jacob Neumann, felt it necessary to publish in 1837 a pastoral letter entitled " A Word of Admonition to the Peasants in the Diocese of Bergen Who Desire to Emigrate." [1] This pamphlet, which took as its text the Biblical injunction " So shalt thou dwell in the land, and verily thou shalt be fed," seems to have been rather widely distributed. At least three editions were printed; and a newspaper item mentions that 550 copies were sent to congregations in the Bergen diocese and 50 to Stavanger. [2] Neumann argued vigorously against emigration; marshaled much evidence about the perils of the voyage and

[1] *Varselsord til de udvandringslystne Bønder i Bergens Stift. Et Hyrdebrev fra Stiftets Biskop* (Bergen, 1837. 16 p.). An English translation by Gunnar J. Malmin is in *Studies and Records,* 1: 95–109.

[2] *Tiden* (Drammen), June 15, 1837. According to *Bibliotheca Bergensis,* 1: 584 (Bergen, 1926), one edition appeared as early as 1836. Internal evidence shows that the edition of 1837, as translated by Malmin, must have been written in the spring of that year.

the difficulties of pioneering; appealed to the people on religious, patriotic, and economic grounds to remain at home; and suggested as an alternative to emigration the colonization of available lands in Finmarken and other northern areas of Norway. He admitted that the earlier emigrants to America had been thrifty, diligent, and successful. In their favorable reports to the home community he found the roots of the prevalent desire to emigrate. "A spirit of restlessness took possession of all," he declares.

All wanted to enjoy a similar fortune. All wanted to go to America. And so great numbers left the coast of Norway — just as they left Germany, Prussia, and Ireland — and steered over the ocean to the distant Land of Happiness, where they hoped to harvest almost without sowing, or, in other words, where they hoped that a luckier star would arise over their families and over their futures.[3]

The *bønder* seem not to have been greatly impressed by the bishop's citation of Biblical authority. An immigrant of 1843 comments amusingly on this point. He had visited Slogvig in 1836; he had read with great interest a German book of American travel; he had spent a few months in England and there secured pamphlets and books relating to the United States and English emigration; and he was familiar with Bishop Neumann's pastoral letter. This immigrant later suggested that the bishop had failed to take into account another Biblical injunction, namely, "Multiply and replenish the earth." "The latter," he continues, "the farmers had adhered to; most of them had large families, and since the land at home was filled, while they now heard that a large part of the new world was unsettled, they decided to disobey the bishop's advice and go to the new Canaan, where flowed milk and honey."[4]

[3] Malmin's translation, in *Studies and Records*, 1:100.

[4] Langeland, *Nordmændene i Amerika*, 20–23. Langeland went to America in 1843, but he had first-hand knowledge about the emigration of 1837.

Another illustration of the emigrant's point of view is given by a Norwegian from Telemarken, who has described the conditions that confronted many peasants in the upper portion of that region. Early in the century much of the land had been concentrated in the hands of a comparatively s m a l l number of owners. "Even a large number of those who w e r e presumed t o o w n their farms had sold their timber and m a d e such contracts that they practically were mere tenants," writes this early immigrant.

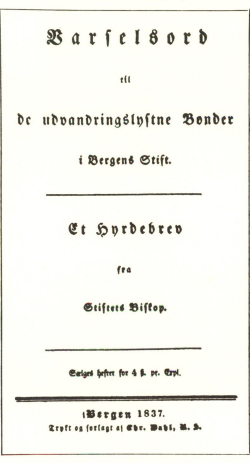

REDUCED FACSIMILE OF THE TITLE-PAGE OF NEUMANN'S "A WORD OF ADMONITION TO THE PEASANTS"

Stock raising, the most natural industry of this part of the country, was neglected. The same is true of agriculture, and the majority of the peasants had no other income than the scant pay they could get for cutting timber and bringing it to the market. . . . Frequent lack of employment, impoverishment, debt, and dissatisfaction were the visible manifestations of this condition. But it was a golden epoch for money-lenders, attorneys and sheriffs. Then the America fever began to rage, and many crossed the sea hoping to find a spot of ground where they could live in peace and enjoy the fruits of their labors without being annoyed by the thoughts of pay-day, rents and foreclosures.[5]

A bitter tone enters into the letters of Hans Barlien, an emigrant of 1837, a disciple of Voltaire, an uncompromising democrat, and a prominent leader in the early political struggles of the peasants against the Norwegian officialdom.   Professor Koht characterizes Barlien as the first *bonde* who tried consciously to become a leader of that class.   He was elected to the Storthing of 1815–16 from Nordre Trondhjem *Amt* and was the only *bonde* in that body.   At one time in his later career he was jailed for sacrilege, revolutionary agitation, and other offenses. In 1836 he wrote a treatise on the Norwegian constitution in which he advocated a thoroughgoing democratic system of self-rule.[6] " Now for the first time am I able to breathe freely," he wrote from America after his emigration.

No one is persecuted here because of his religious faith.   Everybody is allowed to worship God in the manner which accords with his own convictions.   Pickpockets or lawyers, unscrupulous creditors, officials and vagabonds who are morally tainted are without power to harm the people here.   No restrictions are set upon freedom of occupation; and every one secures without hindrance the fruits of his own work and by wise and liberal legislation the American citizen is made secure from the assaults of oppressors.   The so-called free Norwegian constitution has hitherto served only to burden the people with heavier taxes, to increase the gains of public officials, and to promote misery and idleness.   The results of this situation will soon be apparent to all; such a condition must necessarily lead to general ruin.[7]

In another letter he wrote, " Let the government of Norway and some of its officials slander the American gov-

---

[5] This evidence was given in the late sixties to Svein Nilssen, the editor of *Billed-Magazin*, who made visits to the Norwegian settlements and interviewed a large number of early immigrants.   The passage is translated in Anderson, *Norwegian Immigration*, 233–234.

[6] Koht, " Hans Barlien," in *Norsk Biografisk Leksikon*, 1: 378–380.

[7] The letter is quoted by Nilssen, "De Skandinaviske Setlementer i Amerika," in *Billed-Magazin*, 1:34.

ernment as much as they please, their government will never match this." The year after his emigration Barlien was dreaming of securing sufficient lands to accommodate a few thousand Norwegian families and of organizing " a colony with a government in harmony with nature, and in a manner to preclude the thriving of injustice." [8]

Two peasants from Numedal, Ole and Ansten Nattestad, visited Stavanger in 1836 and there, apparently for the first time in their lives, " heard much talk about a country which was called America." " We saw letters," writes Ole Nattestad, " written by Norwegians who were living in America and we were told that Knud Slogvig, who many years before that had emigrated in a sloop from Stavanger, had lately visited his native land and had given so favorable a report about America that about 150 emigrants from Stavanger *Amt* and from Hardanger had gone back with him and had sailed that very summer in two brigs across the ocean. They had gone in spite of all sorts of threats and warnings about slavery, death, and disease." [9] The two brothers had much to think of as they made their way back home to Numedal. Their father, Knud Nattestad, owned a *gaard* or farm, which by right of primogeniture would go to their older brother. While the latter was away at a military school, Ole had been given the management of the farm. He found at the end of a year that he had little or nothing left as a reward for his labor, and he decided that it would be useless to buy a farm and go into debt. He then became an itinerant trader, but because of restrictive laws was forced to abandon this occupation. He then worked for a time as

[8] D. G. Ristad, " A Doctrinaire Idealist: Hans Barlien," in *Studies and Records,* 3:13–22. Mr. Ristad translates a letter of July 14, 1838, written by Barlien at St. Louis.

[9] Nilssen interviewed the Nattestad brothers in 1868 or 1869. He gives a full report of the interviews, with long quotations, in *Billed-Magazin,* 1: 82–84, 94, 102–104.

a blacksmith. Thereupon, with his brother, he made the trip to Stavanger. The following Christmas he visited a prominent man of the community, a member of the Storthing, and discussed with him the economic conditions of the valley, asking him for advice. This man, Even Nubbru, replied that wherever he went in the world, he would nowhere find a people who had as good laws as the Americans. "This information," says Ole Nattestad, "had a magic effect on me, as I looked upon it as an injustice that the laws of Norway should forbid me to trade and not allow me to get my living by honest work as a mechanic wherever I desired to settle. I had confidence in the judgment of a member of the Storthing and I compared his remarks with what I had heard about America in the vicinity of Stavanger. Gradually I got to thinking of emigration while considering the matter on my way home, and the idea matured into a resolution. My brother Ansten did not have to be asked a second time." [10] Back of these considerations was the more general fact of hard times in the thirties. It has been said that not a single year in the decade was a good agricultural year — the first five were poor, the next three miserable; and the result was hunger and want. [11]

Early in the winter of 1837 signs of approaching emigration were noted in Norway. A newspaper report sent from Hardanger in February refers to the busy plans of large numbers in Hardanger and Voss for leaving the following spring, some by way of Bergen and some Göteborg; several farmers had already sold their lands, more intended to do so later: "It seems as if the emigration madness has gripped the people." [12] And in April a Sta-

[10] Nilssen, in *Billed-Magazin*, 1: 83.

[11] S. H. Herbransen, *De første Utvandrere fra Numedal til Amerika*, 11 (Kristiania, 1924).

[12] A note from Utne, Hardanger, February 20, in *Den Bergenske Merkur*, March 14, 1837.

vanger report states that about one hundred were ready to emigrate and that the "fever," especially strong in Ryfylke, was being transmitted from district to district.[13]

The emigration followed hard on the heels of these reports. A party of more than fifty persons started from Tind, Telemarken, for America via Göteborg, sailing from Skien on May 22. They were organized so that they could give mutual help to one another, according to a newspaper report. It was said that two of them were to return the following year, as were two from Numedal. If their reports should prove favorable "every third man in Tind and Numedal intended to emigrate the next year."[14] The "Ægir" sailed from Bergen on April 7 with eighty-four emigrants. The "Stavanger Paqvet" sailed in June for Hamburg with forty-one emigrants, sixteen of whom returned because they had been denied passage at Hamburg on account of disease.[15] "Enigheden" sailed from Stavanger on July 1 with ninety or ninety-one passengers, recruited chiefly from Stavanger and such surrounding districts as Hjelmeland, Hæsbye, Aardal, Ryfylke, and Skjold. These immigrants arrived at New York about September 14 and most of them proceeded at once to Illinois and the Fox River settlement, though some stopped, at least temporarily, at Rochester.[16]

[13] The item, from Stavanger, April 6, is printed in *Den Constitutionelle,* April 15, 1837.

[14] *Den Constitutionelle,* May 27, 1837. A manuscript report by Hans A. Bernaas, *lensmand* at Tind, dated May 15, 1837, tells of the forthcoming departure of fifty-three emigrants, about half of them children under sixteen. There were five *gaardmand* families, four *husmand* families, three bachelors, and two unmarried girls. Their emigration is attributed in part to the influence of letters from westland emigrants of 1831. This is probably an allusion to Hovland. Socialdept., Oslo, Lovkontor: Utv., Kong. Prop. 1845, folder 1.

[15] A list of the "Stavanger Paqvet" passengers is in Socialdept., Oslo, Lovkontor: Utv., Kong. Prop. 1845, folder 1. A letter by Amtmand Aas of July 31, 1837, tells of the return of sixteen of these people.

[16] The New York manifest of "Enigheden," dated September 14, 1837, is published by Cadbury, in *Studies and Records,* 2: 45–52. It lists ninety-one names. A list with more accurate spellings of names, which also indicates the districts in

There were various other minor groups that set off in 1837 by the Göteborg route.[17]

Historical interest in the emigrant ships of 1837 centers in the " Ægir," which left Bergen on April 7 under Captain Christian K. Behrens, with eighty-four passengers, chiefly from Nordhordlen, Søndhordlen, Hardanger, and Søndre Bergenhus. Behrens had made a voyage to New York the previous year with freight and there had examined some emigrant ships. Upon his return to Bergen he learned that a considerable number of Norwegians, some of whom had already sold their farms, were planning to emigrate. He therefore remodeled his vessel for passenger service and made a contract to convey a group of emigrants to New York in the spring of 1837.[18]

Ole Rynning, who was destined to be the leader of this party and an outstanding figure in the history of Norwegian immigration, joined the group at Bergen after the agreement with Captain Behrens had been made. He was born on April 4, 1809, in Ringsaker, where his father,

Norway from which the emigrants came, is in Socialdept., Lovkontor: Utv., Kong. Prop. 1845, folder 1. This list is dated June 29, 1837, and gives ninety names. The sailing from Stavanger is reported in *Stavanger Adresseavis*, July 7, 1837. Among the emigrants were Hans Valder, Knud Olson Eie, Bjørn J. Hatlestad, and Lars Larsen Narvig. ' Most of the emigrants were farmers, but there were also a seaman, an artist, a smith, a shoemaker, two glaziers, and a carpenter. Anderson, Flom, and Cadbury have assembled much biographical information about the various members of this group.

[17] The Göteborg " Landscancellie " reported that more than one hundred Norwegians had booked passage at Göteborg. Thirty-eight or forty had been forced to return to Norway because of lack of funds, however. *Den Bergenske Merkur*, August 20, 1837; report by Borchsenius, June 26, 1837, in Socialdept., Lovkontor: Utv., Kong. Prop. 1845, folder 1.

[18] Langeland, *Nordmændene i Amerika*, 23–29. Cadbury publishes the New York manifest for the " Ægir " in *Studies and Records*, 2: 37 ff. The writer has not found a similar manifest in Norway, but a list of " Ægir " families is in the archives of the Bergen customs office in a package of letters received in 1837. A list of emigrants from Sundhordlen and Hardanger to May 30, 1837, includes a large proportion of the " Ægir " group. Socialdept., Lovkontor: Utv., Kong. Prop. 1845, folder 1. A brief report from the Bergen Toldkammer, dated May 22, 1837, is in the same depository.

the Reverend Jens Rynning, was curate. The father in 1825 became minister of the parish of Snaasen, where he remained until his death in 1857; he was a man of considerable distinction and was noted for his writings in the fields of science and agriculture. Ole Rynning received his education in part under a private teacher, Fredrik Bugge of Trondhjem, and later at the University of Christiania, completing his studies at the latter institution in 1833. Contrary to the expectation of his father he did not choose to go into the ministry but instead returned to Snaasen to conduct a private school for advanced students. His decision to emigrate in 1837 appears to have been occasioned by several reënforcing causes. It has been asserted that the immediate cause was a betrothal which his father regarded with disfavor. Confirmation of this assertion is lacking, but a contemporary newspaper reports that Rynning planned to return to Norway, after he had established himself satisfactorily in America, to marry the young woman to whom he was engaged. According to the statement of his nephew, Ole Rynning had made a contract to buy two small adjoining farms but was unable to raise the required amount of money and hence decided to seek his fortune in the New World. It is possible, however, that Rynning's motives were not purely personal, for the testimony of his fellow emigrants shows that he was interested in helping the economically circumscribed farmers and laborers of his native country to find a permanent solution for their difficulties; and emigration appeared to him to be the key to the problem. Rynning was profoundly in sympathy with the *bønder* and was thoroughly democratic; he was furthermore critical of the state church clergy, of which his father was a typical member. It was unusual for men of Rynning's class and education to join this movement, condemned as it was by most of the educated people of the day. In

Morgenbladet special comment was made on the fact that among the emigrants was " a student with the many-sided cultivation possessed by Ole Rynning." [19]

Only two in the company of emigrants on the " Ægir " were recruited from outside the *bondestand*. Many of this company of farmers were victims of seasickness, but, according to a newspaper report which gave details of the voyage, they were quickly restored to health through the experienced aid of the skipper, who acted as a physician for them though he possessed no " doctor's cap." " With the seasickness all worries seemed to disappear," continues the newspaper account. *" Bønder* who never before had looked upon the sea saw it to be peaceful and lost their fear of its terrors as the ship sailed on toward milder skies. The fiddle was brought out and in the evening the sailors and the farmer folk gathered for a lively dance." That some thought was given to more serious matters, also, may be inferred from the fact that at the outset of the voyage religious books were distributed among the company. On May 17 the emigrants celebrated in interesting fashion the Norwegian national holiday and sang a song composed for the occasion by Rynning.[20]

The ship reached New York on June 9 and on the seventh day after arrival the immigrants set out for Illinois, in accordance with their plan to settle in the Fox

[19] *Cf.* the writer's introduction to *Ole Rynning's True Account of America*, 5 ff. It is possible that the various rumors concerning Rynning's engagement go back to an engagement with Anna Nikoline Lund of Overhalden, who died in 1829. Rynning is said to have sorrowed to the end of his life over her death. Wilhelm Lassen, *Biskop i Lund (1620–1637) Dr. Mats Jenssøn Medelfar's Agnatiske Descendenter af Navn: Wibe og Lund*, 50 (Christiania, 1901). Among Rynning's personal papers is a seven-page manuscript containing reflections on her death. See *post*, n. 30.

[20] Before the " Ægir " left Bergen, Amund Helland distributed religious books among the emigrants. *Den Bergenske Merkur*, April 11, 1837. A vivid account of the voyage, based upon an interview with Captain Behrens, is in *Den Bergenske Merkur*, September 16, 1837. *Cf. Rynning's True Account of America*, 7–8.

River region.[21] They went by steamer to Albany and by canal boat from Albany to Buffalo, whence they continued their journey to Detroit by way of Lake Erie. At Detroit one family dropped out and here Ole and Ansten Nattestad, who had come to America by way of Göteborg and Fall River, joined the party. " On the street I met one of the Norwegians who had sailed from Bergen on the seventh of April preceding," wrote Ole Nattestad in his journal. " In the course of my conversation with him he said that there were about eighty persons of them, who were going to Chicago, and they had remained here five days without securing passage, but they were to leave in two days." [22]

Shortly after reaching Chicago the immigrants received unfavorable reports concerning the Fox River settlement. Rynning, by virtue of his education, his character, and his ability to speak English, was now the leader of the party.[23] Some Americans with whom he talked in Chicago probably suggested the Beaver Creek region — some seventy miles south of Chicago in Iroquois County — as a favorable site. The company delegated four men, including Rynning, to investigate the place. Two of the committee remained at Beaver Creek to build a log house preparatory to the arrival of the party, and Rynning with one companion returned to Chicago to acquaint the party with the results of the investigation.

[21] The following notice appears in the *New York Evening Star* for June 10, 1837, p. 2: " Marine Intelligence. Arrived last evening. Norwegian bark Aegir, Behrens, 62 ds fm Bergen, with 2bls plants and 84 passengers, to order May 8th, lat 39 34, lon 32 18 was run into by Br ship Barelto, fm Madras for London — both vessels received trifling damage." *Cf.* the account in *Den Bergenske Merkur*, September 16, 1837.

[22] *Beskrivelse over en Reise til Nordamerica, begyndt den 8de April 1837 og skrevet paa Skibet Hilda samt siden fortsat paa Reisen op igjennem de Forenede Stater i Nordamerica*, 23 (Drammen, 1839).

[23] Captain Behrens spoke of Rynning's leadership of the group. *Den Bergenske Merkur*, September 16, 1837.

Oxen and wagons were purchased and the members of the party, now reduced in numbers to about fifty, made their way to Beaver Creek, selected land, and built log houses. No other settlers lived in the vicinity, and there was some dissatisfaction because of difficulty of securing supplies, the nearest mill being seventy miles away. For a time considerable criticism was directed against Rynning and others who were responsible for the selection of the site; but when Ole Nattestad returned in the autumn from a short trip he found the settlers in good spirits. Later events proved, however, that a tragic mistake had been made. The ground, which was very low, had been examined in late summer, and, because of the dryness and the overgrowth of grass, the men had been deceived as to its true character. When spring came the flat land of the settlement was soon inundated and the unfortunate colonists were in sore straits.   Ultimately a severe epidemic invaded the settlement and soon began to claim daily victims. Most of the settlers succumbed. Some of the survivors removed to La Salle County in the spring of the following year, but a few remained. The last to leave was Mons Aadland, who in 1840, finding his capital reduced to three dollars, exchanged his farm for a small herd of cattle and went to Wisconsin. In realizing something for his land he was more fortunate than most of his companions. They practically fled from the settlement and could not sell their land. "Only the empty log houses remained, like silent witnesses to the terrors of the scourge, and afforded a dismal sight to the lonesome wanderer who ventured within these domains." [24]   A Norwegian who in the spring of 1839 passed through the Fox

[24] For accounts of the Beaver Creek settlement, see Nattestad, *Beskrivelse*, 23, 25–27; Langeland, *Nordmændene i Amerika*, 29–31, 32; Nilssen's reports of interviews with Aadland and the Nattestad brothers in *Billed-Magazin*, 1: 30, 84, 95; Anderson, *Norwegian Immigration*, 245–247; and Malmin, in *Decorah-Posten*, February 27, 1925.

River region wrote, "Here I met also some Norwegians who had emigrated by way of Bergen two years before and who first settled farther south in Illinois at Beaver Creek, but who, after student Rynning and many others died as a result of the unhealthful climate, fled from their houses and lands after having lost nearly everything they owned." [25] This traveler returned to Norway, and on October 26, 1839, his story was made public in *Morgenbladet,* confirming an earlier report written by the father of Ole Rynning on September 4, 1839.[26]

Ole Rynning is an interesting and important figure in the history of Norwegian immigration. Ansten Nattestad, who knew Rynning well, wrote:

A great and good idea formed the central point of all his thinking. He hoped to be able to provide the poor, oppressed Norwegian workman a happier home on this side of the sea, and to realize this wish he shunned no sacrifice, endured the greatest exertions, and was patient through misunderstandings, disappointments, and loss. . . . Nothing could shake his belief that America would become a place of refuge for the masses of people in Europe who toiled under the burdens of poverty.[27]

How Rynning came to write his *True Account of America for the Information and Help of Peasant and Commoner* has been told by Nattestad. Rynning had gone out on a "long exploring expedition." "Frost had set in during his absence," according to Nattestad. "The ice on the swamps and the crusts of snow cut his boots. He finally reached the colony, but his feet were frozen and lacerated. They presented a terrible sight, and we all thought he would be a cripple for life." [28] In this

[25] *Peter Testman's Account of His Experiences in North America,* 55.

[26] Rynning's father incorporated in his account a letter from Hans Barlien telling of the death of the leader of the party and the disaster which had overtaken the community.

[27] Nilssen in *Billed-Magazin,* 1: 84, 95.

[28] *Billed-Magazin,* 1: 95. In an account from 1841 Dr. H. C. Brandt writes of Rynning: "In the middle of the winter he walked almost barefoot across a prairie; he was near his house, but he could not reach it without help; and he was almost

condition he wrote the manuscript of his book in the winter of 1837-38. As soon as he completed a chapter of it he would read it aloud to Nattestad and others in order to get their opinions. A Norwegian doctor who visited the western settlements in 1840 asserts that if Rynning had lived he would have altered considerably his account of America. This appears to be a conjecture that can be neither verified nor disproved. The interesting thing, however, is that at the time when the book was written, its author, though ill in a settlement that already had had a taste of misfortune, was able to rise above local circumstance and to view broadly the American situation that awaited the immigrant from Europe. Though it is of course conjecturable that a later account might have paid more attention to the problem of disease in the frontier settlements, it is also possible that the critic of 1840 failed to do justice to the breadth of vision and the courage of Ole Rynning.[29] He regained his health and resumed his work among the settlers, but in the fall of 1838 he " was again confined to the sick-bed, and died soon thereafter to the great sorrow of all." Only one man in the settlement was well at the time — late in September; he chopped down an oak from which he fashioned a coffin, and in this Rynning's body was buried in an unmarked grave on the prairie.[30]

Meanwhile Ansten Nattestad, in the spring of 1838, had set off for Norway to visit friends and relatives, going

frozen stiff when people found him and brought him home." *Morgenbladet,* September 18, 1841.

[29] *Morgenbladet,* September 18, 1841.

[30] Muus, in Anderson, *Norwegian Immigration,* 204. The man who buried Rynning was Sjur Rosseland. Later he returned to Norway, taking Rynning's personal papers with him. They are now in the possession of Arne Larsson Rosseland of Kvam. They contain a manuscript booklet of verse (16 p.), a manuscript about the death of Anna N. Lund (see *ante,* n. 19), a letter of 1830 attesting Rynning's studies under Fredrik Bugge, a large number of Latin exercises, and some other items.

by way of New Orleans and Liverpool. He took with
him "letters from nearly all the earlier Norwegian emigrants" whom he had met; and he also carried with him
the manuscripts of two books, one by his brother Ole
Nattestad telling of his journey the preceding year and
some of his experiences in America, the other Rynning's
True Account of America. The Nattestad book was published at Drammen in 1839; the Rynning volume was
brought out at Christiania in 1838.[31]

So important an influence did Rynning's book have
upon Norwegian emigration that an analysis of its contents is necessary to an understanding of the movement.[32]
In his preface, dated February 13, 1838, Rynning explains
that he has been in America eight months and is in a
position to answer many of the questions raised by prospective emigrants. He recognizes the need of a "trustworthy and fairly detailed account of the country," for
he himself has learned in Norway "how great the ignorance of the people is, and what false and preposterous
reports were believed as full truth." His book contains
thirteen brief chapters each of which answers in a concise
manner a question or group of questions put very specifically. There is conclusive evidence that Rynning prepared
a fourteenth chapter which was stricken out in Norway
before the book went to press. The fact is important
because the chapter in question dealt with the religious
situation in Norway. Nattestad himself tells of it: "Dean
Kragh in Eidsvold read the proofs, and struck out the
chapter about the Norwegian ministers, who were accused
of intolerance in religious matters and of inactivity in
respect to the improvement of the condition of the people
in temporal matters and in questions concerning the ad-

[31] *Billed-Magazin*, 1: 94.
[32] For the original text and an English translation see the writer's edition of
the volume, *Ole Rynning's True Account of America.*

vancement of education." [33]   It would be distinctly en-
lightening to have the testimony of so competent an observer as Rynning on the religious situation.   The facts
that he wrote such a chapter and that it was stricken out
by a prominent clergyman of the state church certainly
point to a larger part played by the religious factor than
has usually been recognized in connection with the emigration after 1825.

In the first chapter Rynning answers the question: " In
what general direction from Norway is America situated,
and how far away is it? "   He then asks, " How did the
country first become known? "   After telling of the
early Norse discovery of Vinland the Good, he mentions
the establishment of the English colonies and the independence won through the Revolution.   He next devotes a
chapter to an interesting brief account of the early Norwegian immigration.   Having thus furnished an appropri-
ate background, he proceeds in his third chapter to discuss
the size of the United States, its climate, soil, products,
and general nature.   In chapter 4 he shows that rumors
that the United States would soon be overpopulated were
false and that America had plenty of room for all immigrants who might come.   He also refutes the rumor circulated in Norway that the United States government intended to forbid immigration, pointing out that the
government especially wanted good immigrants, but that
beggars were not welcome.   " The Norwegians in general," he adds, " have thus far a good reputation for their
industry, trustworthiness, and the readiness with which
the more well-to-do have helped the poor through the
country."

After explaining in chapter 5 where the Norwegian
immigrants have settled in the United States, he asks in

[33] *Billed-Magazin*, 1: 94.

the next chapter, " What is the nature of the land where the Norwegians have settled? What does good land cost? What are the prices of cattle and provisions? How high are wages? " This chapter is compact with valuable practical information, and one can easily imagine with what eagerness its contents were studied by Norwegian peasants. Prairie land, grass, timothy, clover, the quality of the soil, the kinds of vegetables and grains produced, the amount of crop yields, the uses made of the various grains, the keeping of cattle and hogs — these and other similar topics are intelligently discussed. Rynning does not deal in generalities, and his details were taken seriously by the Norwegian readers of the book. " If a settler is furnished with a good rifle and knows how to use it," he writes, " he does not have to buy meat during the first two years. A good rifle costs from fifteen to twenty dollars. The chief wild animals are deer, prairie chickens, turkeys, ducks, and wild geese. Wild bees are also found. The rivers abound with fish and turtles." [34] He discusses fruit culture, the kinds of timber available, minerals, water supply, climate, and the price of government land, and gives suggestions as to American land measurements, deeds, and claims. He especially warns the immigrant to beware of land speculators. He then discusses prices and wages, pointing out that they vary widely at different places. " At Beaver Creek," he writes, " a fairly good horse costs from fifty to one hundred dollars; a yoke of good working oxen from fifty to eighty dollars; a lumber wagon from sixty to eighty dollars; a milk cow with calf from sixteen

[34] " In the winter of 1839 there was a party at the house of Mr. Gilderhus in Voss, and one man read aloud out of Ole Rynning's book. All listened attentively. It is said that wherever Ole Rynning's book was read anywhere in Norway, people listened as attentively as if they were in church. Several Vossings resolved to emigrate that year, and in obedience to instructions in Rynning's book all took guns or rifles with them to be prepared for all the wild game they expected to find in America." Anderson, *Norwegian Immigration*, 331.

to twenty dollars; a sheep two or three dollars; an average-sized pig from six to ten dollars; pork from six to ten cents a pound; butter from twelve to twenty-four cents a pound; a barrel of the finest wheat flour from eight to ten dollars; a barrel of corn meal from two and one-half to three dollars; a barrel of potatoes one dollar; a pound of coffee twenty cents; a barrel of salt five dollars." Servant girls were paid " from one to two dollars a week," and they did no outside work " except to milk the cows." Capable workmen could earn from half a dollar to one dollar a day in winter, and twice as much during the summer. Here was exactly the sort of information most desired by the prospective immigrant who by necessity was forced to think primarily of the economic problem.

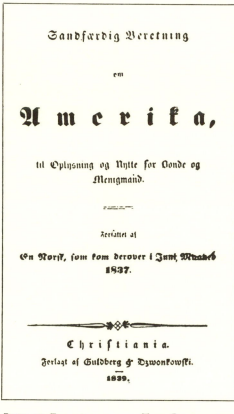

REDUCED FACSIMILE OF THE TITLE-PAGE OF THE 1839 EDITION OF OLE RYNNING'S "TRUE ACCOUNT OF AMERICA"

Chapter 7 has a naïvely phrased title: " What kind of religion is to be found in America? Is there any kind of order or government in the land, or can every one do as he pleases?" Rynning assures his countrymen that America is not a land of heathens. "Every one can believe as he wishes," he writes, "and worship God in the manner which he believes to be right, but he must not persecute any one for holding another faith. The government takes it for granted that a compulsory belief is no belief at all, and that it will be best shown who has religion or who has not if there is complete religious liberty." He speaks of the various sects to be found in America and adds, "There are also various sects among the Norwegians, but they do not as yet have ministers and churches. Every man who is somewhat earnest in his belief holds devotional exercises in his own home, or else together with his neighbors." After describing the nature of the American national government he continues:

For the comfort of the faint-hearted I can, therefore, declare with truth that in America, as in Norway, there are laws, government, and authorities. But everything is designed to maintain the natural freedom and equality of men. In regard to the former, every one is free to engage in whatever honorable occupation he wishes, and to go wherever he wishes without having to produce a passport, and without being detained by customs officials. Only the real criminal is threatened with punishment by the law.

Rynning defends the native American against such charges as faithlessness and deceitfulness, and asserts that the American in fact is "more accommodating, more obliging, more reliable" than the Norwegian. Then follows a remarkable passage on slavery:

An ugly contrast to this freedom and equality which justly constitute the pride of the Americans is the infamous slave traffic, which is tolerated and still flourishes in the southern states. In these states is found a race of black people, with wooly hair on their heads, who are called negroes, and who are brought here from Africa, which is their native country; these poor beings are bought and sold just as other property, and are driven to work with a whip or scourge like horses or oxen. If a master whips his slave to death or shoots him dead in a rage, he is not looked upon as a murderer. The children born of a negress are slaves from birth, even if their father is a white man. The slave trade is still permitted in Missouri; but it is strictly forbidden and despised in Indiana, Illinois, and Wisconsin Territory. The northern states try in every Congress to get the slave trade abolished in the southern states; but as the latter always oppose these efforts, and appeal to their right to settle their internal affairs themselves, there will in all likelihood come either a separation between the northern and southern states, or else bloody civil disputes.

This passage, written twenty-three years before the outbreak of the Civil War, foreshadows the position that the Norwegian immigrants were to take on the issues involved in the slavery controversy. It presages their affiliation with the Free Soil Party, and, later, the Republican Party, an affiliation that was to last long after the echoes of the great sectional conflict had died away. Furthermore, Rynning's view is representative of the views of the great mass of Norwegian immigrants, an important fact in accounting for their tendency to go to the North and the Northwest, rather than to the South and the Southwest.

Chapter 8 deals with education and with the care of poor people. Rynning also touches upon the language question:

Two schools have now been started among the Norwegians at Fox River, where the children learn English; but the Norwegian language seems to be destined to die out with the parents. At least, the children do not learn to read Norwegian. At Beaver Creek no school is yet established, but most of the children who are old enough are taken into American homes, where their instruction is usually well cared for.

In writing of the problem of poverty, Rynning says, " In this state I have not yet seen a beggar. The able-bodied man is in no danger of poverty or need."

The importance for the immigrant of acquiring the use of English is pointed out in the ninth chapter. In the following chapter he gives assurance that danger from unusual diseases, wild animals, snakes, and Indians is slight. He then enumerates, in chapter 11, various classes of

people for whom it is advisable to emigrate.   Among these
he places the Norwegian peasants, mechanics, tradesmen,
blacksmiths,   tailors,   shoemakers,   turners,   carpenters,
wagon-makers,   itinerant   traders,   and   servant   girls.
" Women are respected and honored far more than is the
case among the common people in Norway," he writes.
" So far as I know, only two or three Norwegian girls have
been married to Americans, and I do not believe that they
have made particularly good matches.   But there are
many Norwegian bachelors who would prefer to marry
Norwegian girls if they could."   Thereupon follow some
suggestions as to the cost of transportation.   " Expenses
for each adult from Norway to Illinois must be figured
at about sixty dollars, in addition to expenses for board
across the sea."   He advises certain kinds of persons on
no account to come to America.   Among these are drunkards, " who will be detested, and will soon perish miser-
ably," and " those who neither can work nor have sufficient money to carry on a business."   He writes, " The
person who neither can nor will work must never expect
that riches and luxurious living will be open to him.   No,
in America one gets nothing without work; but it is true
that by work one can expect some day to achieve better
circumstances."

In the next chapter he disposes of some exaggerations of
the dangers connected with crossing the ocean.   There is
little danger of shipwreck.   Seasickness is not a fatal
malady.   In truth, tediousness on the voyage is worse than
seasickness.   A rumor in Norway to the effect that the
immigrants were in danger of being enslaved is exploded
in a few lines.   The final chapter is entitled " Guiding
advice for those who wish to go to America."   It contains
good advice concerning ships, fare, contracts with ship
captains, the exchange of money, the proper time for
leaving Norway, the best routes to the West, and medicines and other supplies with which the immigrant should

equip himself. It is of some interest to note the kinds of articles which Rynning especially advises the immigrant to take with him. He mentions bedclothes, fur, clothing of wadmol,[35] a *baxtehelle*,[36] a spinning wheel, a hand mill, silverware, tobacco, pipes, tools, and rifles. Among the provisions, especially for the ocean voyage, he enumerates pork, dried meat, salted meat, dried herring, smoked herring, dried fish, butter, cheese, *primost*,[37] milk, beer, flour, peas, cereals, potatoes, rye rusks, coffee, tea, pots, pans, and kettles. In the final paragraph of the book, Rynning writes, " It is a good thing if the immigrants can have a dependable guide and interpreter on the trip from New York to the interior. For those who wish to leave next spring, there is a good opportunity to go with Ansten Knudsen Nattestad from Rolloug parish in Numedal, who is now on a trip back to Norway."

The book was compact, informative, definite, clear; a few misstatements may be detected in it, but in general it was reliable, justifying its name. No book of the sort had appeared in Norway before, and therefore it has a special importance. Doubtless it omitted much detail that would have been useful to emigrants, but on the whole it is an unusually successful condensation of a vast amount of information.

Ansten Nattestad found himself a second Knud Slogvig in the popular estimation. He records:

I remained in Numedal throughout the winter and until the following spring. The report of my return spread like wildfire through the land, and an incredible number of people came to hear news from America. Many traveled as far as twenty Norwegian miles to talk with me. It was impossible to answer all the letters which came to me containing questions in regard to conditions on the other side of the ocean. In the spring of 1839 about one hundred persons from Numedal

---

[35] A coarse hairy woolen cloth similar to frieze.

[36] A round iron plate used by the Norwegians in baking *flatbrød* (flat-bread).

[37] A cheese made from skim milk.

stood ready to go with me across the sea. Amongst these were many farmers and heads of families, all, except the children, able-bodied and persons in their best years. In addition to these were some from Telemarken and from Numedal who were unable to go with me as our ship was full.[38]

Important as was the personal influence of Nattestad, however, the effect of the little book which he brought to Norway to be printed was far greater. It was published in 1838, reprinted in 1839, and apparently had a very considerable circulation. Naturally its most noticeable early effects were in Numedal and the adjoining parts of southern Norway, but there is evidence of a gradually expanding area of influence. Very striking is the testimony as to the combined effect of Nattestad's return and the publication of Rynning's book. The following statement is a record of an interview with an immigrant of 1839, Gullik O. Gravdal:

Hardly any other Norwegian publication has been purchased and read with such avidity as this Rynning's *Account of America*. People traveled long distances to hear " news " from the land of wonders, and many who before were scarcely able to read began in earnest to practice in the " America-book," making such progress that they were soon able to spell their way forward and acquire most of the contents. The sensation created by Ansten's return was much the same as that which one might imagine a dead man would create, were he to return to tell of the life beyond the grave. Throughout the winter he was continually surrounded by groups who listened attentively to his stories. Since many came long distances in order to talk with him, the reports of the far west were soon spread over a large part of the country. Ministers and bailiffs . . . tried to frighten us with terrible tales about the dreadful sea monsters, and about man-eating wild animals in the new world; but when Ansten Nattestad had said " Yes and Amen " to Rynning's *Account*, all fears and doubts were removed.[39]

An eyewitness has left a record of the effect of Rynning's book upon the people of Snaasen, his home town. He reports:

[38] *Billed-Magazin*, 1: 94.
[39] *Billed-Magazin*, 1: 154.

For a time I believed that half of the population of Snaasen had lost their senses. Nothing else was spoken of but the land that flows with milk and honey. Our minister, Ole Rynning's father, tried to stop the fever. Even from the pulpit he urged people to be discreet and described the hardships of the voyage and the cruelty of the American savage in the most forbidding colors. This was only pouring oil upon the fire. . . . Ole Rynning was one of those philanthropists for whom no sacrifice is too great if it can only contribute to the happiness of others. He was, in the fullest sense, a friend of the people, the spokesman of the poor and one whose mouth never knew deceit. . . . But then came the news: Ole Rynning is no more. This acted as cold water upon the blood of the people. The report of his death caused sorrow throughout the whole parish, for few have been so commonly loved as this man. Now the desire to emigrate cooled also, and many of those who formerly had spoken most enthusiastically in favor of emigration now shuddered with fear at the thought of America's unhealthful climate.[40]

In connection with the attitude of Rynning's father it is interesting to note that in 1839 he published in the leading Norwegian newspaper a tabular comparison of the advantages and disadvantages of both Norway and America and reached the conclusion that the balance between the two countries was so even " that none save speculators or those who are dissatisfied with the established order or are persecuted will be willing, when all is considered, to pay from seventy to eighty specie dollars to exchange their position here with one there." [41]

There can be no doubt that the Beaver Creek tragedy tended to counteract some of the more glowing reports that came from immigrants. Indeed, Reiersen, a contemporary, declares that Rynning's death caused a temporary cessation of emigration from Norway in the years from 1839 to 1841, and it is true that the larger movement did not get into full swing until 1843.[42] Neverthe-

[40] *Billed-Magazin*, 1: 45.

[41] *Morgenbladet*, October 10, 1839; *cf.* introduction to *Rynning's True Account of America*, 19.

[42] *Veiviser for norske Emigranter til de forenede nordamerikanske Stater og Texas*, 151. Cf. Flom, *Norwegian Immigration*, 152; Babcock, *Scandinavian Element*, 37, 40.

less, the emigration of 1839 was twice as large as that of 1837. There was a decline in 1840, but in 1841 the number equaled that of 1839, and the next year it nearly doubled. Rynning's book probably went to many who did not learn the circumstances of his death. There was no cessation, but the movement as a whole was in its preliminary stages; large numbers of people who felt the pressure of conditions in Norway were seriously considering emigration; many were marking time pending the arrival of more favorable news.

Ole Nattestad's journal is a simple and unsophisticated peasant's description of the sights that passed before his eyes as he made the journey from the Old World to the New. It bore the title (in translation) " Description of a Journey to North America, begun April 8, 1837, and written on the ship Hilda, and also continued later on the trip up through the United States in North America." One can find nowhere a more illuminating picture of the attitude of the shrewd and honest peasant from the interior of Norway as he reacted to the new environment of America. Unconscious humor, gullibility, and astonishment are apparent on every page of the book. The author looks upon the changing panorama with eyes wide open and he sees much. With unpracticed pen he sets down on paper what he has seen, serenely confident that his friends of the Norwegian countryside will read what he has written and marvel at the wonders he has seen. He tells of his trip with his brother from Numedal to Göteborg, where they secured passage on a freight boat bound for Fall River. The ship itself, scenes during the voyage, icebergs, the Newfoundland banks, and many incidents of the journey are described. The immigrants went to Providence and then to New York. For the first time in his life Ole Nattestad saw a train. " Now I am going to report something that I have neglected, namely: when we had come on board the steamboat in Provedens, and just as we left the shore we saw an engine go from the carhouse and draw 10 cars with it and all were filled with people; this we stood on the deck and saw; it went to the city of Boston." [43]   From New York the Nattestads went to Albany, Rochester, Buffalo, and Detroit, where, as has been noted, they fell in with the Rynning party.   Characterizations of Indians and Negroes, a brief account of the Beaver Creek settlement, reports on work and wages, and comments on the religious situation in America occur in Nattestad's journal.   After describing land conditions, the author discloses his pioneering spirit by writing, " But I also have in my mind to go more to the west to look for land." [44]   He gives his countrymen the benefit of his experience.   In four months he earned fifty dollars.   He states that he has been offered one hundred and ninety dollars a year, together with board " as good as an official has in Norway "; that a workingman can earn from twelve to sixteen dollars a month in winter, and almost twice as much in summer; and that a girl can earn from one to two dollars a week if she has some knowledge of English. [45]   Nattestad does not leave his reader with the view that the American streets are paved with gold; he utters a distinct note of warning instead.   " It is my opinion," he writes, " that everyone who has his youth and is unmarried certainly can make up his mind in regard to the journey; but one must consider that he is leaving his home and his relatives and friends.   I have heard many, especially among the women, say that if they have ever so good days, they are homesick for Norway."   Emigrants

[43] Ole Nattestad, " Description of a Journey to North America," translated by Rasmus B. Anderson, in the *Wisconsin Magazine of History*, 1: 178 (December, 1917).

[44] *Wisconsin Magazine of History*, 1: 186.

[45] *Ibid.*, 1: 186.

are reminded that " one must first taste the bitter before he can drink the sweet." Ignorance of English presents one difficulty; but inability to work is a more serious one.[46] Nattestad's journal was a personal record, whereas Rynning's was a general account. In influence and historical importance the latter was far more important than the former, but the two supplemented each other effectively. They mark a step forward in the emigration movement as a whole and they are of much historical interest for those who wish to know what the Norwegians were reading about America in the period when emigration was on its first upward swing.[47]

Many of the immigrants of 1837, when they reached Rochester on their way to the interior, stopped to visit and to consult with Lars Larsen, the shipbuilder, and their poverty prompted him to address a note of warning to his countrymen in October, 1837. He states that of some ninety emigrants who had arrived on the vessel from Stavanger, the majority had come to his home in Rochester and remained with him for three days. He had sent about thirty on to Illinois; the rest were still there and had been augmented by twelve more, whom he was housing temporarily on one of his boats. Many of these people had evidently been aided by the consul in New York; and were again in need of help when they reached Rochester. Larsen was a generous man and gave them as much help as he could, but their numbers were so great that it was impossible for him to meet the problem. In his open letter he urged Norwegians to bear in mind the difficulty that

[46] *Ibid.*, 186. The writer has made a slight change in translation after comparison with the original.

[47] Nattestad's *Beskrivelse over en Reise til Nordamerica* was reprinted by S. H. Herbransen in 1926 (Numedal Sogelags Forlag, 45 p.) with valuable critical notes and comments. For information about the Nattestads see also Mr. Herbransen's brochure *De Første Utvandrere fra Numedal til Amerika*, 9–34, and numerous contributions by him in *Dølaminne*, vols. 5–8.

many immigrants faced: lack of sufficient funds to complete their journey.   Ignorance of English added greatly to the seriousness of the problem, for it made it difficult for the immigrants to get work easily.[48]   In a private letter of October 11, 1837, Larsen's wife tells of trudging the streets in search of employment for immigrants and reports that her husband had taken many out into the country, presumably to near-by farms.   She declares that they will spare no effort to aid their countrymen, but that nearly all the immigrants come to their home and they are not able to aid so many.   These letters give an attractive picture of the kindness of the Larsens, whose home had become in a sense an immigrant station, but they also reveal the great economic need which many of the immigrants faced and which caused them unusual hardship.[49]

It is of interest to note that occasionally a well-to-do immigrant aided poor Norwegians to emigrate.   Thus in 1838 — a year in which the emigration from Norway was slight [50]— Ole Aasland, a rich farmer from Flesberg parish, Numedal, took a group of poor emigrants with him on condition that they should repay him in labor.   From Kendall, New York, he proceeded to Noble County, Indiana, where he bought a large tract of land.   The sickness and deaths of a considerable number of his as-

[48] Lars Larsen to his countrymen, October, 1837, in *Stavanger Adresseavis*, December 15, 1837.   An immigrant letter of October 2, 1837, from Rochester, published in the same paper, tells of the experiences of the Stavanger immigrants, complains of an overcharge by the captain of the vessel, says that the consul in New York lent them money to help them to get to Rochester, and adds, " Then two Norwegians, Lars Larsen and Ole Eie, took them in charge, supplied them with room and food for a number of days in several houses, and also lent them money to get on to Illinois."

[49] Martha Larsen to Elias Tastad, October 11, 1837, in Tastad Papers, Quaker Archives, Stavanger.   The letter is published by Malmin, in *Decorah-Posten*, December 12, 1924, and is translated in part in *American-Scandinavian Review*, 13: 361 ff. (June, 1925).

[50] The official Norwegian figure for emigration in 1838 is 100.   *Utvandringsstatistikk*, 101.

sociates defeated his plan and he later exchanged his Indiana lands for a small tract in the Kendall settlement.[51]

The emigration of 1837, which aroused the concern of
Larsen in New York, was also observed with alarm by
public officials in Norway; and the finance, trade, and
tariff department of the government instituted an inquiry
as early as April 3 of that year, calling upon the *amtmænd*,
or sheriffs, in certain districts to report on all sides of the
movement, including the numbers of emigrants, the classes
to which they belonged, their motives, the nature of the
reports that had come from earlier emigrants, and the
like. Two purposes underlay this investigation: the government desired to study the problem of how to deal with
the situation and it wished to be in a position to give reliable information to prospective emigrants.[52] The inquiry brought together a large amount of specific information about emigrants, copies of some "America letters,"
and opinions about causes — the latter stressing usually
the influence of favorable letters and the hope of winning
a better livelihood, with occasional mention of social dis-
affection.[53] Departmental action seems to have gone no

[51] Anderson, *Norwegian Immigration*, 264–266. Anderson states that Aasland
took twenty poor people with him, but it is possible that the number was smaller.
Herbransen has found records of Aasland's emigration, with his wife and five
children, and of five other Numedal emigrants from Flesberg in 1838, and suggests
that these five were aided by Aasland. *De Første Utvandrere fra Numedal til
Amerika*, 38–41. Three manuscript letters by Aasland, dated September 2, 1845,
August 17, 1846, and November 8, 1847, are preserved in the Historiografisk
Samling, Oslo.

[52] A draft of the department's circular of April 3, 1837, to Stavanger and
Søndre Bergenhus *amter* is in Socialdept., Lovkontor: Utv., Kong. Prop. 1845, folder
1. Mr. Malmin gives an account of this investigation, based upon the archival
materials, in *Decorah-Posten*, December 19, 1924.

[53] The reports received by the department may be found in Socialdept., Lovkontor: Utv., Kong. Prop. 1845, folder 1. Particularly valuable are those by N.
Hertzberg of Ullensvang for May 9 and July 6, 1837, the latter containing copies
of five "America letters," one by Gjert G. Hovland. Reports from Tind, May 15,
and Vigøer, April 25, are also of special interest. A number of valuable papers
occasioned by the investigation in Stavanger *Amt* are in Bergen S. A.: Stavanger

further than the newspaper publication of some reports, which it was probably hoped would dampen the ardor of prospective emigrants. Late in May there was published in Stavanger a department announcement based mainly upon information supplied by a Norwegian recently returned from New York, who declared it as difficult to earn a livelihood in America as in Norway, commented on the dangers to Norwegians of the American climate, and reported that the emigrants of 1836 were without money and in unfortunate circumstances when they arrived at New York.[54] Later in the year the department made public a report on the 1836 emigrants received from the Norwegian-Swedish vice consul in New York. This report was fair in tone, pointing out that a pioneer settler in the West could be expected to have a very difficult time of it for the first year or two, but that thereafter his position ordinarily would rapidly improve. Farmers could count on making a good living. For laborers also the American situation in general had been favorable. Nevertheless, the vice consul explained, the panic of 1837 had caused a great reverse in normal conditions and neither laborers nor skilled workmen should now be advised to come.[55]

Amt, eldre afdeling, Pakkeafdeling, no. 678. These form a part of a collection of papers for the years 1836–1844. A draft of the department's letter of May 11, 1837, is in R. A., Oslo: F. D., Kopibøger, 1837D 219/301.

[54] *Stavanger Adresseavis*, May 26, 1837. The report of Stavanger *Amt*, April 20, 1837, is published in *Den Bergenske Merkur*, May 21, 1837. The original draft is in S. A., Bergen: Stavanger Amt Copie-Bog, 1836–37.

[55] The report of Vice Consul Zacharison, dated August 7, 1837, appears in *Stavanger Adresseavis*, October 13, 1837, and *Den Norske Rigstidende*, October 1, 1837; the original is in Socialdept., Lovkontor: Utv., Kong. Prop. 1845, folder 1. Zacharison mentioned the emigrants of 1825 as honorable people who were now in good circumstances. He also expressed the opinion that most of the immigrants were becoming Quakers.

V. THE SPREAD OF WESTERN SETTLEMENT

THE story of Norwegian immigration from 1837 to the middle of the century is one of increasing volume and of steady expansion in settlement from the Illinois nucleus to the West, Northwest, and Southwest. The total American figure for Norwegian-Swedish immigration from 1831 to 1840 is 1,161; Norwegian figures for the last five years of this decade reach 1,200. For the forties the Norwegian and Swedish arrivals, according to American statistics, total 13,903; but for the same decade the emigration from Norway alone amounted to 17,000. There is good reason for considering the Norwegian round numbers approximately correct. The European statistics are no guarantee, however, that the people enumerated actually reached the United States, though that was the intended destination with comparatively few exceptions. On the other hand, as arrivals at American ports in the earlier period were carelessly tabulated, it is probable that the American figures are too low. The first years of the forties represent a gradual increase in Norwegian emigration, with a definite upward swing in 1843, followed by declines in 1844 and 1845, a slight rise in 1846, a downward reaction in 1848, and thereafter a marked increase.[1]

In 1838 Rynning wrote that the Fox River colony, the first nucleus of Norwegian settlement in the West, numbered from sixteen to twenty families.[2] One of the immigrants of 1836 relates that when he and his companions

[1] *Utvandringsstatistikk*, 100–101; *Statistical Review of Immigration 1820–1910*, 17 ff.; " Angaaende Udvandringer til Fremmede Verdensdele," in *Kongeriget Norges Ellevte Ordentlige Storthings Forhandlinger i 1845*, vol. 1, part 6, p. 23–24.

[2] *True Account of America*, 78.

first saw the settlement they were bitterly disappointed, not only because of the bare and unattractive living conditions which they found, but also because the land was already well taken up and it seemed necessary for the newcomers to look elsewhere for desirable locations.[3]   Out of this disappointment grew an attempt to establish a Norwegian settlement in Missouri.

Cleng Peerson was engaged by a group of dissatisfied immigrants to search out a new place for settlement. Curiously, instead of going north he went southwest, and he selected a spot in northeastern Missouri — Shelby County — as the new Eldorado. The immigrants trusted Peerson because, as one of them wrote, he " knew the language and had much knowledge of conditions in the country." [4]   Upon his return from his journey of investigation Peerson reported that he had found good land aplenty west of the Mississippi and as a result, in the spring of 1837, a party of twelve or fourteen Norwegians, including Peerson, Jacob and Knud Slogvig, and Sjur J. Haaeim, left the La Salle County settlement. After reaching Hannibal, the settlers still had a sixty-mile drive, with wagons and horses, before they came to their destination, a place some twenty-five miles from Shelbyville, Missouri. Claims were taken and rude log houses erected, but, lacking money and faced with all the difficulties of the initial pioneering stage, the immigrants had a hard time. Since the nearest mill was fifty miles away and the nearest village twenty-five, marketing was rendered unusually difficult. Haaeim, after one year's trial, gave up and returned to Norway thoroughly disillusioned about the American prospects.[5]   Meanwhile, Peerson was attempting to recruit

---

[3] Sjur Jørgensen Haaeim, *Oplysninger om Forholdene i Nordamerika*, 2 (Christiania, 1842); translated and edited by Malmin as " The Disillusionment of an Immigrant: Sjur Jørgensen Haaeim's ' Information on Conditions in North America,' " in *Studies and Records*, 3:1–12.

[4] Haaeim's account, in *Studies and Records*, 3:4.

[5] *Ibid.*, 4–5.

settlers for the colony. In the spring of 1838 he was in New York and persuaded a party of newly arrived immigrants, including Peter and William Testman, to accompany him west. This little group had come by way of Bremen. One of its members tells of the arrival in New York: " Here we met several Norwegians and Danes, including a Norwegian named Kleng Pedersen, who has been in America about twenty years and has much knowledge about the country since he has traveled about in nearly all the states of the union and speaks fairly fluent English." [6] Before the party left Rochester it numbered twenty-two persons. Some of these went on to Chicago after reaching Buffalo, but a number of them followed Peerson to Cleveland and, via the Ohio Canal, the Ohio River, and the Mississippi, to St. Louis, Hannibal, and the Shelby County settlement. Testman has left a vivid description of the difficulties which met the immigrants in Missouri, and he, like Haaeim, gave up after a short trial. [7] Several other recruits were added to the colony in 1838 and 1839, but on the whole the settlement was unsuccessful and after a few years it began to disintegrate. It is true that as late as 1879 one of the original Shelby County pioneers, Andrew Simonsen, declared that " no settlement ever founded by Norwegians in America had a better appearance or better location than this very land in Shelby County, of which the Norwegians took possession at that time, and which they in part still own." [8] The fact is, however, that Missouri as a place of settlement

[6] A letter from Missouri dated October 15, 1838, in *Stavanger Amtstidende og Adresseavis*, February 1, 1839.

[7] Peter Testman, *Kort Beskrivelse over de vigtigste Erfaringer under et Ophold i Nordamerica og paa flere dermed forbundne Reiser* (Stavanger, 1839); translated and edited by T. C. Blegen as *Peter Testman's Account of His Experiences in North America* (Norwegian-American Historical Association, *Travel and Description Series*, vol. 2 — Northfield, 1927).

[8] It is noteworthy that Simonson himself deserted the Missouri settlement and moved to Iowa in 1840, although he indicates that he gained nothing by the exchange. Anderson, *Norwegian Immigration*, 186.

received little attention from Norwegian immigrants. In the sense that it attracted few settlers, the Shelby County settlement did fail. The reasons, however, are probably other than those that account for the disillusionment of Haaeim, Testman, and other settlers in Missouri. The basic causes seem to have been the distaste of the majority of the Norwegian immigrants for a slave state and the increasing pressure of population into Wisconsin and Iowa. The Missouri region was not on the highways of population expansion in the upper Mississippi Valley. The immigrant was like other human beings in his liking for following the crowd, and his unfamiliarity with the English language accentuated his tendency to flock with his countrymen. The crowd was thronging to the fertile, unoccupied lands of Wisconsin, and the Norwegian immigrant naturally joined in this movement.

While Ansten Nattestad was in Norway in the summer of 1838, his brother Ole left the Beaver Creek colony, went to northern Illinois, and after a short time, believing that as one moved toward the north and the west one always faced the better land, he crossed the Wisconsin line and on July 1, 1838, located in what is now Clinton Township, Rock County, where he entered a claim and set about making for himself a temporary abode. By remaining in this region he became the founder of an important Wisconsin settlement of Norwegians, the Jefferson Prairie settlement. Thousands upon thousands of Norwegians were to follow in the footsteps of Nattestad, and Wisconsin soon became the objective of the majority of the immigrants from Norway. Meanwhile, however, Nattestad lived alone, out of touch with his countrymen in Illinois. " Eight Americans," he writes, " had settled in the town before me, it is true, but these persons lived in a condition almost as isolated and lonely as mine. The soil I found to be exceptionally fertile, and the dreary uniformity of the prairie was broken here by intervening clumps of woods. Flocks of deer and other wild animals were to be seen almost every day, and the mournful howl of the prairie wolf disturbed my sleep regularly, until custom fortified my ears against interruptions of this sort." [9]

The sensation created by the return to Norway of Ansten Nattestad and the publication of the Rynning and Nattestad pamphlets has already been described. When it became known that Nattestad would personally conduct a party of emigrants from Drammen in the spring of 1839, throngs of people made known their desire to join it. In fact, a considerable number were unable to secure accommodations on board the ship in which Nattestad was to sail. Some of these, under the leadership of an energetic emigrant named John Nelson Luraas, were from the Upper Telemarken region, chiefly from the Tind and Hjertdal parishes. Approximately forty persons were in the group and of these perhaps half were members of the four Luraas families represented. Luraas and his companions went to Göteborg, where they fell in with a party of emigrants from Stavanger. The two joined forces and, now numbering approximately sixty persons, they engaged an American captain, whose ship, loaded with iron, was ready to sail for Boston, to give them passage at a cost of forty-two specie dollars per adult. After a nine weeks' journey they arrived at Boston. The antecedents of the Luraas emigration, told in the words of its leader, throw an interesting light on the general situation:

I was my father's eldest son and was therefore heir to the estate of Luraas. The farm was considered one of the best in the district, but it was burdened with a debt of $1,400. Up to my twenty-fifth year

[9] *Billed-Magazin*, 1: 84.

I had worked at home and consequently had had no opportunity to save money. Obviously my future would be a precarious one if I should take over the estate with its burden of debt, care for my brothers and sisters properly, and finally supply my father with an annual allowance. I viewed with alarm the way in which one farm after another was falling into the hands of the *lendsmand* and other money lenders, and this increased my fear of assuming charge of the estate. But I married, and was forced to find a solution of the problem. Then it occurred to me that the best thing for me to do was to emigrate to America. I was strengthened in this plan by letters from Norwegian settlers in Illinois, and the idea became a definite resolution when I read a book written by a Norwegian emigrant who had lived two years in America. These things led me to desert my native land and I take it that the other " America travelers " who were in my company reached the same conclusion as a result of similar motives.[10]

Another member of the same group has left an account of the forces that eventuated in his emigration, which it is interesting to compare with the Luraas statement. John Evenson Molee writes:

My oldest brother, according to the old law of primogeniture *(odelsret)*, would take the farm unincumbered, and there was not enough cash or personal property on hand for me and my sisters with which to buy another farm, for we were seven children. . . . The labor market was so overstocked that strong young men could hardly obtain work for more than five dollars and clothing a year. . . . The professions and trades were also overstocked. A laborer was not allowed to eat at the same table with a land-owner. Labor commenced before sunrise and lasted till after dark — no time for the enrichment of the mind by reading newspapers or good books evenings.

He tells of leaving his home in Tind, Telemarken, and going to Stavanger, where he obtained work with a farmer, Gitle Danielson. " In 1839," he writes, " the ' America fever,' as it was called, commenced. Gitle Danielson, my master, and his family, were smitten badly by the ' America fever '; that is, an intense desire to emigrate to America. Mr. Danielson sold his farm and personal prop-

---

[10] *Billed-Magazin*, 1: 6–7. A note in *Tiden* (Drammen) for May 12, 1839, mentions the clearing of a vessel on the previous day with forty emigrants for Göteborg, where they intended to join other emigrants on a ship for America.

erty and made himself ready for the daring undertaking." [11]

When the Luraas party reached Boston its members seem to have been the objects of a peculiar curiosity. The following account of the reception of the immigrants is based upon the testimony of the immigrants themselves, who apparently derived some amusement from the situation and probably indulged in exaggeration:

In Boston these newcomers occasioned considerable surprise. Few had heard of Norway, and the inhabitants came in throngs to the wharves to see the ship on which were emigrants from the high north. The foreign language of the emigrants, their clothes, and their customs were marveled at, but the visitors were even more astonished to find that people who came from a land so near the ice region as Norway looked like other human beings! They thought that men and women alike would be clad in skins from head to foot, that they would eat raw meat and, like the Eskimos, drink oil. [12]

The immigrants went west by way of New York and Buffalo, and after a perilous voyage on the Great Lakes reached Milwaukee seventeen weeks after they left their native land. Their original plan was to go to the Fox River settlement in Illinois. Why they altered it is not entirely clear, but one of the immigrants has put on record a story which, if true, indicates that only the chance landing at Milwaukee and an American ruse diverted the party. According to this tale, the Norwegians were preparing for their departure from Milwaukee when several Americans from that city came on board the boat and inquired of them where they intended to go. When informed that their destination was Illinois, one of the Americans replied that of course they were at liberty to do as they pleased in a free country, but they would do well, before starting for Illinois, to look carefully at the two men who accompanied him. One was robust and

[11] A letter by Molee, including the passage quoted above, is printed in Anderson, *Norwegian Immigration*, 300–326.
[12] *Billed-Magazin*, 1: 7.

blooming with health. He was from Wisconsin. The other, sick, decrepit, and obviously miserable, was an Illinois man — a specimen of the effects of Illinois heat and malaria.[13] Whatever may have been the cause, the immigrants did decide to remain in Wisconsin. A guide conducted a committee representing the party to the north end of Muskego Lake in Waukesha County, and since the lakes were inviting, the woods plentiful, and the swamps dry, the committee carried back a favorable report. As a result, most of the members of the party went from Milwaukee and established the Muskego settlement, on land that could be purchased from the government at $1.25 per acre. By autumn much of the land was under water and the immigrants had occasion to rue their hasty choice. Unfortunate as the land selection was, a beginning had been made, and the Muskego settlement, destined to become one of the best-known Norwegian settlements in America, was in existence. The name was retained after most of the settlers moved away from the low lands originally selected and settled in Norway Township and adjoining townships of Racine County.[14]

The route by way of Göteborg was followed by several minor groups of emigrants in 1839. Thus Johannes Johansen and Søren Bache left that port on July 15, on the " Skogsmand," and arrived at Newport on September 2, the first stage of a journey that was to bear important results. Bache was the son of Tollef Bache, a devout Haugean of Drammen, who like Hauge himself had a keen business sense. The elder Bache became one of the prominent lumber dealers and shippers of Drammen, and

[13] The story is recorded in *Billed-Magazin*, 1: 8. The exact words of the American are quoted: " Look! The robust man is from Wisconsin, where there is a healthful climate and food in abundance. The sick man is from Illinois, where people are destroyed by the burning summer heat and die like flies from the malarial fever."

[14] *Billed-Magazin*, 1: 8, 10.

his son set off for America in 1839 well supplied with money. Both he and Johansen, in fact, were in a position to play the part of philanthropic friends to poor immigrants in the West. It is certain also that accounts of their experiences and their conclusions with respect to the advisability of emigration were awaited in and about Drammen with keen anticipation. Bache has been characterized as a dreamer, but the records indicate that he was a careful and systematic observer of men and events. Recently his diary came to light, one of the most detailed and valuable records in existence for the pioneer Norwegian period.[15] Earlier in 1839, on May 27, three emigrants, Anders and Johannes Wiig and Brynnild Leqve, together with some others, left Göteborg. They arrived at Fall River on August 2 and started for the West.[16] Yet another group, consisting of twenty-six persons, sailed from the Swedish port on May 25 on an American vessel which was later damaged by a heavy storm, put into an English port for repairs that took a month, and did not reach New York until September 4. The voyage was one of hardship and misery for the passengers. The crew, writes one of the immigrants, " apparently did not consider us people, but usually called us devils." [17]

Early in June, 1839, the main Nattestad party assembled at Drammen. From 130 to 140 people, " most of them

[15] Bache's diary for the period from 1839 to 1847 is published under the title " Sören Baches dagboksoptegnelser under sit ophold i Amerika " in the monthly magazine *Norsk Ungdom* (Minneapolis) beginning with the issue for December, 1927. Preceding the first installment are brief biographical sketches of Tollef and Søren Bache written by the latter's daughter, Marie Bache of Oslo. The diary is in the archives of the Norwegian-American Historical Association at Northfield, Minnesota. Bache and Johansen give a lengthy account of their journey in a letter written at the Fox River settlement on December 31, 1839, printed in *Tiden* (Drammen), March 3, 1840. This letter is analyzed *post*, p. 203.

[16] A letter by the three individuals mentioned, written from " Iowe County, Wis. Territory " on January 11, 1841, tells of this emigration. *Bergens Stiftstidende*, July 29, 1841.

[17] An undated letter by Halvor J. Nymoen in *Tiden* (Drammen), January 7, 1840.

from Rolloug, Veglie, and northern Numedal and some from Tind and Heddal," were there about June 5, according to a newspaper item. When people attempted to frighten these emigrants by terrifying stories about America, they merely smiled and said that they had received first-hand reports from returned emigrants, who did not lie.[18] Nattestad's party, one hundred in number, sailed on June 12 on the "Emilia," captain Thomas Anchersen.[19] A smaller group, consisting of some thirty people, went by another vessel to Göteborg, where they caught the brig "Bunyan" for Boston. After they reached Chicago, they fell in with the main Nattestad group.[20]

A newspaper, commenting on Nattestad's emigrants at the time when they left Drammen, states that most of them were in good circumstances and a couple of them owned several thousand specie dollars. "As a whole they were vigorous and well-appearing people; there were no old people, few children, and sixteen young unmarried girls." They "put their firm faith in the guidance of Providence and hoped for a better livelihood in the new world." [21] An earlier newspaper article spoke of the emigrants of 1839 as representing the "best youth" of the land.[22] As the "Emilia" sailed out from Drammen a young university graduate in theology, Peter Valeur, who accompanied the group to Göteborg, delivered a farewell sermon.[23] Typical of the piety of the emigrants was their

---

[18] *Tiden* (Drammen), June 6, 1839.

[19] *Tiden* (Drammen), June 13, 1839.

[20] An interesting account of the journey of this group is "Halvor P. Haugens Reiseskildring," in the *Aarbok* of Numedalslaget for 1920, p. 54–59. The author was a member of the party. It should be noted that in the spring of 1839 Captain Willemsen had conveyed a group of forty-four emigrants from the west coast, according to an item dated Bergen, April 8, in *Morgenbladet*, April 16, 1839.

[21] *Tiden* (Drammen), June 13, 1839.

[22] *Tiden* (Drammen), April 2, 1839.

[23] Knud Knudsen, *Beretning om en Reise fra Drammen til New York*, 9–10 (Norlie ed., Minneapolis, 1926).

petition to the church department, drawn up on June 3, more than a week before their departure, requesting the ordination of Valeur for service among them in America as a minister. Valeur had declared his willingness to accept such a position and the majority desired him to be ordained first. The emigrants desired assurance that their children would be brought up in their own faith. The church department was in a quandary, for this " call " did not originate in an organized congregation and no departmental control could be exercised over a minister in America. Nevertheless, after getting opinions from the theological faculty of the university and from a bishop, it moved the authorization of the request, and on December 23 it was granted by royal resolution.[24]

The " Emilia " carried its passengers to New York at a cost of 33½ specie dollars per person. From June 13 to 22 it remained at Göteborg, where a cargo of iron was secured. The vessel arrived at New York on August 26 and three days later the emigrants were on a Hudson River packet. They followed the usual route to the West, stopping at Rochester to consult with Lars Larsen.[25] They

[24] R. A., Oslo: Kirkedept., Referatprotokoller, 1839, no. 64, res. 244; and Gunnar J. Malmin, " Litt norsk-amerikansk kirkehistorie fra de norske arkiver," in *Lutheraneren*, January 16, 1924, p. 75.

[25] Knudsen, in the pamphlet cited in n. 23, gives an interesting account of the party's experiences. Among other things he mentions the custom of the emigrants on board the " Emilia " to have prayer and religious songs each evening. At Albany on September 1 Knudsen and Claus Stabæk, on behalf of the emigrants, wrote a letter of thanks to Anchersen, who seems to have been a model ship captain. He aided them in making arrangements for their journey to the interior and took leave of them at Schenectady. They wrote that it was as touching to say goodbye to the captain as it had been to leave their relatives in Norway. The letter was printed in *New-Yorker Stats-Zeitung*, September 4, 1839, and reprinted in *Tiden* (Drammen), December 31, 1839. In *Tiden* for the same date Knudsen gives an account of the trip. See also *Billed-Magazin*, 1: 94. In the *Aarbok* of Numedalslaget, 1919, p. 58–61, Mr. H. L. Skavlem published a critical note seeking to prove that the " Emilia " went not direct to New York from Drammen, but via Göteborg, and that the voyage took twelve weeks. On both points he differed with earlier writers. On the first he was right; but the duration of the voyage was less than twelve weeks. The date of departure from Drammen was June 12; the

reached Milwaukee shortly after the earlier group from Telemarken. Although Norwegians and Americans alike tried to persuade Ansten Nattestad to go to the Muskego region, he firmly refused, and, with his party, went on to Chicago, where he was apprised of the fact that his brother had moved north into Wisconsin. Some of the immigrants in the group remained in Chicago and some went to the Fox River colony, but the majority followed Nattestad to Jefferson Prairie, where they bought land. " Toward the end of September, 1839," records Ole Nattestad, " I received the group of people from my home community who as emigrants had followed my brother Ansten from Norway. Most of them settled on Jefferson Prairie and in this manner this settlement in a comparatively short time got a large population." [26]   On November 6 Ansten Nattestad wrote to Valeur explaining that he feared that the settlers, though they were still together and had not yet selected land, would be too scattered to form a compact settlement that would support a minister. They would therefore be unable to carry out the plans with reference to a " call."   The Fox River colony, he added, represented such various religious views that it would not accept a Lutheran minister. Should Valeur decide to come despite these considerations, Nattestad felt that he would probably be able, without official ordination, to carry on such ministerial work as opportunity might afford. Thus ended what was probably the first move looking toward Lutheran church organization among Norwegian immigrants in the West. Valeur, so far as is known, never came to America.[27]

date of arrival at New York, August 26. This makes the length, inclusive of these two dates, ten weeks and five days; but as has been noted, the voyage was broken at Göteborg from June 13 to 22.

[26] *Billed-Magazin*, 1: 84.

[27] Nattestad's letter is printed in *Den Norske Rigstidende*, March 1, 1840. *Cf.* Malmin, in *Lutheraneren*, January 16, 1924.

The effort to secure an ordained minister of the state church suggests that the emigrants of 1839 were wholly orthodox, but there is evidence of a considerable Haugean influence. Gullik O. Gravdal, one of the emigrants, pointed out this fact when interviewed many years later. He said:

The great majority of those who in 1839 emigrated from Numedal belonged to the Haugeans. We were not actually persecuted because of our beliefs . . . but the "readers" were nevertheless in bad repute and we had to endure much contempt and scorn from those who were other-minded. I will not say that this intolerance was the cause of our emigration, but it contributed to the ripening of our resolution to leave a country where we were exposed to many annoyances because our conceptions of religious teaching did not entirely conform with the beliefs of the great majority. Still, the motives which were clinching for the most of us were the hope of finding cheap and fertile land in America and the stories about high wages.[28]

On the latter point specific confirmation is given, for one case, by another emigrant. " My father lived on a little farm and had many children," writes Gullik K. Laugen (Springen).

The products of our farm gave us only the barest necessities. We were five brothers and I worked at home for my father until my twenty-first year. For my labor I could never hope to get more than food and clothes. . . . I began to think seriously about the future and then the thought of emigration came. My father . . . encouraged me to try my luck in America. Ansten Nattestad, who had made a trip to Norway from America, stayed in our community in the winter and spring and it was his accounts especially that wakened the desire among us to emigrate. I borrowed twenty specie dollars and got ready for the journey.[29]

Incidentally, Laugen confirms the evidence already cited from a contemporary newspaper that people in Drammen were hostile in their attitude toward the emigrants. Stories about poisonous snakes, savage Indians, pestilential air, and fearful storms were in circulation among the

[28] *Billed-Magazin*, 1: 161–162.
[29] *Billed-Magazin*, 1: 171.

inhabitants of that city. In this connection it is worth noting that Nattestad seems to have aroused the ire of certain local Norwegian officials because of his stimulation of the emigration. They are reported to have threatened him with punishment should he return to Norway and to have spoken ominously of the prospect of an absolute prohibition of further emigration. It is apparent that the emigrants themselves attributed this alleged hostility to the fact that their emigration removed from the district a source of profit for local officials.[30]

In 1839, only five years after the original Norwegian settlement in Illinois had been established, Norwegians were moving into Wisconsin by two approaches, the Lake Michigan shore and the Illinois boundary. The Jefferson Prairie settlement was augmented in numbers steadily in the years immediately following its founding; but it became almost at once a point of departure for settlements farther west and north. In fact, the Rock Prairie settlement, embracing the region west of the city of Beloit, in the towns of Beloit, Newark, Avon, Spring Valley, and Plymouth, was established almost as early as the Jefferson Prairie settlement, its founders being Gullik O. Gravdal and Gisle S. Hallan, two individuals not content with the general location selected by Ole Nattestad.[31] They were joined in the spring of 1840 by several of the 1839 emigrants who had stopped in Chicago but were now ready to buy land, among these being Lars H.

---

[30] *Billed-Magazin*, 1: 94, 171. There is probably some exaggeration in the recollections of many immigrants with reference to the attitude of government officials, but there is ample contemporary evidence of hostility to emigration propaganda. An article in *Morgenbladet*, March 21, 1839, refers caustically to individuals who were encouraging emigration but who had not previously shown themselves to be interested in improving conditions among their countrymen. It asserts that stimulators of emigration were making "missionary journeys" in Numedal, Gudbrandsdalen, and various other mountain districts.

[31] H. L. Skavlem, *Scandinavians in the Early Days of Rock County*, 424–427. This is a reprint from *History of Rock County* (Chicago, 1908).

Skavlem, Gjermund Skavlem, and Knud Christbinusen. By the fall of 1840, five homesteads had been taken by Norwegians in the Rock Prairie region, and in the following years this settlement grew by leaps and bounds, especially after 1843, and became itself a starting point for settlers seeking lands farther in the interior.[32] Meanwhile, a settlement in Illinois, partly in Stephenson County and partly in Winnebago County, which had begun in 1839 as an offshoot of the Nattestad enterprise, was developing under the leadership of Clement Torstenson Stabæk, who, with three other immigrants, selected the Illinois lands in preference to the lands of Nattestad's choice.[33]

Bache and Johansen, after a trip of investigation in Wisconsin in the fall of 1839 — in the course of which they did not visit the Muskego area, but confined their attention to lands lying to the north of the Jefferson Prairie settlement [34] — returned to Fox River, where they remained until the summer of 1840, meanwhile writing to their friends in Drammen letters that were influential in bringing out a party of immigrants in 1840. Early in June Bache and Johansen left Fox River for Chicago and then proceeded north searching for good lands. The Muskego site seemed to Bache to be unfavorably located, and with Johansen he now selected lands on the shores of Wind Lake in a township that became known as " Norway." [35] This choice influenced most of the settlers on Lake Muskego eventually to move farther south, where

[32] Skavlem, *Scandinavians in the Early Days of Rock County*, 427 ff. A great deal of material on the Rock Prairie settlement is printed in *Billed-Magazin*, 1: 154-155, 171–173, 182–183, 186–188.

[33] " The smith, Knud Knudsen from Drammen, and Clement Stabek have settled about thirty English miles west from here," wrote Ansten Nattestad from Jefferson Prairie on November 6, 1839. *Den Norske Rigstidende*, March 1, 1840. Cf. Reiersen's account of 1844 as translated in *Studies and Records*, 1: 114.

[34] See *post*, p. 203.

[35] See Bache's diary, in *Norsk Ungdom*, March and April, 1928.

land conditions were better; and the "Muskego settlement" spread into Norway, Waterford, Raymond, and Yorkville townships of Racine County.[36]   Elling Eielsen, the noted Haugean lay preacher, seems also to have investigated the situation in the Muskego settlement in 1840. It has been suggested that the real purpose of Tollef Bache, who supplied the funds for his son's journeys and land purchases, was to establish a colony of Haugeans in America, where there would be no possibility of state-church antagonism.[37]   There is no suggestion of any such plan in Bache's diary, however, nor does Bache speak of any association with Eielsen in the first period.   The latter was bent on making a thoroughgoing investigation of the Norwegian settlements, was well aware of the fact that a considerable number of Haugeans were coming to America, and was filled with zeal for meeting their religious needs.   If there is no evidence of a specific plan for a Haugean colony, it yet remains true that Bache and Johansen were themselves Haugeans, and the friends in and about Drammen who awaited their verdict included many Haugeans.[38]

In the spring of 1840 a group of emigrants who had been influenced by Bache and Johansen left Norway for Wisconsin.   Their leader was Even Heg, a well-to-do innkeeper of Lier, near Drammen.   After having received encouraging letters from Bache and Johansen, Heg sold

[36] *Billed-Magazin*, 1: 11.

[37] Nilssen makes the suggestion of a possible colony of Haugeans. *Billed-Magazin*, 1: 12. On Eielsen see Mørstad, *Elling Eielsen og den " Evangelisk-lutherske Kirke " i Amerika*, 83–86.

[38] Various writers assert that Bache and Johansen established themselves at Wind Lake in the fall of 1839. The Bache diary proves, however, that they did not arrive until the following summer. The "dug-out" in the sides of a large Indian mound, where they made their home, was made, or built, in the summer and fall of 1840. Bache notes that twelve or fourteen skulls were found in the course of the excavation. Rohne writes that the "dug-out" served as "a land office, a general store, a center of culture, and a clearing house for aid and information to the immigrants." *Norwegian-American Lutheranism up to 1872*, 47. *Cf.* Bache's diary in *Norsk Ungdom*, April, 1928.

his property and assumed leadership of a group including about thirty persons from Drammen and a smaller number from Voss. These emigrants sailed from Drammen on May 17 in the "Emilia," and after a swing to Göteborg and a stormy trip across the Atlantic, they reached New York, went west, and arrived at Milwaukee, where they were met by people from Muskego. The Voss element continued to Chicago but most of those from Drammen followed Heg to Muskego. In the latter group was Ole K. Trovatten, who later won considerable fame in Norway as a writer of influential "America letters." In a manuscript journal he tells of this emigration of 1840. Many people in Drammen, he writes, ridiculed him, and one woman accused him of planning to get rid of his wife and children by exposing them to dangers that meant certain death. A minister asked him if "he believed that he would find a shorter road to Heaven from America than he could find from Norway," and Trovatten replied that since he would be able to worship God with entire freedom in America he really felt that he might be able to worship God better there than in his native land. In all he paid 189 specie dollars and 60 skillings for the expenses of the trip. The price for transportation was $33 apiece for himself and his wife and $25 each for his children; for board during the voyage he paid $12 apiece for himself and his wife. The contract for the journey from New York to the interior called for $13 for adults, half that amount for children under twelve, and nothing for children under two.[39]

The joy at Muskego upon the arrival of Heg is suggested in Bache's diary in an entry for August 28, 1840:

[39] This journal of thirty-six pages, written by Trovatten probably in 1842, is in the possession of Mr. Halvor Skavlem of Janesville, Wisconsin, and a photostatic copy is owned by the Minnesota Historical Society. The manuscript is not signed, but internal evidence proves that it was written by Trovatten. The problem of its authorship was solved by Mr. Skavlem.

I heard the voices of Even Heg and Johansen outside and our servant boy came rushing in to report that Even Heg had arrived. I hastened to meet them and great was the joy in meeting such old friends in so distant a land. Even Heg and his companions had arrived in the morning at Milwaukee, and guided by a Norwegian he had come on to meet us. Luckily we were able to treat him to a fresh fish that our boy had caught and to a cup of tea. After the meal we finally had to go to bed, but because our house was so little we had to move the bed outside and make up beds on the floor. But there was little sleep that night, for there was an unceasing flow of questions and answers.[40]

Even Heg was a man of marked ability, resourceful and helpful, a genuine leader among immigrants, and he won fame as a sagacious adviser to hundreds of immigrants who in the following years stopped temporarily at Muskego on their way to settlements farther west.[41]

Men like Heg, Bache, and Johansen gave much aid to less fortunate immigrants; and Muskego was a congregating point for newcomers whose funds had been exhausted by the expenses of the journey. At one time in 1843 the swarm of such new arrivals was so great that every house in the colony had to accommodate from fifteen to twenty persons — and this was at a time when the settlement was ravaged by disease.[42] Land was purchased in considerable amounts by such men as the three named, and by them divided into small lots. How far this process might sometimes go is illustrated in the Wisconsin Domesday Survey, which maps the farms of Norway Township for 1860. For example, " The southwest quarter of section 28, bought by Søren Backe in 1841, was divided into twelve different portions and resold from 1849 to 1859. Practically all the land as resold was divided." [43] Though poverty and small beginnings were the rule, some of the impecunious Norwegians who came to the Muskego settlement became

---

[40] Bache's diary in *Norsk Ungdom,* April, 1928.

[41] *Cf.* the writer's article, " Colonel Hans Christian Heg," in *Wisconsin Magazine of History,* 4: 140–165.

[42] Bache's diary in *Norsk Ungdom,* November, 1928.

[43] *Wisconsin Domesday Book: Town Studies,* 1: 91.

prosperous farmers in the course of a decade or two. For example, Mons K. Aadland, who in 1840 went north from the Beaver Creek settlement with three dollars and a few head of cattle, was worth forty thousand dollars eighteen years later and had eight hundred acres of land and much valuable farm equipment.[44] The tendency on the part of many in Norway was to pass judgment on emigration on the basis of the results of the first year or two, but such judgments often had to be revised in the light of the results of ten or fifteen years of effort. It may be noted that it was Johansen who drafted the famous Muskego manifesto of 1845, which served notice on the people of Norway that the settlers saw further than the immediate present, that despite sickness, privations, and suffering, they rejoiced in having come to the United States and faced the future with confidence.[45] Johansen himself, however, less than a year after writing the manifesto, fell victim to disease and died. Bache returned to Norway in 1842 to visit his father at Lier, but went back to Muskego in 1843 and played a prominent part in the affairs of the colony until his final departure for Norway in 1847, when he was called back because of the illness of his father. After the latter's death Bache remained in Norway and there became a successful farmer.[46] It is said that he left an investment of six thousand dollars in Muskego land, most of which he never regained.[47]

The Muskego settlement is one of the most noted Norwegian settlements in America, not because of prosperity — in the forties it was scourged with sickness, its land was not the choicest Wisconsin land, and in its material achievements it did not equal certain other midwestern

[44] *Billed-Magazin*, 1: 30–31.
[45] See *ante*, p. 119, and Bache's diary in *Norsk Ungdom*, January, 1929.
[46] See the biographical sketch of Bache by his daughter, Marie Bache, in *Norsk Ungdom*, December, 1927.
[47] *Billed-Magazin*, 1: 12.

settlements — but because it was a " mother colony " to numerous other settlements and because it witnessed during the forties and fifties some significant beginnings in the field of Norwegian-American religious, social, and cultural activities. By virtue of his character and his financial means Even Heg became the acknowledged leader of the colony. Shortly after his arrival he purchased the farm of John Nelson Luraas, the leader of the settlers of 1839. This farm became the Mecca of hundreds of Norwegians in search of homes in Wisconsin and the West.

Of the settlement itself in the forties, a pioneer of the community wrote, " This settlement was the journey's goal for the majority of the emigrants and it thus became a common assembling place and point of departure for most of the older colonies in America. It was later that the settlers went directly from their native land to the newer settlements in Wisconsin, Iowa, and Minnesota." [48] At the Heg farm a helping hand was always offered the immigrant. Especial interest attaches to the large barn which Heg erected in 1843. The small log cabins of the settlers could not accommodate the great numbers of immigrants who passed through Muskego, and Heg's barn was therefore utilized for the purpose. Every summer saw it thronged with large parties of newcomers who made it their home during the first days and weeks after the long journey from Norway. After consulting with the Muskego settlers in regard to the best lands for settlement, they started westward. Not only was the Heg barn a haven for new arrivals, but it also served for a long time as the social and religious center of the community. Before the arrival of a minister, lay services were conducted in the barn, at which Heg and Bache, among others, preached. The pioneer minister, C. L. Clausen, preached there upon his arrival at Muskego in 1843, and there he

[48] *Billed-Magazin*, 1: 11.

organized a congregation during the same year. Sunday school classes were held in the barn, and in 1844 the Reverend Mr. Clausen confirmed the first class of children there. In 1844 an interesting double wedding was celebrated in " Even Heg's new, home-sawed, oak frame barn." During the epidemic of disease which desolated the colony in the late forties the barn served as a hospital. Many of the religious influences among the Norwegians in the United States go back to their origin in Muskego. There for a time lived the Haugean preacher, Eielsen; and there was built the first Norwegian Lutheran church in America, a structure begun in 1843 and dedicated in the spring of 1845. It may be noted that a gift of $400 from Tollef Bache in Drammen aided the Muskego settlers in erecting this church building.[49]

One of the most interesting developments in the Muskego settlement was the establishment there in 1847 of a Norwegian newspaper. As early as 1845 James D. Reymert, a prominent member of the community, and several others urged the publication of a paper. Two years later it became a reality, the necessary funds having been supplied by Heg and Bache, who, with Reymert, were the publishers, the latter serving as editor. The early numbers of this paper were printed in Even Heg's log cabin. The name of the newspaper was *Nordlyset* (The Northern Light). The first number contained among other matters a translation of a portion of the Declara-

[49] The most valuable contemporary record of life in the Muskego settlement is Bache's diary, previously cited. In the installment published in *Norsk Ungdom* for January, 1929, an entry for March 13, 1845, describes the dedication of the church by Clausen and Dietrichson. It is interesting to note that Gustaf Unonius of Pine Lake and James L. Breck, later Episcopalian bishop in Minnesota, were present. An illustrated sketch of the Muskego settlement is A. O. Barton, " Muskego, the Most Historic Norwegian Colony," in *Scandinavia*, 1: 22–29. Light on its religious and social history is shed in H. G. Stub, " Reminiscences from Bygone Days," in *North Star*, 4: 12 ff. Contemporary material of first importance is in Dietrichson's *Reise blandt de norske Emigranter*, 25 ff. A sketch by H. R. Holand is in *Symra*, 3: 187–196.

tion of Independence and at the head of its editorial column appeared a cut of the American flag. Naturally the office of *Nordlyset* became the political center of the community. The significant point with regard to *Nordlyset* is that it became the Norwegian organ of the Free Soil Party. In supporting the principles of this party, the paper forecast the general course that the rank and file of the Norwegians were to take in the stirring political controversy centering about the slavery issue in the next decade and a half.[50] Though *Nordlyset* was, strictly speaking, the first Norwegian newspaper published in the United States, the researches of Mr. Malmin have recently brought to light the fact that the Scandinavian colony in New York City inaugurated a newspaper earlier in 1847. This paper, *Skandinavia*, with Christian Hansen as one of its promoters, was intended to serve the needs of Norwegians, Danes, and Swedes, and it employed both Norwegian-Danish and Swedish in its columns.[51]

[50] A file of *Nordlyset*, nearly complete, is in the library of Luther College, Decorah, Iowa, and an incomplete file is owned by Luther Theological Seminary, St. Paul. A good account of the ante-bellum Norwegian-American press is Carl Hansen, " Pressen til Borgerkrigens Slutning," in Wist, *Norsk-Amerikanernes Festskrift 1914*, 1–40.

[51] Mr. Malmin learned of the publication of an earlier Scandinavian-American newspaper than *Nordlyset* while engaged in editing the Munch Ræder travel letters. An illustrated sketch telling of *Skandinavia* is contributed to *Nordmands-forbundet*, 22: 14–17 (January, 1929) by J. Dieserud, who found a partial file of the paper in the Library of Congress.

VI. RISING EMIGRATION AND WESTWARD EXPANSION

A SIGNIFICANT rise in Norwegian emigration occurred in the early forties. The official figures are
300 emigrants in 1840, 400 in 1841, 700 in 1842, and 1,600
in 1843. Emigration interest was flaming in Telemarken
and Numedal especially. In 1841 Anchersen sailed on
June 1 with 90 emigrants, largely from Telemarken. The
next year he again undertook the voyage, this time with
115 passengers, largely from Numedal. On the bark
" Ellida " in 1842 went 176 emigrants — 77 from Numedal, 70 from Telemarken, and the rest from scattered
southern districts. The vessel reached New York on
August 8 after a voyage of misery: nine passengers had
died from cholera or typhus; thirty were transferred from
the " Ellida " to a New York hospital. Sixty-three immigrants from Telemarken reached New York on July 30
on the brig " Washington " and about seventy made the
journey by way of Havre. These immigrants of 1842
seem to have been in general very poor and their poverty
added greatly to the economic difficulties of the settlers in
the West, upon whose hospitality they were thrown.[1]

In the winter of 1842–43 many signs pointed toward a
considerable expansion of emigration the following spring
and summer. One of the emigrant ships of 1842 brought
back to Norway an emigrant whose narrative of American
experiences was given wide publicity. He was Knud

---

[1] *Stavanger Amtstidende og Adresseavis*, May 31, June 2, 10, 30, July 28, September 12, 1842; *Morgenbladet*, May 14, June 2, 1842; *Tiden* (Drammen), June
24, September 8, 14, 25, 1842; *Bratsberg Amtstidende*, December 16, 1842. Emigration statistics are in *Lov om utvandring m. v.*, 129. Typical of emigrant
poverty was the situation among the 63 passengers on the " Washington," who
averaged only 15 specie dollars each. Interesting letters telling of the experiences
of these emigrants are in *Skiensposten*, July 22 and September 5, 1842.

Aslaksen Svalestuen, a Telemarken *bonde* who had emigrated in 1839. In publishing his story one newspaper
warned its readers that many emigrants had pictured
America in darker colors than those employed by Svalestuen. It adds that he left Norway a poor farmer but
returned a well-dressed seaman with the glow of health
in his cheeks. One of a party of thirty Norwegians, he
had set off for America three years earlier via Göteborg
to "achieve a new and more independent existence." His
experiences had been varied. He was in debt when he
reached Illinois, where he was employed by an American
farmer at fifteen dollars a month. He asserts that probably
none of the Norwegian aristocracy have better food on
their tables than he received in this farm home. After
a month he went to Chicago, where he found work at
$1.50 a day. Later he earned seventy-five dollars in six
months at farm labor. Then he tried his luck as a Great
Lakes sailor, but was taken sick with malaria and returned
to Chicago. Soon he was well enough to accompany Elling
Eielsen, the Haugean preacher, to the Fox River settlement. The Norwegians there, he said, "neither regretted
having emigrated nor wished to return to Norway." His
travels then took him to St. Louis and north to the Sugar
Creek settlement in Iowa, which numbered thirty families.
After an expedition west into Indian country, he returned
and bought two hundred acres of land at Sugar Creek,
built a house, and remained a year. Before returning to
Norway he again visited the Fox River settlement and he
also made a tour to the Muskego settlement. He urged
those to emigrate who were in a position to buy land and
to meet the expenses of the first year. And he announced
his intention of going back to America the following
spring.[2]

2 "En Hjemkommen Tellebondes Beretning om hans Reise og Udvandrede
Normænds Befindende i Nordamerica," in *Skiensposten*, October 25, 1842; reprinted
in *Tiden* (Drammen), October 30, 1842, *Christianssandsposten*, October 31, 1842,

In November, 1842, newspapers announced that Hans Gasmann, a former member of the Storthing, had sold his *gaard* and mill for seventy-five hundred specie dollars in preparation for emigration. " The people talk of nothing but America," said a Laurvig news item, " and artisans and others are busy taking lessons in English." [3] " The emigration desire in this vicinity and in Telemarken is so great," it was reported from Skien, " that if it is realized many vessels will be employed next spring in carrying the emigrants from here." Another Skien item mentions the arrival at the local post office of some fifty letters from " Telemarkian emigrants " in America.[4] Shipowners advertised extensively in the newspapers their plans for emigrant voyages.[5]

Meanwhile great interest was aroused on the west coast by the return in 1842 of the redoubtable Cleng Peerson, who had come by way of London and Hull. He was soon under fire for his alleged efforts to stir up emigration interest. An anonymous writer sent to *Bergens Stiftstidende* a long letter picturing Peerson as an emigration agent and demanding a public explanation of his purposes and methods. This writer tells of finding Peerson in a certain tavern surrounded by eager listeners one evening early in March. He was clad in a long coat and wore a fur cap; in broken " English-Norwegian " he was telling of the glories of America and his own fortune, damning Bishop Neumann and praising Ole Rynning, generally acting the part of an apostle of wisdom, and greatly exciting the simple-minded *bønder* who listened to him. The critic suggests that Peerson was in reality a Mephistopheles with

and *Den Constitutionelle,* November 4, 1842. It is also reprinted in *Telesoga,* no. 43, p. 15–20 (March, 1920), and by S. B. Hustvedt in *Decorah-Posten,* April 3, 1925.

[3] *Tiden* (Drammen), November 27, 1842.

[4] *Skiensposten,* November 1, December 6, 1842.

[5] *E.g., Bratsberg Amtstidende,* December 9, 23, 1842; *Christianssandsposten,* December 21, 1842.

a carefully concealed cloven hoof.[6] To this curious attack Peerson promptly replied, declaring that he was in no sense an emigration agent and that the purpose of his return was simply to visit relatives. Nevertheless he was wholly for America; his long experience there justified him in confirming Rynning's account; the bishop's letter, he said, was not supported by facts.[7] The attack on Peerson, whose offense seemed to have been that of expressing his opinions, prompted the editor of *Christianssandsposten* — one of the few pro-emigration papers in Norway — to declare, " One is tempted to believe that one lives in a land of the inquisition, not a state whose constitution is based upon freedom of thought and of speech." [8]

It was implied that Peerson had visited Voss and Hardanger as an emigration agent. This he denied. But a spirited public discussion developed with reference to certain skippers of emigrant ships, who, it was said, had visited these districts in order to enroll emigrants. Such activity, which involved picturing America in the brightest colors, was sharply condemned by *Bergens Stiftstidende*. Skipper Bendixen of the " Juno " — the vessel on which Peerson returned to America — declared that he had visited Voss in response to a request to come there to arrange for the passage of some fifty or sixty persons. He found many more than he could accommodate and later another skipper went to the district to arrange for the rest. The Voss *bønder* had received favorable " America letters," were determined to emigrate, and had simply responded to a newspaper announcement of the " Juno." Several other skippers also explained that they had gone to Voss and Hardanger. One had held a general

[6] *Bergens Stiftstidende*, April 27, 1843. The communication is signed " B."

[7] Peerson's reply, dated April 28, is in *Bergens Stiftstidende*, April 30, 1843. This letter and the article which prompted it are reprinted by A. R. Brækhus, " Cleng Peersons Norgesbesøk i 1843," in *Normands-forbundet*, 18: 227–231 (April, 1925).

[8] *Christianssandsposten*, May 12, 1843.

meeting in a local church yard, where he explained conditions. Bendixen asserted that the sea was open and emigration legal and that there was no general agreement that conditions in America were unfavorable. Someone replied that the skippers, in making financial arrangements, had even taken over the debts of some prospective emigrants. This, it was declared, was a questionable type of encouragement of emigration. The controversy affords an interesting illumination of contemporary opinion. Two facts stand out: the skippers did make journeys to inland districts to enroll emigrants; and there was a widening interest in emigration.[9] Earlier in the winter Peerson's return had occasioned a public discussion in Stavanger of the causes underlying the whole movement.[10]

The promise of a comparatively large emigration was fulfilled in the spring and summer, when not less than nine emigrant vessels sailed from Norwegian ports for New York and seven for Havre.[11] Local officials in upper Telemarken had issued passes to approximately fourteen hundred persons by the middle of May; and in lower Telemarken and Bamble more than four hundred had been passed before June.[12] Numedal was also represented; for example, fifty-seven of the ninety passengers on the brig " Hercules," which sailed from Drammen on May 11, were from that region. Prominent among the emigrants were Cleng Peerson, who sailed on May 11 from Bergen on the " Juno "; Svalestuen, who was on the " Washington,"

[9] For the controversy see *Bergens Stiftstidende*, April 23, 27, 28, May 4, 7, 11, 14, 1843; and for echoes of it, *Christianssandsposten*, May 12, 1843.

[10] *Stavanger Amtstidende og Adresseavis*, January 5, 8, 1843.

[11] One of the Norwegian vessels that went to Havre was there engaged to carry the immigrant party direct to New York. *Stavanger Amtstidende og Adresseavis*, July 20, 1843.

[12] *Den Norske Rigstidende*, May 18, 29, 1843. In the issue for May 29 an analysis of the 429 passed in lower Telemarken and Bamble is given. It may be noted that 109 were from Gjerpen and 110 from Seufde. A report later in the summer from the Telemarken *Foged* office on 689 emigrants states that 52 families were *bønder* and 67, *husmænd*. *Christianssandsposten*, July 17, 1843.

leaving Langesund eight days later; and Hans Gasmann, who took his brother's vessel, the " Salvator," reaching New York on July 13. The stir and bustle of emigrant departures in 1843 are adequately reflected in the newspapers of the day; in them, too, a little later, are letters telling of the voyage and the arrival at New York, of novel experiences and of prospects in America; from Havre, where 200 of 841 Norwegians were in need of financial assistance, came not only written and printed reports, but also some emigrants who were compelled to return. Norway, viewing all these events, began to realize that it had on its hands an emigration problem of magnitude.[13] And there were signs of an unending and widening circle: while echoes of departures were still sounding, Norwegians learned that yet other earlier emigrants had returned, optimistic over America, planning re-emigration the following spring.[14] When that season came emigration was reduced, but nevertheless it included over a thousand people. In fact, never again after 1842 did the number of emigrants in one year total less than a thousand.

The early Norwegian emigration was recruited largely from country districts in the southwestern and south central portions of Norway. In the period from 1836 to 1845 the emigration totaled 6,200. Of this number 2,800, or 45.1 per cent, were from Bratsberg *Amt*, a preponderantly agricultural district, substantially the Telemarken region. Buskerud *Amt*, situated north of Bratsberg and representing the Numedal district, contributed 1,100, or

[13] Reports of the 1843 emigration are in *Den Norske Rigstidende*, March 15, April 10, 20, 27, May 15, 16, 1843; *Tiden* (Drammen), May 25, August 15, 20, September 8, 1843; *Stavanger Amtstidende og Adresseavis*, May 8, July 20, August 21, 24, September 14, 1843; *Christianssandsposten*, May 26, 1843; and various other Norwegian newspapers of the time.

[14] Two earlier emigrants from Voss and one from Ryfylke had returned. *Tiden*, October 6, 1843.

17.9 per cent of the total. The three counties in the southeastern corner of Norway sent only a half hundred emigrants up to 1845. South central and southeastern Norway as a whole contributed 3,950, or 63.7 per cent of the total. Three counties on the southwest coast sent 35.9 per cent of the total: Stavanger *Amt*, with that city as a nucleus, 950, or 15.3 per cent; South Bergenhus, with Bergen as an outlet, 750, or 12 per cent; and North Bergenhus, 530, or 8.5 per cent. Thus by 1845 substantial beginnings had been made in two general areas — the coastal region embracing the three *amter* on the southwest, and the south central *amter*, mainly Bratsberg and Buskerud; the emigration had its roots in the situation in the more populous south and southwest. Though the movement by 1845 had had many psychological repercussions throughout Norway, the country outside the specified regions was almost untouched so far as one may judge by statistics of departures.[15]

The Norwegian settlers in Wisconsin in the earlier period probably were not as shrewd as the Yankees in selecting their land. Dr. Joseph Schafer, in connection with the Wisconsin Domesday Survey, raises the question whether the American settlers were " more averse than Europeans to pay the enhanced price for land which its speculative ownership implied " and therefore avoided, when they could, " the necessity of purchasing speculator lands by going farther afield to procure Congress land." Speaking of one Wisconsin township, he writes, " The great bulk of the settlers, who entered the left-over lands and bought, usually in small tracts, the speculator lands, were Norwegians." [16] He points out that the foreigners

[15] A. Kiær, " Den norske Udvandring til Amerika," in *Aftenbladet*, November 25, 1864.

[16] *Wisconsin Domesday Book: Town Studies*, 1: 11.

were less expert than the Yankees in judging the quality of wild lands and that the tendency to delegate the choice of lands to one or two persons resulted in poor selections. Dr. Schafer's generalization appears to be true with reference to the Norwegians. Unskilled in the business of land selection, they did not understand the true value of prairie land and only slowly gave up their prejudice against it. Such colonies as Fox River, Beaver Creek, Jefferson Prairie, and Muskego were established as the results of trips of investigation by individuals or small delegated groups, whereas the common practice among Americans was individual choice. This difference helps to explain the fact which Dr. Schafer states: " Whole settlements of foreigners, however, might be planted in poor townships." [17] One other factor, however, deserves attention: The immigrant was handicapped by ignorance of the English language as well as of American land conditions and therefore fell prey more easily than the Yankee to the machinations of unscrupulous land speculators. There is no definite evidence that speculators profited by the Norwegian settlement at Muskego, but there is reason for believing that they were responsible for the selection of the site of the Beaver Creek colony in Illinois and that in this case the immigrants were deliberately deceived. The Norwegians learned from experience, however, and they were quickly infected with the spirit of the frontier quest for better lands farther west. A Norwegian who in the sixties studied conditions among the early immigrants describes their psychology as follows:

It seems as if the words: " To the West! " " To the West! " continually ring in their ears, and scarcely have they overcome the initial difficulties of pioneer life before they again set out for the wilderness to prepare the way for cultivation and for less hardy immigrants. Just when they have reached their goal and can look hopefully toward an old age which will be free from economic sorrows

[17] *Wisconsin Domesday Book: Town Studies,* 1: 12.

many of them grasp the pilgrim's staff for the second or third time and take up again the fight against raw nature and for conquests in the service of civilization.[18]

Perhaps the most important of all the Wisconsin settlements — certainly the most prosperous — was the " Koshkonong settlement," which was established in 1840, taking its name from Koshkonong Creek and Lake, and having its nucleus in the southeastern portion of Dane County, the southwestern part of Jefferson County, and the northern part of Rock County. The name was applied to a general region that extended a considerable distance from Lake Koshkonong, the more important townships involved being Albion, Christiana, Deerfield, Dunkirk, Pleasant Springs, and Cottage Grove. After the initial settlements had been made, waves of immigrants moved into a second Dane County area, embracing the northern townships of Vienna, Windsor, Bristol, Burke, and Westport; and a third area in western Dane County, including Blue Mounds, Springdale, Primrose, and Perry townships. Settlement soon overflowed into Columbia County on the north and Iowa and other counties on the west, and as time went on the Koshkonong settlement became a mother colony to num rous settlements in Wisconsin and in other parts of the Middle West. Thus a Koshkonong settler, Even O. Gullord, became in 1848 the founder of the well-known Coon Prairie settlement in Vernon County.[19] The fame of Koshkonong spread far and wide among the Norwegian immigrants in the United States and, in books, pamphlets, and letters, was carried across the ocean.

---

[18] *Billed-Magazin,* 2:114. B. H. Hibbard declares that the Norwegian settlers in Dane County were "keen in the choice of land." They "soon learned to take the oak openings in preference to the more thickly wooded land, while many of them settled on the border of the prairie." *History of Agriculture in Dane County, Wisconsin,* 108 (Madison, 1904).

[19] H. R. Holand, *Coon Prairie,* ch. 3 (Minneapolis, 1927).

In general the type of settlement in Dane County was individual, but the prosperity of the settlers was perhaps due to the superior quality of land in the entire area rather than to any marked success of the Norwegians in securing the best lands within it. Analyses of land entries indicate, in fact, that as usual the Americans, who were on the ground earlier than the Norwegians, made the best selections.[20] The beginnings of the Koshkonong settlement represent three elements in the stream of Norwegian immigration, the Voss, Numedal, and Stavanger groups. Three " Vossings " who arrived at the Fox River settlement in 1839 — Nils Bolstad, Nils Gilderhus, and Magne Bystølen — planned a trip north to Wisconsin in search of better lands and secured the services of Odd J. Himle, an immigrant of 1837, as guide. When the trip was made Bystølen was physically unable to go; the other three walked north to Milwaukee and then west to the Koshkonong area, where they selected a site near Cambridge. They returned to the Illinois settlement for the winter, but the next spring, in covered wagons, Gilderhus, Bolstad, Bystølen, and one other made their way to Koshkonong, where claims were taken out in Deerfield and Christiana townships. Individual beginnings were thus made.[21] Another expedition by Norwegians to the Koshkonong region was made late in 1839 by Johannes Johansen and Søren Bache, recently arrived immigrants from Drammen. The prairie, they thought, resembled the

---

[20] In the *Wisconsin Domesday Book: Town Studies*, 1: 11, Dr. Schafer writes: " We have the entry records for twelve townships in Dane County. Six of these show a large proportion of speculator land, taken early; and of the six, two were practically absorbed by speculators, so they need not be considered. Of the other four, two were almost wholly settled by Norwegians, who took up the remaining government lands and bought the speculator lands, and two others received a large proportion of Norwegians along with a good many Americans. Five of the other six, which were left open by speculators, were taken up, in the forties, prevailingly by settlers having American names. The sixth had more Norwegian entrymen than American, and Norwegians were also interspersed among the American entrymen in the other five townships."

[21] *Billed-Magazin*, 1: 387.

finest meadow lands in Norway, but since it was lacking in woods they decided not to settle there.[22]

A Numedal immigrant of 1839, Gunnul Olson Vindeg, who had passed the winter in the Jefferson Prairie settlement, visited the Koshkonong region in the spring of 1840, found a place to his liking in Christiana Township, and shortly thereafter took his wife and two sisters to the settlement. Thus connections were established with the settlement founded by the Nattestads. Incidentally, it may be noted that Vindeg is one of the group of writers of " America letters " who had sufficient influence to stand out distinctly from the multitude. Of him Nilssen wrote in 1868:

Vindeg often wrote to his friends in Norway, who were thereby encouraged to emigrate. He seems to have been one of those who occasionally indulged in exaggeration, and many curious stories are in circulation concerning the contents of his " America letters." A number of people apparently found that the reality did not come up to their hopes, and Vindeg, who advised emigration, has sometimes been criticized because he allowed his friends in Norway to see the new world in colors altogether too bright.[23]

The third element connected with Koshkonong beginnings was a group of Stavanger immigrants who broke away from the La Salle County settlement in Illinois. A group of seven men, possibly acting upon suggestions received from the " Vossings " who investigated Koshkonong in 1839, visited the Wisconsin settlement in the spring of 1840, selected land, and returned to Illinois. The following spring several of the group returned and settled in Albion Township, Dane County. The composition of the group of seven investigators is of interest. One of its members was Thorstein Olson Bjaadland, a member of the " sloop party," who had farmed in the Kendall settlement, in Michigan, and at Fox River, and

[22] Johansen and Bache to relatives, December 31, 1839, in *Tiden* (Drammen), March 3, 1840. See *post*, p. 203.
[23] *Billed-Magazin*, 1: 387.

now joined the Wisconsin settlers. One was an immigrant of 1839, Lars A. Dugstad; and the other five were immigrants of 1836: Bjørn Anderson Kvelve, Amund Anderson Hornefjeld, Lars Schei, Amund Anderson Rossaland, and Erik Savik. The entrymen in the Koshkonong district in 1840, twelve in number, were soon joined by immigrants who went north from the Illinois settlements, who pushed farther into Wisconsin from the Muskego, Jefferson, and Rock Prairie settlements, or who arrived direct from Norway. A period of rapid growth followed. Professor Flom points out that by the end of 1842 there were in the town of Christiana alone, " perhaps more immigrants found together . . . than in any of the other settlements founded during the preceding years, 1839–1840." [24] The same author has recorded the names of large numbers of the settlers who reached the Koshkonong area in the early forties and has also made available much biographical information concerning the extension of the settlement into other parts of Dane County.[25] Though the purpose of the present work is not to present a biographical record, some typical cases that throw light upon general tendencies may be considered. The settlement expanded widely between 1842 and the end of the decade, the chief accretions to the population being from Voss, Numedal, Telemarken, and Sogn, with some arrivals from Norwegian regions which had as yet been only slightly associated with the emigration.

The movement to Koshkonong and the adjacent region seems to have resembled, in some respects, a stampede, the character of which has been caught by Nilssen, who came into contact with the earliest settlers. He writes:

In 1842 and the years immediately following people came streaming to this place from all directions and as a result all the tillable

24 *Norwegian Immigration*, 188.
25 *Ibid.*, chapters 18–20, 28–29, 36–39.

public land here was bought up in an unbelievably short time. "We scarcely had time to orient ourselves in our new home," says one of the first settlers of the town of Dunkirk, "before we were surrounded by neighbors on all sides." "The corn attains a growth here which is unknown elsewhere," it was claimed, "and on the prairies grows grass which is man-high, while in the woods are lumber and fuel in abundance, and the marshes afford excellent grazing ground for the cattle. . . ." These and similar reports spread near and far, setting people in motion and producing an excitement which somewhat resembled the gold fever occasioned by the discovery of California's rich mineral wealth.[26]

Back of the excitement was the eager desire of the immigrants to get good land. "It had been my wish, ever since I left Norway," said Knud H. Roe, who after seeking his fortune in the Fox River and Muskego settlements arrived at Koshkonong in the spring of 1843 with a few head of cattle and not a penny in money, "to get a piece of land in this country which I could call my own. But nearly all the good land in La Salle County had by this time been bought by speculators and was held at high prices." And the Muskego land he did not like.[27] Alexander N. Bækhus was a Norwegian school teacher who received only a few dollars a year for his services and, despite the outspoken opposition of the local minister, gave up his position and left for America, enticed by tales of Koshkonong.[28] Two of his brothers went the next year, one of whom, Aslak O. Bækhus, has left a record of his emigration. "Hard times and a dearth of work obtained at that time in Vinje," he says. "Under good circumstances one could earn from four to six skillings a day in winter; but a great many people were idle and sought work for their board only." Wages during the summer, he admits, were somewhat better, twenty-four skillings a day, but the season lasted only a short time.

---

[26] *Billed-Magazin*, 2: 114.
[27] *Billed-Magazin*, 2: 15–16.
[28] He emigrated in 1842. *Billed-Magazin*, 2: 293–294.

Many of the farmers were in debt, and to make matters worse there was a numerous class of *husmænd*. The consequence was that there was much public support of the poor. The situation, in his opinion, summed itself up in the fact of overpopulation. He himself was a shoemaker, but could not earn more than enough to pay his ordinary expenses. When he learned about the prospects in America he decided to turn his back on his difficulties in Norway.[29]

Gaute Ingebrigtsen of Tin, Telemarken, influenced by good tidings in letters from early emigrants from his home district, joined a throng of 120 emigrants in the spring of 1843, went to Skien, Havre, New York, and Milwaukee, settled in Muskego, and then went on to Koshkonong. " I was not satisfied with Muskego," he says. " The land was low, swampy, unproductive. The settlers were in poor circumstances and much sickness visited the colony. . . . But rumors of Koshkonong's fertility had reached this region and a number of people had even made a trip west to see that section." [30]   Knud A. Juve, an emigrant of 1844, was a man of forty-four years and possessed a capital of six hundred specie dollars when he left his home in Telemarken. " I was a farmer in Norway and lived in fairly good economic circumstances," he relates. " By means of letters and pamphlets, reports on the situation in America were widely circulated in the mother country and the thought of my family's future caused me to emigrate." The original plan of the group which he joined was to go to Illinois, but in Milwaukee the immigrants were informed that the Norwegian settlers in Illinois were discontented and were flocking north to take advantage of the fruitful soil and healthful climate of Wisconsin. Juve went to Muskego but was dissatisfied with conditions there. Finally he met a settler who gave him this pithy

[29] *Billed-Magazin*, 2: 294.
[30] *Billed-Magazin*, 2: 123.

advice: " Go farther west; not until you reach Koshkonong will you find America! " Juve went.[31]

A considerable emigration from Sogn had been opened
up in 1843 and 1844 and some of the emigrants from this
district took the lead in founding a settlement in Illinois
some distance south of Jefferson Prairie, known as the
Long Prairie settlement. In 1845 a larger emigration
from the same district began, and, although some of these
later immigrants went to Chicago and a considerable number to Long Prairie, not a few settled at Koshkonong. In
the middle forties, in fact, a large proportion of the new
settlers at Koshkonong were from Sogn. One of the
1845 emigrants, Ole Olsen Menes, has left the following
illuminating account of his emigration:

The emigrants of the preceding year wrote from America to friends
in the home community advising emigration. They told of the fertility of the soil, the low prices of land, and the good chances for employment. In a letter which I received from Iver Hove he wrote that
he received thirty-five bushels of wheat per acre and that the grass
was so thick that it was possible in a single day to cut enough for
the winter's provision for a cow. . . . The America fever grew
worse with each letter that came from the land of wonders. . . .
Early in the spring of 1845 about seventy persons from Vik parish
were in readiness for the journey.

Chicago, Long Prairie, and Rock Prairie each received
some of this emigration party, but a number, including
Menes, went to Koshkonong. " America offers the poor
workman many advantages," said Menes some years later.
" With persistence and industry he can here attain well-
being." Cheap land promotes agriculture, he pointed out,
and this in turn leads to a general development which
opens up opportunities for artisans and tradesmen. Evils
there are in America, he admitted, particularly in the matter of dishonest public servants, but after all the possibilities of reform are in the hands of the people if only
they will exercise their power.[32]

[31] *Billed-Magazin*, 2: 23–24.
[32] *Billed-Magazin*, 2: 131–132.

Nils H. Fjeld was a fairly well-to-do farmer of southern Aurdal in Valders, but as his family increased in size, a succession of lean years darkened his prospects. "Meanwhile rumors about America's fertile soil and cheap land reached Aurdal also and there was much discussion about the advantages and drawbacks of America in comparison with Norway," writes Nilssen in summarizing an interview with Fjeld.

Opinion was divided. Some saw everything pertaining to the world across the sea in rosy colors, while others were astounded that anyone should venture to emigrate to a land full of poisonous snakes, bloodthirsty animals, and even more dangerous wild men. . . . Imaginary pictures furnished the stuff for the most exaggerated accounts of America's glories, while the enemies of emigration drew from the same sources materials from which they put together terrifying stories of the sorrow and misery which awaited the foolhardy persons who, despite warnings, went to meet their certain doom. With the exception of two individuals about whose fate nothing was known, nobody had yet emigrated from Aurdal.

He explains that the emigration fever reached the district in the middle forties and soon spread in all directions, but that the circulation in the community of a book on America was the final stimulus needed to produce actual emigration. In April, 1847, with his wife and seven children, Fjeld joined a party of a hundred emigrants from Toten, Modum, and Telemarken, and after a perilous voyage from Christiania reached New York, made his way to the interior, and eventually appeared at Koshkonong.[33] The spirit of adventure seems to have brought Hans Andreas Haaversen to Koshkonong in 1848, for he says, "I had a desire to look about in the world, and then the thought came that America was the land best suited for the Norwegian emigrant." His father was a well-to-do farmer in Lunde parish, Jæderen, and Haaversen, speaking of his own emigration, says, "So far as I know, no

[33] *Billed-Magazin*, 2: 237–238.

one had hitherto emigrated from this part of Harald Fairhair's dominions to build and live in America." [34]

In some cases the Norwegians proceeded with admirable caution. In 1844, for example, Elling H. Spillum, accompanied by his son and Lars E. Survigen, went to America to investigate the situation. All three returned the same year. Survigen strongly advised people not to emigrate, and it was rumored that he had been subsidized by the Norwegian government to use his influence to check the movement — an interesting indication of the popular feeling with reference to the attitude of the government. Spillum sold his farm, however, and the next year, with a party from the northern parish of Overhalden, he set out for America, and in after years he exerted considerable influence upon the emigration through the writing of many "America letters." [35]

The case of Anders Johannesen Tømmerstigen, who went to Koshkonong in 1846 from Vardal, Norway, influenced by letters written by his brother who had emigrated several years earlier, throws light upon the nature of the opposition to emigration. "There was no lack of pessimistic predictions, and the chorus in all such prophecies was that those America travelers who escaped death in the waves would be sold as slaves to the Turks or to the even more fearful cannibals," he testifies. The minister in Vardal "was especially active, thundered against all emigration, and told a great many stories about the terrible fate which met the fools who disregarded all admonitions and went to that land of sin and aberrations, which was called America." "I was constantly exposed to importunity," continues Tømmerstigen, "and in the last two months before my departure my children could hardly leave the house without being jeered at and teased

[34] *Billed-Magazin*, 2: 162.
[35] *Billed-Magazin*, 1: 34, 45.

by those with whom they came in contact. I did not allow myself to be frightened, however, but with my family, consisting of my wife and four children, I went from Christiania to Havre, France, where I met about three hundred emigrants from the Westland (especially from Telemarken). From here we got a ship to New York and continued our journey to Milwaukee." Later he went to Koshkonong. By the sixties Tømmerstigen was worth twenty thousand dollars. " I thank God," he told Nilssen, " that it was written in my book of fate that I should come to America." [36]

It was natural that, as the dissemination of Norwegian immigrants proceeded in the early forties, a number of small settlements should spring up and that not a few Norwegians established themselves upon a purely individual basis in regions where no group settlements were made. Some of the smaller settlements in Wisconsin have received considerable attention in Norwegian-American annals because of prominent individuals connected with them or because of their relation to religious and cultural movements. The development of these " lesser colonies," however, need not be followed in the present work. Suffice it to call attention to a few examples. The lead mines attracted a considerable number of immigrants to Lafayette County, while not a few settled in the adjacent Illinois County, Jo Davies. In a region embracing portions of southern Dodge and northern Jefferson counties, Wisconsin, a Lutheran minister estimated that there were a hundred church members in 1844–45.[37] Walworth County, Wisconsin, in the southern portion of which is the beautiful Lake Geneva, counted four distinct, small Norwegian settlements which took their rise in the early forties. One of these, Skoponong, extending north into

---

[36] *Billed-Magazin*, 1: 388.

[37] J. W. C. Dietrichson, *Reise blandt de norske Emigranter*, 74–75 (Anderson ed.).

Jefferson County, was estimated by the same minister to have approximately a hundred church members in 1844–45.[38]   To the Skoponong settlement at the end of the forties went a humble emigrant woman from Voss whose son, Knute Nelson, was destined to become famous as United States senator from Minnesota.   Hans Gasmann and various other Norwegians joined in 1843 the Swedish colony established in 1840 at Pine Lake by Gustaf Unonius.[39]   Mineral Point, Blue Mounds, and various places in Iowa County attracted settlers moving west and northwest from the older Koshkonong and Rock Prairie settlements.   A survey of the entire situation in Wisconsin shows that in the forties the tendency was to fill up the lands in the south central portion of the state generally, with a very definite trend toward the west and northwest which near the end of the decade caused a flow into northeastern Iowa.

While the bulk of the Norwegian immigrants were streaming into Wisconsin in the forties, beginnings were being made in southeastern Iowa, but in the main the latter state was outside the area of the earlier distribution of the contingent from Norway — a fact sufficiently indicated by the census of 1850, which shows that there were only 361 Norwegians in Iowa as compared with 8,651 in Wisconsin in that year.   The first point of entry into Iowa was in the southeast, where in Lee County the Sugar Creek settlement was established about 1840.   It appears to have had a double origin.   Some of the dissatisfied settlers in Shelby County, Missouri, moved north in

[38] Dietrichson, *Reise blandt de norske Emigranter,* 83.

[39] The founder of the colony, which was called "New Upsala," tells the story in his *Minnen fran en Sjuttonarig Vistelse i Nordvestra Amerika.* See also Norelius, *De Svenska Lutcrska Församlingarnas och Svenskarnes Historia i Amerika,* 1: 1–14. Mabel V. Hansen, in an article entitled " The Swedish Settlement on Pine Lake," in *Wisconsin Magazine of History,* 8: 38–51, devotes considerable attention to certain romantic features of the colony's history and quotes Fredrika Bremer's account of her visit to the Pine Lake settlement in 1850.

1840 and selected a site a few miles north of Keokuk, Iowa; a little earlier a few immigrants from the Fox River settlement, under the leadership of Hans Barlien, moved westward into Iowa; and the two groups joined forces in the Sugar Creek settlement. Cleng Peerson was associated with this settlement, but his precise relationship to it has not been ascertained. He had returned from the east with the Testman party of immigrants in 1838. Professor Flom states that Peerson was probably the first Norwegian to enter Iowa, since he had passed through its southeastern corner on his way to Missouri in 1837; but he does not credit Peerson with any important relation to the Iowa settlement on the ground that the famous pioneer did not actually settle in Iowa.[40] But Peerson himself in a signed statement records the fact that he " has resided in the states of New York, Illinois, Missouri, and Iowa." [41] In view of this claim it is practically certain that he was for a time a member of the Sugar Creek settlement. Reiersen in 1844 wrote that Hans Barlien and one of the Testmans were " presumably " the founders of the settlement.[42] Professor Anderson believes that Peerson was sent by the other settlers in Missouri to inspect the land in Iowa and that this investigation resulted in the founding of the settlement.[43] The question of priority is of little importance, the significant fact being that the Iowa settlement was begun about 1840 and drew upon both the Missouri and Illinois colonies for recruits, but in view of the character of Peerson, his position of leadership in the Missouri colony, and his own claim of residence in Iowa, it is safe to conclude that he played a part of some importance in the Iowa venture.

[40] *Norwegian Immigration*, 190–192.
[41] From *Hamars Budstikke*, in *Morgenbladet*, June 18, 1852.
[42] Reiersen's account, as translated in *Studies and Records*, 1: 117.
[43] *Norwegian Immigration*, 186–187. Mr. Anderson bases his view upon an account by one of the original settlers.

The Sugar Creek settlement did not lead to any considerable Norwegian migration into southeastern Iowa. The more important movement of Norwegian immigrants into northeastern Iowa did not occur until the late forties and was a result chiefly of the expansion of the Wisconsin settlements of Rock Prairie and Koshkonong. The nucleus of the Norwegian element in Iowa was to be in Winneshiek County, with lesser contingents in Allamakee, Clayton, Fayette, and neighboring counties. Although some foreshadowing of this movement occurred before 1849, the beginnings on a large scale date from 1849–50.

VII. EMIGRATION CAUSES AND CONTROVERSY

EMIGRATION seems to have caught Norway by surprise, not unmixed, on the part of many, with consternation. Its beginnings were followed by a period of bitter controversy in which numerous writers trained their guns on emigration and the United States, while others with equal zeal sought to defend the movement. Bishop Neumann, whose pastoral letter of 1837 calling upon people to remain in their native land has been mentioned, is typical of the clergy. In the spring of 1840 he defended his earlier views on emigration and published a mournful letter by an emigrant of 1836, Sjur Jørgensen Haaeim.[1] Two years later be brought out in pamphlet form Haaeim's narrative of his experiences, written after he returned, dejected and broken, in 1841. This pamphlet is a doleful wail from beginning to end: sickness is a fearful enemy to success in the western settlements; the cost of transportation is high; the best land has been taken; wages are good, but the work demanded is extremely hard; the settler begins at the bottom and material difficulties are severe; few of the immigrants are independent; most have to work for wages; many take claims and are unable later to produce the cash to buy the lands that they have improved; the language situation adds to the general difficulty; the American religious situation is good, but on the western prairies there are no churches. Haaeim declares that many Norwegians in America would like to return to Norway, but cannot do so.[2]

---

[1] *Bergens Stiftstidende*, March 5, 8, 1840. The letter and the bishop's views are further discussed in the issues for March 19, 22, and April 9, 1840.

[2] Haaeim's pamphlet, *Oplysninger om Forholdene i Nordamerika især forsaavidt de derhen udvandrede Norskes Skjæbne angaaer* . . . (Christiania, 1842. 10 p.), is translated by G. J. Malmin in *Studies and Records*, 3: 1–12.

The newspapers of the time were filled with earnest warnings of the perils of emigration, reënforced frequently by gloomy letters from immigrants.[3] When, despite all such discouraging items, Norwegian *bønder* continued to emigrate, some writers insisted that they were impervious to reason, caught in the grip of a scourge, like the Black Death. The great nationalist poet, Wergeland, was enraged. " Yes, the ' emigration frenzy,' " he wrote in 1843, " that is precisely the word for this desire to emigrate to America which like a general epidemic has swept over large sections of our country. It is the most dangerous disease of our time, a bleeding of the Fatherland, a true frenzy, because those whom it seizes follow neither their own nor others' reason, disdain arguments and examples, give up the present for a still more threatening, dark future, and let themselves be driven by it into the vortex of that future's unknown sufferings." [4] " What, in God's name, is it that draws the calm, wise, and phlegmatic Northman over to the New World?" exclaimed another perturbed writer.[5] Yet another Norwegian ironically described the symptoms of the disease as dreams and fantasies, dizziness, a noticeable disarrangement of one's normal thinking processes, coupled with the expectation of quick transportation to Paradise.[6] There is an almost hysterical note in the appeal of the Reverend J. W. C. Dietrichson to his countrymen in 1845. Speaking especially to those " infected with the desire to emigrate," he declared that they would lose in every respect by going to America — from the religious point of view, " for where can the Christian life be better developed than in the peaceful, dear fatherland! "; politically, " for where

---

[3] Haaeim's narrative, for example, appeared in various newspapers. *Christianssands Stiftsavis*, May 8, 12, 15, 1843, reprinted it from *Skiensposten*.

[4] " Om Udvandrings-Raseriet," in *For Arbeidsklassen*, February 6, 1843.

[5] *For Arbeidsklassen*, May 17, 1844.

[6] A. G[røtting], " Den nye Landfarsot," in *Norsk Folke-Kalender*, 1848, p. 121–124.

is there a more law-bound liberty than in fortunate Norway! "; and economically, " for where will the Lord, to whom the silver and the gold belong, bless your industry more than in that circle where He has placed you! " [7]

Not all agreed with such diagnoses and opinions, however. One writer, rejecting the view that emigration was " a mania, insanity, or sickness," declared that he had interviewed emigrants and found that they knew why they went: they were loaded with economic burdens and expected better opportunities in America.[8] One liberal journalist asserted that the opponents of emigration damaged their own cause by publishing only the worst letters received from immigrants.[9] On one occasion an audience of people interested in America voted to burn Haaeim's pamphlet, which they considered a tissue of lies and misrepresentations.[10] One investigator reported that the *bønder* regarded the writings against America much as they had regarded earlier outpourings of officialdom against the election of *bønder* to the Storthing. The emigrants said, " Show us by authentic accounts that Ole Rynning and the other letter writters have lied — and we will remain at home. But don't come with fairy stories and nursery tales to grown men; if you have nothing else to set up against the reports that we have, then don't call us fools and dreamers if we, following our best convictions, choose to go to a country where there is a market for labor and where the land rewards the farmer, rather than to remain in a country in which, though it is called free, our children can become at best cotters or beggars." [11]

---

[7] A letter of December 28, 1844, in *Stavanger Amtstidende og Adresseavis,* April 10, 1845.

[8] *Nordlyset* (Trondhjem), August 9, 1847.

[9] *Christianssandsposten,* October 14, 1842.

[10] *Morgenbladet,* April 23, 1843.

[11] *Christianssandsposten,* March 13, 1843.

There is no doubt that partisanship colored both sides of the controversy. A writer in 1846 declared that the defenders of America had been looked upon as egotists and traitors to Norway, while they in turn had treated their opponents as if they were wolves in sheep's clothing, enemies of the people and of freedom.[12] The controversy, coupled with growing emigration, aroused general interest, and by the beginning of 1844 one Norwegian newspaper asserted that emigration and American conditions had become the theme of the day.[13] If this was the case it was to a large extent due to the pertinacity and polemical vigor with which the chief defender of emigration, Johan R. Reiersen, presented his views, baited his enemies, and drew the discussion away from the superficial symptoms and toward the basic conditions that gave rise to emigration. In 1839, in the first issue of *Christianssandsposten,* of which he was the founder and editor, he declared his position on emigration. He declined to join those who pictured America only in dark colors; emigration, he said, showed that the *bønder* had spirit; they craved, not gold and luxury, but bread and freedom; among them in Norway success was the unusual thing, while the accumulation of debt and virtual loss of freedom were normal.[14] He opened the columns of his newspaper to numerous articles about the United States.[15] In 1842 he began a discussion of Norway's overpopulation, said that the emigrants were the most progressive and energetic of Norway's working people, and suggested the desirability of planned colonization.[16] Gradually the condition of Nor-

[12] *Nordlyset* (Trondhjem), October 30, 1846.

[13] *Bratsberg-Amts Correspondent* (Skien), January 1, 1844.

[14] *Christianssandsposten,* June 3, 1839.

[15] " De nordamerikanske Fristater," in *Christianssandsposten,* September 20, October 11, 1839; and " America letters " in *ibid.,* September 30, 1839, March 9, 13, 16, 1840.

[16] " Betragtninger i Anledning af vore Landsmænds Udvandringer til Amerika," in *Christianssandsposten,* October 14, 17, 19, 1842.

wegian agriculture, America, and emigration became the central topics of discussion in his paper; and his views provoked a newspaper controversy that echoed throughout Norway. Organized colonization abroad needed to be supplemented, he believed, by the settlement of uncultivated, waste, and state lands at home. The farmer should be aided by the state even to the extent of loans without interest. While exploiting such ideas Reiersen attacked the official class boldly and vigorously and took advanced liberal positions on most of the public questions of the day. When in the summer of 1843 he gave up the editorship of his paper, it was to make a trip of investigation to the United States and to launch a colonization plan in an attempt to prove his theories in practice.[17] The next year he declared it to be his " unwavering and proved conviction " that " Norway's present overpopulation, in connection with social and political conditions, — which make possible no self-dependence and hence no general freedom and independence, — seem to make a partial emigration both desirable and advisable. . . ." [18]

An able modern investigator finds " the chief influences that have promoted Scandinavian immigration to the United States in the nineteenth century " to be the following, in the order of their importance: " first, the prospect of material betterment and the love of a freer and more independent life; second, letters of relatives and friends who had emigrated to the United States and visits of these again to their native country; third, the advertising agents of emigration; fourth, religious persecution at home; fifth, church proselytism; sixth, political oppres-

[17] Some of the more significant articles in *Christianssandsposten* are those in the issues for November 16, 1842; January 12, 19, February 9, 20, 23, 27, March 6, 9, 20, and June 16, 1843. The last is entitled " Et Overblik og en Afskedshilsen." Later the controversies, especially with *Granskeren* and *Morgenbladet*, were continued.
[18] *Veiviser*, p. xxiii.

sion; seventh, military service; and eighth, the desire for adventure." [19]

Such a category is interesting and suggestive, but it leaves unexplained several important questions, such as why emigration developed when it did rather than at an earlier time.   At best, therefore, it offers only a partial explanation.   To elucidate the causes of emigration, for an individual or a movement as a whole, is difficult; for reliable information is usually lacking, often various motives coalesce and it is impossible to judge their relative weight, and the emigrant himself may appreciate only partially the forces back of his decision and may be blind to the larger movement in which he appears as a figure. As early as 1853 a Norwegian commentator sensed the relationship between numerous small forces and large results when he said of emigration:

It proceeds prosaically and unconsidered, like the great changes in the earth's surface, which are not studied until they appear as if they were a result of unexplained earthquakes or revolutionary changes. For this colossal movement is a result of innumerable small and unappreciated causes, which exercise on human life the same disintegrating and transforming power that the chemical elements do on the earth's crust.[20]

The emigrant is a dissenter, either in an economic or in some other sense of the word, for emigration grows out of discontent and restlessness occasioned by burdens of some kind or the hope of improvement through change, usually both.   He is necessarily also a separatist in one sense or another, for his act means a sharp break with familiar conditions; he turns his back on his accustomed environment.   Contemporary Norwegian critics often attributed emigration solely to the so-called " America fever."   This was of course a superficial view, but there is no doubt

[19] Flom, *Norwegian Immigration*, 88.
[20] *Den norske Tilskuer*, March 12, 1853.

that certain causes created in the minds of many people a predisposition toward emigration. This was fashioned out of some kind of dissent; it was a potential separatism; and it needed but an " America letter," an " America book," the influence of a returned immigrant, or some other type of immediate agency to bring it to a head. It is important to study all the influences that were brought to bear upon the prospective emigrant, but the essential question in explaining his action is that concerning the backgrounds of the predisposition in question. An emigration movement is based upon hundreds and thousands of individual decisions. In each case the primary problem is psychological.

Norwegian emigration can be understood only by seeing it in its relation to other movements and forces of its time, for Norway in the period when emigration took its rise was the scene of stir and change; new political and religious forces were making themselves felt; the time was one of growth and transition; but Norwegian economic life did not keep step with other aspects of the scene.

The generation responsible for the upward swing of Norwegian emigration in the thirties and forties had breathed the air of protest and had felt the force of the cause of that protest, both in religious and in political spheres. The Norwegian *bønder* in the thirties were discontented with church and state; they were articulate; they felt their own possibilities of power; they had leadership; and they also had a definite reform program. Discontent in church matters coalesced with political discontent; both with economic discontent; and all three have relations with emigration and emigrants. The period was one of self-assertion by the *bønder,* and it would be unsafe to mark off too sharply the boundaries of this spirit. It took one form in Haugeanism; another in the battle of the *bønder* with officialdom and the struggle for political and economic reform; and yet another in emigration. The rise of emigration, drawn from the class that furnished the power behind the other movements, cannot be divorced from the history of a time when the *bønder* were speaking out and taking action on the broad national stage of Norwegian affairs.

Haugeanism was at heart a pietistic revival. Rationalism, intelligent and broad but lacking " spirituality," was dominant in the state church; Hans Nielsen Hauge's aim was to substitute within that church a " living " faith for the prevalent formalism. He was persecuted, but he traveled indefatigably about the country before his imprisonment in 1804 and had tremendous influence upon the humble country people with whom he came in contact. " In six years," writes Gjerset, " he traveled over 10,000 miles, mostly on foot, preached from two to four times a day, and wrote hundreds of pamphlets and devotional books." [21] A recent biographer writes of Hauge, " There is perhaps no name in Norwegian history more familiar to the common man, especially of the rural communities, of Norway than the name of this first herald of Norway's new day." [22] A distinguished Norwegian bishops asserts, " What Eidsvold is to Norway's political history, that Hauge's birthplace is to her religious history." And Georg Brandes goes so far as to say, " Hans Nielsen Hauge introduced Christianity into Norway." [23]

The work of Hauge was wider in its implications, however, than a religious revival. Everywhere he stimulated interest among his hearers in social reform and in the improvement of material conditions. Of Hauge, the practical man, one writer says:

[21] *History of the Norwegian People*, 2: 403.

[22] Wilhelm Pettersen, *The Light in the Prison Window: The Life Story of Hans Nielsen Hauge*, 3 (Minneapolis, 1921).

[23] Quotations in Pettersen, *op. cit.*, 3. The standard life of Hauge is by the bishop cited, Anthon C. Bang, *Hans Nielsen Hauge og hans Samtid*.

He established a paper mill, a stamping mill, a bone mill, a flour mill, a tannery, a foundry for church bells and small cannon. And during the English blockade he was released from prison to manufacture salt as he was about the only one in the land who could do this. He engaged in trade in Bergen and along the sea coast, and in thousands of ways helped his adherents in their practical affairs. An indefatigable worker himself, he demanded industry and thrift, not laziness and idleness, from his adherents.[24]

It is of interest to note that Hauge was imprisoned for violating not only the Conventicle Act of 1741, which prohibited lay preaching, but also the Monopoly Act of 1797, restricting coastal trading to those granted special royal privileges. Hauge left his followers with a specific issue to work for, the repeal of the Conventicle Act; he left them aflame with his own spirit of piety; and he was looked upon as a martyr. Haugeanism was a kind of Puritanism, with many of the characteristics that so strongly stamped the earlier movement. Very shrewd was the comment of a Norwegian student four years after Hauge's death, " If Norway only gets a Cromwell, it already has its Independents." [25] The early immigrants from Norway " generally sided with Haugeanism against the State Church." [26] One of the important Norwegian lay preachers who spread the Haugean gospel, Elling Eielsen, emigrated, as has been noted, in 1839; in the pioneer western settlements he carried on the same type of missionary activity that Hauge himself had initiated; and his work resulted eventually in the establishment of a Norwegian-American synod. Many other lay preachers voiced Haugeanism among the immigrants, thousands of whom were

---

[24] Rohne, *Norwegian American Lutheranism*, 11.

[25] L. K. Daa, quoted in Koht, *Norsk Bondereising: Fyrebuing til Bondepolitikken*, 351–354.

[26] Rohne, *Norwegian American Lutheranism*, 16. It is of interest to note how often contemporary writers attributed the emigration wholly to religious persecution. Thus a writer in *Statsborgeren* for May 26, 1836, declared that the basic cause of emigration was religious compulsion. This explanation was coupled with a plea for freedom of religion, speech, and occupation.

influenced by the Haugean movement. Many traces of resentment by the common people against the state church clergymen crop out in the early history of the emigration movement. Perhaps the most significant fact of all, however, is simply that the Haugean ferment was working vigorously in Norway when emigration got under way; and it was intimately connected with a bold challenge by the *bønder* of the political power of the official class.

The connection of Haugeanism with the political battle of the *bønder* was not confined to a single issue. As Professor Koht asserts, it was a living bond.[27]   Haugeanism sharpened the issue of the *bønder* with officialdom; it blazed the trail of popular agitation; and in the political movement it both furnished and supported leadership. Perhaps the broadest significance of Haugeanism lies in its awakening of the self-consciousness of the *bønder*. The *bønder* and the official and urban class " had become sharply differentiated," writes Dr. Gjerset, " not only in customs and language, but also in views and sympathies. The men of Eidsvold had created liberal institutions suited to the most democratic society, but during the great European reaction, 1814 – 1830, it became evident that the old spirit of class prejudice, desire for special privileges, and the antipathy to the common people still prevailed in higher social circles. The officials showed strong bureaucratic tendencies, and continued to rule in the old spirit, even under the new constitution." [28]   But in the hard times after 1815, suffering need, paying high taxes, and feeling that he had not derived the advantages that he anticipated from the constitution, the *bonde* launched a sharp political protest. Haugeanism itself was a movement directed against officialdom and the clergy as well as a struggle of orthodoxy against rationalism.[29]   Two sig-

[27] Koht, *Norsk Bondereising,* 351–354.
[28] Gjerset, *Norwegian People,* 2: 465.
[29] Edv. Bull, *Grunriss av Norges Historie,* 92 (Oslo, 1926).

nificant developments in the promotion of the *bonde* campaign came in 1830. The July Revolution, writes the historian of the *bønder,* was like a fresh spring breeze in Norway and gave " new courage and new hope to all those who were laboring for the *bonde* uprising against the old rule." [30]   And in 1830 a *bonde* leader, Jon Neergaard (1795–1885), published a book that presented a *bonde* platform: *An Odelman's Thoughts on the Present Condition of Norway.*[31] This was an attack on the official class and a call to the *bønder* to employ political means to improve their status. It pictured them as suffering for lack of money, with avenues of profitable production closed to them, and yet with increased taxes to pay. Neergaard asserted that there never had been a time when distraints, foreclosures, and auctions had been so numerous and so ruinous to the people. He distributed his book widely, traveled like Hauge in various Norwegian communities, and agitated for the election of *bønder* to the Storthing. In 1830 the movement got an organ of its own in *Statsborgeren,* edited first by Peder Søelvold, the son of a *husmand,* and later by Wergeland. The first fruits of the agitation came in the election of 1833, when for the first time the *bønder* outnumbered the official class in the national parliament. With Neergaard and Ole Gabriel Ueland as *bonde* leaders, the way was now paved for the first great reform — the local self-government act of 1837. Ueland, himself a Haugean, rose to great prominence; and in the long struggle of the *bønder* he was a consistent spokesman and leader of his class, advocating economy, reduction of taxes, trial by jury, limitation of the power of officialdom, and numerous democratic reforms in state and church. Many of these reforms —

[30] O. A. Johnsen, *Norges Bønder,* 353.

[31] *En Odelsmands Tanker om Norges nuværende Forfatning . . .* (Christiania, 1830). The book was popularly known as *Olaboka.*

for example, the repeal of the Conventicle Act — were eventually won. The movement gained great force and ultimately brought about — but not until the middle eighties — the triumph of the principle of responsible ministries and the introduction of genuine parliamentary government. Meanwhile, however, large numbers of the common people were turning to America. Their going synchronized with this period of political and religious ferment. Among their numbers were even some *bonde* leaders, like Hans Barlien; Neergaard himself seems to have thought of emigration; and few of the emigrant rank and file were untouched or uninfluenced by the movements described. The sensation caused among Norwegian commoners in 1835 and later by the letters of Hovland, for example, telling of the liberal institutions in the United States can only be understood in the light of the backgrounds here sketched.[32]

An interesting development in Norwegian population growth synchronized with these religious and political changes and with the rise of emigration. The Norwegian population was almost stationary in the period from 1801 to 1815, advancing only from 883,038 to 885,431; but after the critical war years it increased more rapidly, reaching 1,051,318 in 1825, 1,328,471 in 1845, 1,818,853 in 1875, and 2,097,328 in 1895. One of the most interesting aspects of the growth of population in the first half of the century is the fact that in the period when emigration took its upward swing the age group from 20 to 30, which contains ordinarily a comparatively large

[32] Neergaard in his later years is said to have expressed the wish that he might be laid to rest in the soil of America, a country "where the spokesmen of freedom are better appreciated" than in Norway. J. Brøvold, *Forhenværende Lensmand, Storthingsmand John Neergaards Liv og Virken,* 83 (Kristiansund, 1877). Søelvold nearly became an emigrant in 1834. A convenient summary of the *bonde* movement may be found in Johnson, *Norges Bønder,* 347–357. The Conventicle Act was repealed in 1842.

number seeking labor and employment and always leads in emigration, had a disproportionately large increase. This group, which comprised 15.5 per cent of the total in 1800, 16.7 per cent in 1825, and 14.4 per cent in 1835, leaped to 18 per cent in 1845. In other words the age group from 20 to 30 increased in numbers from 1835 to 1845 by approximately one-third, in a period when the population as a whole increased by about one-tenth. It is curious to note that a similar, though less pronounced, bulge in the same age group occurred a generation later, in the late sixties and early seventies, synchronizing with another large upward swing in emigration; and yet again in the early years of the twentieth century. Importance must be attached to an unusually high proportion of persons in the vigorous ages of 20 to 30 in the period that marked the rise of Norwegian emigration, for, given hard times and the opening up of an emigrant road to the West, this was the class that would be the first to respond.[33]

The emigrants themselves, in explaining their action, emphasize the economic difficulties in Norway and the hope of winning a better livelihood in America, but they frequently touch also on social, political, and religious issues. Reiersen in 1843, after visiting many Norwegian immigrants in the West and inquiring about their motives for emigrating, drew up a list of particulars.[34] Ruling out many special reasons, he presented the following causes:

[33] *Utvandringsstatistikk*, ch. 6. This chapter is a study of emigration causes. On page 84 is a table showing age distributions in the Norwegian population from 1800 to 1900. Proof that the age group from 20 to 30 predominates in emigration is hardly needed, but it may be pointed out that this age group contributed 39.85 per cent of the total Norwegian emigration from 1866 to 1915: the group 20 to 25 giving 26.80 per cent, and 25 to 30, 13.05 per cent. Next in importance was the group from 15 to 20, with 22.18 per cent. Taking the ages from 15 to 30, we get 62.03 per cent of the whole emigration. Going further, 78.79 per cent of the total emigration was made up of people in the age group from 1 to 30. Clearly emigration was a young people's movement. *Utvandringsstatistikk*, 108–109.

[34] A letter of December 12, 1843, in *Veiviser*, v–vi. Christian Gierløff, in *Folket som utvandrer*, 99–101 (Oslo, 1925), also summarizes these points.

1. The gloomy prospects in Norway for the future of the rising generation, coupled with the hope of independence and happiness in America.

2. The fact that for the " producing and working class," Norway is too circumscribed; that there is not room enough; and that the time is not distant when " a slavish dependence " will become general.

3. General dissatisfaction with the administration of Norwegian law, especially with reference to relations between debtors and creditors, where the regulations in force work the ruin of the former.

4. A general feeling that the state does too little to promote agriculture and the welfare of the common people, though it devotes large sums of money to other purposes.

5. Dissatisfaction with Norwegian officialdom and the clergy, which form a caste that looks upon an ordinary citizen as an inferior.

6. Failure in Norway to realize the freedom and equality that the constitution of 1814 promised.

7. The pressure upon the *bondestand* of poor-relief burdens.

8. The pressure upon the same class of burdens connected with the Norwegian road system.

9. Uncertainty of crops and sterility of the soil.

10. Idealization of America.

Economic conditions in Norway, difficult in the period after 1814, were unusually oppressive in the thirties. From 1836 to 1840 only the last year was a fairly good grain year; the rest were particularly bad. Emigrant evidence, as quoted in the foregoing chapters for this period and the forties, is conclusive that conditions for many were nearly intolerable. An economic historian characterizes the thirties as a period of stagnation in Norwegian agricultural history.[35] Lands were divided until in vari-

[35] J. Smitt, *Det norske Landbrugs Historie i Tidsrummet 1815–1870*, 36 (Christiania, 1874).

ious Norwegian districts the patches were too small to support those who cultivated them. Thus in 1802 the number of farms was 79,256; by 1820 it had increased to 93,621; in 1845 it was 112,930; and by 1860 more than 135,000; this process, to a large extent, was a result of the break-up of old holdings, though there was also cultivation of new lands.[36] If a plot of ground was too small to support a family, it was necessary for the owner to supplement its proceeds with such profits as he could secure through labor for others. If no extra work was to be had, he faced impoverishment and the necessity of poor relief — unless he could raise sufficient funds to emigrate. The *amtsmand* of Bratsberg in 1846 declared that emigration had been advantageous in that it had checked the process of land division, which already had gone to extreme lengths.[37] When crops failed bad conditions became worse and there was serious danger of starvation. In the summer of 1838, for example, a report from upper Telemarken tells of almost general *Hungersnød*, or famine, and of people who were forced to share in the food of their cattle as a result of bad years. And a local historian of Numedal, another district prominent in the early emigration, writes thus with reference to the late thirties: " The need was terrible in many places. Cattle and horses starved to death for lack of fodder and in some parishes as many as one-third of the people went hungry." [38] It was in 1839 that Wergeland wrote his poem " Famine " — a lament to the cold-hearted stars, which look down so smilingly on the bitter famine and

[36] *Morgenbladet*, May 25, 1866; " Er Udvandring begrundet i de stedfindende Forholde i Norge?" in *Norge og Amerika*, 1: 23–24 (August, 1845). The Odel law of June 26, 1821, is considered by Norwegian students a primary cause of much of the disintegration of the Norwegian *gaarder*.

[37] *Beretning om Kongeriget Norges økonomiske Tilstand i Aarene 1840–1845*, p. 89.

[38] *Ugeblad for Skien og Omegn*, September 12, 1838; cf. *Bratsberg Amtstidende*, March 23, 1841; Herbransen, *De første Utvandrere fra Numedal til Amerika*, 11.

suffering in Norway.[39]   In the face of such conditions
came reports of boundless fertile lands available for settlers in the West.   These reports came to the ears of
people who may be presumed to have had the Teutonic desire to own land and perhaps that deep-rooted impulse,
so often found among dwellers in Norway's narrow valleys, to go beyond the grim barriers between them and the
world's broad acres.   And there came also reports of good
wages!   When Rynning, for example, reported American
wages for men as fifty cents to a dollar a day in winter
and twice as much in the summer and for servant girls
from one to two dollars a week, he dazzled his Norwegian
readers by the contrast that he suggested.   In the period
from 1836 to 1840, a servant girl in Telemarken received
eight to twelve specie dollars a year, a man servant fifteen
to thirty dollars a year, an ordinary laborer twelve to
twenty cents a day with board and twenty to thirty-two
cents without board.   Skilled workmen in Nedenes received thirty-six cents a day.   These wage scales were not
quickly changed: for example, in the period from 1846
to 1850 wages were reported for various parts of Nordre
Bergenhus as seven to ten and eight to twelve dollars a
year for servant girls; ten to sixteen and fifteen to twenty
for men servants; and twenty-four to thirty-six cents a
day for laborers in the summer.   And from 1856 to 1860
in Stavanger *Amt* workmen received twelve to sixteen
cents a day in winter and twenty to thirty-six in summer;
while artisans might receive thirty-two to forty-eight
cents a day.[40]

Lacking as yet any considerable industrial development
or an advanced agriculture, Norway faced a serious pop-

[39] Wergeland, *Udvalgte Skrifter,* 96.

[40] *Beretning om Kongeriget Norges œconomiske Tilstand i Aarene 1836–1840,*
p. 94, 99, 108, 111; *ibid.,* 1846–1850, p. 8; *ibid.,* 1856–1860, p. 11; "Norges
Økonomiske Udvikling indtil 1850," in N. Rygg, ed., *Norges Banks Historie,*
1: 285–287 (Oslo, 1928).

ulation problem. A later Norwegian writer, discussing the causes of emigration, said:

The mass of our people live under such restricted and hard circumstances that the burden discourages them both physically and mentally; there are too many mouths for the bread that our resources produce; if our population were not so large our resources would yield more for each one; many farms which yield a bare but sufficient livelihood for one family must now provide a miserable livelihood for two; many laborers must long seek in vain for work; we have too numerous a working population in proportion to our capital and the present development of our natural resources.[41]

In the middle forties it was estimated that two-thirds of the Norwegian *gaard* owners had mortgaged property.[42] Borrowing money, which necessary buying on credit often forced, was an extremely expensive thing because of the tangle of official transactions connected with borrowing. It was said in 1843 that to borrow fifty specie dollars one had to pay eight dollars and eight skillings for the official fees thereto attached.[43] It was doubtless the numerous exactions attendant upon money loans and taxes, centering in the office of *lensmand,* that caused one emigrant to write, " The best thing about America is that we do not have *Lensmand* Blank here." [44] Usury is a Norwegian evil complaints of which often creep into the " America letters." Coupled with this is bitterness over the public exactions connected with inheritance of property, the demands upon the *bonde* in the matter of supplying transportation to travelers, numerous special fees that had to be paid the clergy and public officials, and restrictions upon freedom of entry into various trades.[45] Thus burdened with debts and forced to pay high taxes to the commune, many a *gaardsmand* sold his property at such prices

[41] *Morgenbladet,* May 20, 1866.
[42] *Nordlyset,* October 9, 1846.
[43] *Morgenbladet,* March 31, 1843.
[44] Quoted in *Morgenbladet,* May 25, 1866.
[45] *Morgenbladet,* May 25, 1866.

as he could get and left.   Advised to work out his own
salvation, he noted that the official class seemed to receive
a favored treatment from the state.   The *bonde,* wrote a
commentator in 1843, is a man of deep pride and is not
satisfied with empty glitter.   " This pride of his causes
him to prefer to bury himself in the deserts of America
and to accept all its woes rather than to see himself and
his family face a future in his native land that promises
him no betterment."   What he wants is independence:
he will get it in America; he will prove to all that he actually is what officials do not acknowledge him to be.[46]
The social revolution involved in Haugeanism and the
bonde movement stimulated the *bonde's* belief in the essential dignity of man, though his class had proud traditions
of independence and self-assertion, reaching back to a
much earlier period.[47]

One prospective emigrant in an interview complained
thus: " Our government does altogether too little to promote the earning of a livelihood, and the Norwegian
bonde has always to pay, without receiving any fruits
thereof; whereas in America a large share of the state's
funds is devoted to the aid of railroads, the building of
canals, the construction of new roads, and the like, and
all this serves to promote the welfare of the inhabitants
and to multiply the sources of employment." [48] The fact
that the main burden of compulsory military service fell
upon the *bønder,* while the urban and official classes were
exempted, did not add to the contentment of the former,
who recalled the constitutional provision of 1814 placing
the duty in theory upon every citizen.   The principle of
general military service was embodied in a law of 1845,
but exemption through a money payment furnished a

---

[46] " Hvorfor vandre man ud? ", in *Morgenbladet,* March 31, 1843.

[47] Koht, *Norsk Bondereising, passim.*

[48] *Morgenbladet,* November 23, 1853.   *Cf.* a letter by an early emigrant,
Johannes Nordboe, published in part in *Statsborgeren,* July 13, 1837.

loophole for those able to pay. Not until the middle seventies was this loophole closed. Military service in times of peace seems to have been in general disfavor among *bønder,* aside from grievances over its inequitable apportionment. " In earlier times," observed a caustic writer in the sixties, " many a young *bonde* maimed himself to escape military service; in these more civilized times he emigrates." [49]

Norwegian agriculture as well as the general social and economic welfare of the country appears to have suffered a serious setback as a result of a law of 1816 passed in supposed aid of agriculture, legalizing distilling on Norwegian farms and prohibiting importation of liquor. " This distilling," writes a student of emigration causes, " was carried on with small kettles on every *bondegaard* and the result was that the whole country was turned, so to speak, into one great public house, and the common people were demoralized and impoverished." [50] Not only did the practice increase drunkenness and attendant economic waste, but it also turned Norwegian agriculture disproportionately toward the cultivation of potatoes and grains. There is no doubt that the prevalent home distilling ruined many small farmers, who turned to emigration as an avenue of escape. The decade of the thirties again occupies the center of the stage. Norwegian drunkenness is estimated to have reached its highest point either in 1833 or in 1837. [51] In 1846 the *amtmand* of Nordre Bergenhus sought to explain the high emigration from

[49] *Morgenbladet,* May 25, 1866. See also " Værnepligten i Norge," in *Christianssandsposten,* November 9, 1842.

[50] *Morgenbladet,* May 25, 1866.

[51] Erling Tambs Wicklund, *Bøndene og Brennevinsspørsmålet i Norge 1800–1850,* 62–63 (Oslo, 1925). The average consumption of alcohol in 1833 was sixteen litres per person, according to this authority, an increase of some four hundred per cent over the average before the law of 1816 was passed. " The *gaard* owners and *husmænd* distilled and drank up most of their potatoes and corn," writes the author of a Norwegian school history. Jens Hæreid, *Norges Nyere Historie (efter 1814),* 4 (Oslo, 1926).

Sogn in the period from 1843 to 1845: from Nordfjord
and Søndfjord only six persons had emigrated to America,
whereas more than four hundred and fifty had emigrated
from Sogn, not including nearly three hundred who had
removed to Nordland and Romsdal. The *amtmand* found
the first cause in overpopulation, for, he said, agriculture
was so restricted by nature that it could not keep up with
the population increase. A second cause was drunkenness
and sundry evils connected therewith, including poverty
and discontent. He reports emigration heaviest in the
districts where *gaard* distilling was most prevalent.[52] If
home distilling was thus directly and indirectly a cause
of emigration, it is interesting to note that emigration
in turn forwarded the reform movement that culminated
in 1845 with the passage of a law the conditions of which
practically abolished *gaard* distilling. The temperance
movement seems to have drawn much inspiration from
America. Immigrant letters from the West warned
against the evils of drunkenness. Rynning sternly advised
drunkards that they would receive no welcome in the
United States. Returned immigrants expressed their horror over the prevalence of drunkenness in Norway.
American writings in the interest of temperance, including some of Benjamin Franklin's, were translated into
Norwegian.[53] As early as 1839 an emigration play by an
advocate of temperance reform appeared in Norway,
with American ideas voiced by American and Norwegian-
American characters.[54] A Norwegian scholar, in a book
on the *bønder* and the liquor question from 1800 to 1850,
emphasizes the influence of the American temperance
movement and especially of the emigrants in promoting

[52] *Beretning om Kongeriget Norges økonomiske Tilstand i Aarene 1840–1845*,
p. 143–144. Report by H. Tostrup, June 1, 1846.

[53] Wicklund, *Bøndene og Brennevinsspørsmålet i Norge 1800–1850*, 60–61.

[54] Hans Allum, *Broder Ebbern i Fødelandet, eller Amerikareisen* (Christiania,
1839. 130 p.). In the fourteenth scene of the second act a prospective emigrant
presents his reasons for wanting to go to America.

reform in Norway. Meanwhile numerous Norwegian influences were at work to convince the *bønder* themselves and the Norwegian people as a whole of the need of reform, and eventually it became a *bonde* demand, led by Ueland.[55] It may be noted that some prominent emigrants, for example, Mrs. Wærenskjold and Reiersen, were active workers for temperance in Norway.[56]

Emigrant evidence shows that many family heads, who were themselves in good economic circumstances and not in special degree personally discontented, went to America primarily in the interests of their children's future. Here the fundamental fact was the ease of acquiring good land in the United States contrasted with the difficulty in Norway. A Norwegian writer, analyzing emigration causes in the sixties, puts the matter thus:

A man with one thousand dollars and five children reasons as follows: one thousand dollars divided among five children amounts to little or nothing here in this country. But if I go to America, where there is plenty of fertile land to be had for next to nothing, my little capital, combined with the industry of myself and my children, is sufficient to furnish all of us an independent and satisfactory position.[57]

It was not only those in good circumstances, however, who were concerned about their children's future. Lack of opportunity in Norway, contrasted with the unusual opportunity in the American West, probably had even greater force than in the suggested hypothetical case as a motive for emigration in the cases of parents with nearly empty hands who were sharply discontented.[58]

Once emigration was under way it naturally responded in its rise and fall to the swings of economic conditions

---

[55] Wicklund, *op. cit.*, 44–63, 109–121.

[56] Mrs. Wærenskjold published a pamphlet entitled *Opfordring til alle ædle Mænd og Kvinder at forene sig i Maadeholdsselskaber for at udrydde Brændeviinsdrik og Drukkenskab* (Christianssand, 1843).

[57] *Morgenbladet*, May 25, 1866.

[58] See the article "Er Udvandring begrundet i de stedfindende Forholde i Norge?", in *Norge og Amerika*, 1: 24–26 (August, 1845).

in Norway and in the United States. In business cycles economists find the central explanation of the fluctuations of emigration. A statistician says that " emigration increases when times are poor in Norway and decreases when they are good "; but even though times are hard in Norway, " this is not enough to cause people to emigrate if at the same time economic conditions in America are unattractive."

When emigration, for example, in 1858–59 drops to about 2,000 a year as compared with 6,000 in 1857, it is believed that this is because prospective emigrants were warned by relatives and friends against immigrating to America, where times were bad after the great crisis of 1857, which took its beginning in America and caused stagnation in industry and railroad building. One might expect that as Norway gradually developed its industry and bettered its means of communication, these new branches of industry would in part relieve superfluous labor within other branches of industry, especially agriculture. But this does not appear to have been the case; simultaneously with the expansion of industry the Norwegian emigration seems to have increased, because cycles in the economic life have so strong an influence.[59]

The upward swing of emigration at the end of the forties was doubtless in part due to the prevalence of potato rot in Norway coupled with high prices, generally unfavorable conditions, and specially inviting prospects in the United States.[60]

It was no accident that Norwegian emigration, inaugurated in 1825, swung upward in the late thirties and early forties, for that period witnessed an unusual conjunction of favoring circumstances: a sharp increase in the age-group from 20 to 30 (people in whom the desire for adventure might be expected to join hands with other motives); an unprecedented stir of religious and political

[59] *Utvandringsstatistikk*, p. 83. For an interesting statistical, economic explanation of the swings in Norwegian emigration, see Gottenborg, in *Nordmands-forbundet*, April, 1913, summarized and translated by Rohne, *Norwegian American Lutheranism up to 1872*, 19.

[60] *Morgenbladet*, March 19, 1849.

discontent and agitation among the *bønder;* severe pressure of unfavorable basic economic conditions brought to a sharp point by special circumstances of undue severity; numerous collateral irritations that added to the irksomeness of these basic and special conditions; and finally the arrival of " America letters " and returned immigrants, the influence of relatives, the publication of " America books," the beginnings of a spirited controversy about emigration — these and other forces conspiring to bring into action the magnetic pull of the United States.   Discontent became focused: emigration was a cutting of the Gordian knot.   The influence of letters, books, agents, propaganda, and many other special factors is traced in other chapters of the present book.   Suffice it to repeat here that certain fundamental conditions seem to have given rise to an emigration viewpoint in the minds of many Norwegians.   In the following periods Norwegian conditions naturally changed in many respects; Norway was to experience an expansion of its economic life; agriculture and industry were to make possible the more adequate support of its people; *laissez-faire* was to give way to vigorous programs of economic and social reform; the *bønder* were to proceed from victory to victory; but meanwhile the earlier immigrant pioneers had cut the pathway to the West broad and clear.   As that road was more and more traversed, it became easier and more natural for succeeding generations to contemplate its use in the effort to improve their circumstances.

VIII. SOUTHERN COLONIZATION AND THE
WESTERN SETTLEMENTS

THE forties witnessed an attempt by Norwegians to establish an immigrant colony in the South. This experiment centers about the activities of Johan R. Reiersen of Christianssand, the most vigorous defender of emigration in Norway in the early forties, a pronounced liberal, and a firm believer in the desirability of organized colonization. In 1843 he made a journey to America on behalf of a group of interested persons who raised a fund to aid him in meeting the costs.[1] His object was to survey the American situation, prepare a handbook of information, and if possible select an ideal colonization site. He was energetic, able, and fired with lofty purpose. The bitter opposition that his journalistic liberalism had bred against him in Norwegian official and newspaper circles added to the zest with which he set out to prove his theories in practice. The book that resulted from his travels occupies an important place in the general history of Norwegian emigration and is discussed elsewhere in the present study. Here attention must be centered upon his investigation and its relation to southern colonization. Probably no other Norwegian investigator on behalf of prospective emigrants made so careful and wide a search as Reiersen. What he did therefore takes on a more general significance. An interesting aspect of early Norwegian immigration is the part played by " advance agents," investigators, leaders. Other American immigrant elements occasionally undertook colonization projects sponsored by high authority and backed by large funds. Other immigrant elements have also had men of the type of Peerson and Reiersen, but published records

[1] *Studies and Records*, 1: 110.

devote comparatively little attention to their influence. It is therefore of added interest to trace in detail the work of an investigator sent out by a group of humble prospective emigrants.

Reiersen left via Havre for New Orleans in 1843. A letter written by him at Iowa City, on January 24, 1844, tells of his travels in the upper Mississippi Valley.[2] He had gone north to St. Louis and then — after a trip into Ohio — to Galena and Mineral Point, and to Madison, where he met Governor Doty of Wisconsin Territory. A week was spent in the Koshkonong settlement as the guest of Ole Knudsen Trovatten. Thereupon he visited the Pine Lake settlement, where he spent eight days with Hans Gasmann, whom he found in thriving condition. His tour was continued to Milwaukee, at that time a city of 6,700 inhabitants, and to Muskego, where he spent a week. He then returned to Milwaukee, went north to Fond du Lac, down the Wisconsin River, and back to Mineral Point and Galena. He spent Christmas at the Wiota settlement and visited Jefferson Prairie and other near-by communities. He next visited Dubuque, interviewed Governor Lucas, investigated the Iowa " Neutral Ground," and went to Davenport and Iowa City. He was thinking seriously of California as a suitable place for colonization, but concluded that the transportation problem was as yet too difficult. Meanwhile the Texan consul in New Orleans had suggested Texas and made an attractive offer of land for Norwegian colonization purposes there, and Reiersen therefore concluded to investigate the northern area of Sam Houston's domain. He was working out a plan for a colony and was convinced that for thousands of Norwegians then " gathering crumbs from the table of the aristocracy " relief was in sight. Before following Reiersen southward it will be of interest

<hr>

2 Reiersen to friends, January 24, 1844, in *Christianssandsposten*, July 1, 1844.

to note his characterizations of the Norwegian communities in the Northwest.

Reiersen describes the La Salle County settlement in Illinois as " the first Norwegian settlement of any importance." [3]   It " numbers at present about six hundred inhabitants, chiefly emigrants from the vicinity of Stavanger and Bergen," most of whom " have passed the initial stage, have erected good houses, and live in a comfortable and independent position," he writes.   " Although agriculture constitutes the main support of the settlement, many persons carry on cattle raising as their most important means of subsistence and keep large herds of cattle and droves of swine, which find food in abundance on the grassy prairies." The marketing of products was well cared for through Ottawa and Chicago, he states. The digging of the Illinois Canal increased land values, and settlers, chiefly American, soon took up the available lands, forcing the Norwegian immigrants after 1838 to go farther north, where unoccupied land was plentiful. " The Norwegians . . . have schools in common with the neighboring Americans," he writes, " but in 1842 they built a church, or chapel, of their own, where the well known Elling Eielsen conducted devotional services for a time. The majority understand the English language, however, and usually attend the American churches in the vicinity, where their church rites and affairs are cared for."

Reiersen then speaks of the group of settlements near the Wisconsin-Illinois boundary line: Jefferson and Rock Prairies and Rock Run, together with small settlements near the Pecatonica River and in the vicinity of Mineral Point. As to the first three he writes, " Most of the inhabitants . . . have made very good progress when one

[3] Reiersen, *Veiviser for norske Emigranter til de forenede nordamerikanske Stater og Texas*, ch. 10 (Christiania, 1844). This chapter, on " The Norwegian Settlements," is Englished in *Studies and Records*, 1: 110–125.

considers the short time they have lived there. Many good and substantial houses have been put up in place of the inadequate log huts; and enclosed wheat and corn fields stretch far out on the prairie and yield all the necessaries for an independent and carefree existence." He calls attention to the preponderance of Numedal people in these settlements and comments upon their religious activities: " They have a few schools of their own and during my visit they united in sending a call for a minister from Norway, with an offer of an annual salary of three hundred dollars, a farm of eighty or one hundred and sixty acres, a free parsonage" and various other inducements.

The Muskego settlement seemed to Reiersen to be unfavorably situated. " The whole region is flat, with many marshes," he writes.

Immigrants from Voss, Telemarken, Numedal, and elsewhere, have settled in this region and have begun to till the land, but the crops are not yet sufficient to supply the needs of all the settlers. No signs of malaria appeared in the settlement during the first year, but in the following two years, when large numbers of poor immigrants swarmed into the colony — chiefly because it was the nearest Norwegian settlement to Milwaukee — and were lodged, many of them sick as a result of the ocean journey, in the small pioneer huts, a general wave of sickness swept the colony, attacking almost everyone and laying a great many in the grave.

He indicates that about two hundred families have purchased land, " chiefly in small lots of forty acres each." " The population in the winter of 1843," he adds, " was estimated at between fifteen hundred and two thousand, but of these a large number planned to push on into the interior in the spring." Visitors who judge the new lands in the West by Muskego form " an extremely unfavorable opinion " of American conditions, in Reiersen's opinion.

The Koshkonong settlement, " almost in the heart of Wisconsin, on the prairies which border the capital," receives a more favorable judgment: " The region is health-

ful, the soil fertile, and the land beautiful. The few who
have lived here for some time have made very good progress and have been able to dispose of a large part of their
crops in the nearest villages." The Pine Lake settlement,
according to Reiersen, " is being developed with ability,
insight, and power " and has the advantage of fertile soil
and healthful conditions.

"From thirty to forty families live along " Sugar Creek,
Lee County, in southern Iowa, he states. "The land is
chiefly woodland, difficult to clear, but possessing good
soil. The majority have occupied claims for several years
and are liable to suffer losses unless they can secure the
title when the land is put up at auction." Apropos of
the Mormons, whose headquarters were in Nauvoo, only
a short distance away from the Sugar Creek settlement,
Reiersen remarks, " That their evangelists have not failed
to work among our credulous and simple countrymen who
live in their near vicinity goes without saying."

Meanwhile Reiersen continued his investigations. After
further travels in Iowa he went by wagon through northern Missouri. At Independence he encountered a Major
Adams, who was leading a party of eighty emigrants over
the Oregon Trail to Walla Walla; a group of merchants
was also setting off for Santa Fé; from both he derived
information. Reiersen nearly decided to make the western
trip to Fort Hall, but gave it up, went to St. Louis, and
then to Texas. At Austin he met Governor Houston, who
told him that he was much interested in the possibility of
a Texas Norwegian colony and that the Texan government would extend every aid. Reiersen went to Houston
and Galveston and back to New Orleans. He then left
for New York to catch a vessel for Norway. In a long
letter written at Cincinnati on March 19, 1844, he tells
of these travels.[4] His mind was not made up as to the

[4] The letter appears in *Christianssandsposten*, July 5, 1844.

wisest choice of a colonization site, but in balancing advantages and disadvantages he seemed most interested in Texas. He writes that it was very difficult to choose; when he was in Wisconsin he favored that territory; in Iowa his opinion changed; Missouri seemed better than Iowa; and when he reached Texas his enthusiasm for Missouri had waned.

Late in 1844 Reiersen's book, which included an informing chapter on Texas and advised the New Orleans route for all emigrants to America, was published; and throughout the winter Reiersen's views on American conditions were given prominent newspaper attention in Norway, especially in his own organ, *Christianssandsposten*. In January, 1845, formal announcement was made of his intention to lead a party of emigrants to America the following summer via Havre and New Orleans and those who were interested were invited to enroll.[5] In the spring a small group, including Reiersen, his father and brother, Christian Grøgaard,— a man of good family and education who, it was hoped, would become the teacher and minister of the colony,— and several others emigrated as an advance guard. The final decision as to their destination was delayed until after their arrival at New Orleans early in June. The emigrants wanted assurance that Texas would become a state of the Union and in New Orleans they learned of the Congressional resolution of March 1, 1845, providing for Texan annexation. In New Orleans one of the party bought a Texan land patent for 1,476 acres, with the privilege of selecting unclaimed land whereever the emigrants chose to settle. About ten in number they then started on the laborious journey to San Augustin. Reiersen selected a first site for settlement at Brownsboro in northeastern Texas, giving to his colony the name

[5] *Christianssandsposten*, January 28, 1845. The invitation, dated at "Vestre Haave i Eide Sogn" on December 9, 1844, was signed by Reiersen, Peder Nielsen, Osuld Enge, and Anders N. Holte.

" Normandy." He anticipated the arrival of a considerable body of emigrants in the fall, including his own
family, and he returned to New Orleans to meet them.
One Norwegian group was forced to remain in Norway
until the next year and most of those who actually went
to New Orleans concluded to ascend the Mississippi to
the Missouri country. Consequently there were only a
few accessions to the Texas colony.[6]

It is characteristic of Reiersen's energy and enthusiasm
that he established in Norway the summer of his departure
a little monthly magazine to serve as a medium for his
own and other reports from America and for discussions
of social and economic conditions among Norwegian
farmers and laborers. It was called appropriately *Norge
og Amerika,* and the first issue appeared in July, 1845, the
same month in which Reiersen and his party arrived in
northern Texas. During the first year of the existence
of the paper, Reiersen was its editor and much of its contents came from his pen. America was the home of liberty
and the defender of human rights, in his opinion. Believing that the emigration of a portion of Norway's population was absolutely essential, he proposed to use this paper
to contrast American and Norwegian conditions and to
afford a vehicle for the publication of " America letters."
He published a series of informative " Sketches from
Western America " and brought out reports from Texas,
letters from immigrants in the North, and vigorous
polemical articles on emigration. Of special interest is a

---

[6] O. Reiersen to his wife, New Orleans, June 9, 1845, with a postscript dated
June 12, in *Norge og Amerika,* 1: 17–19 (August, 1845); " Beretning fra Texas,"
ibid., 1: 126–127, 138–144, 145–160, 171–175 (February-May, 1846) — an account
by J. R. Reiersen. It is worth noting that the San Saba Colonization Company, a
Texas project of this period, was definitely interested in promoting Scandinavian
immigration. Its leaders proposed to bring to Texas a thousand families of " German,
Dutch, Swiss, Norwegian, Swedish and Danish immigrants." It seems to have
been concerned chiefly with German colonization, however. *Cf.* R. L. Biesele,
" The San Saba Colonization Company," in *Southwestern Historical Quarterly,*
33: 175 (January, 1930).

vivid account of the journey to Texas and the first experiences of the pioneers.[7]

Another emigrant party went out in 1846, and though some of its members decided to go up the Mississippi to the Northwest, about fifty made their way to Texas. Meanwhile the sudden death of Grøgaard, whose expected leadership in the colony had been a factor of importance in winning adherents in Norway, had discouraged prospective emigrants.   One of the most interesting and influential Texan Norwegians was Elise Amalie Wærenskjold (1815–1895), who with some others emigrated in 1847.   She had been a pioneer school teacher in Norway, from 1834 to 1839; and in 1846–47 she brought out the second volume of Reiersen's *Norge og Amerika*.   She and her husband, J. M. C. W. Wærenskjold — an emigrant of 1847, whom she married in Texas — were both good writers, and their letters together with Reiersen's writings, published in Norwegian newspapers, gave Texas a prominence in Norway quite out of proportion to the numerical importance of the Norwegian settlements in that state as compared with those in the Northwest.   Early in 1848 Reiersen founded a second settlement in Van Zandt and Kaufman counties, not far to the southwest of Dallas, and established as its nucleus the village of Prairieville. The Wærenskjolds joined this settlement the same year and in 1850 it received a reënforcement of fourteen families from Norway.   Neither the Brownsboro nor the Prairieville settlement compared in ultimate importance with the Bosque County Norwegian colony,— in central Texas, a short distance northwest of Waco,— founded in 1853 by Ole Canuteson, a farmer who had gone to Texas three years earlier from the Fox River colony in Illinois. By the end of the forties, however, little progress had been

---

[7] *Norge og Amerika, Et maanedligt Flyveblad,* vol. 1 (Arendal, 1845–46). Copy in the library of the University of Oslo. A copy of volume 2 is in the library of Luther College, Decorah, Iowa.

made in inducing Norwegians to go to the South; in 1850 there were only 105 Norwegians in the state of Texas.[8]

Just as the decade of the forties came to an end the Texas project was given considerable impetus by the ubiquitous immigrant leader, Cleng Peerson. In 1849 he went from the Fox River colony to Texas. During his investigations in that state he visited a Norwegian, John Nordboe, pioneer immigrant from Gudbrandsdalen, who in 1841 had settled in Texas a short distance south of Dallas. In 1850 Peerson was back in Illinois endeavoring to interest Norwegian immigrants in Texas. In a letter written on August 20, 1850, he gives an account of his journeys in Texas, describes the land, and tells in detail about the prospects.[9] He states that he visited the Norwegians settled in eastern Texas, and although he does not approve of their choice of land he concedes that they have raised good crops. He had the true frontiersman's fondness for ample elbow-room. " But I can not approve of the method of settlement practiced by the Norwegians in establishing themselves so closely together instead of spreading out more so as to have greater freedom in their sphere of action," he writes. He regrets to hear that

[8] An informing chapter is devoted to Mrs. Wærenskjold in Anderson, *Norwegian Immigration*, 379 ff.; and a biographical summary, with references to her writings, is in Halvorsen, *Norsk Forfatter-Lexikon 1814–1880*, 6: 702–703. Mrs. Wærenskjold published in 1870 a valuable historical account entitled " Beretning om de norske Setlementer i Texas," in *Billed-Magazin*, 2: 58–60, 66–67, 75–76 (February 19, 26, March 5, 1870). Various historians state that the Prairieville settlement was founded in 1847, but the date 1848 is confirmed in the account by Mrs. Wærenskjold cited above and in a letter by J. M. C. W. Wærenskjold, March 30, 1857, published in *Emigranten*, May 27, 1857.

[9] The letter was written at Norway, La Salle County, Illinois, to Knud Langeland, and is printed in full in the latter's newspaper, *Democraten*, for September 7, 1850. *Cf.* Blegen, in *Mississippi Valley Historical Review*, 7: 323 ff. Anderson and Norlie (*Norwegian Immigration*, 139; *Norwegian People in America*, 175) state that Nordboe, whom they designate as the first Norwegian to settle in Texas, went there in 1838; but Nordboe himself in a letter written in 1851 states that he had then lived in Texas ten years. This letter, or statement, was written as a supplement to Mrs. Wærenskjold's letter of July 9, 1851, and appears in *Morgenbladet*, June 18, 1852.

thousands of Norwegian immigrants are pouring into the upper Mississippi Valley states while, only a thousand miles to the south, better land and a more favorable climate give distinct advantages to Texas over these northern regions. He writes that he intends to return to Texas in the following September; and so, in fact, he did, with a small party of immigrants. Curiously enough, Peerson made no reference whatever to the institution of slavery. Many circumstances combine, of course, to explain the enormous advantage gained by the North over the South in the matter of attracting the northern European immigrants — for example, the lines of trans-Atlantic commerce, the development of the transportation routes from the Atlantic seaboard to the upper Mississippi Valley, the opening up of the northwestern states, and the historical tendency to follow the northern routes. There can be no doubt, however, that one of the potent reasons why the Norwegian settlements in the Southwest never gained any great headway was the deep-rooted hostility of the Norwegians toward slavery.

In 1851 a Norwegian newspaper translated and published a series of American travel letters by A. Tolmer, which originally appeared in France, in which Texas was pictured in particularly dark colors. These letters were called to Mrs. Wærenskjold's attention and on July 9, 1851, from "Four-mile-Prairie, Vanzandt Kounty i Texas," she wrote a long and vigorous refutation of Tolmer's views and a defense of Texas, discussing its soil, climate, crops, and people. Touching on social conditions she declared, " It is not here as in Norway, where equality and freedom are found only on paper, but not in real life." She expressed her horror of slavery, but asserted that the slave-holders, who were the Americans, treated their slaves kindly and that often the latter were better off than laborers in Norway. Still, she added, there can be no

compensation for the loss of freedom. She favored Texas
above all other states and maintained that thousands of
people — especially laborers, *husmænd,* and poor *bønder*
and artisans — would greatly improve their status by
joining the Texan colonists. With her letter, which was
published in at least two Norwegian newspapers, were
statements by various other Norwegian settlers, including
Nordboe and Cleng Peerson, attesting its accuracy.[10] Her
husband also wrote an effective reply to the Tolmer
account.[11]

Late in 1852 and early in 1853 Texas was again the
subject of thoroughgoing newspaper discussion in Norway,
this time in the organ of the Norwegian labor movement,
which printed letters from Mrs. Wærenskjold, J. R. Reiersen, and others. The views of Reiersen, five years after
he had founded the Texas colony, are of interest. Writing
on July 27, 1852, he declares that he has learned to love
the land to which he had come more than his native land,
with its " monarchic, aristocratic, and hierarchical institutions." " I am free and independent," he continues,
" among a free people who are not bound by the chains
of old class and caste conditions, and I feel proud to belong
to a mighty nation, the institutions of which must necessarily conquer eventually the entire civilized world because
they are based upon the only principles which reason can
acknowledge to be right." He declares that the emigrants
who arrived in 1847, though most of them were very poor
then, are now in good circumstances, with land, houses,
cattle and horses, and yearly crops. With the land in the
Four-mile Prairie settlement, however, he was not satisfied
and he reports a search for a more favorable site in the

[10] The Wærenskjold letter with an introduction explaining its origin was reprinted
from *Hamars Budstikke* in *Morgenbladet* for June 17 and 18, 1852.

[11] J. M. C. W. Wærenskjold to T. A. Gjestvang, March 1, 1852, in *Morgenbladet,* June 30, 1852.

western part of the county.[12]   That the spirited exploitation of Texas in Norway was not without influence was
disclosed the next summer, when a considerable number
of emigrants started for Texas. " In the early part of
April," ran a report from Galveston, " 150 Norwegian
emigrants arrived here and 250 are expected on the next
steamboat from New Orleans. This band intends to establish a Norwegian colony on the Trinity River." [13]   These
figures are probably exaggerated, however, for the Texan
settlements grew very slowly.   A letter by Wærenskjold
in 1857 estimates that there were then not more than
three hundred and fifty Norwegians in the three principal
settlements — about two hundred in that in Henderson
County and one hundred in Reiersen's Prairieville settlement, while the Bosque County settlement was yet in its
beginning stages.[14]   Mrs. Wærenskjold, the following year,
put the number at approximately three hundred and wrote
that there were only sixteen families in the Four-mile
Prairie colony.   Incidentally she mentions the fact that
this colony " called " a Norwegian minister as early as
1854 and erected a church which was dedicated upon the
arrival of the pastor, A. E. Frederichsen, in 1855.   Five
years after the end of the Civil War she was still an enthusiast for immigration to Texas, which she thought had
great advantages over Minnesota, then the Mecca for Nor-

[12] *Arbeider-foreningernes Blad,* January 15, 1853. Other Texas letters are in
the issues for December 11 and 18, 1852, and January 1, 1853. It should be
noted that in 1860 a Dane, J. S. Smith, made the charge that Reiersen was a land
speculator.   Smith said that sixteen years earlier, with other emigrants, he fell
into Reiersen's hands. Reiersen, he asserts, took their money and then disappeared;
the summer heat and the prevalence of disease broke up the colony. No confirmatory evidence has been found of the charge here made against Reiersen. The
latter certainly did not disappear from Texas. He died at Prairieville in 1864,
a respected citizen. *Berlingske Tidende,* May 30, 1860, quoted in *Morgenbladet,*
June 7, 1860.

[13] *Morgenbladet,* June 24, 1853.

[14] Wærenskjold's letter, dated March 30, 1857, is in *Emigranten,* May 27, 1857.

wegians. "For poor people," she wrote, "Texas is a Paradise." [15]

Immigration to Texas had early beginnings and the state was adequately advertised among prospective emigrants in Norway, but the attraction of the South never became strong. Not until 1890 did the number of Norwegian-born in Texas exceed one thousand and it has never been in excess of two thousand. Though the Bosque County settlement ultimately became a thriving and prosperous one,[16] it is obvious that Reiersen's selection of the Southwest did not win popular ratification among the Norwegian common people. His dream of a large, compact colony that would attract thousands of oppressed and poor families from the North was never realized. The upper Mississippi Valley and the West continued, as before, to be the great magnet. The Texan colonization plan must therefore be regarded as an episode — though an interesting one — in the larger story, important chiefly for the light that it throws upon the comparative attractions of two great American regions for Norwegian immigrants.[17]

It is significant of the trend of settlement that when the Norwegian-Swedish consul general, Adam Løvenskjold, visited the "Norwegian settlements in the western districts of the United States" in the summer of 1847, he confined his attention almost wholly to Wisconsin.[18] In his pub-

[15] See Elise Wærenskjold, "En Hilsen fra Texas," in *Morgenbladet*, February 26, 1858; and her "Beretning om de norske setlementer i Texas," in *Billed-Magazin*, 2: 76. Mrs. Wærenskjold, a cultured frontier woman, lived until 1895. Her unusually charming letters, picturing social, economic, and religious conditions in Texas and recounting her own story have been published by Mr. Emil Olsen in *Tønsbergs Blad*, May 11 to 26, 1925.

[16] A modern account of the colony is "Bemerkninger om norsk indvandring til Texas og om Bosque settlementet isærdeleshet," in *Nordmands-forbundet*, 5: 94–105.

[17] Cf. Norlie, *Norwegian People in America*, 174–176.

[18] Løvenskjold's *Beretning om de norske Setlere i Nordamerika* was published at Bergen in 1848. The quotations above are taken from Dr. Knut Gjerset's translation of the document in *Wisconsin Magazine of History*, 8: 77–88.

lished report he devotes scant attention to the Jefferson Prairie settlement, however, merely pointing out that the city of Beloit, situated west of it, promises to become an important trading center. The Rock Prairie settlement, west of that city, is reported to number " about two hundred families from Numedal, Hallingdal, and Land." " Many well-to-do people are found in this settlement," he wrote. " As usual there are only log houses; but those who have settled on the prairie dwell, to a large extent, in sod huts almost under ground, with only the roof projecting above the surface."

The Koshkonong settlement, Løvenskjold reports, " is the largest in Wisconsin, and numbers about four or five hundred families from Telemarken, Voss, and Numedal." A comment on the choice of land is interesting and bears out the general view that the Norwegians usually avoided the prairie land. The region, says the government official, " consists mostly of prairie with a little timber." " Only a few Norwegians," he writes, " live on the prairies, which are mostly inhabited by Irish and Americans. The Norwegians have bought their land in such places that they have a little of the timber which fringes the prairies — that is, clearing land. At present even those who live on the prairies are not in want of fuel, as there is still government land, where they can cut as much wood as they need."

About two hundred families from Telemarken and Voss are reported for the Muskego settlement, which Løvenskjold in common with most other observers condemned because of its location in an unhealthful region of " many lakes and large swamps." Some " thirty families from different districts in Norway " were living in the Pine Lake settlement. At Ashippun, northwest of Pine Lake, he found some thirty families, chiefly from Sogn. " As I was personally acquainted in Norway with many of the settlers here," he writes, " I had an opportunity to observe how quickly they have grown old in a few years, due, no doubt, to sickness and toil in a hot climate. But the homes here are cleaner and better than in most of the other settlements." Of the minor settlements he notes Skopon-ong, five miles northeast of Whitewater, with " twenty or thirty families from Voss and Telemarken "; Heart Prairie, a few miles southeast of that city, with fifteen or sixteen families from Holden, Telemarken; Rock River, east of Watertown, with about fifty families from Modum, Sætersdal, and Gausdal, Gudbrandsdalen; Sand Prairie, with fifty or sixty families from Sogn, Telemarken, and Voss; Blue Mounds, west of Madison, with eight or ten families; Washington County, with about an equal number; Hamilton, south of Mineral Point, with " ten or twelve families from Voss and Sogn "; and Rock River, west of Beloit, with about fifty families chiefly from Numedal.

He comes to the conclusion that in all these settlements there are about fifteen hundred Norwegian families with a total population of approximately seventy-five hundred people; and that Norwegians scattered about in other states bring the total up to ten or twelve thousand. He discusses the religious situation at some length and observes that in " the Norwegian settlements are found members of nearly every religious sect in America " and that " unless drastic measures are taken the Norwegian settlers will within a short time be lost to the Evangelical Church." His testimony indicates that there was a lively interest in religion among the settlers despite their lack of unity. Two " so-called churches " at Koshkonong are described: " On the outside they resemble barns, but inside they present a neat and tasteful appearance."

The emphasis placed by Løvenskjold upon families was an entirely natural one, for the early Norwegian emigration was preëminently of the family type. An excellent illustration of the situation is afforded in a Norwegian government report which deals with the totals of the emigration from Norway up to December 15, 1844, not including the 1836 and 1837 emigrations. Of a total emigration of 3,940, the respective numbers of men, women and children are 1,451; 1,061; and 1,428. The proportion represented in these figures is typical of the emigration through the fifties and indeed the entire period before the Civil War.[19]

The importance of the individual as a leader appears to be declining by the end of the forties and the migration, although not yet swelling into great numbers, begins to take on some of the aspects of a mass movement. Emigration was of course a novel experience for every individual who essayed it; pioneering was an adventure in the unknown; the removal to new frontiers, even though they were but a short distance from established settlements, meant a taste of a fundamental American experience that has left its impress on the national character. Nevertheless Norwegian immigration as a general movement was following a worn channel by the mid-century. Yet as one surveys the forties one finds ample evidence of the influence of Norwegian immigrant leaders — of men like Cleng Peerson, Ansten and Ole Nattestad, Knud Aslaksen Svalestuen, John Nelson Luraas, Søren Bache, Even Heg, Elling H. Spillum, and Johan R. Reiersen.

Perhaps the most arresting personality among these immigrant leaders was the veteran Cleng Peerson. It is interesting to note how prominently Peerson figures at various crucial points in the earlier development of the movement. He appears as the trail blazer of the " sloop folk "; he is in a sense the founder of the Fox River settlement; he is responsible for the colonization experiment in northern Missouri; his career is associated with the be-

[19] *Storthings Forhandlinger i Aaret 1845*, vol. 1, pt. 6, p. 23–24.

ginnings of Norwegian settlement in Iowa; he frequently appears in the rôle of guide, interpreter, and adviser; and in Norway in 1842–43 he is a factor back of the deepening of the tide in 1843.   He joined the famous communistic settlement in Henry County, Illinois, — the Swedish Bishop Hill colony, — in 1847.   Shortly thereafter, " robbed of all he possessed, and sick in body and mind," he left that colony and returned to the first Norwegian settlement in the Mississippi Valley — that in the Fox River region.   But, as has been noted, in 1849 he made an expedition to Texas, and when he returned, in 1850, he was an enthusiast for settlement in that state. To Texas he went finally, and there, in Bosque County, he died in 1865.   An eccentric, perhaps something of a Peer Gynt, a droll and entertaining story teller, a restless follower of the frontier, a lover of adventure, Peerson has been a hazy figure in the history of Norwegian immigration and many legends have been twined about his name, some born of admiration, some of hostility.   His leadership in the early movement is substantiated, however, by dependable documentary evidence.   Svein Nilssen, after his investigations in the late sixties, came to the conclusion that Peerson exercised a greater influence upon early Norwegian immigration and settlement than any other man. His goal was " to work with all his power for the temporal happiness of his fellow-beings."   On the whole Peerson merits this praise.   He was indisputably the pathfinder for the first group emigration from Norway to the United States.   He was the leader of the vanguard of the Norwegian migration to the upper Mississippi Valley.   His incessant travels, his reports of conditions, and his personal influence are of great importance in the first twenty-five years of the history of the movement.   And yet it is obvious that the great majority of the immigrants who swept into Wisconsin in the forties were following the trails of other pathfinders.   Peerson turned to Missouri,

southeastern Iowa, finally Texas — and the great bulk of
the immigrants, responding to forces greater than any
individual, ignored his counsels.[20]

By the end of the forties the dissemination of Norwegian settlers in the Middle West was well under way.
The first of their settlements in the Mississippi Valley was
no longer the nucleus of the Norwegian element. Ex-
periments had been made in Missouri, southern Iowa, and
Texas settlement, and individual immigrants of Norwegian blood were to be found in many other parts of
the country. But the main tide of the incoming immigrants was flowing into Wisconsin, chiefly through Milwaukee, while there was also a distinct movement
northward from the earlier settlement in Illinois. In
Wisconsin the settlements near Lake Michigan and the
southern boundary had yielded primacy to the south central settlement of Koshkonong, and from that new nucleus
radii were being extended both west and northwest, with
some beginnings of Norwegian settlement in northeastern
Iowa. The census of 1850 illustrates the trend of Norwegian settlement. Of the total population of Scandinavian-
born in the United States in that year, 70 per cent were
Norwegian. The three Scandinavian countries were represented as follows: Norway, 12,678; Sweden, 3,559;
Denmark, 1,837; total, 18,074. Illinois and Wisconsin
had 11,066, or 87 per cent, of the 12,678 Norwegians —
Illinois, 2,415, Wisconsin, 8,651. That is, Wisconsin had
more than three times as many as Illinois. The number
of Norwegian-born in Iowa was 361; in Missouri, 155;
in Michigan, 110. All but 986 of the total number of
Norwegian-born in the country lived in the five states
mentioned, but it is interesting to note that Norwegians
were reported in the population returns of twenty-eight

---

[20] See the writer's "Cleng Peerson and Norwegian Immigration," in *Mississippi
Valley Historical Review*, 7: 303–331.

states and four territories.   New York had only 392, evidence that only a small percentage of the immigrants tarried in the state in which they landed after their arrival. Some came by way of Boston, but there were in 1850 only 69 Norwegian-born in Massachusetts.   Texas with 105, Louisiana with 64, and California with 124 offer clues to special immigration trends.[21]

[21] See the statistical table of racial distribution in *Seventh Census of the United States, 1850*, p. xxxvi.

IX. EARLY " AMERICA LETTERS "

THE gradually increasing number of bonds between the Norwegian communities and the American settlements led inevitably to a constantly widening dissemination in Norway of information about the United States. As one surveys this steady development from the middle thirties on through the forties and fifties one gets the impression of a vast advertising movement. Through the medium of Norwegian immigrants and travelers in the United States the people of Norway were having their horizon widened; they were " finding out " about the New World. There was of course no advertising campaign in the sense that it was unified and directed by any agency. The writers of letters and books about America were not consciously fitting their testimony in with the whole and taking into account all that had been said and written before. But hundreds of individuals were sending back independent reports of things seen and experienced; and the result, taken as a whole, was a report on a grand scale to the people of Norway. Naturally, errors and exaggerations were corrected on the one hand, while on the other, unduly pessimistic and discouraging reports were checked by the recorded experiences of the more fortunate and successful.

Gjert G. Hovland, whose influential letters of 1835 have already been described, continued to be a writer of importance. " I am glad that I came here," he wrote from Illinois in 1838, " though everything has not always gone according to my wishes since I left New York, where I first settled." He recognized that many people were unfitted by temperament to meet the trials of the pioneer; he advised no hasty decisions about emigration; he urged those who were in comfortable circumstances in Norway or were no longer young not to emigrate. Throughout his letter there ran a conservative tone, and yet his basic enthusiasm breaks forth now and then: " I and others who have been accustomed to work since we were children think of this as a Canaan when we consider the fertile soil, which without the use of fertilizer brings forth fruits of every kind. Norway can no more be compared with America than a desolate waste with a garden in full blossom." He advises a certain writer to refrain from producing any more books about America until he has actually visited that country and ascertained the truth by first-hand observation.[1] Four years later he wrote again, telling of his one hundred and sixty acre farm, renewing his assurance of the great advantages of America, but warning those who expected fortunes to drop in their laps that they would be bitterly disappointed. Apropos of the many denunciations of America then common in Norway, he reminds his correspondent that these proceed from prejudices rooted in class antagonism.[2]

Ole Knudsen Trovatten was as notable a writer of " America letters " in the early forties as Hovland was in the late thirties. He was an immigrant of 1840 who first settled in Muskego, and after three years at that place and a few months at Pleasant Spring removed to Cottage Grove in the Koshkonong settlement, where he became a school teacher with much influence over his neighbors. " He was very popular and was reputed to be an upright and trustworthy man," writes Nilssen.[3] His writings indicate that he possessed a strain of the pedantic, but his pompous-

[1] Hovland to a friend, July 6, 1838, in *Den Bergenske Merkur*, November 30, 1838. The letter was written at " Medel Point," Illinois. On Hovland's letters of 1835, see *ante*, ch. 3.

[2] Hovland to Peder Johannesen Sætten, July 9, 1842, in *Christianssandsposten*, February 23, 1843; and an undated letter, possibly a postscript to the one to Sætten, published in the same paper.

[3] The opinion is derived from Gunder T. Mandt, an immigrant whom Nilssen interviewed. *Billed-Magazin*, 2: 38.

ness did not lessen his influence. He wrote many letters
to Norway, and in some regions — particularly northern
Telemarken — they not only were influential but actually
created a distinct sensation. An immigrant has left a
record of the effect of Trovatten's letters upon the minds
of the Norwegians in one district.[4] The people of this
district were in grave doubt as to the advisability of
emigration. Some argued for it and some against it, and
the clergy were unsympathetic. Among the people of this
community were circulated copies of " America letters "
written by Trovatten. Gunder Mandt, an eye-witness,
describes their effect: he declares that gradually Trovatten
" came to be looked upon as an angel of peace, who had
gone beforehand to the New World, whence he sent back
home to his coutrymen, so burdened with economic sorrows, the olive-branch of promise, with assurance of a
happier life in America. . . . ' Ole Trovatten has said
so ' became the refrain in all accounts of the land of wonders and in a few years he was the most talked of man
in Upper Telemarken. His letters from America gave a
powerful impulse to emigration, and it is probable that
hundreds of those who are now plowing the soil of Wisconsin and Minnesota would still be living in their ancestors' domains in the land of Harold Fairhair, if they
had not been induced to bid old Norway farewell through
Trovatten's glittering accounts of conditions on this side
of the ocean." [5]

It is interesting to turn from this description of the
effect of Trovatten's letters to the letters themselves.

---

[4] The district in question was Mo parish in Upper Telemarken. Trovatten's
letters seem to have exercised much influence on the emigration situation throughout
all Upper Telemarken.

[5] *Billed-Magazin*, 2: 38. Translated in Flom, *Norwegian Immigration*, 82–83.
The evidence of another contemporary on Trovatten's influence is in *Billed-Magazin*,
2: 218; and Nilssen presents a character sketch of Trovatten in the same magazine,
2: 283.

One, written at Vernon, Wisconsin, on June 28, 1842,[6] was carried back to Norway by an " America traveler," Knud Aslaksen Svalestuen, who was prepared to indorse the accuracy of Trovatten's reports and to supplement them with accounts of his personal experiences.[7]   In his letter Trovatten suggests that perhaps his friends censure him for having emigrated and believe that he himself regrets the step. "No! not so," he writes. " Under no circumstances would I return to live in Ødefjeld, not even if I could be the owner of half the Annex.   Ødefjeld is such a wretched place that one ought by no means to live there.   Every inhabitant would do better by selling his farm to people from Lower Telemarken.   It seems rather questionable to me to abide by one's ancestors' ignorance of better districts and their fear of emigration. . . ." Meanwhile, he writes, " fertile fields lie uncultivated in America " and a " much better mode of living is open to every honorable citizen."   " Every poor person who will work diligently and faithfully can become a well-to-do man here in a short time."   To clinch the case Trovatten tells about his own experiences.   He gives specific details which may be passed over; the important point is that despite sickness and early losses and suffering, he has " made good."   As he himself put it, " Although I have been sick almost half a year and have a family to care for, still I have accomplished more than a worker can do

[6] The letter has been printed in the original Norwegian in *Telesoga*, no. 5, p. 2–9 (September, 1910), together with another Trovatten letter dated July 7, 1842.   A complete translation of the letter of June 28, 1842, made by the present writer, appears in the *North Star*, 2: 76–77 (March, 1920).   It is addressed to " Tollef Olsen Juve and family, dearly beloved friends from my birthplace in Norway, Ødefjeld Annex."

[7] An immigrant of 1843, Ole K. Dyrland, tells that there was considerable doubt about the whole matter of Trovatten's reports but that when Svalestuen came back, even the most skeptical had to give way. Delegations of visitors came to interview Svalestuen throughout the following winter. Dyrland's testimony is in *Billed-Magazin*, 2: 218.

in Norway." He relates that he has forty acres of land and some other property, his children are learning English, and his wages are " from sixteen to eighteen dollars [a month] and board." His main cause of dissatisfaction, he states, is the absence of a church in the community in which he lives. He offers the opinion that the end of the world is drawing near, but he does not believe in a certain American sect which has the event timed for the following summer. Many details concerning climate, crops, wages, and farm possibilities are given. For example: " Every man here has a large number of pigs and also chickens. There are some who have as many as a thousand chickens." What Utopian dreams such a recital must have stimulated! The letter is signed, " Your devoted true friend in America, Ole Knudsen [Trovatten]."

One " America letter " writer of 1841, in order to give force to his testimony, states that he had promised to take his wife back to Norway if she were not satisfied with America. She does not care to return, he adds. He gives his indorsement to Rynning's *True Account of America* in all matters save that relating to sickness.[8] A mass of detail is incorporated in a letter written by Anders Larsen Flage at Chicago in 1840 and signed by himself and three other immigrants. Flage states that he has written a much more detailed account, but cannot send it by mail because that would cost too much. He therefore intends to send that document with some returning emigrant. Homely details concerning sickness and death among the Norwegian immigrants, work, the discharging of debts, and settlement fill the letter — " Let the man without a *gaard* come — if only he have the desire, the courage, youth, strength, and willingness to work," is the advice of the letter writer. Room and work are available, and the na-

---

[8] Mons L. Skutle to Anve K. Skutle, June 22, 1841. *Vossingen*, vol. 4, no. 3, p. 12–13. The letter was written from La Salle County, Illinois.

tive American will not discourage the Norwegian; still, the writer adds, it is " not easier to work here than in Norway." He adds that it is easier to support oneself, however, for wages are higher and supplies cheaper than in Norway. He reproves one immigrant who is reported to have said, " I live here like an honored guest and I would not return to Norway again and eat the dog's food which they eat there." It is not necessary to criticize the fatherland, he says, but neither is it necessary to misrepresent America, as some have done. He asks that all people in the Voss district who have relatives in America be allowed to see the letter and he closes by pointing out that Norwegians need not bother to bring pipes with them to America, for they will soon discard their own pipes in favor of the universally used clay pipes and cigars.[9]

" It is true that those who come here must go through various trials at first," writes another immigrant.[10] " But as regards making a living, the difference between America and Norway is very great. Wages are high and the means of life cheap. . . . Wisconsin is the best and most healthful place for the Norwegians." And another:

I can inform you that I and my brother John have bought three hundred and twenty acres of land, six of which are broken and planted. . . . I am glad that so many are coming from Norway this summer. I can tell you that I would not come to Norway to live there even if I were given the *gaard* of Erik Olsen Rokne, my nephew. You may tell him this. All young, free, and independent persons should come to America. . . . I should be glad to see all my relatives and friends in America.[11]

A tone of discouragement enters into a letter written by an immigrant in Chicago in 1843. " I do not advise

[9]Anders L. Flage, Sjur Sjursen Ulven, Elling Hallesen Væthe, and Peder Davidson Skjærvheim to Anders Størksen Flage and Knud Olsen Reque, November 23, 1840. *Vossingen*, vol. 4, no. 3, p. 4–11. See also Lars Johannessen Møen of Muskego to Anders T. Graue, February 1, 1842. *Vossingen*, vol. 4. no. 4, p. 9–15.

[10] Mons L. Skutle to Lars K. Takle, 1842. *Vossingen*, vol. 4, no. 4, p. 15–16.

[11] Anders B. Lassehaug to Tosten A. Kyte, Chicago, June 20, 1843. *Vossingen*, vol. 5, no. 1, p. 10–11.

anyone to come here who has a good *gaard* and has a
tolerable income for himself and his family," he writes,
" for it is a hard journey and there are difficulties." There
is much sickness, much death; and indeed the climate is
so unhealthful, he adds, that " everybody looks pale and
worn." [12]   Reverses failed to weaken the courage of
Anders Kløve, however, who wrote to his mother in
December, 1843, that two of his children died during the
ocean voyage, a third died in New York, and a fourth died
in the Muskego settlement in Wisconsin.   Two other
children and his wife had been near death from malaria,
but were better now.   " I have suffered a great loss in the
death of my children," wrote Kløve, " but now I and my
family are glad to be in America. If only God will give us
health, I believe that we will have easier and better circumstances here than we had in Norway."   He then tells
optimistically about a piece of land which he has purchased
and about the organization of a congregation in his
community.[13]

A servant girl can earn in America in one year the
equivalent of what she can earn in ten years in Norway,
writes an immigrant in the spring of 1837 in a letter
telling of his farm of 160 acres and advising various persons, including a sister, to emigrate.   His relatives are all
invited to live with him during the first period after their
arrival.[14]   The little money that immigrants have with
them disappears like smoke in the wind, according to
another letter of the same period.   Their ignorance of
English is a great obstacle to their success; and the Norwegian farmers have no conception of the difficulties that

[12] John Haldorson Qvilequal to his relatives, Chicago, December 22, 1843.
Vossingen, vol. 5, no. 1, p. 8–10.

[13] Anders Kløve to his mother, Racine County, Wisconsin, December 22, 1843.
Vossingen, vol. 4, no. 3, p. 14–16.

[14] Halvor Knudsen to relatives, April 9, 1837, in *Den Bergenske Merkur*,
November 25, 1837.   From the Fox River settlement.

they will have to face in America. Still, this individual
notes that he has worked for nine months for a Norwegian boat builder in Rochester at wages of sixteen to
twenty dollars a month.[15] Another immigrant of a year's
standing writes in 1837 from Rochester that he has already made more progress for himself than he had been
able to do in many years in Norway.[16]

Many of the " America letters " were obviously frag-
mentary, but occasionally fuller reports were made. Thus
on December 31, 1839, Johannes Johansen and Søren Bache
wrote a very long letter describing in detail their journey
to America the previous summer. They tell of conditions
in the Fox River settlement, especially of the miserable
huts in which the immigrants had to live and of malaria
and other sicknesses that had ravaged the settlements. The
two men had made a long excursion into Wisconsin, first
to the Jefferson Prairie settlement founded by Ole Nattestad, and then northward to the lands that later became
the nucleus of the famous Koshkonong settlement. They
give precise information about conditions as they had
observed them. After an investigating tour of three weeks
they were back at the Fox River settlement, where they
intended to remain until the following spring. Though
they report fully the darker side of the situation, especially as regards sickness, they are on the whole favorably
impressed and they leave no doubt in the mind of the
reader that they consider the possibilities for the industrious immigrant very good, especially in Wisconsin. In the
spring of 1840 this entire letter was published in a Drammen newspaper.[17]

15 John Johnsen Aga to Samson Johnsen, June 23, 1837, in *Den Bergenske
Merkur*, November 8, 1837. The boat builder was doubtless Lars Larsen.

16 Sjovat Poulsen to relatives, June 24, 1837, in *Den Bergenske Merkur*, November 8, 1837.

17 *Tiden* (Drammen), March 3, 1840.

A long letter of January 11, 1841, from " Iowe County, Wis. Territory," contains a detailed chronicle of the adventures of three immigrants who went to America by way of Göteborg in 1839. Much of the account is devoted to the prevalence of malaria in the West. " But though we believe that no one who is determined to come should be frightened away by fear of sickness and though we are convinced that every industrious and able-bodied man can live better here than in Norway, we do not seek to persuade anyone to come, but rather to advise against it in the cases of those who are earning a good livelihood there." [18] This note of caution is typical of the " America letters " in general.

" The native-born Americans are called Yankees," wrote an immigrant of 1840 from Muskego. " They have such cold houses that the snow blows into them. They eat three times a day, always at a decked table. No matter how simple a workingman they may have with them, all eat at the same table, without distinction as to persons. These people work daily at their various tasks, even though they are merchants or officials." This immigrant had purchased a farm of about 250 acres, of which eight or ten had been broken and in 1841 planted with winter wheat. " We have built a house of oak, thirty feet long and twenty feet wide." [19]

" God be thanked, I can report that I and Anlaug have been well all the time and have been satisfied from the first day we stepped on American soil," wrote a Wisconsin immigrant in 1843. He had joined the Swedish colony at Pine Lake and owned 160 acres. He goes on to discuss in orderly fashion the climate, local conditions and soil,

[18] The letter, by Anders Wiig, Brynnild Leqve, and Johannes Wiig, is printed in *Bergens Stiftstidende,* July 29, 1841.

[19] Johannes Evensen to " Sorenskriver " Ellefsen, May 14, 1842, in *Morgenbladet,* September 16, 1842.

manner of living, language, customs, and religion. If all
shared his view of things and were in circumstances similar
to his, he would without hesitation advise all who had felt
the hard times in Norway, who had little capital, were
young and in good health, to emigrate to America. " But
since human beings have such different ways of looking at
things that some are never satisfied I will not involve myself in that matter."   On the other hand he sounds the
familiar warning that America is not Paradise. As to
religion he points out that a large number of Americans
are very active in the worship of God. The man who
fears and loves God can do so in America as well as he
can in Norway, where, he adds ironically, he is " surrounded by covetous ministers who often give more an-
noyance than edification to the common people." [20]

New York was a lively and populous commercial town
but also seemed to be " a genuine home for all arch-
pickpockets and swindlers," wrote a disillusioned and unhappy immigrant in 1843. He adds that the pickpockets
whom he and his companions had had the honor of meeting were not Americans but Norwegians — runners in the
employ of transportation agencies. Conditions among
the Norwegians in Wisconsin, as described in his letter,
were wretched. Sick, poor, and miserable, he says, people
go about, lacking house and home, the one scarcely able to
help the other. Many families that were well-to-do in
Norway are almost reduced to beggary, in part because
they have been too liberal in helping others, in part because
they have been cheated by swindlers. Climate, soil, living
conditions, in short, nearly every phase of the American
situation is unsatisfactory. The writer sweepingly con-
demns America; his hope is that his lines will cause some
of those who are suffering from emigration fever to give

[20] Ellev Bjørnsen Tungen to relatives, January 6, 1843, in *Christianssandsposten*,
May 15, 1843. From " Vinn Township per Milwauki V. T. i Nordamerika."

up their project. His letter was printed by a newspaper editor in documentary support of an anti-emigration article.[21] The truth of the indictment so far as the temporary situation was concerned was acknowledged by such an immigrant letter writer as Johannes Johansen, who explained that great numbers of poor Norwegians, just arrived, were thrown upon the mercy of the settlement. Those who had been there for some time were as yet barely able to meet their own needs, but when poverty-stricken immigrants streamed in, the little that they had must be shared with the arrivals.[22]

The testimony of few letter writers was awaited with so much interest as was that of Hans Gasmann of Foss in Gjerpen, who emigrated in 1843 and settled at Pine Lake in Wisconsin. He was a well-to-do Norwegian; the sale of his home *gaard* and mill brought him seventy-five hundred specie dollars.[23] Gasmann was a man of prominence, both as a large property holder and because he had twice been elected to the Storthing. He was known as a man of cool judgment, and many who were in doubt about the wisdom of emigrating awaited his reports with the confidence that they could trust his word. It is significant of the interest in Gasmann's emigration that he was honored by a long farewell poem from the hand of a writer named Pavels Hielm.[24] The poet could not understand why Gasmann should wish to emigrate; he suggests one possible cause after another, but the matter remains a riddle to him. Apparently he did not grasp the implications of the fact that the emigrant set off with a family of thirteen children. On October 18, 1843, Gasmann wrote a long

[21] A letter by Anders Brynildsen, October 11, 1843, in *Tiden* (Drammen), December 19, 20, 1843.

[22] Johansen to friends, October 11, 1843, in *Tiden* (Drammen), December 20, 1843.

[23] *Tiden* (Drammen), November 27, 1842.

[24] *Smaalehnenes Amtstidende* (Frederikshald), April 25, 1843.

letter from Pine Lake.[25]   He had arrived safely with his
large family, had taken out a claim to 160 acres of land
and had bought a tract of 1,000 acres.   " The woods are
not dense here," he wrote, " but have pleasant openings,
that is, the trees are scattered so that one can plow between
them; and when one sees this land, it looks like a garden
full of large fruit trees."   He lived in a humble cabin.
He points out that the first essential is to cultivate one's
ground so that one can make a living.   Fine buildings must
come later.   " My house, therefore, consists merely of a
living room, kitchen and dining room, with two small
upper rooms and a little clothes closet."   But he also built
a barn, something not yet common among the farmers.
He tells of the Swedish colony at Pine Lake and of his
neighbors.   He recognizes the shortcomings of the immigrant's position in the West,— especially in the cases of
those who come with empty pockets,— yet he says, " I am
well pleased with my decision to come to this place and
I hope that with God's help, I shall never have cause to
regret it."   The next summer, on July 27, 1844, Gasmann
again wrote from Pine Lake.[26]   "I believe I have achieved
that which I desired: a higher welfare for all my children,"
he says.   He misses the social and cultural contacts that
he had enjoyed in Norway, but he is pleased with the
friendships of the frontier.   He writes that he has erected
a sawmill on a stream that runs through his lands and
that he intends to build a flour mill.   The profits from the
sawmill range from six to eight dollars a day.   He has
divided most of his land among his four grown sons, retain-
ing 260 acres for his own use: " I am now building houses
on my own tract and I expect to move there some time in
the fall."   Two years later, in 1846, Gasmann wrote a
long letter about the emigration controversy then raging

[25] To A. P. Limie and others, in *Christianssandsposten,* December 22, 1843.
[26] *Morgenbladet,* December 19, 1844.

in Norway.[27] He attacked the Reverend J. W. C. Dietrichson, who violently opposed the emigration movement,
and he declared that the emigrants in the settlement where
he lived were well contented with America. Needless to
say, these letters of Gasmann were brought out in contemporary newspapers and played their part in the advertising of America among Norwegians.

Thus the process went on: letters praising America;
letters condemning; letters expressing cautious, tentative
judgments; letters reflecting special local conditions; occasional letters essaying more general conclusions. In constantly increasing numbers such reports were brought before the Norwegian reading public. One immigrant in
1843 represents himself so satisfied that even if he could
have the best *gaard* in Norway he would sell it and emigrate, thus echoing the opinion of Trovatten.[28] Another
urges his acquaintances not to emigrate and summarizes
his arguments in such points as the great amount of sickness; the unhealthful climate; the extreme heat of the
summers; the prevalence of snakes; the unattractiveness
of the land in Wisconsin, with its woods and swamps;
burdensome governmental taxes; the danger of contamina-
tion by Mormonism; lack of money in the settlements; and
the necessity of almost unendurably hard work.[29] Yet
another proceeds to classify mankind in eight divisions, for
each of which he has a shrewd word of advice. Growing
youth are advised to come; for working people under fifty
years of age the prospects are on the whole good, though

27 A letter of March 20, 1846, in *Bratsberg-Amts Correspondent*, June 16,
1846; also in *Norge og Amerika*, 1: 180–191 (June, 1846). This letter was from
the Ashippun settlement, to which Gasmann had removed.

28 Knud Ellingsen Dokenæs, Koshkonong, to Knud Ellingsen Liane, December,
1843, in *Christianssandsposten*, March 4, 1844.

29 Jon Nielsen Bjørndalen to his parents, January 5, 1844, in *Morgenbladet*,
May 28, 1844. With this letter is printed a postscript by a widow with six
children, who tells of the recent deaths of her husband and one son.

they are urged to weigh all sides of the question; people who are not workers are advised to remain at home unless they have capital and are experienced tradesmen; people over fifty years of age are advised to stay at home even though earthly cares and democratic aspirations make them dissatisfied where they are; those who are so poor that they will not be able to meet the first needs in America receive the writer's sympathy but no encouragement to come; those with fortunes will be placed in a doubly advantageous position by investing in American soil; those who are healthy, strong, and determined, and do not belong to any of the banned classes, are in an excellent position to come; those who are weak or sickly are invited to continue to endure their lot in ther native country.   Thus this immigrant, long before restrictive immigration became a serious issue, proposed a program of voluntary restriction in the home country.   America in his eyes was for the young and strong, the best classes that the common people of the Old World could produce.[30]

Meanwhile the emigration controversy continued to resound, with much emphasis by some writers upon the difficulties that the immigrant was forced to contend with in the United States.   Many immigrants were greatly disturbed by the dismal chorus of anti-emigration writings in Norway and not a few individuals raised their voices in protest against what they considered misrepresentation or hasty judgment.   Finally, on January 6, 1845, eighty men of the Muskego settlement attached their names to an open letter addressed to the people of Norway.   This document, which was published in full in *Morgenbladet* for April 1, 1845, is a noble statement of the faith that

[30] Ellef Bjørnsen Tungen to relatives, January 14, 1844, in *Bratsberg-Amts Correspondent*, April 1, 1844.   From Pine Lake, Wisconsin.   See *ante*, n. 20.

was in the Norwegian pioneers, one that could only have been written by men with traditions of self-assertion. Discouragement and need there had been in the colony because poverty-stricken people had descended upon the settlers in swarms; sickness and suffering, too; but these trials did not justify reports generally condemning America, which through centuries had been a haven for the oppressed from all Europe and where nearly all, once the first difficulties were overcome, had done well.

There are complaints over the difficulties which meet emigrants here at the outset; but in truth all who make such complaints should feel a sense of shame when they recall what history has to tell of the sufferings of those earliest immigrants who opened the way for coming generations by founding the first colony in the United States, the Virginia colony.

The seventeenth century settlers faced sickness, hunger, and dangers from wild beasts and Indians; their colony seemed doomed. But it was not God's will that it should be destroyed; reënforcements came; with fresh courage the pioneers continued the struggle and won. " Nearly all the obstacles which met the first settlers have been removed," declared the eighty Norwegians. " Should not therefore we, who have brighter prospects than they had, cherish the hope, through persistence, of winning the fight and of gaining a simple livelihood." They believe that God will crown their venture with success, for has He not made this land more fruitful perhaps than any land in the world? And is not the need of America greater than ever before, since the European countries are over-populated and emigration is rooted in necessity? The pioneer faith is summed up in these words:

We have no expectation of gaining riches; but we live under a liberal government in a fruitful land, where freedom and equality are the rule in religious as in civil matters, and where each one of us is at liberty to earn his living practically as he chooses. Such opportunities are more to be desired than riches; through these opportunities we have a prospect of preparing for ourselves, by diligence and industry a carefree old age. We have therefore no reason to regret the decision that brought us to this country.[31]

The Muskego manifesto is an example of an immigrant colony banding together to defend America before the court of Norwegian opinion. Almost equally interesting are the efforts of a group of Chicago Norwegians from Voss to organize the writing of " America letters." This element was to a considerable extent concentrated in Chicago from the earliest period in the history of Norwegian settlement in the West. From Chicago in 1840 Anders Flage, as has already been noted, sent a vigorous letter to his home district in Voss. Several other " Vossings " attached their names to that letter, which perhaps was in a sense a reply to critics on behalf of all the Chicago Vossings.[32] Eight years later this element, prompted by zeal for the defense of America against hostile criticism, organized a Correspondence Society, the chief object of which was to send regular " America letters " to Norway. The association for this purpose is of interest not only in relation to the subject of " America letters " but also as an early example of a type of organization that was to become very common among Norwegian-Americans — the *Bygdelags,* or district leagues, " organizations for social and cultural purposes among emigrants or their descendants from the various *Bygds* or districts of Norway." In true American spirit, these Chicago Vossings, as a preliminary to their letter writing, adopted a constitution and elected officers. One letter was to be written each month by some individual selected by the executive committee. The first letter, sent on September 30, 1848,

[31] This document has been translated into English by S. B. Hustvedt, " An American Manifesto by Norwegian Immigrants," in *American-Scandinavian Review,* 13: 619 (October, 1925). Among the signers of the manifesto were such men as Even Hansen Heg, Joh. Johansen, and Bjørn Hatlestad.

[32] See *ante,* p. 201, and n. 9.

was addressed "To our dear Fatherland and old Norwegian Friends." It frankly presented the society's constitution, which opened thus:

Since many erroneous impressions exist in our fatherland concerning
the political as well as the religious situation in America, particularly
as relating to the emigrated Norwegians, and in order that these may
be dispelled through correct advices from the immigrants here, which
can be brought about only through a systematic correspondence, we
have agreed and decided as follows: 1. That to attain the end sought
we form ourselves into a Correspondence Society of Chicago, Ill., for
the mutual purpose of meeting the costs which will ensue upon writing to Norway, and, possibly, of obtaining correspondence therefrom.

In the series of letters that followed, the views of an alleged hostile critic were vigorously refuted; the Chicago-
ans declared that the Norwegian government had sought
to frighten the working class with dire reports about
America and thus hinder emigration; precise information
was given about the Vossings in Chicago; one letter was
devoted to the subject of political equality; another reported the contemporary gold rush to California; yet another depicted the general religious situation; and one or
two related to church matters among the immigrants.
Three members of this Correspondence Society were in
Norway in 1849–1850 to supplement the written with
the spoken word, and they led back to the United States
a party of some eight hundred emigrants.[33]

The "America letters" were unquestionably a factor
of great importance in the history of Norwegian emigration. They contributed powerfully to the spread of
enlightenment among Norwegian commoners. They kept
fresh the connection between the Norwegian *gaard* and
the American farm. And they were undoubtedly the
decisive influence in ripening many a decision to emigrate.

[33] The history of this Correspondence Society, with many extracts from letters,
is told in A. O. Barton's article, "Norwegian-American Emigration Societies in
the Forties and Fifties," in *Studies and Records,* 3: 23 ff.

For the historian they possess a threefold interest: they are valuable records of the details of the emigrant's experiences; they help one to understand the reaction of the immigrant mind to the new environment of the West; and they illustrate a type of influence that was brought to bear upon the mind of the prospective emigrant in Norway.

X. THE NORWEGIAN GOVERNMENT AND THE EARLY EMIGRATION

THE emigration problem was a novel one for Norwegian officials who in the late thirties and early forties felt obliged to take it under consideration. The government was at first uncertain how to proceed. Should it attempt to regulate emigration or keep its hands off? In 1837 it undertook a preliminary investigation but took no action save to give publicity to some of the items gathered; [1] from 1843 to 1845 it attempted to secure the passage of a general regulatory law.

The first steps in the direction of emigration legislation were taken as a result of the poverty of many emigrants, their lack of preparation for the voyage, and the overcrowding of vessels. Evils of this type were especially marked in 1843 and a description of them sent to the government by the Norwegian-Swedish consul at Havre on June 30 of that year convinced officials of the need of an investigation. Consul Broström reported that of 841 Norwegian emigrants who had arrived at Havre up to June 30, not less than 200 were in dire need and 28 had to be returned to Norway. Nearly 5,000 francs had been used in alleviating the needs of the 200 emigrants in question. Vessels were frightfully overcrowded — for example, one of 140 tons carried 210 passengers. The consul criticized the skippers for taking advantage of the ignorance of the *bønder*. Meanwhile he suggested that ministers and public officials should be urged to warn emigrants of the perils that they faced. Regulations were needed to prevent overcrowding and the emigration of persons unable to meet the necessary expenses of the trip. The

[1] See *ante*, p. 109.

legal minimum for each emigrant, the consul believed, should be fifty specie dollars.[2]

The finance, trade, and tariff department[3] took up the matter with F. C. Borchsenius, sheriff of Bratsberg *Amt*, who suggested the appointment of a commission to study the situation and draft a law. He believed the emigration had not yet reached its highest point, that on the contrary it would spread like a contagious disease over Norway. Consequently the causes of emigration ought to come within the scope of the investigation, and legislation should be aimed at the correction of the fundamental evils. So remarkable a phenomenon, he believed, was rooted "not only in the national character but also in defects in the economic and social conditions" of the country. The land question seemed to him particularly important, for the emigrants were drawn chiefly from the poorest districts.[4]

The finance department took the view that the causes of the movement were temporary and would disappear as soon as the general economic life improved. Legislation, save in the direction of removing hindrances to a free economic development, was not advisable. The department accepted the implications of the *laissez-faire* theory, for it held that "if laws are passed you hinder the free

---

[2] The manuscript records of the investigation of 1843–45 are in Socialdept., Lovkontor: Utv., Kong. Prop. 1845. The consul's report is in folder 2. In the notes to the present chapter this source will be referred to as U. K. P. The printed records are in "Angaaende Udvandringer til Fremmede Verdensdele," in *Kongeriget Norges Ellevte Ordentlige Storthings Forhandlinger i Aaret 1845*, vol. 1, part 6. The consul's report is summarized on p. 1. This source will be abbreviated in the present chapter as *Stort. Forh. 1845*, vol. 1, pt. 6. Details of the Havre complications are reported in *Morgenbladet*, July 31, 1843. Some material on the investigation in Stavanger *Amt* is in S. A. Bergen: Stavanger Amt, Eldre Afdeling, Pakkeafdeling 678.

[3] To be referred to as the finance department from this point on.

[4] The finance department to Borchsenius, August 28, 1843, and Borchsenius to the department, September 12, 1843, in U. K. P., folder 2; *Stort. Forh. 1845*, vol. 1, pt. 6, p. 1.

development of business." Nevertheless, the protection of creditors was considered imperative, no less than the protection of the emigrants themselves. The department, therefore, although it specifically said that the " government does not want to hinder the emigration or to make it more difficult," proposed the following:

(1) That in the limits of Bratsberg *Amt* a commission be appointed which shall be empowered to draw up a proposed law embodying what should be done in respect of emigration to foreign countries, with a view both to protecting the emigrant on the journey and to protecting the public and private interests affected by the emigration; and that the commission be authorized to correspond directly with the various authorities in order to secure from them the needed information and explanations. (2) That as members of this commission the following be named: F. C. Borchsenius, procurator and sheriff in Bratsberg *Amt*; J. Gasmann, vice consul and broker in Porsgrund; and Dr. F. C. Faye of Skien.

These recommendations were approved by the government on November 8, 1843, and on November 11 the commission was appointed by the king.[5]

In a preliminary report dated December 27, 1843, the commission stated that two difficulties had arisen in connection with emigration. People in debt had " run away without satisfying their creditors," and on at least two ships typhus had developed. The commission advised the issuance of an executive order as a temporary measure before the emigration of 1844. In the meantime a full investigation would be made. The commissioners state that they have already familiarized themselves with the American immigration law of March 2, 1819. The movement may be rooted in some serious " condition of the state's organism " or in evil social conditions. Or it may be based — and the commission is inclined to believe that this is the case — upon the " hope of an easier liveli-

[5] *Stort. Forh. 1845*, vol. 1, pt. 6, p. 3–5. The formal instructions to the commission, dated November 16, 1843, are in U. K. P., folder 2.

hood in the new world." In any event, it is "impolitic and not right to put legal hindrances in the way of immigration," for it "will not serve the state to force people to stay" in their own country. Apropos of conditions on board ships, the commission reports that on one emigrant ship thirty persons died during the voyage and that on another five died and three times that number were ill. As soon as the latter ship reached America the sick emigrants were taken to a hospital. Attention is called to a letter from an emigrant in which "people who are in tolerable circumstances" are advised not to come to America. Special attention is also given to the situation reported by the consul at Havre.

In a report of January 7, 1844, approved by the king on February 7, the government took the view that the condition was not sufficiently serious to warrant a provisional order. The subject matter of the proposed regulations was novel and it was unwise to deal with it in haste. The government therefore called for a continued investigation to be reported by October, 1844, in time for action by the Storthing of 1845, so that a law might be put into effect before the spring emigration of 1845.[6]

The commission therefore continued its investigation and on December 15, 1844, submitted a final report to the king.[7] The main portion of this report consists of a proposed emigration law, but this is preceded by an interesting and important consideration of the emigration movement. Emigration from Norway, the commis-

---

[6] Stort. Forh. 1845, vol. 1, pt. 6, p. 6–21. The commission included in its report a draft of rules to be embodied in the provisional order. These are similar to the later proposed law, which is analyzed in the present chapter.

[7] Stort. Forh. 1845, vol. 1, pt. 6, p. 23–47. The commission's journal, or "Forhandlingsprotocol," is a valuable detailed manuscript source of information on the investigation. This and numerous reports sent to the commission are in U. K. P. Malmin, in Decorah-Posten, December 26, 1924, and January 2, 1925, gives an account of the investigation with quotations from the archival sources.

sion points out, has for a long period been practically unknown. "Only in very recent times has it appeared, almost like a contagious disease, and with few exceptions it is to the North American Free States and especially to the uncultivated regions of the interior of that country that the Norwegian common people have turned their eyes, wishing to win a better livelihood there than they believed they could find in their native land." Emigration in any considerable volume is an occurrence of " the very last few years." The earlier emigration from Stavanger, which led to the later movement, is mentioned; but, the commission reports, " First in the year 1836 the migrations began to be more frequent, especially in Stavanger *Amt,* until in 1843 in several parts of the kingdom, especially in North Bergenhus, Buskerud, and Bratsberg *amter,* they seem to have reached their high points, since they have been falling off largely during the past year." The commission states that it has made a study of reports from ministers and bailiffs, from surveyors of the customs, and from chiefs of police, those from the latter being the most dependable and complete.[8]

According to the reports from ministers and bailiffs, the total emigration has amounted to 1,565 individuals — 597 men, 476 women, and 492 children. Reports from collectors of the customs — supplemented by statements from skippers — give a total of 1,599. These totals are " much too small," however, for the police chiefs, using records of passports, give a total of 3,940 — 1,451 men, 1,061 women, and 1,428 children. The latter figures are somewhat high, however, for " some travelers may have

---

[8] *Stort. Forh. 1845,* vol. 1, pt. 6, p. 23. Many of these reports are in U. K. P. One of special interest is that by the noted minister, M. B. Landstad, dated March 12, 1844, on emigration from Sillejord parish. Two emigrants left that parish in 1839, 2 in 1840, 2 in 1841, 37 in 1842, and 186 in 1843. Drafts of the commission's circulars are in the " Forhandlingsprotocol " in U. K. P.

been included who have not intended to leave the country permanently, and on the other hand some individuals who have requested passports may later have decided to turn back." But they are "fairly reliable for approximate figures." The total of about four thousand has been recruited chiefly from the *amter* of North Bergenhus, Buskerud, and Bratsberg, the sources being as follows, respectively: (a) from Nordhorlehn, 504; Søndhorlehn, 156; total, 660; (b) Numedal and Sandsværd, 432; Buskerud *fogderies*, 129; Drammen, 741; total, 1,302; and (c) Upper Telemarken, 1,054; Lower Telemarken and Bamble, 682; Skien and Porsgrund, 102; total, 1,838; grand total, for the three districts, 3,800. The commission also calls attention to the fact that those listed from the towns of Drammen, Skien, and Porsgrund, have come, with few exceptions, from the neighboring land districts of Buskerud and Bratsberg *amter*. Essentially, therefore, the emigration has been confined to country people from the three districts named. Less than 140 individuals — according to these reports — were from the " upper regions of the kingdom." The figures given above do not include the emigrants who went to America in 1836 and 1837 in " Den Norske Klippe," " Norden," " Enigheden," and " Ægir." The commission had access, however, to reports from 1837, including that from Stavanger *Amt* for April 20, giving information about the earlier emigration; and it took under consideration the antecedents of the migration of 1836 and 1837, touching, among other things, on the question of intolerance toward the Quakers as a factor in causing emigration. The commission expressed regret " that the principle of religious freedom for all Christian religious sects was not more clearly expressed in paragraph 2 of the constitution or carried through in private legislation." It calls attention to the unfortunate treatment

accorded the Quaker sect and cites one specific case.
" Meanwhile it must, however, be admitted without question," the report continues, " that even though the first
sprouts of the migrations must be sought to a certain
extent in imperfections in the law, which have produced
dissatisfaction among certain individuals, their growth in
recent times is the result of other causes, especially of the
common need, affecting the great majority of the emigrants, of seeking a less difficult existence in a new
country." [9]

The commission is not prepared to say that the emigration has been brought about " by any absolute lack in
the conditions in our native land, either in institutions or
in the physical character of the land." It considers it a
very reasonable development " that the countries of the
Old World by their very progress should in the long run
become overpopulated and that the surplus should seek
escape to the newly discovered and unsettled parts of the
world where one can secure the possession of fertile tracts
of land for practically nothing." If, in addition to this,
" a more healthful climate and richer soil are available
there than in the mother country it is undeniable that in
this fact alone there lies so great an attraction that neither
surprise nor anxiety should be awakened if such emigration develops." The commission believes that " it is not
the political institutions of our country which occasion
the desire to leave the country, for they must be considered among the freest in Europe, and the country people
— especially in the recent period — seem to have known
very well how to exercise their political rights." [10] The
commission does not deny, however, that Norway " in
physical respects puts obstacles in the way of the mass of

[9] *Stort. Forh. 1845*, vol. 1, pt. 6, p. 25.
[10] To the Storthing of 1842 the elections returned fifty of the official class and
forty-two *bønder*. Gjerset, *History of the Norwegian People*, 2: 486.

the people in their attempt to win a good livelihood without extreme difficulty and trouble." Nor does it deny " that a certain indolence in respect to industry obtains among the Norwegian people with the result that many of our fellow citizens are willing to risk hazards in the hope of winning more successfully than is possible here at home the fruits of the earth and thus securing the necessaries for the demands of life." [11]

To some extent emigration might be offset, in the opinion of the commission, " by helpful measures on the part of the government, by the encouragement of business in general and agriculture in particular." But the proposals in these respects necessarily would coincide with " what in general should be done for the good of the country," and this naturally lies outside of the scope of the commission's work. It is pointed out, however, that the study of emigration " might give a clue to the defects that are present in social and economic conditions." In this connection attention is called " to the possible relation between the first migrations and intolerance toward the separatists. . . . Similarly the commission, as a result of the fact that the emigration has occurred especially from those parts of the kingdom where landed property is greatly subdivided, has come to the conclusion that perhaps through legislation a limit should be set upon further subdivision of the land holdings." [12]

Reports of conditions in America, as contained in the letters of emigrants, are stated to be " very incomplete and contradictory." [13] But " they leave no doubt that

[11] *Stort. Forh. 1845*, vol. 1, pt. 6, p. 25.

[12] *Stort. Forh. 1845*, vol. 1, pt. 6, p. 26.

[13] The full texts of two " America letters " collected by the commission, Gunder Jørgensen Heisholt to relatives from Pine Lake, October 21, 1844, and Ole Olsen Huuset to relatives from New York, July 7, 1844, are in R. A., Oslo: F. D., D, Journalsaker 1844/1915. Many of the commission's letters are summarized in its " Forhandlingsprotocol," U.K.P. Malmin, in *Decorah-Posten*, January 9, 1925, publishes abstracts of the more important letters listed in the commission's journal.

the destiny which awaits the emigrants is highly uncertain and that for a large number of them it has been a very unhappy one." The discouraging reports, it is indicated, have come especially in the more recent period from people who left Norway " without sufficient resources." The commission further states that such reports " are largely responsible for the fact that the emigration as a whole must now be considered to be declining." On the basis of the emigrant letters which have been examined by the commission it is granted " that those emigrants who have been good people and who have possessed the necessary means not only to purchase an adequate area of land and to clear and cultivate it but also to subsist for the first couple of years until the newly cultivated soil can give the needed products, have been satisfied, and this is particularly true of those who have been fortunate enough to select a settlement where malaria has not attacked them and laid them low; but on the contrary the majority of those without means, who have not had special qualifications in some kind of skilled work, have been the victims of great distress." [14]

The commission then attempts to estimate the financial loss brought about through the emigration. It estimates the number of emigrants in the last decade at 4,500, and the value of their possessions on the average at fifty to sixty specie dollars each. Thus " the emigration has brought about a direct loss in national wealth of 225,000 to 270,000 specie dollars." The loss is not unbalanced, however. For example, " account must be taken of the amount which has come back to the country in transportation costs, since the transportation has been chiefly direct to New York by Norwegian ships." Furthermore, it is suggested, the passenger and freight traffic thus

[14] *Stort. Forh. 1845*, vol. 1, pt. 6, p. 26. The commission reports that the mortality among emigrants from Tind, Telemarken, had been particularly high.

stimulated may have " given the opportunity for more profitably using the American market for the disposal of Norwegian iron products." This in turn may be considered a very good thing for the iron industry and its employees. " Similarly this trade may be the beginning of a more active direct connection with that important part of the world, and this may in the far future have a good influence upon our mercantile and naval conditions." Yet another factor must be given consideration, according to the commission: " Among the majority of the emigrants, so far as can be learned, there has been a considerable proportion of the less industrious and in part useless and discontented citizens." Therefore, " it can hardly be assumed that the emigration has especially weakened the resources of the nation." The commissioners go further and say: " There may even be some question as to whether it has caused any loss at all to society, especially since it is noted, among other things, how the emigration has served to level out certain conditions, for example, to remove the excess population in certain mountain districts, to reduce the disproportionately high cost of land, — as a result of which several broken-up holdings have been brought together again, — and so forth." [15]

The commissioners then raise the question whether a law is needed or not. The emigration appears to them to be in process of decline, as " few are getting ready to go." But the reasons for this decline are probably temporary, and it is uncertain " whether the emigration will not spread like an epidemic." Two good years have stimulated Norwegian agriculture and the fishing industry, but on the whole there are great uncertainties in Norwegian agriculture, and if emigration should set in, many people with slender means would certainly go to America. Unfavorable conditions in the United States,

[15] Stort. Forh. 1845, vol. 1, pt. 6, p. 26.

furthermore, have caused many to defer their departure, but better reports will probably be received before long and the emigration may then develop rapidly. Some officials in the city of Bergen, according to the commissioners, have questioned the advisability of passing the proposed law and have offered three specific criticisms: (1) it would be possible to elude the law by taking indirect routes to America; (2) in enforcing the law it would be difficult to distinguish emigrants from travelers; and (3) people might regard the restrictions embodied in the law as a prohibition of emigration. The commissioners, however, regard the " danger of eluding the law slight as compared with the dangers to society in giving the emigrants an absolutely free hand." Incidentally, the emigrants themselves must not be neglected simply because they have chosen to leave the country. It is pointed out, in this connection, that they are usually ignorant of sanitary questions.[16] Thereupon, in the report, follow the provisions of the proposed emigration law. On March 10, 1845, the finance department recommended to the king that the measure be put before the Storthing for action, and on the same date the king submitted the draft to the national legislature.[17]

The draft contains thirty-eight clauses, the first seventeen of which relate chiefly to the problem of the emigrant in relation to the country and the home community which he is about to leave.[18] The right of every citizen to emigrate is recognized, but it is to be conditioned upon the provisions of this measure in the interests of both the state and the emigrants. Certain classes of people are

---

[16] *Stort. Forh. 1845*, vol. 1, pt. 6, p. 27–30.

[17] *Stort. Forh. 1845*, vol. 1, pt. 6, p. 49–55. The justice, army, and navy departments approved the clauses relating to their specific fields of interest and jurisdiction.

[18] The text of the proposed law is in *Stort. Forh. 1845*, vol. 1, pt. 6, p. 42–47, 55 ff.

forbidden to emigrate without having first received due release or discharge from their duties: officials of the state; others who serve the state even though they hold no royal appointment, such as special trustees, executors of wills, men in military service or called out for military or naval service; and those in the salaried public service, such as parish clerks, schoolmasters, bailiffs, and constables. A similar prohibition extends to such semi-public officials as cashiers and other officials of banks.

Parents are not permitted to take with them children fifteen years of age or older if the latter object; and children between the ages of fifteen and eighteen may not emigrate without the permission of their parents; they must, furthermore, be accompanied by responsible relatives or guardians. If both parents are dead the relatives may not take with them the surviving children under fifteen years of age without the permission of the appointed guardian. A husband is not permitted to emigrate with his wife and with children under fifteen years of age against the will of the wife. If he is determined to go, notwithstanding her opposition, she has the right to demand a division of their joint estate. If such a division be made, she has the right to obtain — apart from the estimated sum — the permanent improvements that would ordinarily come under the rules of primogeniture and also the necessary means of livelihood. A sufficient sum shall be subtracted from the husband's share to assure the support of any children who are left behind until they are fifteen years of age. When parents emigrate and leave behind them legitimate children or when a mother leaves illegitimate children under fifteen years of age, they (the parents or the mother) shall be required to set up such security as the poor-law administration of the place shall find necessary to avoid having children become a burden to the public. A similar duty rests upon the husband with reference to his wife if she is left behind. An emigrant who leaves illegitimate children, as well as one who leaves a divorced wife who receives alimony either by law or by agreement, shall be obliged before his departure to set up such security as the poor-law administration decides to be necessary in order that the payments may be made regularly. He may, if he wishes, pay the entire amount of his obligation to the poor-law administration, which will superintend its later distribution. As to payment of a minor's funds to a parent who has emigrated with the minor in question, the general law concerning the sending of funds of minors to foreign countries shall be observed. These proposed regulations (clauses 3–9) constitute an interesting commentary on some of the possible domestic complications brought about by emigration.

The next clause of the proposed law represents an attempt to safeguard the interests of creditors. It requires the emigrant to make a public announcement of his intention to emigrate during the six months before his departure and at least twelve weeks before that event. It must be printed in the newspaper of the place where he has last lived, or, if there is none there, in that of the nearest town having one. If the prospective emigrant lives in the country the announcement is to be made in the church to which he belongs. The public announcement is unnecessary, however, in case the emigrant shall satisfy the proper public authorities that he has made arrangements which assure the meeting of all legal demands upon him.

Those liable to military service (clause 11) and who have been enlisted for line service or have gone over to the militia or who have been enlisted for naval service cannot be discharged from the armed forces to emigrate except with the permission of the king or an authorized deputy. Nor can men liable to military service who have been excused because they hold civil positions or teach school emigrate without permission. Those who have not been called to fulfill their military duty need not secure special permission to emigrate unless the king in time of war should forbid the emigration of all men liable to military service who are on the rolls of line troops from their twentieth year or who have been enrolled for sea service from their sixteenth year (clause 12). If an emigrant who was enlisted for line service or entered in the militia or who has been excused from service in his capacity as a teacher or civil officer shall return to the kingdom, he shall be required to serve out the remaining time of his service. Nevertheless, he shall not be required to give line service beyond his thirty-second year or militia service beyond his thirty-seventh. Other emigrants who return before the expiration of their military-service age shall be liable not only to enlistment in the regular legal order but also to preference for such enlistment (clause 13).

Only the proper authorities in the place where the emigrant has last resided shall issue a passport to him, and they shall see to it that the regulations in the emigration law are met before the passport is issued. Persons who are guardians or who have not yet fulfilled their military service must have certificates from the proper authorities. Furthermore, before the passport is made out, the police officer shall see to it that the emigrant has received an emigration certificate from the pastor of his district (clauses 14–17).

Most of the remaining twenty-one clauses of the measure relate to emigrant ships and the conditions of the ocean journey. They represent an attempt to protect the emigrant from certain outstanding evils connected with emigration. No ship intended to be used for carrying passengers from any port in Norway direct to lands outside Europe must carry more than one person for each commercial last of the ship's tonnage, the skipper and the crew not included in the estimate (clause 18). Ships having American bills of admeasurement, the passengers of which are without exception bound for the United States, may carry two persons for each five tons, the skipper and the crew not included.[19]

With reference to the room in the ships, the following space shall be allotted to each passenger: in the steerage at least ten square feet if the ship does not pass through the tropics, twelve if it goes to the tropics and the voyage is estimated at fourteen weeks, and fifteen if it is to last longer; and on the orlop deck, thirty square feet for every passenger. The clause specifies that the space thus provided for the passenger must be entirely free from encumbrance, save the passenger's own effects and the bed. On ships carrying passengers to other European countries who are bound for other parts of the world, the space allotted each passenger in the steerage shall be at least six square feet and on the *Naierdæk* at least twelve. The total number of passengers on such ships, excluding the skipper and the crew, may be in proportion to two for each commercial last of the ship's tonnage. In assigning space two children under twelve years of age shall be considered as one passenger and children under one year shall be left out of consideration. This provision, however, shall not apply to ships bound for the United States (clauses 19–21).

In the next clause (22) provision is made for safeguarding passengers from dangers connected with the overloading of ships with merchandise. It is specified that a ship carrying its full allotment of passengers must not be loaded with light goods, the stowage room of which is reckoned according to volume, to a greater extent than

[19] This was in accord with a provision in the American immigration law of March 2, 1819. One of the most interesting documents among the commission's papers is a letter by Captain J. Gasmann of the emigrant vessel "Salvator," dated December 18, 1843, giving his views and describing the methods followed on the "Salvator." U. K. P., folder 3.

two-thirds of the full cargo; or with heavy goods, which are reckoned according to weight, so that the ship shall be weighed down more than two-thirds of the distance between the water line when it is empty and the water line when it is loaded with a full cargo of heavy goods; or with anything harmful to the health of the passengers. If the number of passengers is less than the total permitted, the amount of merchandise carried may be increased proportionately. The passenger deck, cooking facilities, and equipment in general (clause 23) must be dependable and solid. In the matter of sleeping accommodations, each bunk — for one passenger — shall be at least five and one-half feet in length and one and one-half in width, not more than three such bunks shall be placed side by side, and there must be at least eighteen inches between them. If the bunks are built in tiers there must be at least two feet between the tiers; and bunks with three feet of space between tiers must be provided for one-eighth of the total number of passengers on board — to be used, in case of need, for the sick.

No ship of less than forty commercial lasts may be used for the direct transportation of emigrants to foreign parts of the world, cabin passengers and the families of the skipper and captain excepted. If ships of forty to sixty commercial lasts carry both freight and passengers they should not be loaded with more than half a cargo measured by volume, or, measured by weight, with goods weighing the ship down to more than half the distance between the water line when the ship is empty and the water line when the ship is fully loaded (clause 24).

The officer in charge of the ship must furnish the passengers with good water and must supply good, wholesome food to those passengers who have engaged board for the passage. Calculations as to the supplies must be made with due regard to the number of passengers to be boarded and the length of the voyage, according to the following amounts per week for each individual: twenty-one quarts of water; seven pounds of bread; one of butter; three of meat; one and one-half of salt pork; three quarts of barley groats; two of peas; and an ample amount of vegetables if possible. For provisions easily spoiled in hot weather, other nourishing and good foods may be substituted, for example, " food oil " for butter, or rice and beans for barley groats and peas. The provisioning shall be based upon the following time schedule for voyages: to North Africa and North America, but not to the west coast of the latter country, twelve weeks; to the West Indies, twelve weeks; to the Gulf of Mexico, Central and South America, but not the western coast of South America, fourteen weeks; to the west coast of Africa, fourteen weeks; to the Cape of Good Hope or the Falkland Islands, seventeen weeks; to places in the Indian Ocean, twenty weeks; and to places in the Pacific Ocean, twenty-four weeks. The captain is also obligated, in case those passengers who furnish their own board do not have enough to last them through the voyage, to supply them with needed food; and for this service he is to receive adequate compensation. The ship authorities, furthermore, must have an adequate supply of medicines and take every precaution in the interest of cleanliness and sanitary conditions on board during the voyage. No spirituous liquors are to be sold on board ship (clauses 25–28).

Before an emigrant ship may sail it must be examined by the police and by other authorized officials appointed to test its seaworthiness, its equipment, its supplies, and its general readiness for emigrant service. No clearance papers shall be issued until after such inspection. The skipper must prepare two lists of the passengers, giving the names of the emigrants, totals of adults for both sexes, the number of children under twelve years and the number under one year. One of these is to be forwarded by the police to the central government. Furthermore, the skipper must present to the customs officers a certificate from the police stating that the provisions of the present law have been observed. The skipper is also obligated to deposit with the customs officials a sum of money (not under three hundred specie dollars or more than one thousand, the exact amount to be determined upon the basis of eight dollars for each commercial last) as security for the payment of any fine or violation of the regulations and for the payment of legitimate claims against the ship by passengers. The second list of passengers is to be returned to the skipper when clearance papers are issued and by him is to be presented to the Norwegian-Swedish consul or agent at the port of destination, together with a report on the time of passage, health conditions, and mortality during the voyage. The consul or agent shall send this list at once to the Norwegian government and also forward a report on complaints from passengers, discrepancies between the passenger list and the actual number of arrivals, and similar matters. The consul is to " give all possible aid and advice to the passengers with respect to their further journeys unless the passengers object to such guidance"; and to act as arbiter in disputes among the passengers as well as between the passengers and the skipper. If any emigrant has been wronged the consul shall help him to secure legal redress and report the case to the Norwegian government. In the case of the death on board ship of an emigrant unaccompanied by relatives, the consul is to take charge of his effects, which are to be disposed of in accordance with the Norwegian inheritance laws (clauses 29–33).

One of the most interesting clauses in the entire proposed law is that by which the officials of the ship are made responsible for keeping the emigrant from becoming a public burden after his arrival in a foreign country. The ship authorities must see to it that the emigrant, if he leave the ship at some port outside Europe, have a sum of at least fifteen specie dollars, or, if he leave the ship at a European port, have not less than forty specie dollars. Children under twelve years of age must have at their command at least half of the indicated sum. Presumably it was intended that no emigrant should be accepted for the passage who could not satisfy the skipper of the ship that he had the minimum amount of money required by this clause. Passengers must not be landed against their will at any other than the place for which they have purchased passage. They are to have forty-eight hours in which to leave the ship at the port of destination (clauses 34–35).

The last three clauses of the measure relate to the public posting of copies of the law and the giving to emigrants of printed leaflets about sanitary regulations on board ship, exemptions of certain types of ships from the foregoing rules, and penalties. Violations of the law are punishable by a fine of twenty to two hundred dollars in addition to the payment of damages (clauses 36–38).

It is clear that the proposed law was an honest effort to protect both the emigrant and the home community from the dangers of unregulated emigration. On the whole the measure was both liberal and comprehensive. The most novel part of the scheme is embodied in its first clauses. Their weakness lies in the fact that they become entangled in the whole complicated system of Norwegian civil law, but they represent a courageous attempt to deal with an unusual set of domestic problems. The provisions of the intended law covered the needs of the situation as the commissioners, in the light of their investigation, saw it.

The measure was introduced by the ministry in the Odelsthing, the larger branch of the Storthing, and was referred to the committee on trade, the members of which were A. M. Schweigaard and Hans P. Jensen. After a careful examination of the proposal this committee returned the measure to the Odelsthing on May 26, 1845.[20] The committee first called attention to the difference between the two main parts of the bill: the first seventeen clauses were regulations to protect the public and to prevent impositions by the emigrant upon others, whereas the remaining clauses were intended to afford protection to the emigrants themselves. The finance department originally planned only such supervision as the second part of the measure provided and the committee believed that it would be wise thus to limit the regulation. The real problems of emigration, the committee believed, were concerned with mass emigration to countries outside Europe. It was this type of emigration that involved special dangers to the health and life of the emigrant and it was entirely proper, therefore, to make this movement the object of special legislation. It was manifestly improper to regulate emigration to other European states on the basis of conditions occasioned by emigration to America. Should a general regulatory law be passed, applying both to the home situation and to the conditions of the journey, it would be necessary to go to the foundations of civil law, for example, the marriage laws, and this the committee considered unwise. Only a few points from the detailed criticisms in the report need to be mentioned here. The danger that public officials will give up their offices in order to emigrate is considered slight. Parents are not likely to leave their children behind when they depart for America. In some cases perhaps the woman who refuses to emigrate with her husband is at fault. A public announcement of the intended emigration would prob-

[20] The report of the committee is in *Stort. Forh, 1845*, vol. 8, p. 87–95; and it is summarized in *Storthings-Efterretninger 1836–1854*, 2: 762 (Christiania, 1893).

ably be a good thing, for when thousands of people leave, it is inevitable that some of them should be debtors. But an honest man with an established place in the community would find it difficult to keep his plans for emigration secret; and the irresponsible debtor could probably evade the law in any event. The clauses relating to military service are considered unnecessary.

The second part of the proposed law is compared to the English emigration law of 1842.[21] The committee points out that emigration conditions in Norway are not unlike those which have made legislation necessary in England. Ships have been too heavily loaded; there have been sickness and suffering; and there is a danger that ships will not carry adequate supplies of water. The committee believes that the emigration is not a passing phenomenon; it probably will continue to develop, perhaps on a smaller scale, but on a surer foundation. The immigrants in the United States will undoubtedly come to the aid of prospective emigrants and make emigration even more inviting than before. The upshot of the committee's reasoning is that legislation should be restricted to the protection of the emigrant and it therefore advised the passage of a " Law Regarding Passenger Traffic to Foreign Parts of the World," and drafted a bill in ten sections, based essentially upon clauses 18 to 38 of the law proposed by the commission, though with numerous changes in details. One passage of the committee's report deserves quotation:

In the opinion of the committee there are two classes of emigrants, the one consisting of people who believe that the Scriptural injunc-

[21] For a brief summary of the English act of 1842 see Stanley C. Johnson, *A History of Emigration from the United Kingdom to North America, 1763–1912,* 112 (London, 1913). Compare also the English act of 1835, *ibid.,* 105–106, and Dr. Johnson's chapter on the transport of emigrants. *Ibid.,* 101–130. The Norwegian commission studied not only English legislation but also German, for example, the emigration regulations in force at Bremen. The latter are reported in a letter from the consul at Bremen, July 6, 1843, in U. K. P., folder 2. A similar report from Havre, dated November 11, 1843, is in the same folder.

tion, " In the sweat of thy brow shalt thou eat thy bread," applies to only one part of the world and not another, and who, therefore, listening to exaggerated reports about the Paradise on the other side of the ocean, leave their homes without definite plans, without adequate funds to maintain them through the first period, and without connections in the new home which they seek. The second class consists of persons who do not decide to seek homes in distant America before they have weighed the difficulties and hardships of a settler's life but who nevertheless accept the prospects for economic well-being open to them, since they can become masters of fruitful lands by doing little more than ask for them.

The committee believed that the first class would diminish, but that the second could be expected to increase.[22]

An interesting debate occurred in the Odelsthing on June 5, 1845, after the trade committee had reported out the revised bill.[23] It was opened by Nicolaysen, who moved that the bill be tabled. Such a law, he said, was unnecessary both from the state's and the emigrant's side. Up to 1845 emigrants had not cost the state treasury more than a paltry forty-five specie dollars. The emigrants, in his opinion, were sufficiently protected by the fact that the emigrant ships were good ships; and the restrictions in the proposed law, he believed, would cause these good ships to withdraw from the trade. This would force the emigrants to go by way of Göteborg or some other Swedish port where no such regulations were in force. Some of the provisions in the law were made unnecessary, he added, by American laws.

An argument for the law was advanced by A. M. Schweigaard, a member of the trade committee and prominent in the Storthing.[24] He urged its passage because the American laws contained nothing on the two most crucial points of all: the seagoing quality of the ship and guar-

[22] *Stort. Forh. 1845*, vol. 8, p. 90.

[23] The debate is summarized in *Storthings-Efterretninger 1836–1854*, vol. 2, p. 762–764.

[24] For a characterization of Schweigaard, see Gjerset, *History of the Norwegian People*, 2: 486–489.

antees of an adequate supply of drinking water for the
emigrants. To give the passengers sufficient room on the
ship was futile if the ship was so heavily loaded that it
became necessary in heavy seas to close the portholes and
thus shut off the supply of pure air. It was even more
important to guarantee the supply of drinking water.
Another speaker, Borchsenius, supported Schweigaard's
views, and called attention to the losses which local communities sustained through receiving poverty-stricken
emigrants back again and being forced to support them.
But these losses, he said, represented only one side of the
matter; the other was the pitiful condition of the emigrants themselves. That the condition on board ships
was often very bad he brought out by reading passages
from letters of emigrants telling about the ocean voyage.[25]

An interesting turn to the discussion was given by
Falsen, who spoke chiefly about the background of the
movement. His analysis reveals the point of view of an
upper-class official. He looked upon the emigration as a
disheartening spectacle and bewailed the fact that the
country's inhabitants, famed for their love of country,
should now — after thirty years under a free constitution,
which had yielded excellent fruits — desert their country
and flock to the New World. The inhabitants, he said,
were too often without training in the virtues of industry
and orderly conduct. They were allowed to roam from
place to place, to dabble in trade, to peddle goods. When
a man with such a background was placed in charge of a
farm he was not steady enough to use it wisely and poverty
was likely to become his lot. The speaker indicated that the
changes in financial conditions caused by the war from
1807 to 1814 had considerably influenced the situation.
People were extravagant in prosperity. When conditions

[25] *Storthings-Efterretninger 1836–1854*, vol. 2, p. 763.

became stabilized, their extravagant desires remained, but it was no longer easy to get money. Without considering the needs of the future, they tilled the soil unwisely, with the result that they got poorer crops each year. They borrowed money, fell into the clutches of money lenders, and lost their credit. Property was broken up, small patches of land were sold, and the money thus gained was squandered. An added cause of general misery was the immoderate use of liquor. The result of all this was emigration to America. In Falsen's opinion, high taxes, large salaries paid to officials, and the conduct of public officials had no effect upon the emigration. Probably it would be a long time before the general condition of the common people would improve and meanwhile emigration was bound to continue. The speaker declared himself in favor of the emigration law. "If these emigrating citizens turn their backs on the fatherland," he said, "the country should not turn its back on them, but should protect their lives and their happiness as far as possible." [26]

One speaker suggested that the Norwegian-Swedish *chargé d'affaires* in America should be required to submit a true, official report on American conditions as a means of counteracting false reports that were prevalent. Before a vote was taken a number of other speakers voiced their opposition to the proposed law. Nicolaysen's motion to table the measure was then carried and the matter was therefore dropped. [27]

Thus ended the Norwegian attempt to regulate emigration in the forties. As the movement continued to develop and the volume of emigration to increase, the need of legislation became imperative, and eighteen years later

[26] *Storthings-Efterretninger 1836–1854*, vol. 2, p. 764.
[27] *Storthings-Efterretninger 1836–1854*, vol. 2, p. 764. An official investigation of conditions among the settlers in the West was made in 1847, perhaps as a result of the suggestion in this debate. See *post*, p. 257.

Norway passed a law that resembled the measure rejected in 1845. The investigation of 1843–45 brought together a considerable body of facts regarding the movement, called official attention to the migration as a whole, paved the way for later legislation, and is of historical interest for its illumination of the official point of view in the forties.

XI. "AMERICA BOOKS" AND FRONTIER SOCIAL AND ECONOMIC CONDITIONS

IN the early fifties a newspaper asserted that the "North American Free States " were that part of the world the geographical and statistical conditions of which were most investigated and studied by Norwegians — both by prospective emigrants and by those remaining at home.[1] This curiosity about the western world seems to have been provoked primarily by the emigration movement and the contacts it set up. Emigrants were eager to report, through letters and books, about the remarkable country to which they had gone; and Norwegians at home were eager to supplement these reports — often superficial, prejudiced, and extremely local in scope — with more comprehensive and dependable information. The result was a steady stream of books and pamphlets following those by Bishop Neumann, Ole Rynning, and Ole Nattestad, and supplementing letters and newspaper articles. From 1836 to the mid-century there came from Norwegian presses a series of "America books" of curiously diverse origin. Among the authors were a Norwegian bishop; a university-trained school-teacher; several unschooled farmers; a tinner; a smith; a publicist; a Swedish immigrant leader who became an Episcopalian minister in Wisconsin; a liberal newspaper editor; a state-church clergyman; a former Danish official; a consul-general; a jurist and scholar; and the director of a Norwegian agricultural school. Some of these writers were themselves immigrants; some were travelers who later returned to Europe; and some were moved to write about the West

---

[1] *Stavanger Amtstidende og Adresseavis*, August 29, 1853.

though they had no first-hand knowledge of it. The books form a chapter in the history of Norwegian emigration; they played an important rôle in influencing people to emigrate — or to remain at home; they are in some cases historically interesting as narratives of personal experience and observation; they throw light upon social and economic conditions among the immigrant pioneers; and they give one glimpses of the building up of the Norwegian concept of America.

Peter Testman's " Brief Account of the Most Important Experiences during a Sojourn in North America . . . ," published in 1839, was the narrative of an immigrant who had met disillusion in the Shelby County settlement in Missouri. A Stavanger tinner, he emigrated in the spring of 1838; he arrived in the United States in a period of economic depression; he was guided to Missouri by Cleng Peerson and joined one of the least successful Norwegian colonies; and after a year's trial he gave up and returned, empty-handed, to his native land. If the Norwegian *bønder* needed an antidote after reading the encouraging reports by Rynning and Nattestad, Testman supplied it, with warnings of the perils of the journey, its heavy costs, the dangers of the climate, and the difficulties of pioneering. He found no streets paved with gold; he was soon convinced that the dreams of emigrants were too bright. His little book contains some vivid passages describing his travels: for example, the arrival at New York after an eight weeks' journey from Bremen, the washing of clothes before landing, the escape from the vessel as from a prison, the swarms of runners and agents at the wharves. " The crowd and the confusion were so great," he writes, " that we could scarcely make our way forward." Returning from Missouri in 1839 he visited the Illinois metropolis: " Though Chicago not more than five or six years ago consisted of only a few simple log houses, one can now see there more than four hundred respectable buildings on foundations, a fact which sufficiently indicates its rapid progress." [2]

The Haaeim pamphlet of 1842, brought out by Bishop Neumann, was, like Testman's, a tale of disillusionment by a Missouri colonist.   Yet the gloom was not wholly unrelieved: " As far as religion is concerned, I really must praise the American states, both as regards the Americans themselves and the immigrants from Europe."   Haaeim hastens to add, however, that " in the wilderness there are neither schools nor churches." [3]

An " Account of a Journey from Drammen in Norway to New York in North America " by a smith, Knud Knudsen, is a narrative in the form of two letters written by him and signed by various members of Ansten Nattestad's emigrant party of 1839, carrying the story — in defiance of the title — as far as the arrival at Detroit.   The pamphlet, published at Drammen in 1840, resembles Ole Nattestad's narrative in the naïve wonderment that it reveals. " Everything astonished us," wrote Knudsen of New York; " here was a numberless fleet of steamboats and ships; here are buildings which are constructed of hewn marble and elaborately built, most of them seven or eight stories high.   In my opinion it would take days and years to give an adequate account of this city; for in the short time we were there, it seemed incomprehensible to me and the others." [4]

[2] A facsimile of the original and an English translation are in the writer's edition of *Peter Testman's Account of His Experiences in North America* (Northfield, Minnesota, 1927).

[3] Malmin, " The Disillusionment of an Immigrant," in *Studies and Records,* 3: 1–12. See *ante,* p. 154.

[4] Knud Knudsen's *Beretning om en Reise fra Drammen til New York,* 19 (Norlie ed.).

Significant of the new interest in the West was the appearance in 1842 of a general Norwegian work entitled " America: An Historical-Political Account of America's Past and Present Condition," by Jørgen Hansen, which included within its scope not only the United States, but also Canada, Texas, and Central and South America. The author pictured the Yankee as energetic, ingenious, and practical, with a bent for trade and industry, his abilities given free play in a country not bound by the traditions and artificial restrictions common to the Old World. Liberty extended to all fields, including religion, a point much emphasized by the author, who finds in it a partial explanation of the religious zeal that he asserts characterized Americans. An attractive picture of the United States emerges from the pages of this informing volume.[5]

In 1843 two works from Swedish sources and one from English supplemented the number of " America books " already available for Norwegians. " Accounts of America, Especially Those States Where Emigrated Norwegians Have Settled " was turned into Norwegian from Swedish, but an analysis of it discloses the fact that it is derived primarily from Rynning's *True Account*. Thus Rynning, whose Socratic method made him an effective teacher, had apparently been a factor in forwarding Swedish interest in America and now he appears again, though in altered form, on the Norwegian scene.[6] Echoes of the Swedish

[5] [Jørgen Hansen], *Amerika. En historisk-politisk Skildring af Amerikas Fortid og nærværende Tilstand* (Christiania, 1842, 216 p.), originally published in *Skillings Magazin* for 1841. The author was a theologically trained publicist, who in 1844 became resident chaplain at Rollag, Numedal.

[6] *Underretninger om America, fornemmelig de Stater, hvori udvandrede Normænd have nedsat sig, samlede af en Emigrant-Forening i Stockholm, først udgiven paa Svensk af Foreningens Secretair og nu tildeels i Extract oversatte med nogle Rettelser og Tillæg* (Christiania, 1843). The book was advertised in *Tiden* (Drammen), January 26, 1843. The work appeared in *Skiensposten*; it is reprinted in *Lillehammers Tilskuer* for January 24, 27, 31, February 3, 17, 21, 1843; and it also appears in part in *Christianssandsposten*, January 12, 19, 1843.

colonization project sponsored by Gustaf Unonius were heard in Norway in 1843 when a pamphlet entitled "Letter from a Swedish Emigrant, Containing Useful Information about North American Conditions" was brought out. Written from "New Upsala" in Wisconsin on October 13, 1841, this letter gives the impressions of the founder of the Pine Lake colony a month after his arrival. He condemned those who passed judgment on all America after a hasty visit to a few places. Few understood the American people: "For that, in my opinion, one would need ten years, with constant traveling and contact with all classes of the people." To those interested in reading the conclusions of a competent observer he suggested De Tocqueville. The pamphlet was packed with solid advice and good sense.[7] It is interesting to note that Unonius sounded this warning against hasty judgment in the same year when Charles Dickens' famous *American Notes* were made available to Norwegians in translation.[8]

The testimony of Unonius was used by J. R. Reiersen when in 1844 he brought out his "Pathfinder for Norwegian Emigrants to the United North American States and Texas," for he included in the volume a letter by the Swedish minister attesting its accuracy. Reiersen's book was the most comprehensive Norwegian handbook about America published up to its time.[9] It contains chapters on natural conditions; agriculture; the general problem of establishing oneself on a farm; trade and industry; minerals and mining; the public lands; geographical conditions in Illinois, Missouri, Iowa, and Wisconsin; the

[7] G. Unonius, *Brev fra en svensk Emigrant, indeholdene gavnlige Oplysninger om de nordamericanske Forholde* (Christianssand, 1843. 12 p.).

[8] Dickens, *Amerikanske Antegnelser,* tr. by Albert Antenrieth and C. R. Unger (Christiania, 1843. 192 p.).

[9] *Veiviser for Norske Emigranter til De forenede nordamerikanske Stater og Texas* . . . (Christiania, 1844. 166 p.).

government of the states and their relation to the Union; the republic of Texas; and the Norwegian settlements in the West. For the prospective Norwegian emigrant the most interesting chapter was doubtless the last, in which, after describing conditions in the chief Norwegian settlements in the West, the author sums up his observations and gives advice.[10] On the whole his judgments appear to be well considered; unlike some writers of his time, he points out both the good and the bad sides of the situation. He writes:

All those who have been in America for a few years, with a few individual exceptions are in a contented and independent position. Anxiety and care with respect to daily bread and subsistence for their families burden them no longer. Their cultivated fields yield them a sufficiency of bread stuffs, their cows give them milk and butter in abundance, and their swine furnish them fully with meat. They do not suffer want. Taxes and rent encumber no one, and fear of distraints and seizures does not trouble their minds. Poor rates and begging are practically unknown, and even the children of deceased poor people are eagerly received by the Americans, who support them and give them instruction. But, all things considered, this is as much as one can say.

He then calls attention to the less satisfactory features of the situation:

The majority still live in their original log cabins, which, however, are always a good deal better than the mountain huts in which they lived in Norway. They have only a little money because of the indolence with which many carry on their farming; and the old manner of conducting their household affairs, to which they were accustomed in the old country, is continued. Insanitary conditions obtain in many cases. Lack of efficiency and enterprise — qualities upon which success in America altogether depends — and in general of information and education is among the primary causes which explain why our countrymen have not yet progressed further than they have.

More specifically, some of the reasons for the difficulties and hardships of the Norwegian immigrants, in Reiersen's

[10] Translated by the writer in *Studies and Records*, 1: 110–125.

opinion, are unusually heavy traveling expenses, sickness, unfamiliarity with American agricultural methods, and a " deficiency in mutual helpfulness, harmony, and unity." He states that " a family of five or six persons has often expended from three to four hundred specie dollars in traveling expenses alone, thereby losing the greater part of the capital which they intended to employ in beginning their business in America. Unable to purchase land, they have been forced to seek employment as laborers, in this way making a new start, and continuing until they have been able to save a sufficiently large sum of money to buy a small farm; this process has used up at least two years, however." Sickness is sometimes caused, he says, by unhealthful conditions in the

REDUCED FACSIMILE OF TITLE-PAGE OF REIERSEN'S " PATHFINDER FOR NORWEGIAN EMIGRANTS TO THE UNITED NORTH AMERICAN STATES AND TEXAS "

American settlement, but more often by insanitary conditions on board ships; lack of cleanliness; changes in climate and diet; tainted drinking water; living " in damp

or moist houses or cabins "; and failure to employ medicines at the right time.

Reiersen pays a tribute to the native Americans. " They
possess a powerful spirit of enterprise, which drives them
steadily on, with enthusiasm and persistence, to the
achievement of their goal," he writes. " They possess a
versatile — if often superficial — culture, with a knowledge of practical affairs and an extraordinary genius for
everything relating to public life." They are able to unite
in undertakings of common interest, he says, and when
a new settler arrives their first question " is not whether
he is rich or poor, but whether he is a man of activity, of
enterprising spirit, a man determined to succeed." The
American farmer, he writes, " fully understands that the
best possible progress for the settlement as a whole is the
best guarantee for the welfare of each individual settler.
It is from such a farming class that justices of the peace,
jurymen, representatives to the legislative assembly, and
other officers holding responsible and honorable positions
are chosen." He criticizes the Norwegians severely for
their deficiency in many of these qualities. The older Norwegian immigrants find it difficult to absorb the American
spirit, but " those who emigrate in their younger years
live in constant touch with the Americans, fully understand their language, acquire some of their characteristics, and fully enter into their conditions of life." He continues, " A new spirit is awakened in these immigrants, a
feeling of independence and freedom, a spirit of tolerance
in matters of religion, and an open mind for information,
together with that conviction of their worth as men and
citizens which is the cornerstone of the moral virtues."
Reiersen clearly understood that the spirit of American
frontier life would make a strong appeal to the Norwegian.
In conclusion he deals with the problems connected with

the voyage from Norway to the pioneer settlements in the new states of the West. His advocacy of the New Orleans route apparently won few converts, for the Norwegian immigrants continued to come mainly by way of New York.

Reiersen's book was widely read in Norway and exerted much influence upon emigration. It contained a mass of information, far more detailed, though less compact, than that in Rynning's book. It was based in part upon first-hand knowledge of actual conditions in America. Unlike the average " America letter " and some of the little books by immigrants, it represented contact with practically all the Norwegian settlements as well as careful study of American conditions generally. The author, moreover, had studied various American writings: in his preface he mentions Lewis and Clark, Schoolcraft, Flint, Long, Peck, Lea, Delafield, and James Hall as writers with whose works he is familiar. On the whole his book ranks among the more substantial contributions to the advertising of America among Norwegians in the period before the Civil War.

An example of the specific influence of Reiersen's book has been given by a contemporary, Nils Hansen Fjeld of South Aurdal, Valders, who came to America in 1847, among the earliest emigrants from that district. He describes the economic conditions which caused him to listen with great interest to reports about America. The " America fever " was only beginning to make itself felt. Contradictory reports were in circulation, some of them exceedingly " rosy-hued," and others very dark, — he speaks of reports about poisonous snakes, dangerous wild animals, and more dangerous " wild men," — until finally there came to the district two copies of Reiersen's book. People now began to say, " We now have the printed word to rely upon," and many of the doubters were won over to

the " orthodox faith " in the promised land beyond the sea.
" This book, which came from America, caused many to
forsake their homes and the land of their fathers in order to
participate in the good things of the New World." [11]   As
has been noted in another connection, Reiersen continued
his public agitation in the monthly paper " Norway and
America," the two volumes of which, brought out in from
1845 to 1847, may be regarded as supplements to the
book.[12]

The next " America book " of importance came from
the hand of the Reverend J. W. C. Dietrichson, a divine
of the Norwegian Lutheran State Church, and has its
setting in a significant religious development among the
immigrant pioneers. A Lutheran church historian des-
ignates the period from 1836 to 1843 as one of unor-
ganized lay activity in the Norwegian settlements in the
West.[13] Though, as has been noted in a foregoing chapter,
an emigrant party as early as 1839 attempted to secure
the services of an ordained minister of the state church,
nothing came of the project in view of the unorthodoxy
of the settlers in the Fox River Valley and the scattering
of those who might be favorable to such a minister, though
the state church itself, after sundry heart-burnings,
sanctioned the proposed step.[14] Meanwhile lay preachers,
for the most part carrying with them deep-rooted antagonism to the established church of their native land, met
the first religious needs of the settlers. Prior to the ad-
vent of Elling Eielsen in 1839, the ablest and most zealous of the Haugean-inspired lay preachers in the West,
such men as Ole Olson Hetletvedt, Bjørn Hatlestad, Jørgen

---

[11] Billed-Magazin, 2: 237. For Reiersen's comments on the various Norwegian
settlements see ante, ch. 8.

[12] See ante, p. 183.

[13] Rohne, Norwegian American Lutheranism up to 1872, ch. 2, 3.

[14] See ante, p. 121–122.

Pedersen, Ole Heier, and Hans Balder, were active and prominent. The number of such laymen-leaders and their great zeal testify to the power of the Haugean ferment and the fervency of religious feeling among the pioneers.

It is not to be wondered at that there soon arose a state of affairs that Lutheran writers have described as chaos and confusion. The elements in the pioneer settlements were heterogeneous, including some Quakers, different shades of Haugeans, and some who were not unfriendly to the state church. Once in the United States the dissenting groups could not thrive on opposition to the established church; the air of religious toleration was like a heady wine to many; and in the West, which has cradled and nourished so many types of religious behavior, the pioneers naturally came in contact with sundry sects. The Illinois colony was in the vicinity of the Mormon capital, Nauvoo, and it was not long before there were Norwegian converts to the Mormon teachings, including such lay leaders as Pedersen and Heier, whose affiliations were later to result in intensive Mormon missionary work in Norway. Balder went over to the Baptists; while in Wisconsin some of those who joined the Pine Lake colony followed its able Episcopal leader, Unonius. Eielsen became an effective religious leader in the Fox River colony, where, according to Lutheran historians, the brand of Haugeanism was more intense than that in colonies where the Stavanger element was less pronounced. In the Muskego settlement such Haugean laymen as Heg, Bache, and Johannesen, with Heg's barn as a temple, furnished Haugean leadership to the pioneers. " On the whole," writes Dr. Rohne, " it must be said that by the middle of 1843 there was a conscious or unconscious desire for services by a regularly ordained clergy. The lay preachers had performed a most useful labor of love and mercy, but the increasing population and the bitter experiences of pioneer life demanded more systematic and thorough spiritual work."[15] There is no doubt that many immigrants looked across the sea for religious leadership; it is a coincidence that there was a contemporaneous stir of religious interest in Norway with reference to the immigrants, coming to a head in 1843, the year marking the first considerable rise in emigration. The transition to pastoral leadership is signalized by the arrival at Muskego in the summer of that year of C. L. Clausen, a young Dane. He had gone to Norway hoping to join a Norwegian missionary to Africa, Norway having witnessed from 1826 the rise of missionary interest culminating in the organization of the Norwegian Mission Society in 1842. In Drammen Clausen met the well-known Haugean, Tollef Bache, who suggested that he go to the United States instead of to Africa, for in the Muskego settlement there was a demand for a schoolteacher. Clausen decided to accept this proposal, but at Muskego the settlers persuaded him to become their minister rather than their teacher. A call was issued to him in September, 1843, and in the following month he was duly ordained. Shortly before Clausen's ordination, Eielsen, too, was ordained.

About the same time a young Norwegian theological candidate, J. W. C. Dietrichson of Stavanger, applied to the Norwegian church department for ordination in order to carry on religious work among the Norwegian immigrants; his request was granted by royal resolution on October 12, 1843; in February, 1844, he was ordained; and in May he left for the United States. In the month when Dietrichson was ordained, settlers at Rock Prairie, Jefferson Prairie, Rock Run, and Hamilton dispatched a joint letter to a Norwegian bishop asking that a minister

15 Rohne, op. cit., 55.

be sent out.[16] Dietrichson, an aristocratic, imperious, high-church divine, of a military family, had also been inspired by the missionary movement, and was influenced to go to America by a dyer who offered to pay the expenses of the journey. His central object was to bring religious order out of disorder, to form congregations on the basis of the state-church ritual, in short to organize Norwegian-American Lutheranism. After his arrival he visited the various settlements; [17] made Koshkonong his headquarters; reproved those who, like Unonius, had led Norwegians away from the Lutheran fold; became involved in sharp controversy with Eielsen, the validity of whose ordination he denounced; and proceeded to organize congregations on the principle of insuring " to those who valued the Church of Norway, its ritual and history, an unbroken continuity of this Church upon American soil." [18] He carried through his program with an almost military precision before he departed for Norway in the spring of 1845; and while engaged in all this work he found time to write a series of letters, given wide publicity in Norway, denouncing the entire emigration movement with almost fanatical fervor.[19] Before his return to Norway,

[16] Malmin, " Litt norsk-amerikansk kirkehistorie fra de norske arkiver," in *Lutheraneren*, 8: 76 (January 16, 1924). It is of interest to note that another theological candidate, Lagaard by name, requested permission in 1844 to be ordained for ministerial work in America. He had been unable to find a position as a minister in Norway and had been forced to teach for a living. He was in effect a prospective emigrant, who hoped for a better future in the United States. The church department refused his request on the ground that he had received no call from America.

[17] Dietrichson was a gifted writer and a long series of letters by him appeared in Norwegian newspapers beginning with one written at Muskego on September 25, 1844, telling of his arrival and preliminary visits to the pioneer settlements. *Morgenbladet*, December 8, 9, 1844.

[18] Rohne, *op. cit.*, 69–70.

[19] See especially his letter of December 28, 1844, in *Stavanger Amtstidende og Adresseavis*, March 30, April 3, 7, 10, 1845, a passage from which is quoted *ante*, p. 155–156.

Dietrichson had been called as pastor to Koshkonong. In Norway he appealed to young theologians to go to America as missionaries;[20] published a book telling of his travels; and took up with the church department the problem of getting subsidies and traveling expenses for himself and perhaps three other ministers. He suggested two hundred specie dollars for expenses and a yearly stipend (for five years) of one hundred and fifty to two hundred dollars. The church department took up the matter with the finance department, and when the latter refused the request for expenses on the ground that the immigrants were no longer Norwegian citizens, the church department argued that since many immigrants would doubtless eventually return, the Norwegian state ought not to be indifferent to their welfare. Furthermore, it suggested, Dietrichson would familiarize himself with conditions in the West and could perform a useful service by setting them forth " in the right light " through letters and reports, thus counteracting " the disturbing and frivolous emigration desire."

The upshot of the matter was that Dietrichson petitioned for and received a grant of two hundred dollars for traveling expenses on condition that he should transmit such reports. The department must have known that Dietrichson already, on numerous occasions, had published violent denunciations of emigration and pictured pioneer conditions in the darkest colors; hence it was probably in no doubt that the " right light " would be unfavorable. In connection with his journey of 1844 Dietrichson had in fact been accused by the staunchly pro-American Reiersen of having been bought by the government to denounce emigration, a charge which he scornfully denied in his

[20] The appeal is published in *Morgenbladet,* August 16, 1845.

published book.[21]   In 1846 the zealous minister accepted, on the stipulated condition, the grant of two hundred dollars.   In supplying the desired reports Dietrichson was without doubt honest and conscientious.   He was appalled by the sickness and the evidences of misery which he had found among the immigrants.   He believed emigration to be a calamity, and on this issue, as indeed on all others, he did not hesitate to voice his convictions, notwithstanding difference of opinion and opposition.[22]   He returned to the United States in 1846 and remained there until 1850, a storm center of theological controversy.   In 1848 the Reverend Hans A. Stub joined him and in succeeding years many other able young theologians, trained at the University of Christiania, responded to calls from immigrant congregations, laid the foundations of Norwegian Lutheran church institutions, continued and expanded the tradition of theological controversy inaugurated by the militant Dietrichson, and, it must be added, served their far-flung frontier congregations with ability, courage, devotion, and sympathy.[23]

[21] Dietrichson, *Reise blandt de norske Emigranter i " De forenede nordamerikanske Fristater,"* 4 (Stavanger, 1846. 128 p.).   The book was reprinted by R. B. Anderson at Madison, Wisconsin, in 1896.

[22] The documents relating to Dietrichson's request for financial assistance from the government are in Riksarkivet, Oslo, Kirkedept., Journalsaker, July–August, 1846, res. 1556, and are discussed by Malmin, in *Lutheraneren,* 8: 76–77 (January 16, 1924).   In Dietrichson's fourteen-page letter of April 3, 1846, to the chief of the church department arguing for traveling expenses and subsidies, he declares that such aid would discourage, not encourage, emigration, for it would expose the need of the settlers.   Malmin, p. 77, n., suggests that the church department saw in Dietrichson a good agency for working against emigration.

[23] Dr. Rohne, professor of Christianity at Luther College, traces the theological development in his *Norwegian American Lutheranism up to 1872. Cf.* a review of this work by Dr. George M. Stephenson, in *Studies and Records,* 2: 104–109.   A much needed work, to supplement Dr. Rohne's study, is an objective analysis of the social and religious activities of the pioneer pastors in their direct relations with their congregations, where the theological controversies seem on the whole to have

The primary interest of Dietrichson's "Travels among the Norwegian Immigrants in the United North American Free States," published at Stavanger early in 1846, lies in the contrast that it shows between the orthodox high-church view and that of the Haugean school, its full report of the author's work as a church organizer, and its descriptions of the various settlements. Dietrichson was horrified to find that nearly one hundred and fifty Norwegians had become Mormons, and of these some had already obtained high ecclesiastical positions. At Fox River he took occasion, in the presence of the Mormons, to deliver a slashing attack on their teachings, and in his book he writes an interesting account of the sect and his own collision with it. Dietrichson recorded faithfully what he saw, heard, and believed, and his account, written in the stately ministerial style of his age, though dogmatic, is informing. His descriptions of the voyage, New York City, the journey to the interior, Muskego, Koshkonong, and Fox River are especially interesting. On the economic situation, which he discussed at length in his published letters,[24] he has little to say in his book, though he does not fail to make it clear

been subordinated. An engaging picture of this side of the frontier minister's activity is furnished, for example, in the manuscript letters of the Reverend Olaus Duus from 1855 to 1858, written from Waupaca, Wisconsin, to relatives in Norway. The originals are in the Historiografisk Samling, Oslo, and transcripts are in the archives of the Norwegian-American Historical Association at St. Olaf College, Northfield. Another source of the greatest interest in this connection is *Fra Pioneertiden: Uddrag af Fru Elisabeth Korens Dagbog og Breve fra Femtiaarene* (Decorah, Iowa, 1914), which contains the contemporary reflections from the fifties of a gracious and cultivated woman who cheerfully shared the hardships and privations endured by her husband, the Reverend Vilhelm Koren, pioneer preacher in Iowa.

[24] See *ante*, notes 17, 19. A letter of May 10, 1845, is in *Stavanger Amtstidende og Adresseavis*, July 21, 24, 1845. Important letters from the later period are those of October 15, 1846, in *Bergens Stiftstidende*, December 17, 1846; of January 29, 1847, in *Stavanger Amtstidende og Adresseavis*, April 10, 1847; of April 9, 1848, in *ibid.*, June 23, 1848; and of June 7 and August 23, 1847, in *Nordlyset* (Trondhjem), September 6, 13, 17, and November 19, 1847.

that he regarded emigration as a snare and a delusion.[25] It is not unlikely that the letters, which were given much prominence in Norwegian newspapers, had greater influence upon prospective emigrants than the published volume. In 1851, after his final return, he brought out a second book, entitled "Some Words from the Pulpit in America and in Norway," including three sermons preached to immigrant congregations.[26]

While more serious books were thus appearing, Norwegian compilers were not willing to let the *bønder* go unassisted in their struggles with the intricacies of the speech which they would be compelled to use as immigrants in the United States. Thus a "Guide to Self Instruction in the English Language" was published at Bergen in 1846, with suggestions for making profitable use of the time during the sea voyage. The foundations of a Norwegian-American version of English were well laid. Should the immigrant, for example, desire to say, "In general the Americans deserve to be called models of a religious people," he had only to follow phonetic directions: "In dsjenneræl te æmerikæns diserv tu bii kaaeld moodels ov æ rilidsjøs piip'l." If worst came to worst and he fell a victim to sickness in the malaria-infested settlements, he need not be at a loss to describe his symptoms. Should he have occasion to say, "I am not well at all. My head is giddy, and I can hardly stand on my legs," he had but to recite: "Ai æmm naat uell ætt aael. Mei hedd is giidi, ænd ai kænn hærdli stænd onn mei leggs."[27] The Norwegian had

---

[25] Dietrichson, *Reise*, 112–113.

[26] *Nogle Ord fra Prædikestolen i Amerika og Norge* (Stavanger, 1851. 86 p.).

[27] C. Rudolph, *Ledetraad til Selv-Underviisning i det engelske Sprog. Emigrantens Tidsfordriv paa Amerika-Reisen* . . . (Bergen, 1846. 72 p.). This manual was a translation from the German. Numerous other handbooks of this type were soon made available, for example, F. W. Günther, *The Little American: Den lille Amerikaner* . . . (2d ed., Christiania, 1851. 80 p.).

his troubles, but he soon learned that there were numerous other immigrants who found English a difficult problem. " My word! " exclaimed a Norwegian in Chicago after hearing French, Italian, and Scandinavian assaults on the language. " How the English language is mutilated here! " [28]

" All should go to Wisconsin," advised Laurits J. Fribert in a comprehensive volume entitled " Handbook for Emigrants to the American West," published at Christiania in 1847. Iowa, he declared, was too far away, lacked woods, and was unhealthful; and in Illinois religious conditions were disturbed, there were heavy state debts, and besides, many people were moving west from that state. Snakes, alligators, crocodiles, fevers, and negro slavery constituted the main indictment against Texas. A few of the forty-five chapters of the book were devoted to a refutation of certain " Untrue Rumors about Wisconsin." These, briefly, were that the immigrant in that favored region was exposed to much danger from Indians, poisonous snakes, and epidemics; that the territory had no law or courts; and that it lacked religion, churches, and ministers. The manual helps one to understand why many Norwegians selected woodland rather than prairie land, for Fribert advised all poor immigrants, if they could not find combinations of the two, to choose forest land. The book touched on nearly every side of the emigrant's problem, giving special attention to agricultural methods in the West. One of the collateral effects of emigration was the knowledge that Norwegian farmers obtained about American farming methods, and such books as Fribert's probably played their part in this process of education. Fribert was an educated Dane, a former official, who lived in the Pine

[28] B. J. Hovde, "Chicago as Viewed by a Norwegian Immigrant in 1864," in *Studies and Records*, 3: 67.

Lake settlement and had had several years of practical experience as a farmer.[29]

On October 15, 1847, the Norwegian-Swedish consul-general, Adam Løvenskjold, reported to the Norwegian government on a visit that he had made to the Norwegian settlements the preceding summer.[30] Thus the request made in the Odelsthing in 1845 was answered: the Norwegians received an " official " account of the situation of the immigrant pioneers. It was printed at Bergen in 1848 and it also appeared in various newspapers.[31] Løvenskjold opens with a summary of the names, locations, and conditions of the chief Norwegian settlements.[32] His more general conclusions were pessimistic, and many immigrants maintained that his object was not to give an impartial report, but to check emigration from Norway. The publication of his account was in part responsible for the organization in Chicago of the Vossing Correspondence Society, which attempted to refute his views.[33] The consul-general believed that his countrymen were much influenced by temporary conditions and that they therefore passed quickly from one extreme to another in their judgments: " In regard to the prevailing sentiment among

[29] *Haandbog for Emigranter til Amerikas Vest, med Anvisning for Overrejsen samt Beskrivelse af Livet og Agerdyrkningsmaaden, nærmest i Viskonsin* (Christiania, 1847. 96 p.). Chapters are devoted to the religious work of Clausen and Unonius and the need of additional ministers in the Scandinavian settlements. Another Danish account of 1847, published in Denmark, was Rasmus Sørensen, *Om de udvandrede Nordmænd i Nordamerika.*

[30] The manuscript report is in R. A., Oslo: Indredept., Journalsager, 1847/2395.

[31] *Beretning om de norske Setlere i Nordamerika, efter den norske Generalkonsuls, Adam Løvenskjolds, til Departementet under 15 October 1847 indgivne Beretning, om hans i afvigte Sommer i de nordamerikanske Fristaters vestlige Provindser, i de norske Setlementer aflagte Besøg* (Bergen, 1848. 16 p.). The report appears in *Morgenbladet,* November 22, 1847. It is translated by Knut Gjerset in the *Wisconsin Magazine of History,* 8: 77–88 (September, 1924).

[32] This material is discussed *ante,* ch. 8.

[33] See *ante,* p. 211.

the people I have found it to differ much, depending upon their economic well-being or the condition of their health. Any misfortune with regard to either of these makes them complain and wish that they were again in Norway; on the other hand, any little success will make them praise their new country very highly." The author stresses the difficulties of the immigrants. "Some are quite well-to-do," he writes, "others are very poor." The poverty is due to "lack of systematic effort or to sickness." He speaks particularly of the ravages of the ague in the preceding year among Wisconsin settlers. Another enemy is intemperance; and yet another trouble is the fact that "everything is so different from that to which they [*the immigrants*] were accustomed: language, climate, tools, and implements, even the way in which the work is done." Of course the younger people adapt themselves more

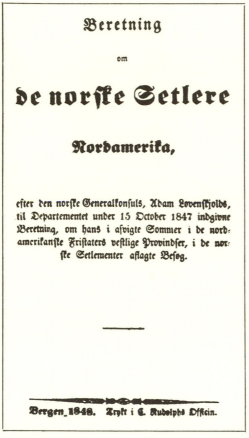

REDUCED FACSIMILE OF THE TITLE-PAGE OF LØV-ENSKJOLD'S "REPORT ON THE NORWEGIAN SETTLERS IN NORTH AMERICA"

quickly than the older. Laborers in the towns are ordinarily well satisfied, for they receive good wages, yet they have to spend much for their living. Tradesmen have an advantage, but " even if they know a trade quite well, they will have to learn it over again, when they come here."

Løvenskjold reports that many settlers — " older and respectable persons " — told him privately " that if they had known that they would have to endure all the hardships which they have suffered in America, they would never have left their native land, that many a time during the first years here they wished that they could have returned to Norway, that they cursed the persons who through glowing accounts led them to come here." He adds that, although they would now like to return, they are unable to do so, and stay on in the hope that their children will know better days. " For their own part they felt that they had gained nothing by exchanging Norway for America."

The Norwegians have not taken part in politics, the author explains, and because of their " general ignorance " they are termed " Norwegian Indians " by the natives. Land can be purchased at small cost, but " the difficulty lies in cultivating and fencing the new land." He offers the opinion that " those who come here with means are the least successful, and that in a few years they lose everything, as they do not know how to use their means in the right way." On the whole he presents a sorry picture of the Norwegians as farmers, stating that they have profited but little from their crops. " It struck me," he writes, " that many of the settlers had brought with them their native and habitual squalor, though this can be said chiefly of the settlers from the mountain districts of Norway." Finally the author dismisses the entire gloomy subject with the following conclusion:

From what has been stated it will be seen that the condition of the
Norwegians in America in general is not so bad as many describe it,
but it is far from being as good as others would have us believe.
Some complain already that liberty here is not as great as they had
expected, either in one respect or another. Some who dwell in settlements which are quite well populated are saying that they intend to
move farther into the country, as their cattle are hampered by the
fences of their neighbors.[34]

With Løvenskjold on his travels in the West went a
gifted young jurist and scholar, Ole Munch Ræder, who
was engaged in an intensive study of the jury system, with
a governmental stipend. His investigations of that institution in England, the United States, and Canada were later
embodied in an important three-volume work that helped
to make Norwegians familiar with a system that ultimately — though not until the eighties — was to be embodied in Norwegian law.[35] While traveling about in the
United States Munch Ræder also wrote a series of spirited
letters which were published in various Norwegian newspapers and which comprise one of the keenest and most
comprehensive American travel accounts ever made available to Norwegian readers. They are of special value for
their portrayal of conditions on the American frontier in
the late forties, especially in Wisconsin and among the
Norwegian pioneers; on the whole they present a far more
detailed and perhaps more reliable report than that of
the consul-general. But Munch Ræder's interest was
broader than a section or group; his travels took him not
only to the Middle West, but to Washington, New York,
Philadelphia, New England, Montreal, and other places;
and his commentary reaches out constantly from local to
regional and national considerations. He admired Ameri-

[34] These quotations are taken from Dr. Gjerset's translation, cited in note 31.

[35] Munch Ræder, *Jury-Institutionen i Storbritanien, Canada og de forenede
Stater af Amerika: Indberetning i Anledning af en efter offentlig Foranstaltning
foretagen Reise* (Christiania, 1850–52. 696, 828, 432 p.).

can democracy, was a competent observer of social customs, and recorded his experiences skillfully and shrewd-
ly.[36]

Characteristic of the trend of public opinion in Norway was the appearance at the mid-century of an anti-
emigration book by the director of an agricultural school.
Jan Ádolph Budde, the author of " From a Letter about
America," was the head of the agricultural school of
Stavanger *Amt*, which had been established in 1844.[37] He
was a trained student, primarily interested in modernizing agricultural methods in Norway; emigration to him
seemed folly; and he painted a dark and dismal picture of
the American scene.

Budde presents estimates of the cost of farming in the
vicinity of Milwaukee and comes to the conclusion that
there is " absolutely no advantage in owning land far in
the West." In the eastern states the situation is somewhat
better, he believes, for there the prices paid for corn and
other products are higher. Land is more expensive in some
eastern sections, however, than it is in Norway. The author asserts that in some years corn and other products
have brought such low prices that American farmers have

[36] The Munch Ræder letters, as published in *Den Norske Rigstidende* in 1847
and 1848, supplemented by manuscript letters in the possession of Dr. Ulrik A.
Ræder of Asker, Norway, have been translated by Mr. Malmin and published under
the title *America in the Forties: The Letters of Ole Munch Ræder* as volume 3 in
the *Travel and Description Series* of the Norwegian-American Historical Association (Minneapolis, 1929). Some of the letters appeared also in *Stavanger Amtstidende og Adresseavis* from August 4 to September 8, 1848, and in *Drammens
Adresse* from November 16 to December 30, 1847. Munch Ræder's itinerary is
reported in *Den Norske Rigstidende* for September 18, 1850. He left Norway in
the fall of 1846, went to the United States from England in the spring of 1847,
and remained until the fall of 1848.

[37] [J.] A. Budde, *Af et Brev om Amerika* (Stavanger, 1850. 16 p.). The
pamphlet has been translated into English by A. Sophie Bøe and published, with an
introduction by the present writer, under the title " Emigration as Viewed by a
Norwegian Student of Agriculture in 1850," in *Studies and Records*, 3: 43–57.

preferred to let the crops rot in the fields rather than
harvest them, and incidentally he declares that the de-
composing crops have poisoned the air and caused diseases!
He then produces figures intended to show that land
ownership is more remunerative in Norway than in
America. Those who work for daily wages in America
are better off than their fellows in Norway, he says,
but he adds that much depends upon their success in
warding off disease and their ability to compete with the
native Americans. He states that unbiased observers believe
that a person in America must do several times the amount
of work per day that is customary in Norway. In fact,
some people kill themselves with work! And if sickness
attacks the worker, the game is up. " Rynning, who had
helped many people," he writes inaccurately, " died help-
less not far from his house door, which he was unable to
reach." Sickness attacks a great many of the Norwegian
immigrants, and it is well known, he says, that most of
those who emigrated the previous spring are dead. Contrast this with the situation in Norway, where the average
life is longer than anywhere else in the world. Surely, if
people live longer in Norway than in any other country,
it must be " good to live in Norway." True, it may seem
crowded for many people, but there is still sufficient room
on the Norwegian farming lands. The author then paints a
gloomy picture of life in an American log cabin, with all
its discomforts, and tells of a returned immigrant who
was accustomed, in his western cabin, to waken on wintry
mornings with a sheet of snow covering his bed!

What, then *are* the advantages in America, if they do
not include money, health, or convenience? Well, for one
thing, people in that country eat wheat bread! But rye
bread, Budde gravely assures his readers, is very good. There
is plenty of meat to eat in America. But what of fish, asks
Budde. Maple sugar is available in America — but as a

matter of fact beet sugar is the kind ordinarily used. The emigrant says that he goes for the sake of his children, that he gives them broad acres in the West in place of cramped spots in Norway. Budde answers that if the Norwegian is not yet actually suffering from crowded conditions he had better let his children, in their day, decide for themselves about emigration. The American soil is just as subject to exhaustion as the Norwegian. The author, to support his contention, tells about the experiences of a returned emigrant, and he quotes an opinion concerning the exhaustion of soil in Virginia, Maryland, and North Carolina. The immigrant in America must change his farming methods completely. Why not change methods in Norway? Norwegian stones are not harder to clear away than American roots, according to Budde.

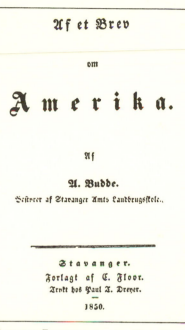

REDUCED FACSIMILE OF THE TITLE-PAGE OF BUDDE'S "FROM A LETTER ABOUT AMERICA"

Of course there are some places in Norway that are overpopulated but in many instances if the farms were properly developed they could support many additional persons. And in some cases distressing conditions in Norway may be caused simply by laziness or foolish farming methods.

Why is America praised so much, asks Budde. He discusses seven reasons. (1) Many immigrants have won success through industry and persistence, but these virtues would be equally rewarded in Norway. (2) Many people praise America because, having gone there, they are too proud to admit that they were mistaken. (3) Many are homesick and long for their relatives; therefore, in order to heal their own wounds, they induce their relatives to come and join them. (4) Many people are by nature discontented; they must move away from that to which they are accustomed, hoping vainly for greater happiness, and forgetting the words of Horace: *Qui trans mare vehunt, coelum, non animum mutant.* Budde's point is that the basic conditions of human disappointment and sorrow lie in the mind, and not in external circumstances. (5) There is external unrest in America; people are always moving. An immigrant is quoted: " I have sold my first farm and bought another farther west." These changes stimulate speculation — a fever which seizes the immigrant himself, even though, from the moment he lands, he is victimized by speculators; not even when he buries himself in the western wilderness does he escape from their clutches. (6) The Americans like to praise themselves at the expense of the Old World. They are able people, Budde admits, but they are addicted to exaggeration and the habit is quickly learned by the immigrants. One wrote home that he owned nine pigs, whereas actually he had one sow which was expected to bring forth eight pigs! Actually many emigrants come home empty-handed. Why, asks the author, are Norwegians at home asked to raise money to send ministers to the immigrants and to help them to build schools and churches? Surely these " rich, boasting people " are able to take care of themselves. Incidentally Budde reminds his readers that the native Americans sometimes call the Norwegians Indians! (7) Those who have something to gain from emigration naturally stimulate it. Budde states that some ships' officers have traveled into the country and deceived the peasants with "rain bow-colored pictures of America." In the author's opinion, the people best suited for emigration are young men who are skilled workers, but even men of this type have returned from America disillusioned.

America offers the emigrant, according to Budde, more meat to eat, a larger area of land to cultivate, more exertion, less comfort, and a shorter life. Emigration necessitates giving up one's traditions, language, and birthplace. The author hopes that if he cannot restrain the Norwegian from emigrating, he will at least make him less extravagant in his hopes and therefore less liable to disappointment. He closes by calling attention to "America's great scandal" — slavery.

The book by Budde is a gloomy and pessimistic study based in part upon misinformation; and the author's obvious bias leads him into some naïve claims. Yet he was doubtless right when he asserted that changes in agricultural methods, had they been made by the *bønder* in Norway, would have brought them good returns. It is interesting to observe that by the mid-century, emigration was thus provoking public discussion of Norwegian agricultural reform. In other writings Budde urged farmers to use up-to-date machinery on their farms, to employ fertilizers for their soil, and to modernize their methods in general.[38]

By 1850 the advertising of America in Norway, forwarded by books, newspaper discussion,[39] letters, and other means, was far advanced. In the main this interesting development grew out of an emigration movement that was

[38] Halvorsen, *Norsk Forfatter-Lexikon 1814–1880*, 1: 507–508.

[39] Of numerous newspaper accounts of American conditions, mention may be made of "Kort Oversigt over de nordamerikanske forenede Stater," in *Bratsberg-Amts Correspondent*, March 11, 1844; "En skotsk Haandværkers Reiser i de nord-

still in its infancy. That it had widely ramifying social and intellectual consequences is certain. For the common people of Norway, as of all Scandinavia, emigration lifted the curtain on the United States, until then little more than a name to them. Now they began to take an intelligent interest in the strange and stirring drama of life that was being enacted on the broad stage of the New World. The reports that came to them were frequently contradictory, but the multiplication of sources of information tended toward the gradual correction of misrepresentation, whether on the one side or on the other.

amerikanske Fristater i Aarene 1840–42," in *Stavanger Amtstidende og Adresseavis,* October 5 to November 10, 1849; and "De norske Colonier i Wisconsin," *ibid.,* January 26, 1850. An interesting account of the settlements at Muskego, Koshkonong, and Pine Lake, was published in the forties by A. Van der Straten Ponthoz, a secretary of the Belgian legation at Washington, in a book entitled *Onderzoek naar den Toestand der Landverhuizers in de Vereenigde Staten van Noord-Amerika,* 101–108 (Utrecht, 1847). Norwegian translations of this account, perhaps derived from an earlier edition of the book or from a newspaper source, appeared in *Bergens Stiftstidende,* December 31, 1846, and in *Nordlyset* (Trondhjem), January 4, 1847.

XII. EMIGRANT GOLD-SEEKERS

UNREST and transition characterized Norway about the middle of the nineteenth century. New forces in the country's economic and social life were stirring; echoes of revolutionary change on the continent were sounding in the North; and labor was responding to a preliminary effort at organization. Emigration from western Europe was approaching its highest peak before the American Civil War; and Norwegian popular interest in the West was mounting. " In no year have we seen the newspapers so full of reports about emigrants," commented an observer in 1849.[1] Norwegian emigration leaped from fourteen hundred in 1848 to four thousand in 1849; the highest total reached in any previous year was sixteen hundred. The direct emigrant traffic with New York in 1849 required a fleet of not less than twenty-four sailing vessels.[2] A typical emigrant load was that carried by " Harmonien," which sailed from Stavanger in May with 114 passengers, all from Skaanevigs parish, Hardanger, their destination Illinois and Wisconsin, where many of them had relatives. They comprised nineteen families, three of ten persons each, and the party as a whole had a capital of four thousand specie dollars.[3] In eastern Norway there was likewise a stir of interest in emigration. " From Gausdal parish alone," noted a newspaper, " a hun-

---

[1] *Christiania-Posten*, June 9, 1849.

[2] Probably there were more, but not less than two dozen are mentioned in advertisements and news notes in *Correspondenten* (Skien) and *Stavanger Amtstidende og Adresseavis* for 1849. See the former, February 1, 8, 11, 22, April 1, May 2, 26, June 2, 13, 16, 23. For Norwegian emigration statistics see *Utvandringsstatistikk*, 100 ff. (Norges Offisielle Statistikk. VII. 25 — Kristiania, 1921).

[3] *Stavanger Amtstidende og Adresseavis*, May 16, 1849.

dred persons are said to have engaged ship passage to
America for the spring, and some in Biri, Land, Ringsager,
Faaberg, and several other communities are planning to
go, so that it is estimated that several hundreds of emigrants will go from the best districts in the Eastland." [4]

The reports that came from America in 1849 and 1850
were not altogether propitious, for the dread cholera was
ravaging the Middle West, and the Norwegian settlements
at Fox River, Muskego, Koshkonong, and elsewhere were
attacked with full force.[5] Meanwhile, however, the echoes
of that rush of " forty-niners " which in one year transformed California from a quiet settlement of some six
thousand people to a surging mining frontier of eighty-
five thousand were resounding in the valleys and towns
of Norway. West and East, the world over, the magic of
gold was quickening human pulses, enticing people from
home and friends, nerving them for life in frontier camps.

In the fall of 1848 announcements of the California
gold discovery began to appear in Norway;[6] early in 1849
the press contained more comprehensive accounts of the
mining country.[7] In the spring a book about California
and its riches was brought out at Christiania, a compilation
drawn from various English and American reports.[8] The
compiler apparently did not anticipate an exodus of Nor-

[4] Correspondenten (Skien), March 29, 1849.

[5] Knut Gjerset and Ludvig Hektoen, "Health Conditions and the Practice of
Medicine among the Early Norwegian Settlers, 1825–1865," in Studies and Records,
1: 14–17.

[6] E. g., Correspondenten (Skien), October 26, 1848.

[7] " Guldregionerne i Californien," in Morgenbladet, January 16, 1849; " California og dets Guld," in Correspondenten (Skien), February 15 and 25, 1849;
" California og dets Guld " and " Guldgraverne i Californien," in Stavanger Amtstidende og Adresseavis, February 6, 28, 1849; " Guldlandet California," in Bergens
Stiftstidende, March 4, 1849; " Kalifornien," in Christiania-Posten, March 8, 1849.

[8] Beretning om Californien og dets Guldrigdom. Med et Kart over California
(Christiana, 1849. 124 p.). The book is announced in Christiania-Posten for
May 7, 1849.

wegian gold-hunters, but he had an eye for advantageous trade results. The flood of new gold, he believed, would stimulate world trade; American railroad building would develop the market for Norwegian iron, already in part exploited. Direct Norwegian traffic with New York would increase. A Panama canal would make the American west coast an accessible market for products from Canada and Labrador and relieve Norway from the competition that it was feeling from these quarters in European markets.[9]

California was soon dramatized for Norwegians. On April 26, 1849, the emigrant schooner "Ebenezer" sailed from Stavanger for New York with seventy-five emigrants;[10] when it returned late in the summer it brought back a Norwegian whose story excited widespread interest among the common people. He was Christian Poulsen, a

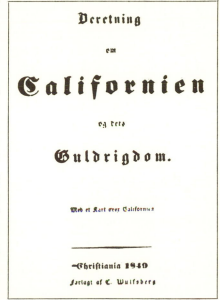

Beretning

om

Californien

og dets

Guldrigdom.

Med et Kart over Californien

Christiania 1849
Forlagt af C. Wulfsberg

REDUCED FACSIMILE OF THE TITLE-PAGE OF A BOOK ON CALIFORNIA PUBLISHED AT CHRISTIANIA IN 1849

shipbuilder of Arendal, who had emigrated in 1841 and had gone to San Francisco while it was still in Mexican hands. He was there when the first reports of gold arrived in the spring of 1848; one month later he was at the diggings. After five months of successful mining he decided to return home with his fortune. Taking hire as a seaman in

[9] *Beretning om Californien og dets Guldrigdom,* 120–124.
[10] *Stavanger Amtstidende og Adresseavis,* April 27, 1849.

November, he sailed from San Francisco around Cape
Horn to New York. The rumor that he had brought with
him to Norway a chest full of money was spread far and
wide. One newspaper felt called upon to publish a serious
discussion of the entire emigration problem by way of
counteracting the effect of this story of fortune. It took
the view that nothing in Norway's condition — economic,
civil, political, or religious — made emigration necessary.
In a period of general European distress Norway had not
known famine; and its lumber, fisheries, minerals,
shipping, and available lands for cultivation placed the
country in a favorable position. Its government was based
upon the same principles as American freedom. In this
discussion it was not denied that America eventually would
reward labor with good returns; but the question was
raised, would the returns outweigh the losses? Those who
were thrilled by the stories of the heavy money chest were
reminded that Poulsen had been in California at the most
opportune time.[11]

Solemn warnings were easy to forget, however, in the
excitement over gold. The next spring, for example, two
Swedes arrived at Mandal from New Orleans on their way
to visit relatives in their native land. They had spent six
months at the mines in California and their reported fortune was thirty thousand specie dollars. The most they
had earned in one day was three hundred dollars, the least
sixty.[12] Letters from other miners, published in various
newspapers, gave details about the journey to the West
and about earnings. " In the month of May I saved $223,
in June $295, and yesterday alone I earned $35," wrote

[11] "Om Udvandringerne til Amerika" in *Stavanger Amtstidende og Adresseavis,*
August 21, 24, September 7, 1849.

[12] The two Swedes, Johan Bjørkgreen and Johan Petersen, reported that there
were many Norwegian sailors in California and they referred to the large number
of deserted ships at San Francisco. *Correspondenten* (Skien), April 27, 1850.

an emigrant on July 15, 1849, in a letter vividly picturing a miner's experiences.[13] Yet another, writing from Sacramento City in 1850, contrasted $15 a day in earnings for two months with ten cents a day in his native Bergen.[14] Meanwhile newspapers were putting before Norwegian readers article after article telling about life at the mines and discussing from different points of view the effect of California gold upon America and the world.[15] Happenings on the Pacific coast, thousands of miles away, were becoming familiar themes in Norway and indeed in all western Europe. Norwegians were also deriving information about this absorbing theme from relatives and friends in the Middle West. Like all other communities the immigrant settlements were excited by the news of gold and many young men from them joined the " forty-niners." From the Muskego settlement, for example, Hans Christian Heg and three companions set forth in the spring of 1849, with wagon and oxen, on the long overland journey. Heg reported his progress in a series of letters published in the Norwegian newspaper of his home community.[16] And the leading topic of the day naturally crept into " America letters " of the time.[17]

Norwegian shipping interests were quick to take cognizance of the new possibilities for passenger traffic. In the spring of 1849 a bark was advertised for a direct

[13] *Christiania-Posten*, November 15, 1849.

[14] *Den Frimodige*, September 14, 1850. The letter was dated June 14, 1850.

[15] See for example reports and articles in *Stavanger Amtstidende og Adresseavis*, September 21, November 24, 1849; January 9, April 10, July 5, August 20 and 23, September 21, and December 24, 28, 1850. Michel Chevalier's " Om Guldminerne i Californien og deres Indflydelse paa Verdens Rigdomme," in *Christiania-Posten*, February 11, 12, 1850, is one of many articles derived from French sources. Cf. *Den norske Rigstidende*, September 18, October 19, 1850.

[16] *Nordlyset*, March 29, May 17, June 7, October 11, 1849. A California letter by Gunder Aadnesen and Ole Knudsen is in *Democraten*, November 3, 1850.

[17] Albert O. Barton, " Norwegian-American Emigration Societies in the Forties and Fifties," in *Studies and Records*, 3: 31–32.

trip from Norway to California at 150 specie dollars per passenger.[18] Freight profits also attracted skippers: thus the brig " Seagull " of Arendal set off in the fall of 1849 for San Francisco via Rio de Janeiro; it later made three trips between California and China; and it returned to Norway in 1852 after sailing around the world.[19] In the spring of 1850 a brig soon to sail from Tvedestrand to California announced that it could accommodate some passengers.[20] In July the " Amerika Paket " left Christiania for California with passengers; more than a year later on September 8, 1851, it reached San Francisco.[21] In September, 1850, the " Amerika " left Arendal for New Orleans with 120 passengers, including a party of ten bound for California.[22] And from the same port the brig " Juno " was advertised to sail for Panama with passengers later in the fall.[23] In the same year some prospective gold-hunters set off for California by way of Liverpool and New York.[24]

Early in 1850 the first steps were taken toward an organized expedition of gold-seekers, and a sequence of events was set in motion that eventuated in a strange and

[18] *Christiania-Posten*, March 6, 1849.

[19] *Morgenbladet*, June 8, 1852. The brig " Nicolay Nicolaysen " of Bergen was engaged in trade in 1851 between San Francisco and Hongkong. In December of that year it rescued eleven Japanese on Guy Rock, a naked rock in the Pacific, where they had been marooned for more than a year. *Christiania-Posten*, February 25, 1852.

[20] *Drammen Adresse*, April 4, 1850.

[21] *Christiania-Posten*, November 20, 1851. The ship remained until midwinter at London, where it was equipped with a copper sheath. One of its emigrants wrote a long letter from the interior of Peru on June 2, 1857, published on the first page of *Morgenbladet*, for September 7, 1857, telling of revolution, personal adventure, and life on a sugar plantation. His name is not given; his initials were J. L. A letter of November 14, 1851, tells of a suit instituted by the passengers against the captain of the " Amerika Paket." *Lillehammers Tilskuer*, May 11, 1852.

[22] *Den vestlandske Tidende*, September 10, 1850.

[23] *Lillehammers Tilskuer*, October 8, 1850; *Den vestlandske Tidende*, July 9, 1850.

[24] *Christiania-Posten*, August 15, 1850.

unexpected experiment in colonization. Three men, O. Eide, A. Finne, and N. C. Tischendorff, of Levanger, a small town north of Trondhjem on the west coast of Norway, conceived the idea of an expedition to California financed and equipped through the sale of shares; and in an invitation of January 19, 1850, published in various newspapers, they brought the scheme to the attention of the public. They declared that in a period of fabulous opportunity, Norwegians ought not be content with the rôle of spectators when by strength of will and far-sightedness they could share the fruits of new discoveries. Why should Norway lag behind other peoples in enterprise? In other lands millions were poured into doubtful schemes; could not the Norwegians invest a more modest sum in an undertaking that offered profits of several thousand per cent? The advantage would be national; the new capital gained would stimulate science, art, industry, and the various trades. The three promoters proceeded to explain the situation of affairs in California and to answer numerous questions. Miners could be expected to make profits of thirty to forty specie dollars a day. They did not fail to mention Christian Poulsen, who, they said, had brought back to Norway a fortune of twelve thousand specie dollars. They anticipated that the cost of living in California would not be high. The fact that the company would not be made up of American citizens would not cause any practical difficulty in acquiring the legal right to mine. But if it did, there were almost equally rich possibilities for exploitation in South America. The fact remained that a gold-seeking expedition could earn large profits in a year or two. A committee to be elected by all the shareholders would form and equip the expedition. The basic principles of the undertaking were laid down: (1) the party would consist of seamen, laborers, persons expert in natural science, a physician, and a minister, all of whom would agree to abide by certain rules; they would take with them provisions for one year and necessary equipment, weapons, and the like. (2) A ship would be chartered for two or three years and would be loaded with articles that would command high prices in San Francisco. (3) The number to go was tentatively set at a hundred men, who would have to satisfy the shareholders that they were industrious, sober, moral, and honest. (4) A hundred shares were to be issued, each holder to be responsible for a hundredth part of the total cost of the expedition. (5) Half of the profits would go to the miners; half to the shareholders. A general meeting would be called after fifty or sixty shares had been subscribed; and it was hoped to dispatch the party in the fall of 1850.[25]

The proposal, though scoffed at in some quarters, was taken seriously by many. A general assembly was held in Trondhjem on April 22; a committee worked out specific rules for the expedition; it was announced that, with full shares selling at a hundred specie dollars and half shares at fifty, fourteen thousand dollars had been subscribed, in part by prospective participants; Tischendorff, who seems to have been the leading spirit, complained of cabals, but it was obvious that the project was booming. " It is not unlikely that the enterprise will be carried out, though it is very doubtful that it will have the anticipated success," wrote a hostile newspaper.[26] An assembly to make final arrangements was held in June, and though the newspapers echoed some difficulties, including disagreement over a proposal to reduce the number of participants to

[25] " A more extravagant idea we have never yet seen presented," commented *Lillehammers Tilskuer*, February 19, 1850, in reprinting this invitation from *Nordre Trondhjems Amtstidende*.

[26] An account of the assembly, quoting from a speech by Tischendorff, is in *Lillehammers Tilskuer*, May 17, 1850. See also *Den Frimodige*, April 16, 23, 1850; and *Drammens Adresse*, May 11, 1850, quoting *Nordre Trondhjems Amtstidende*.

eighty, the plans for the expedition were matured.[27] One newspaper bewailed the folly of so needy a region as Nordre Trondhjems *Amt* pouring money into so wild an enterprise, and it expressed fear that in other parts of Norway similar expeditions might be organized.[28] In Trondhjem during the fall steps were actually taken toward the organizing of a second shipload of gold-hunters, to go the following spring either to Australia or California.[29]

Meanwhile the shareholders had bought a ship, the " Sophie," and were advertising room for some twenty extra passengers at 120 specie dollars a person.[30] Late in September the argonauts began to assemble at Trondhjem. The departure of the main group from Levanger is thus depicted in the local newspaper:

Scenes such as we know from Cooper or W. Irving have in these days inaugurated the California expedition. Powerful men have appeared from all directions, knives in hand, with chests and rifles loaded on wagons. After many conversations with them we are convinced that the Norse spirit is again alive; the California men, handsome and determined, are on their way; there is no dejection or wavering; speak to them of danger and difficulty and they reply that they put their trust first in God and next in themselves and their own courage; thus in certain respects have we imagined the ancient Vikings.

Another newspaper sounded a less sympathetic note:

Many of these people are young innocents, only recently the objects of a mother's tender care. One can only feel the sincerest pity at the thought of the fate that awaits such gold diggers.[31]

A last assembly was held in Trondhjem on September 30 and October 1, with two hundred shareholders and participants present; and on October 19 the expedition, com-

[27] *Trondhjems Stiftstidende*, May 27, 1850; *Den Frimodige*, June 1, 1850; *Drammens Tidende*, July 5, 1850.

[28] *Drammens Tidende*, June 7, 1850.

[29] *Den Frimodige*, October 5, 1850.

[30] *Den Frimodige*, August 20, 1850.

[31] *Den Frimodige*, October 15, 1850, quoting *Nordre Trondhjems Amtstidende*; *ibid.*, October 1; and *Den norske Rigstidende*, October 9, 1850.

prising 106 passengers, sailed for San Francisco by way of Rio de Janeiro and Cape Horn. The departure from Trondhjem offers a strange contrast to the manner in which many gold-seekers set forth on the great adventure. The Norwegians were almost like crusaders; they could not start without the blessing of the church. The day before the sailing a considerable number partook of the Lord's Supper in a Trondhjem church and listened to a farewell sermon. The following day there was another sermon on board the ship. This was followed by a reply and by a song of farewell composed for the occasion by Christian Monsen. Salutes were fired and, watched by some two thousand people, the " Sophie " weighed anchor.[32]

The journey to Rio de Janeiro occupied three months. When the party reached the Brazilian port, on January 20, 1851, after a stormy voyage, its plans were suddenly and drastically upset by the captain, who declared the " Sophie " unseaworthy and refused to continue to California. The emigrants had supposed the stop at Rio de Janeiro would be a brief one, merely to take on fuel and provisions, and they believed the ship seaworthy though in need of minor repairs. There is evidence of ill feeling between the passengers and its officers and crew. Meanwhile the ship was condemned; the delay at Rio de Janeiro of five or six weeks used up the company's provisions; the crew demanded payment; and the upshot of the situation was that the ship and its cargo had to be sold. The emigrants were stranded in Brazil; the ambitious plan of the shareholders disastrously checked; the gold mines of California far away; resources low; yellow fever a menace

[32] *Lillehammers Tilskuer*, October 18, 1850; *Christiania-Posten*, November 2, 1850; *Den Frimodige*, October 28, November 1, 1850. The " Sophie " was secured through a company in Hamburg; its captain was T. V. Leesen. The text of the farewell song is in Christian Monsen, *Samlede Digte*, 346–349 (Trondhjem, 1854).

in the city. At this point a German company acting as the agent of the Prince de Joinville, who owned large tracts of Brazilian land, proposed a solution of the difficult problem facing the gold-seekers. Why not establish a Norwegian colony in Brazil, in the vicinity of Germans on good land available at Donna Francisca in the province of Santa Catharina? Seventy-four members of the party accepted the offer; if they could not be gold-miners they would become tropical farmers, at least temporarily. If the shareholders in Norway sent funds to rehabilitate the expedition, perhaps they could get on to California later. In the meantime some of the others took service on a ship bound for San Francisco and some returned to Norway.[33]

A five-days' sea journey brought the prospective colonists in March to the Brazilian town of Sao Francisco, beyond which, some seven miles in the interior, were the colony's lands. A shipload of more than a hundred Germans arrived at the same time as the Norwegians. Thirteen of the latter remained only a short time; the others took land and began farming. An emigrant letter of July 2, 1851, tells of products in startling contrast to those of Norway: coffee, cotton, rice, oranges, lemons, and bananas. Four of the company were then dead from tropical disease. The others were struggling, among other things, with language difficulties in their relations with French-

---

[33] Consul Morsing, Rio de Janeiro, to the Norwegian government, February 21, 1851. R. A., Oslo: Indredept., Kontor D, Journalsager, 1851/771; *Christiania-Posten*, April 6, May 25, 26, 1851; *Nordre Trondhjems Amtstidende*, May 13, 1851; *Bergens Stiftstidende*, May 25, 1851. The ship was sold for two thousand specie dollars, the cargo for five hundred. An undated letter describes the voyage and tells of the arrival at Rio de Janeiro "on the 20th of this month." A comparison of this letter with other reports proves that the month was January. *Christiania-Posten*, May 25, 1851; *cf.* issue for April 6. The land company was Schrøder and Company of Hamburg. It is curious to note how prominently Hamburg figures in the entire affair. Oddvar Grønli, "Orgelbyggjar Ole Møen pa Ytterøya," in Nordtrønderlag Historielag, *Aarbok*, 1927, p. 81–84, tells of a member of the party who returned to his home in 1851.

men, Germans, and Brazilians. The letter writer, who feels in his strange fate the hidden purposes of God, is still interested in gold and speaks of a prospecting expedition that he and his companions plan to make.[34] Most of the colonists were restless; more than fifty of them left in 1851 and 1852; a letter from Rio de Janeiro of December 7, 1852, tells of eight Norwegians who were taking an American ship for California and incidentally criticizes sharply the promoters of the expedition for not sending additional funds.[35]

A Norwegian minister, Jonas W. Crøger, visited Donna Francisca late in 1854 and formed a pleasant impression of the Joinville colony as a whole. In Hamburg he had been informed that there were thirty-four Norwegians among the German colonists there, but personal investigation reduced this number to ten. Their personal appearance and dress seemed a painful contrast to Crøger's imaginary picture of the " knightly adventurers." Yet he found them on the whole doing well; for two weeks he was the guest of one of them, whom he describes as a prosperous man.[36] Crøger returned to Norway an enthusiast over South America, especially Brazil and Uruguay, and published a book describing his travels. He proposed in 1856 the establishment of a stock company capitalized at one hundred thousand dollars to organize emigration to Brazil, one hundred colonists to pioneer for two years on lands selected through negotiations with Brazil. The Germans, colonizing in southern Brazil, had stimulated their trade through developing new markets. This Norway also could do: buy tropical products from its own emigrants, supply

---

[34] *Nordre Trondhjems Amtstidende*, November 4, 1851.

[35] *Stavanger Amtstidende og Adresseavis*, March 5, 1853.

[36] Crøger, *En Reise til Brasilien og Uruguay, Ophold i disse Lande og en Beskrivelse over dem*, 20–33 (Christiania, 1856). Crøger's diary is published in part in *Christiania-Posten*, May 25, 28, June 3, 1855.

them with needed articles from the north. In 1857 Crøger advertised a projected colony in Uruguay with room for fifty families; and in 1858 Norwegian newspapers reported a proposal for Norwegians to join a Swiss colony at Rosario on the Plata. These plans, though given considerable publicity, seem to have aroused comparatively little interest among prospective emigrants, for whom the United States continued to be the most attractive goal.[37] A few of the colonists at Donna Francisca tarried in Brazil; in 1862 the Norwegian-Swedish consul at Rio de Janeiro reported that seven were left. Some had intermarried with Brazilians and had achieved good circumstances; the colonists as a group had been respectable and law-abiding; the province of Santa Catharina was making good progress; but the consul considered Brazil, in view of the illiberality of its government, an unsuitable field for European immigrants.[38]

It is possible to follow the fortunes of some of the Trondhjem gold-seekers who eventually reached California, one of the most interesting of whom was Theodor S. Støp of Levanger. After three weeks at Donna Francisca he left for Valparaiso, where he worked for three months in humdrum employment at good wages. He was a true argonaut, however. " I was well off there," he wrote to his parents, " and I also learned some English, but I had no peace, for the idea of California was always on my mind."

[37] Crøger, En Reise til Brasilien og Uruguay; Morgenbladet, May 1, 1856; Emigranten, June 6, 1856; " Om Oprettelse af en norsk Koloni i Syd Amerika, helst i Brasilien," in Christiania-Posten, June 10, 1856; Aftenbladet, December 1, 1857; Christiania-Posten, October 19, 1858.

[38] The consul's letter to the Department for det Indre, May 26, 1862, is in Utenriksdept., Oslo: Arkiv, Justitsbygningen, F. D. 1489/1862 C. With the letter is an undated report (in German) by the German Pastor Stapel of Donna Francisca. Of the original seventy-four colonists thirteen soon left; Stapel lists the remaining sixty-one. Of these eight had died in 1851. Not less than nineteen left in 1851 and twenty-four in 1852. By the end of the year 1852 there could not have been more than eleven of the original seventy-four left. Cf. Morgenbladet, July 6, 1862.

And to California he went, on board an American schooner, with two other Norwegians of the party, J. H. Bakke and L. Buch. A letter written by Støp on January 18, 1852, gives a good picture of conditions in San Francisco. He spurned work there at high wages and started for the Sacramento Valley. After eight months in the mines he wrote that he had saved eight hundred dollars; he set his goal at a thousand more; then his fortune would be large enough for him to return home and live independently. And in 1854 he did return by way of Panama, New York, Antwerp, Ghent, Helsingborg, Christiania, and Norway's recently opened railroad. He had made a success as a miner, and newspapers did not fail to mention that he had displayed some gold nuggets to his friends. A few years later three other members of the party of 1850 returned to Levanger, "decorated with massive rings, breastpins, watch chains, and similar expensive gold trinkets." The Levanger newspaper believed to the end that the idea back of the great expedition was sound: what some of the mining Vikings did, the others might have done — if circumstances had been kinder.[39]

The failure of the Trondhjem expedition did not dampen Norwegian interest in California. Newspapers continued to discuss reports from the West, and often the theme of gold led to articles of more general American

[39] Støp's letters of January 18 and September 6, 1852, are in *Trondhjems Stiftstidende*, April 24, 1852, and *Nordre Trondhjems Amtstidende*, December 21, 1852. See also the latter paper for February 24, 1854, and September 4, 1857; and *Christiania-Posten* for January 21, 1852. On August 26, 1856, *Nordre Trondhjems Amtstidende* published a poem entitled "On the Return of a Person Who Has Seen the Free States and California." An interesting case of another return is mentioned in *Christiania-Posten*, November 4, 1854, with sharp criticism of the central management. An inheritance left by one of the party awakened newspaper interest in 1871. *Verdens Gang*, July 29, 1871. One of the argonauts of 1850, Andreas Sakshaug, died in Norway in 1926 at the age of ninety-five. O[ddvar] G[rønli], "Ein gullgravarekspedisjon fraa Trøndelag i 1850," in *Nidaros* (Trondhjem), April 21, 1927.

interest. California played its part in the process of filling out the Norwegian popular concept of America.[40] In " The Gold Thirst or the California Fever in America," a pamphlet of 1852, an author predicted an Atlantic-Pacific railway, declared that San Francisco, St. Louis, and New York would become the three great cities of the world, and praised the United States as the land of opportunity for immigrants.[41] A year later a little book was published at Bergen under the title "Routes between Europe and New York, also to Rio de Janeiro; with an Account of the Sailing Route around Cape Horn to California and to China." [42]

There was widespread interest in immigrant

Guldtørsten

eller

California = Feberen.

America.

Arendal 1852.
Trykt og tilsjøbs hos C. Risum,

REDUCED FACSIMILE OF TITLE-PAGE OF " THE GOLD THIRST OR THE CALIFORNIA FEVER IN AMERICA "

letters from the Far West and many were brought before

---

[40] " Om Guldets Forekomst i Siberien og Californien," in *Christiania-Posten,* January 13, 14, 15, 17, 20, 28, 1851; Michel Chevalier, " Om Guldproduktionens Forøgelse," *ibid.,* January 22, 25, 1852; " Partier i de forenede nordamerikanske Stater," in *Stavanger Amtstidende og Adresseavis,* May 1, 1852; and other articles, *ibid.,* May 8, 11, June 5, August 31, September 10, October 5, 1852.

[41] *Guldtørsten eller California-Feberen i Amerika* (Arendal, 1852. 12 p.).

[42] *Router mellem Europa og New-York, samt til Rio Janeiro; tilligemed Beskrivelse over Seiladsen om Cap Horn til Californien, og derfra til China* (Bergen, 1853. 46 p.).

the public through Norwegian newspapers of the time. A native of Mandal, finding San Francisco too crowded, took a government position at Venicia, receiving $150 a month with board and room.[43]   Anthon Lassen of Drammen, disappointed at the mines, went to Oregon to become a farmer near Portland.   A letter from his hand in 1851 describes a region to which Norwegians were to flock many decades later.[44]   A Levanger gold-hunter reached Texas in 1851, learned that a regiment of soldiers stationed near by was to march to California, and promptly enlisted in order to accompany them.[45]   " Who can dream of the glories of America?" wrote one of his companions from Dallas County, Texas.[46] Disappointed in California, an emigrant from Kongsberg reported in 1851 that he was off for Australia; he writes in detail about Norwegians whom he met at the mines.[47]   " A swarm of Chinese are coming in; every week five hundred of these curious people land here in this city and parade about the streets," wrote an emigrant from Drammen in a San Francisco letter of May 1, 1852. He speaks of the opportunities for those skilled in " languages, music, painting, lithography, mathematics, and bookkeeping," though he admits that Greek, Latin, and philosophy would not produce any considerable income. He declares America to be " undoubtedly the best country in the world." [48]   " Come, and you will regret it; don't come, and you will also regret that," wrote the phil-

[43] A letter of June 27, 1850, in *Den Frimodige,* October 1, 1850.

[44] A letter of March 26, 1851, reports his experiences. *Drammens Tidende,* June 27, 1851.

[45] Foureer Sterten, in a letter of July 31, 1851, quoted in *Christiania-Posten,* October 27, 1851.

[46] A letter of November 14, 1851, in *Nordre Trondhjems Amtstidende,* March 18, 1851.

[47] A letter of November 14, 1851, from San Francisco, in *Lillehammers Tilskuer,* May 11, 1852.

[48] *Drammens Blad,* July 4, 1852. The writer's name was Bing.

osophic Carl Nordbye of Drøbak in a letter written at
" Mission de San Jose " in September, 1852, a letter picturing everyday affairs in detail.[49] Five and a half ounces
of gold dust were inclosed with another letter of 1852,
telling of murder, fire, violence, and discontent.[50] An emigrant whose Norwegian name of Nortvedt had been met-
amorphosed into North was looked upon as the best shipbuilder in California and owned one schooner worth
$17,000, according to a letter of 1854.[51] Fragmentary
items these — but for Norwegian newspaper readers they
gradually filled out the Californian scene with hundreds of
details.

Probably only a small part of the " America letters "
from the Far West, however, appeared in print. And
occasionally miners came back from El Dorado with tales
that aroused keen interest. To estimate their influence
accurately is impossible, but now and then the records afford revealing glimpses. For example, in the spring of 1856
a newspaper, commenting on the departure of the
" Sjofna " from Porsgrund for Quebec with 240 emigrants
on board, most of them from Gjerpen, attributes this emigration in part to the influence of a young farmer from
Rosvald. Some years earlier he had gone to California;
in the fall of 1855 he returned, a finely dressed gentleman,
to tell of his adventures and of his decision to go back to
America in the spring.[52] Such returned "America travel-

---

[49] *Morgenbladet*, December 6, 1852.

[50] Reported in *Stavanger Amstidende og Adresseavis*, December 24, 1852.

[51] *Christiania-Posten*, November 7, 1854.

[52] *Morgenbladet*, May 1, 1856, quoting from *Correspondenten*. Instances of the
return of miners are mentioned in *Christiania-Posten*, February 11, 1852, and April
20, 1853; and *Nordre Trondhjems Amtstidende*, May 17, 1853. A late case, reported in *Morgenbladet*, March 8, 1867, is that of a man worth from eight to ten
thousand dollars. Lonesome in America, he longed for Norway; returned to Norway,
he longed for America. The newspapers said that evidently he loved America better
than Norway.

ers " call to mind the favorite hero of the Norwegian fairy
stories, Askeladden, who always triumphed over difficulties
and won half the kingdom. Not all the miners who went
back to their native land were Askeladdens, however. Some
returned discouraged and with empty hands, with dirges
rather than songs of praise. Thus one in 1858 gratified
anti-emigration newspapers with reports of great economic difficulty, disorder, lawlessness, and godlessness in California.[53]

The discoveries of gold in Australia also stirred the interest of Norwegians, both in California and in Norway.
" The Norwegian-Swedish consul in Sydney has sent an
invitation to the Norwegians and Swedes now in California to come to Australia, and several of our countrymen
have followed this suggestion," wrote a Norwegian miner
in California on December 1, 1851.[54] Another miner,
telling in 1851 of his decision to go to Australia, explains
that conditions in California were not particularly promising and that the mines in Australia were new and unexploited. He had arrived too late in California; he would
not make the same mistake in Australia.[55] A Norwegian,
in a letter from Sidney, October 10, 1852, describes the
voyage from San Francisco and his luck in what he terms
the greatest of all lotteries, gold digging.[56] Interest in the
Australian gold fields was greater in Denmark than in
Norway. One Norwegian in a letter from Melbourne
dated August 26, 1853, describes an expedition of some
eighty Danes which he had joined. They were on the
march: " A wagon drawn by ten oxen, followed by
eighty men in woolen shirts and trousers caught in long

[53] *Aftenbladet,* August 18, 1858.
[54] *Christiania-Posten,* February 25, 1852.
[55] A letter of November 14, 1851, from San Francisco, in *Lillehammers Tilskuer,*
May 11, 1852.
[56] *Christiania-Posten,* May 30, 1853.

boots, with wide hats, and pouches fastened around their necks." [57] Another letter from Melbourne reports, " It is swarming here with Danes, many of them without employment." [58] And in the summer of 1854 a three-masted ship to sail from Denmark for Australia was advertised in Norwegian newspapers.[59] A comprehensive book translated from English, " Australia: An Historical, Geographical, and Statistical Account," by William Hughes, was brought out in Norway in 1854.[60] More interesting for Norwegian readers was a pamphlet written by a Norwegian who had spent seven months in the Australian gold mines up to July, 1853. It was entitled " Guiding Remarks for Those Who Expect to Emigrate to Australia, with Some Words about the Emigration to America." In addition to a general account of the Australian situation, it tells of a small group of Norwegian miners.[61] Thus the experiences of Norwegian emigrants to Australia in the early period were brought to public attention in one form or another.[62]

Echoes of another gold rush were heard in Norway in the late fifties. This was the stampede of miners to the Fraser River gold fields of British Columbia. A long and

[57] *Morgenbladet,* February 20, 1854. An advertisement in *Christiania-Posten,* February 4, 1853, invites Norwegians to join a Danish party bound for Australia.

[58] *Christiania-Posten,* October 26, 1854.

[59] *Christiania-Posten,* July 4, 1854.

[60] *Australien. Historisk, geografisk og statistisk beskreven* (Christiania, 1854. 112 p.).

[61] *Veiledende Bemærkninger, for dem som agte at emigrere til Australien, samt nogle Ord om Emigrationen til Amerika. Udgivet af en Nordmand, der har opholdt sig i Australiens Guldminer i syv Maaneder, indtil Juli Maaned 1853* (Fredrikshald, 1854. 26 p.). On the title page of the only known copy of this pamphlet — that in the library of the University of Oslo — a penciled notation attributes its authorship to a shoemaker named Henriksen, of Fredrikshald. There is a reference to Henriksen in *Christiania-Posten,* June 26, 1853.

[62] See a letter by one Erichsen of Fredrikshald, written at Forrest Creek on November 24, 1854, in *Aftenbladet,* May 26, 1855. Three Australia reports are in *Christiania-Posten,* March 5, 1854, *Nordre Trondhjems Amtstidende,* November 6, 1857, and *Stavanger Amtstidende og Adresseavis* June 15, 1863.

most interesting letter dated at " Whatkom, Whatkom Kounty, Washington Terrytory " on July 12, 1858, records the observations of a native of Bergen at a strategic point on the trail to the fields. It pictures a typical rush of prospectors and the amazing growth of a " boom town," where another Norwegian was offered three thousand dollars for a lot bought six weeks earlier for fifty.[63]

Measured in numbers the early Norwegian emigration in response to the lure of the western gold fields is not of great significance. The census of 1860 showed, for example, that there were only 715 Norwegians in the state of California; there had been 124 ten years earlier. The accidental colonization attempt in Brazil was a failure. And few Norwegians went to distant Australia. The permanent interest of Norwegian emigrants was in fertile farming land; " gold fever " could not divert the main body of these land seekers from their trek to the Middle West. Measured, however, by its repercussions and collateral effects in Norway, by its influence on the development of popular knowledge about America, its lands, institutions, and ideas, the discovery of California gold opened up an important chapter in the history of Norwegian relations with the world to the west.

[63] *Stavanger Amtstidende og Adresseavis,* September 30, 1858.

XIII. OLEANA: A COLONIZATION PROJECT IN PENNSYLVANIA

ORGANIZED colonization projects play a minor rôle in the history of Norwegian immigration. The great body of immigrants followed the familiar routes to the West, went usually to the haphazard Norwegian centers of settlement and from these, singly or in groups, to other areas where good land was to be had at low prices. In the settlement of such groups there was frequently leadership and to a certain extent organization; but centrally planned colonization was conspicuously absent. The history of English and Irish immigration presents several instances of organized colonies in the West.[1] Norwegian efforts of similar nature are not lacking, but they have their setting outside the area of principal Norwegian settlement. In the forties J. R. Reiersen advocated organization of the growing immigration and its concentration in a compact area, though his plan did not involve the central purchase of land with subsequent allotment. When his theories were put into practice, however, the scene of experiment was not the upper Mississippi Valley, but Texas.

The next important Norwegian project in this field occurred in the early fifties and was sponsored by the famous violinist, Ole Bull, whose choice of a site fell upon an undeveloped tract of land in Pennsylvania. His colony is celebrated in story and song; the personality of the founder has cast a certain glamour about the episode; the tale runs its course from Utopian anticipation to disap-

---

[1] An interesting account of an unsuccessful Irish effort in Minnesota in the eighties is given by Alice E. Smith in her article, "The Sweetman Irish Colony," in *Minnesota History*, 9: 331–346 (December, 1928).

pointment and failure; the fortunes of the settlement were watched with interest by observers and prospective emigrants in Norway and by settlers in the West; and when the bubble burst, there was a roar of ironical laughter on both sides of the Atlantic. Though Oleana is an interlude in the drama of American immigration and had no appreciable influence upon the development of the main plot, it is worth examining because of its repercussions in Norway and as a chapter in the history of colonization schemes of paternalistic flavor.

Ole Bull, born in Bergen in 1810, was a native genius whose bow had won him a European reputation before he visited America for the first time in 1843. His violin, coupled with his impulsive nature and captivating personality, quickly made him popular among Americans. He toured extensively in the United States for about two years, traveling in all more than a hundred thousand miles. Some of his impressions were put into such descriptive compositions as " Solitude of the Prairie," " Niagara," and " The Memory of Washington." He returned to Europe an enthusiast over America and incidentally with profits estimated at eighty thousand dollars.[2]

The story of Oleana has connections with the founding of a national theater at Bergen. Ole Bull was the leading spirit in this enterprise, an expression of the rising feeling of nationalism in Norway. The new theater, which opened on January 2, 1850, was to nurture authentic Norwegian drama and music. It is a curious fact that one of the first plays presented was *Fjeldstuen,* Wergeland's emigration play, and that Ole Bull, soon to launch Norway's most ambitious emigration plan, composed the music for the anti-emigration songs. Bull's high enthusiasm over

---

[2] *Morgenbladet,* January 16, 1846. There is an account of " Ole Bulls første Reise i Amerika " in *Amerika, Ole Bull og det nye Norge,* 95–108 (Bergen, 1852).

the national theater was soon dampened by adverse criticism, financial difficulty, failure in 1851 to secure a yearly appropriation for the theater from the Storthing, and an absurd clash with police officials, who were so piqued by the artist's hostile attitude toward their demand for complimentary tickets that they arrested him for smoking a cigar in the streets of Bergen. Disappointed and humiliated, he left Norway in the fall of 1851; and in January, 1852, he sailed from England for America. He did not return to his native land again for five years.[3]

No contemporary explanation by Bull himself of the inception of Oleana appears to be available. That he had a colonization project in mind when he arrived in America in 1852 is implied by one student of the history of Oleana.[4] According to an unverified report of 1853, Bull's attention had been called to colonization sites in northern Africa and in Australia, but he much preferred the United States.[5] In March he visited Washington, primarily, according to one biographer, " to learn more about the inducements and advantages offered emigrants to go to the Western States." [6] Thereafter he made a concert tour in the South; Mrs. Bull remarks that the " representations of his countrymen who had settled in the South and had told him their tales of privation and hardships, to which poor health was added because of the unfavorable climate, had induced him to make the experiment of a settlement

[3] A series of letters from Bull to his wife, in Alexander Bull, ed., *Ole Bulls Breve i Uddrag*, 373–382 (Kjøbenhavn, 1881), chronicles the high hopes and the disappointments over the national theater. See also Oddmund Vik, *Ole Bull*, 287–344 (Bergen, 1890), and Sara C. Bull, *Ole Bull, a Memoir*, 198–213 (Boston, 1883).

[4] Torstein Jahr, " Oleana, Et blad av Ole Bulls og den norske indvandrings historie," in *Symra*, 6: 4 (Decorah, Iowa, 1910). This study by the leading authority on Oleana appears in three installments in *Symra*, 6: 3–37, 129–162, 195–216. It is a documentary compilation of much value.

[5] The *Pennsylvanian* (Philadelphia), quoted by Jahr, in *Symra*, 6: 154. The exact date of the item is not given.

[6] Bull, *Ole Bull*, 216.

in the North." [7] His attorney declares that in 1852 Bull
had practically completed plans for the purchase of
land in Virginia when his attention was directed to northern Pennsylvania.[8]

That Bull did not establish his colony in the West —
then in the upward swing of vigorous development and
generally considered the most attractive area by the immigrants themselves — is probably explained in part by
health conditions, for the settlements in the upper Mississippi Valley were attacked by cholera and malaria in the
forties and early fifties. Thus the Fox River, Muskego, and
Koshkonong settlements were harried by cholera in 1849
and its dismal effects were widely reported in Norway.
Bull is reported to have said that he spent many months
in investigating various sections of the United States and
that among other advantages, the Pennsylvania site had a
climate as healthful as that of Norway. Furthermore he is
said to have considered the West too remote from markets, and to have desired, in the interest of the farmers,
fairly easy access to New York.[9] It was apparently expected that some settlers already established in the West
would join the colony, for an agent in Wisconsin adver-

---

[7] Bull, Ole Bull, 221. According to an account in Watson's Art Journal, translated in Morgenbladet, April 15, 1868, it was the southern trip that caused Bull to
decide to found a colony. Yellow fever and slavery were the reasons for Norwegian settlers' discontent with the South. This account is said to have been based on
Ole Bull's own explanation.

[8] A letter of November 18, 1853, published in the New York Herald, November
21, 1853, as quoted by Jahr, in Symra, 6: 147.

[9] Knut Gjerset and Ludvig Hektoen, "Health Conditions and the Practice of
Medicine among the Early Norwegian Settlers, 1825–1865," in Studies and Records,
1: 16–18. The matter of markets is mentioned in a letter by C. J. Kraby and J.
Haarsle, Neenah, Wisconsin, December 27, 1852, published under the title "Beskrivelse over Ole B. Bulls Koloni i Pennsylvanien, og Betingelserne hvorpaa Norske der
modtages," in Arbeider-Foreningernes Blad, February 12, 1853. For Bull's statement
about climate see Eli Bowen, in The Pictorial Sketch-Book of Pennsylvania, part 3,
193–196 (Philadelphia, 1853), quoted by Jahr, in Symra, 6: 12.

tised the project in a newspaper published in that state.[10] Indeed, a Norwegian biographer sums up Bull's idea of a colony as that of " gathering together Norwegians in America to labor in a Norwegian settlement." [11] He may also have desired a region that would not stand in such startling contrast as the prairies to the mountain valleys from which so many of the immigrants hailed.[12]

Ole Bull's colony was the scheme of a man sincerely interested in bettering the immigrant's lot. His plan was conceived in a spirit of generous idealism, stimulated by disillusionment over the national theater fiasco, made possible by riches accumulated on triumphant concert tours, and lifted to the heights of romance by an artist's imagination. " We are to found a New Norway, consecrated to liberty, baptized with independence, and protected by the Union's mighty flag," he declared.[13]

This conception of the colony might have aroused the enthusiasm of a less sanguine temperament than that of an Ole Bull. Unfortunately for him and for the colonists who were to settle on his lands, there now enters into the tale a man whose motives seem to have been something less than idealistic and humanitarian. He was John F. Cowan of Williamsport; closely associated with him was Joseph T. Bailey of Philadelphia. They were brought into contact with the violinist through a New York lawyer, John Hopper, and Bull was persuaded to investigate in their company a large tract of unsettled land available for purchase in Potter County, lying somewhat to the west in

10 See an advertisement signed by John Holfeldt, " Agent for Ole Bull," Inmansville, Wisconsin, in *Emigranten*, December 24, 1852.

11 Vik, *Ole Bull*, 348.

12 A colonist suggests that Bull believed that Norwegian immigrants could not be contented unless they lived in a mountainous region. *Morgenbladet*, June 17, 1856.

13 The phrase, in Norwegian, is quoted in *Ole Bulls Breve i Uddrag*, 123; the English translation is from Sara Bull, *Ole Bull*, 221.

Pennsylvania's northern tier of counties, with Coudersport as the county seat. It is alleged that by previous arrangement a farmer in the vicinity of the proposed site reported to the investigators, when they stopped to make inquiries at his farm, that land thereabouts was worth five dollars an acre and rising in value — though in fact its market value was probably not higher than from twenty-five to seventy-five cents an acre. Not doubting that Cowan and Bailey were, as they claimed, the owners of the land examined, Bull entered upon arrangements for its purchase, making Cowan a preliminary payment of ten thousand dollars and later paying Bailey twenty-five thousand dollars. A company was formed with Cowan superintendent and business manager, Bailey treasurer, and Bull president.[14] And in September, 1852, newspapers announced that Ole Bull had bought 120,000 acres in Potter County. When the news reached Norway, people were stunned: some Norwegian editors could not accept so huge a figure, and one asserted, in November, 1852, that the correct amount was probably twelve thousand.[15] But the cipher had to be restored. One American account asserts that the violinist intended to have two hundred thousand acres to divide into small farms.[16] And as late as February 6, 1853, Bull, in writing to his brother about " my little state in Pennsylvania," said that he had added twenty thousand acres to his earlier purchase and had negotiated for 112,000 more.[17] There could be no doubt of the geographical magnitude of the colony. In December a Nor-

---

[14] See an article in *Watson's Art Journal* translated in *Morgenbladet*, April 15, 1868. L. E. Bulkeley's letter of November 18, 1853, in the *New York Herald*, November 21, 1853, is quoted by Jahr in *Symra*, 6: 146–150.

[15] *Stavanger Amtstidende og Adresseavis*, November 5, 1852.

[16] Eli Bowen, in *The Pictorial Sketch-Book of Pennsylvania*, part 3, 193–196, quoted by Jahr in *Symra*, 6: 11.

[17] *Ole Bulls Breve i Uddrag*, 383.

wegian newspaper published an immigrant's letter singing the praises of Ole Bull: "We all know the North's greatest artist, but we shall soon learn to know the North's greatest benefactor. . . . He has bought so much land that it can receive our countrymen for many years, even should emigration become many times as large as it hitherto has been; and every industrious and good man can look forward with certainty to a care-free and happy home." [18]

Settlement began promptly. On September 6 the first group of colonists, about thirty in number, arrived at Coudersport on their way to Oleana. Less than two weeks later a party of more than a hundred Norwegians appeared in the same town, having been persuaded at New York to join the colony. It was expected that five hundred more would soon follow. Meanwhile the enterprise had been formally inaugurated in a manner worthy of its founder. The first contingent had arrived before Bull. When the founder appeared on September 7 he was greeted with hurrahs and responded with a speech. On the following day work was begun on a hotel; lots were selected for Bull's own house and twenty-five others, to be erected at once; sites for a mill, a church, and a schoolhouse were chosen; the town thus brought into being was called Oleana (or Oleor-a); the first tree chopped down was used for a flagpole; when the flag was raised, thirty-one cheers were given, one for each state, followed by three for Ole Bull; in the evening the violinist delivered a speech inaugurating New Norway, as the colony was called. Later there appeared on the map of New Norway such names as New Bergen and Walhalla. The name of the first village, Oleana, was applied by popular usage to the entire colony.[19]

[18] *Morgenbladet,* December 7, 1852. The letter, undated, was written by H. Larsen.

[19] See an account in *Morgenbladet,* November 15, 1852, quoted from the New York *Weekly Times* of October 2. The best description of the colony seems to be

Many immigrants on the "Incognito," which arrived at New York on September 11, went to Oleana; and Ole Bull, who had hastened back to New York after the opening ceremonies, persuaded its captain and the Reverend Jacob Aal Ottesen, a passenger, to accompany him to the colony. Ottesen was on his way to Wisconsin, where he was to be the minister for a Norwegian congregation, and Bull desired him to conduct the first religious service at Oleana. A letter by the minister tells of the journey and of the colony. The party went by train on September 17 to Genessee and drove to the village of Wellesville; the next day it reached Coudersport, which, Ottesen remarks, was about twenty-eight miles from the railroad. He observed with interest some manifestations of the American spirit in this village. "Here were perhaps four hundred inhabitants; but still a newspaper four times as large as *Morgenbladet* appeared weekly; there were two churches, and a court house costing from ten to twenty thousand dollars." The trip was continued to Oleana, which Ottesen notes somewhat ominously was situated sixty English miles from the railroad. He states, however, that two railroads were expected eventually to cross the colony's lands. The emigrants, if able to clear the heavy timber, were to receive fifteen dollars a month together with food and lodging. The land was to be sold at three dollars an acre the first year, later at five, then at ten. "It is expected," writes the minister, "that all these impassable woods and steep hills will be turned into cultivated land." He expressed doubt, however, that the land could be successfully cleared and cultivated; he advised "neither for nor

that by Eli Bowen, quoted by Jahr in *Symra*, 6: 11–15. Mr. Jahr has also brought together several informing items about the colony from the local Coudersport newspaper, the *People's Journal. Symra*, 6: 10, 30 ff. The form "Oleona" rather than "Oleana" seems to have been most used by contemporaries, — including Ole Bull himself, — but the latter eventually received the sanction of general usage.

against " emigrating to Oleana, for he did not know whether or not Ole Bull would be able to keep his promises and " to realize his great plans." That Ottesen entertained certain doubts is evident by his remark: " I truly believe that Ole Bull means very well, but he is not a business man, and furthermore politico-democratic plans *en gros* are involved in the scheme." [20]

Shortly after Ottesen's visit Ole Bull startled his friends by taking out his first papers as an American citizen. This act was accomplished on September 25 at Philadelphia with due ceremony, including a speech in which Bull voiced his hope that within a year many thousands of Norwegians would join the settlers in northern Pennsylvania.[21]

It did not take the colonists long to discover that Oleana was something less than Utopia. One of the settlers, Jacob Olsen Wollaug, in a letter dated at Coudersport on April 10, 1853, has recorded his experiences.[22] He writes:

Upon our arrival at New York on September 11, we were engaged to go to Mr. Ole Bull's new colony in Pennsylvania, where all were to get work at a half dollar and board per day or a dollar a day without board; artisans were to receive more — from three-fourths to one dollar and board. Everyone could select land to suit himself, from

[20] The Ottesen letter was sent to Norway and published in *Den norske Tilskuer* for November 20, 1852.

[21] *Amerika, Ole Bull og det nye Norge*, 125–128. This step toward citizenship appears to have been taken by Bull because of a state law establishing conditions to the ownership of land to the amount of five thousand acres or more. Mr. Jahr calls attention to a Pennsylvania act of 1853 specifically authorizing Ole Bull to hold lands in that state. *Symra*, 6: 26–29.

[22] *Christiania-Posten*, May 25, 1853. A letter of somewhat similar tone written by Ole Larsen Sorknæs and O. Pedersen on March 11, 1853, is reprinted from *Friheds-Banneret* in *Stavanger Amtstidende og Adresseavis* for May 6, 1853. In this letter Bull is accused of breaking two promises: (1) to return in eight days after his visit of October 15 and to meet all demands then, and (2) to arrange to have supplies sold to the people at cost. Everyone is reported to be asking, " Where is Ole Bull? Why does he not come? " It is interesting to compare these contemporary impressions of Oleana with the amusing recollections of Carl F. Solberg, "Reminiscences of a Pioneer Editor," in *Studies and Records*, 1: 136–137. Solberg's father acted as Ole Bull's manager and director at Oleana.

twenty-five to fifty acres, at three dollars per acre, to be paid for in three years at the rate of two dollars a month. Bull was to furnish all necessaries, such as houses and the like, against a monthly reimbursement.

The first check to enthusiasm occurred quickly:

Upon our arrival we found ourselves disappointed in our expectations, for the land looked very miserable to us. The road to the colony, which is situated about ten Norwegian miles from the railroad, was very poor and grew worse the farther we went, until at the end we found ourselves in the midst of high mountains and narrow valleys cut by small rivers and streams, with heavy forests . . . so that everyone understood that it would take a generation here to clear a farm or *gaard* that would adequately support a family.

The first month passed quickly, with the colonists hard at work. On October 15 Ole Bull again visited Oleana, this time with forty emigrants. " We were then asked," continues Wollaug, " if we would work for a half dollar a day without board. You can understand the effect of such an offer on the spirits of the colonists." This would have meant starvation for wives and children, he writes, for supplies were expensive despite the promise that they would be sold at cost. Everyone prepared to leave, according to the letter writer; but after some negotiation Bull agreed to continue his first terms and to furnish work for the winter, leaving the colonists " free to buy land in the spring or not."

Apparently funds were scarce. Wollaug writes that affairs went smoothly until the beginning of 1853; the workers then wished their wages, but Bull " remained away and no money came, until the people lost their patience, demanded payment for work already done, and stopped all further labor." Late in February Cowan finally arrived.

He declared that Bull had not sent him any money, but that in order to satisfy the people he would pay us something out of his own pocket. I had to be content with twenty-five dollars, others received fifteen, yet others ten or five on their accounts. I still have more than fifty dollars to my credit.

Many colonists now began to leave Oleana, some going to New York, some to Buffalo and Chicago, Wollaug and others to Coudersport. In that village there were sixteen Norwegians, he says, all satisfactorily employed. Despite his disappointment Wollaug adds, " This much I have discovered, that the man who has strong arms, who can and will work, can earn a better livelihood here than in Norway."

Some took a brighter view of Oleana than Wollaug. For example, Jens Skøien in a letter of January 16 said, " I find myself fully satisfied and I can declare with good conscience that I would ten times rather be here than in Norway. . . . " He adds that for three or four years labor at one dollar a day will be available at the colony. So far as he has heard, people are contented. Nevertheless, he adds, " I absolutely decline to advise anyone to come." [23] Oleana was emphatically condemned, however, by another colonist, H. P. Olsen, who wrote on February 2, 1853:

There is nothing but big woods, high mountains, and narrow valleys; I have not seen such ugly land in Norway; so God help the poor Norwegians who come to Ole Bull's colony. Now we have all quit working, for no one has received as much as a penny for four months. We have appointed a committee to find Ole Bull or his companions, but thus far they have not been successful, so I do not know how things will go. When those who are in Ole Bull's colony have received their money they will all leave. [24]

While discontented colonists were thus beginning to rebel, Ole Bull was away on concert tours replenishing

[23] The letter, written at New Bergen, was published in *Arbeider-Foreningernes Blad*, April 30, 1853. Skøien did not leave Oleana until 1856, when he went west and took a homestead in Freeborn County, Minnesota. *Cf.* Jahr, " Jens Jacobsen Skøiens Livsaga," in *Sønner af Norge*, 20: 103–108 (April, 1923).

[24] *Christiania-Posten*, March 19, 1853. See also a letter of January 24, 1853, quoted in *Den norske Tilskuer*, March 12, 1853.

his purse and fashioning great schemes for the future of
Oleana. A curious contrast to the preceding letters is
offered in one written by Bull at Augusta, Georgia, on
February 6, 1853, to a brother.[25] Oleana was to be more
than a settlement of humble farmers, for Bull wrote:

Of my activity as an artist, politician, and manager of my little state
in Pennsylvania, you can form a conception only when you learn that
I am simultaneously laying out five towns and making a contract with
the government for the casting of some 10,000 cannons in Oleana
for the forts, especially those in California. I have succeeded in getting Philadelphia to subscribe two million dollars to the Sunbury and
Erie Road, which will go near the colony on the south; New York has
also subscribed two millions to a branch of the Erie and New York
Railroad from Elmira to Oleana, to run through the northern part
of the colony, so that Oleana will be only twelve hours from New
York, ten hours from Philadelphia, and about eleven hours from
Baltimore.

The building of these roads and other projects would of
course furnish labor for many thousands of colonists.

Expansion, not retrenchment, was in the air. " So many
have applied for land," he wrote, " that I have been obliged
to look about for more in the neighborhood; nearby, to
the west, I have bought 20,000 acres, and in the adjoining
county (McKean) I have negotiated for 112,000 acres. In
Wyoming County I am contracting for an old, deserted
foundry with forest, water-power, workshops, and dwel-
lings, and I am taking out patents in Washington for a
new smelting furnace for cannon." The letter contains
a passage that throws light on Ole Bull's psychology in all
this. In his interest for New Norway, he had not forgotten his critics in Old Norway. He said:

You ask me how I could have got all this in operation, how I can,

---

[25] *Ole Bulls Breve i Uddrag*, 382–384. The letter is translated in part in Sara
Bull, *Ole Bull*, 223–224. The passages given in the present text are based on Mrs.
Bull's translation, but have been revised after comparison with the original.

so to speak, play with millions. Good Edward, when you see for yourself you will be much more surprised; this is merely a beginning; my powers have grown proportionately with the magnitude of the work; my enthusiasm has triumphed over skepticism. My persecutors have themselves called into play my indisputable right to defend myself, and I answer with facts!

Before long he was thinking of building a great polytechnical school at Oleana, to be staffed with European professors — a civil and military institution combined, which would be open to the youth of America. The United States needed such a school: why not have it at Oleana? School, cannon foundry, and government contracts would go admirably together. Experts in the school would design improvements in military defense; the Oleana foundry would manufacture in accordance with designs submitted; all the government had to do was to buy. Teachers, craftsmen, and laborers would be permit-

Amerika,

Ole Bull

og

det nye Norge.

· Bergen 1852.

C. D. Dahl.

REDUCED FACSIMILE OF THE TITLE-PAGE OF "AMERICA, OLE BULL, AND THE NEW NORWAY"

ted to take shares in the enterprise and thus supplement their salaries or wages by dividends. Ole Bull's ideas were indorsed in one American periodical on the ground that West Point had become exclusive and aristocratic; the Oleana Polytechnical School would be for the people.[26]

Meanwhile reverberations from Oleana were being heard in Norway. The news of the establishment of the colony went the rounds of the Norwegian newspapers, amplified from time to time with additional details culled from American papers and eventually with letters from participants. A book published in Bergen late in 1852 under the title " America, Ole Bull, and the New Norway " brought before Norwegian readers much information about the United States, the violinist's first American visit, and Oleana; and it was obviously intended to create enthusiasm for the New Norway.[27] Its keynote is sounded in a song of which the following three verses are representative:[28]

Here in the old world freedom is but a name: hence this busy stir toward the distant port. For the land there in the West is free both for belief and for practice. And the answers to many difficult problems may be found there.

America! For a long time Norway's sons have been making their way to your blossoming fields to build for themselves new homes; but often, upon landing on your beautiful shores, joyfully and with high hope, they have been deceived by fair words.

Hurrah for the master of the strings, for the brave Ole Bull! He has now taken his stand among you, firm against hatred and strife. He is founding a new Norway for the benefit of his countrymen, which, amply blessed with peace and freedom, will make men marvel.

---

[26] Jahr in *Symra*, 6: 36–37, quotes " Ole Bull and His Colony " in *Dwight's Journal of Music* (Boston), 3: 60–61 (May 28, 1853). Mr. Jahr takes the view (*Symra*, 6: 129–130) that the project for the Oleana Polytechnical School does not prove that Ole Bull was impractical, as some critics have suggested. He thinks, indeed, that it proves the opposite, for such a school was needed, would have been unique, would have aided both the colony and the United States, and would have made Oleana a familiar name throughout the country. It is probably unkind to suggest that the impractical thing about the conception of the school was its association with Ole Bull and Oleana.

[27] *Amerika, Ole Bull og det nye Norge* (168 p.). The material, culled from many miscellaneous sources, includes accounts of America's legal and school systems and of general conditions, a chapter from *Uncle Tom's Cabin*, a section on California, some four or five items about Ole Bull and the colony, and various other matters. A copy is in the library of the University of Oslo.

[28] *Amerika, Ole Bull og det nye Norge*, 122.

In certain quarters, however, the book was singularly ineffective in evoking enthusiasm. One reviewer described it as " a work from which it is to be hoped that the publisher will have as little profit as he has honor." [29] The tone of the Norwegian press toward Oleana was in general skeptical from the first. A typical item declares that one must not put faith in the plans of Ole Bull, though he is a masterly violinist.[30] But Bull had many friends in Norway. In Bergen there was evidence of a desire to give favorable news from Pennsylvania a hearing;[31] some sympathetic notes in other quarters are heard as echoes of anti-aristocratic feeling.[32] And in labor circles a very friendly attitude prevailed. Laborers looked upon Ole Bull as an ally of the common people; the organ of the labor movement, *Arbeider-foreningernes Blad*, gave favorable attention to the colony; and it opened its columns to articles in which the alleged anti-labor attitude of the government was held responsible for the growing interest in America. It hailed Oleana with song and with editorial endorsement. It declared that hundreds of thousands would be willing to leave Norway on Ole Bull's word alone. It anticipated great throngs of emigrants the next spring who would sing: " Farewell my valley and farewell my mountain; long have I been a miserable slave. But now, with a free mind and a full heart, I'm setting off for Ole Bull." [33] In fact,

[29] *Christiania-Posten*, February 17, 1853.

[30] *Stavanger Amtstidende og Adresseavis*, November 5, 1852.

[31] See for example *Bergens Stiftstidende*, November 24, 1852.

[32] *Stavangeren* recommended Oleana and quoted a sharp attack by the Norwegian-American *Friheds-Banneret* on the Norwegian aristocracy. See *Christiania-Posten*, April 23, 1853.

[33] *Arbeider-foreningernes Blad*, November 13, 20, 27, December 4, 1852; January 22, February 12, April 2 and 30, July 30, 1853. On November 13 the paper hailed Ole Bull in song as " Better than Gold," and a week later it published a cartoon picturing a government official who complains that Ole Bull is leading the laboring class away from Norway. A letter by C. J. Kraby and J. Haarsle, Neenah, Wisconsin, December 27, 1852, published in the issue for February 12, 1853, describes the project in glowing terms. It should be mentioned that as late as April 30 and July 30, 1853, the paper published favorable letters from Oleana.

generally among people who felt personally the force of the causes back of emigration, there was a disposition to believe the best. A report from Kongsberg dated February 9, 1853, notes that " In the country districts in this vicinity there is a common belief that Ole Bull will pay the costs of passage for everyone who wants to go to America, with the understanding that the recipient can repay the loan by working on Bull's property Oleana, in North America." [34] And in the spring a newspaper attributes the rising fever of emigration to the " enticing Oleana." [35] Among Norwegian youth Bull's theatrical plans had aroused great enthusiasm and they viewed his venture in America with admiration. "We young men believed that it was the millennium which he was establishing on earth," wrote Professor Dietrichson in his reminiscences.[36]

Among the most merciless critics of Oleana was the humorous paper *Krydseren* of Christiania, edited by Ditmar Meidell. This publication laughed at many contemporary foibles and frequently flashed the sharp blade of satire. It opened its attack on November 20, 1852, with an article ridiculing a glowing report of Oleana. This report had touched on Norse claims to America from the period of the Vikings. "Why not take the whole country," asked *Krydseren,* " dissolve the Union, let the Norwegian bear trample on the American, and thereupon divide the land into states such as Oleana, Mariana, Larsiana, and Pauliana?" After a shrewd analysis of land conditions at Oleana, *Krydseren* remarks, " So far as Ole Bull is concerned, it may be conceded that he can play the violin, but this hardly implies that with his bow he can level the earth, move mountains, and clear primeval forests." [37] In

[34] In *Morgenbladet,* February 13, 1853.
[35] *Christiania-Posten,* April 21, 1853.
[36] L. Dietrichson, *Svundne Tider,* 1: 157 (Christiania, 1896).
[37] *Krydseren,* November 20, 1852.

February it returned to the attack with an ironical description of Oleana: "Though one be as poor as a church mouse, it is the simplest thing in the world to become as rich as Croesus merely by going to Oleana." [38]

The attack was driven home on March 5, 1853, by the publication of a song by Meidell that was received with a roar of laughter in Norway and in America. This rollicking satire, entitled "Oleana," was sung widely among Norwegians, and became indeed a folk song that is still remembered some three-quarters of a century after its day. Many settlers in America joined in the laugh no less heartily for thinking that such a colony might have succeeded had it been established on the fertile open lands of the West instead of on the long-spurned stony and wooded lands at Oleana. Today the song is read with an understanding sharpened by history, for the subtler relation between the satire and the truth with reference both to emigration and to the labor movement in Norway is evident. [39] The song, which is perhaps as important historically as the colony that occasioned it, [40] contains such verses as the following: [41]

In Oleana, that's where I'd like to be, and not drag the chains of slavery in Norway.

> Ole — Ole — Ole — oh! Oleana!
> Ole — Ole — Ole — oh! Oleana!

In Oleana they give you land for nothing, and the grain just pops out of the ground. Golly, that's easy.

> Ole — Ole — Ole — oh! etc.

[38] *Krydseren*, February 19, 1853.

[39] See the comments by Martin B. Ruud in his preface to "Norwegian Emigrant Songs," in *Studies and Records*, 2: 2.

[40] Bjørnstjerne Bjørnson considered "Oleana" a true folk song, one of those that cleared the air in Norway and made possible the writing of the Norwegian national song, "Ja, vi elsker dette Landet." *Norsk Folkeblad*, January 15, 1870.

[41] Translated by Ruud, in *Studies and Records*, 2: 11–13. The original is in *Krydseren*, March 5, 1853, and is reprinted in Ditmar Meidell, *Paa Kryds og paa Tværs, Udvalg af "Krydseren" 1849–54*, 205–206 (Christiania, 1888). Unfortunately the Ruud translation omits two verses of the original.

The grain threshes itself in the granary while I stretch out at ease in my bunk.

And the crops (?)! You just ought to see the potatoes! You can distil at least a quart of whiskey from every one of them.

And Münchener's beer, as sweet as Ytteborg's, runs in the creek for the poor man's delectation.

And the salmon, they leap like mad in the rivers, and hop into the kettles, and cry out for a cover.

And little roasted piggies rush about the streets politely inquiring if you wish for ham.

And the cows they milk and churn and make cheese just as skilfully as Else my sister.

And the calves they kill and flay themselves and turn to veal roast faster than you can take a drink.

And the hens lay eggs as big as a storehouse, and the cocks strike the hour like an eight-day clock.

You bet, they give you two dollars a day for carousing; and if you are good and lazy, they'll probably give you four.

And every last one of us plays upon the fiddle, and dances a merry polka; and that's not so bad!

So come to Oleana, for then you'll live well; the poorest beggar becomes a count over here!

Oh, I'd much rather live in Oleana than drag the chains of slavery over there in Norway.

Ole — Ole — Ole — oh! Oleana!

Ole — Ole — Ole — oh! Oleana!

This satirical thrust at Oleana appeared at a time when the fortunes of the colony were rapidly ebbing. Disillusionment was the predominating note in the letters that came out of Oleana, and these, not a few of which appeared in Norwegian newspapers,[42] did much to persuade emigrants not to go to the colony. Elias Stangeland, an emigration agent who was active in Norway in 1853, carried on a vigorous campaign against Oleana and intimated in February that the land did not belong to Bull but to American speculators. In an emigrant guide he declared that land in the West was cheaper, more fertile, and easier

---

[42] See, for examples, *Stavanger Amtstidende og Adresseavis*, February 12 and May 6, 1853; *Den norske Tilskuer*, March 12, 1853; *Christiania-Posten*, March 19, May 9 and 25, and July 27, 1853; and *Morgenbladet*, May 7, 1853.

to cultivate than that in Oleana.[43] John Holfeldt, Bull's own agent, announced in Wisconsin on March 25 that he could no longer advise emigrants to go to Oleana; and his reluctance was later given due mention in Norway.[44] On April 24 *Morgenbladet* reported that most of the passengers on the emigrant ship " Zephyr " had given up their original intention of joining the Oleana colony and that many others had similarly changed their views.

Affairs at Oleana in the meantime were moving toward a crisis. Ole Bull himself, after long concert tours in the South and West, appeared at the colony on May 17, 1853, the Norwegian national holiday, and participated in a spirited celebration in which many Americans joined the Norwegians. Oleana may have been nearing its collapse, but its promoter's interest in colorful celebrations was still high; great plans were under way for a Fourth of July festival.[45] And when the national holiday arrived it was indeed observed with pomp, some three hundred persons being present. One of the sights was Ole Bull's summer villa, but the master of this " castle " was reported to be ill.[46] Though Bull's land negotiations had been made the previous summer, he did not receive a deed from Cowan

[43] *Stavanger Amtstidende og Adresseavis*, February 5, 15, 19, 1853; Stangeland, *Nogle Veiledende Vink for Udvandrere til Amerika*, 9–12 (Christiania, 1853). The book was reviewed in *Christiania-Posten*, April 7, 1853. Stangeland's motives were impugned in various quarters, for it was known that he had unsuccessfully sought appointment as Ole Bull's agent. See an article in *Emigranten*, December 26, 1852, reprinted and answered by Stangeland in *Stavanger Amtstidende og Adresseavis*, February 19, 1853.

[44] *Emigranten*, March 25, 1853; *Stavanger Amtstidende og Adresseavis*, May 6, 1853. Holfeldt was out of touch with Ole Bull; he said that until Bull explained the Oleana situation to him he could not advise emigrants to join the colony.

[45] The affair is described in a letter of Helge Knudsen Moklebye of June 8, 1853, in *Arbeider-Foreningernes Blad*, July 30, 1853. This is the last favorable letter from Oleana that the writer has found; it speaks of Ole Bull's kindness in aiding Moklebye to send passage money to his wife and family in Norway.

[46] Mr. Jahr prints a long and interesting account of the affair from the *People's Journal* (Coudersport) for July 8, 1853, in *Symra*, 6: 135–140.

until May 24, 1853, and then only for 11,140 acres in scattered tracts; and on September 22 he deeded this land back to Cowan.[47] Between these two events a startling discovery had been made: most of the land in the colony did not belong to Cowan and Bailey, the pretended sellers; the real owner turned out to be a Quaker in Philadelphia named George Stewardson, who had had nothing to do with the negotiations. A fraud of large proportions had obviously been perpetrated on the violinist, who, though Stewardson offered to sell the land at a low price, accepted the advice of a lawyer and withdrew from the entire affair. His losses were estimated variously from $40,000 to $70,000.[48] In August *Emigranten* pronounced the whole scheme a humbug; and in October it was reported that not more than forty emigrants remained at Oleana.[49] Bull was left in serious financial difficulties and at one time was threatened with the confiscation of his precious violin by legal process. Meanwhile the situation in Potter County

[47] Jahr in *Symra*, 6: 134, 144. The price was $10,388; when Bull returned the deed this amount appears to have been refunded.

[48] The clearest account of the fraud seems to be that by Bull's attorney, L. E. Bulkeley, who was not employed until July, 1853. It appeared in the *New York Herald* for November 21, 1853, and is included among Mr. Jahr's documents in *Symra*, 6: 146–150. A long and circumstantial account translated from *Watson's Art Journal* and published in *Morgenbladet*, April 15, 1868 (*cf. ante*, n. 7), asserts that Bull got back $17,000 in 1855 through a suit against Hopper. But Mrs. Bull wrote to her husband on September 9, 1856: "I hear with sorrow that you have lost all your fortune and are very discouraged." *Ole Bulls Breve i Uddrag*, 385. It is possible that there were heavy losses besides the direct investments for land, houses, and supplies. For example, Bull is said to have bought $50,000 worth of stock in the Sunbury and Erie Railroad. C. J. Kraby and J. Haarsle in *Arbeider-Foreningernes Blad*, February 12, 1853. The second Mrs. Bull writes, "Mr. Stewardson was interested in Ole Bull's efforts to found his colony, and offered to make a sale of the land at a very low price; but the artist was able only to buy enough land to protect the people already settled there, and secure the improvements. He brought a suit against the swindlers, who now became his malignant and relentless persecutors." Sara Bull, *Ole Bull*, 227. The price quoted by Stewardson seems to have been thirty-three cents an acre. *Morgenbladet*, April 15, 1868.

[49] *Stavanger Amtstidende og Adresseavis*, September 2, 1853, quoting *Emigranten*; and Jahr, in *Symra*, 6: 144.

was critical, and, with Adelina Patti and M. Strakosch, Ole Bull gave a series of concerts " for the benefit of the Suffering Colonists of Oleona." According to Mr. Jahr, most of the remaining colonists left as soon as they could; a few were there until the late fifties, and one or two remained there as long as they lived.[50]

Thus ended Ole Bull's dream of a New Norway. Oleana is a tale of hope and disappointment; of comedy and tragedy; of idealism and villainy; of very human impulses, strivings, and actions. The evidence indicates that the colony was doomed by its location, natural conditions, unbusinesslike management, and an emigrant poverty that necessitated quick returns from labor. Possibly the tendency of the settlers to depend too much upon Ole Bull and too little upon their own initiative and effort contributed to bring about the failure.[51] The difficulty over the land titles may be said to have administered the *coup de grâce*. Meanwhile emigrants from Norway faced west. The collapse of Oleana did not mean the end of the world for them. Perhaps Utopia was a dream — but there was still the upper Mississippi Valley.[52]

[50] For full information about the last act of the drama and about various persons who were members of the colony the reader is referred to Mr. Jahr's painstaking articles in *Symra*, 6: 151–162, 193–213. It should be noted that though the colony was New Norway, not a few Danes were among the colonists and some other nationalities were represented. A curious fact brought out by Mr. Jahr is that nine Danish Baptists settled there as late as 1854. They are said to have established the first Danish Baptist congregation in America. The Oleana physician, Dr. Edward Joerg, was a German. In 1855 a little group of Germans established the town of Germania in Potter County.

[51] Bull " was altogether too kind; he did far too much for the colonists," was the opinion given Mr. Jahr by a Dane who with his father went to Oleana in 1853. *Symra*, 6: 207. One recalls certain settlements in the West that went through extremely difficult times for the first few years. But the settlers had to struggle on in the face of all odds.

[52] The fantastic Eldorado of Gyntiana, with Peeropolis as its capital, as described in act 4 of Peer Gynt seems to have been suggested to Ibsen's mind by the story of Oleana and Ole Bull. The dramatist, in creating the character of Peer Gynt, undoubtedly drew in part upon that of the dreamer-musician. *Cf.* Koht, *Henrik Ibsen, Eit Diktarliv*, 2: 35–36 (Oslo, 1929).

XIV. EMIGRANT SONGS AND POEMS

THE French-Canadian *voyageur* chanted of love and adventure in rhythm with the paddle of his canoe as he followed lake and stream into the country of furs and Indians. The lumberjack told tales of Homeric vigor and sang heroic songs at the camp fire on winter evenings. The cowboy, at the ranch and on the range or trail, put into song his loneliness, his delight in adventure, and the flavor of life in the open West. The ballads sung by these picturesque figures form an interesting part of their story and are very useful as historical sources. It is not too much to say that American folklore and history have been greatly enriched by the collection and study of such occupational ballads. Less interesting from the literary point of view perhaps, but equally important historically, are the songs and poems thrown off by certain great folk movements, including emigration and immigration. Emigration from Norway produced a very considerable number, and many of them were widely known, sung, and recited.

One of the earliest Norwegian emigrant songs was that composed by Ole Rynning and sung in 1837 on board the "Ægir" in mid-Atlantic at a Seventeenth of May celebration:[1]

The cliffs of Norway lie hidden now behind the waters, but our longings go out to those shores, with their dim and ancient oak-forests,

---

[1] M. B. Ruud, " Norwegian Emigrant Songs," in *Studies and Records*, 2: 4. There are five verses in the original. *Den Bergenske Merkur*, September 16, 1837. As a rule in the quotations given in the present chapter, only a verse or two are drawn from the songs used, since many of them are very long. Mr. Ruud and the writer have in preparation a volume containing the texts and translations of some seventy or eighty emigrant songs. With Mr. Ruud's kind permission some of his translations have been used in this chapter.

where the soughing of the pines and the thunder of the glaciers are music to Norway's son.

And though Destiny should bid him pitch his tent where once Bjørn and Leif pitched theirs, he will cherish always the mountains of old Mother Norway, and yearn with pious longing to see his beloved home once more.

Emigrant farewells help one to understand the poignancy of the leave-taking. A dialect poet of Telemarken sings:[2]

And now farewell to all my folk and parish, for I am going to America, to seek a happier life in the new world. There is no help for it, I must cross the sea. Life has become too hard here for poor folk.

Farewell, now, O valley of Seljord; farewell to church, and woods, and home. Farewell to parson and parish clerk, to kith and kin, and the lovely gardens of home. Would to God this were undone! For the old home lies there grieving. Turn about, hasten, hasten away!

This is typical of many expressions of affection for hill, valley, stream, and folk; one hears echoes of it in songs from both sides of the ocean. In a " Farewell to the Valley of Glommen " by Jonas Lie, an emigrant speaks to a beloved stream of the farmer's struggle against adverse circumstances:[3]

Where are the happy times of yore? And why have all things come to desolation? That you can answer, you deep Glommen, for you wound by the peasant's home and held it mirrored in your waters. You knew of the sorrow that dimmed his eye; you saw him struggle on, strong man that he was, until, weary and with broken courage, he sought a foreign land. The farms remain, half desolate, like melancholy witnesses bearing complaints.

A noted Norwegian poet understood that the sharpest wrench came in parting from the everyday home surroundings. And he causes the emigrant woman, Kari, to sing:[4]

---

[2] Jørund Telnes, *Rupe-ber*, 70–74 (Hamar, 1878). The translation is by Mr. Ruud.

[3] Jonas Lie, *Digte*, 16–18 (Kjøbenhavn, 1889).

[4] From Wergeland's *Fjeldstuen*. The play is in Hartwig Lassen, ed., *Henrik Wergelands Samlede Skrifter*, 4: 439–469 (Christiania, 1854).

Farewell, my old spinning wheel. How I shall miss you: the thought of leaving you breaks the heart in my breast.

No more in the evenings shall we sit by the fireside, old friend of mine, and gossip together.

Ah, all that I see has its roots in my heart. And now they are torn out, do you wonder it bleeds!

A tone of bitterness may be detected in some of the farewells:[5]

Farewell, thou Mother Norway, now I must leave thee. Because thou fostered me I give thee many thanks. All too sparing wert thou in providing food for the throng of thy laborers, though thou gavest more than enough to thy well-schooled sons.

Songs and poems were mediums for the emigration debate, which raged in Norway in the forties, fifties, and sixties. Thus M. B. Landstad, a noted divine, spoke to the people in 1842:[6]

My brothers, hear a word of counsel: remain at home here in the friendly North! From a sorrowful heart I beg you to stay here at home; do not sail over yonder. Little do you know what it is you are doing, nor the bitter disillusioning that may be yours. For when you are buried over there in the deep forests or the wilderness, a restless longing will shatter your peace, and you will remember then what now you forget.

In similar vein another minister, P. A. Jensen, spoke in the sixties:[7]

Think you that you will find in those new lands to which you go the same music in the streams? the same sun? the same summer? Think you the flower that grew by your mother's cot blooms on foreign shores no less?

Nay, be sure, you will not find it so. For clouds will hide the sun from you, and darkness, the stars. Soon will you forget the speech and customs of your father; and however life may deal with you, you will live an exile always.

[5] From an "old emigrant song" printed in Ole Svendsen, *Solør og Solørfolket,* 57–59 (Kongsvinger, 1926).

[6] *Morgenbladet,* June 24, 1842; and in M. B. Landstad, *Sange og Digte af forskjellige Slags, mest fra gamle Dage,* 70–75 (Christiania, 1879); translated by Ruud, in *Studies and Records,* 2: 7–10.

[7] *Morgenbladet,* January 29, 1864; reprinted by Malmin, in *Decorah-Posten,* March 27, 1925; translated by Ruud, in *Studies and Records,* 2: 18–19.

You would go to seek for gold? Assuredly, you shall find more at home. Dig it out of the soil; that will bring you honor. Wrest it from the deeps of the sea and the heart of the mountains, where it glows like burning coals in the darkness.

The conflict of opinion in Norway over emigration is reflected in a group of poetic dialogues. In one the first speaker says:[8]

Norway is a poor and wretched land, and now I am going to America.

Here I have to slave and suffer want: in America everyone can make a living.

There I shall win riches and glory. Farewell, farewell! Here we go.

But he is promptly answered by a second speaker:

Poor fellow! You'll soon regret you've left friends and kin and home behind you.

When the ship bears you far from Norway's coast, deep longings will waken and melt your heart.

For Norway is truly a fostering mother; and you will miss her, miss her more than you can think.

Sometimes a satirical note enters the dialogues. Thus the first speaker in one declares:[9]

When icicles a fathom long hang from the roof and when the force of the wind whirls the snow, filling the kitchen and piling drifts on the threshing floor — then I long for the Mississippi Valley.

When I have worked long with scythe and rake on rocky and almost grassless fields, then I want to get away from our lean soil and go where everything grows without manure.

Why, the hay grows there like vines of hops, and in one day one can cut enough for winter fodder for the cow, which is as large as an elephant. Ah, how wonderful everything is over there!

He is answered by a second speaker:

Every earthly thing has two sides: if one is white, be sure the other is black. Turn over that which you desire to praise: draw from its good its evil thing.

[8] *Morgenbladet,* August 23, 1846; reprinted by Malmin, in *Decorah-Posten,* March 27, 1925; translated by Ruud, in *Studies and Records,* 2: 14.

[9] Johannes Olsen Veseth, "Sang i Anledning af Udvandringen til Amerika," in *Nordlyset* (Trondhjem), March 15, 1844.

An Eden means something more than merely an abundance of worldly goods. How often is not the rich man unhappy in the midst of all his joys.

In a dialect poem from Telemarken,[10] Sveinung speaks first:

I am not going to stay in Norway any longer. I am going to America; that's the best thing for me to do. I have heard that men who know how to use their hands can live well there. Land is cheap, and heavy taxes don't eat up everything a farmer makes.

You hear in this country a lot of fine talk about liberty and equality and that the people hold the purse-strings; but the bureaucrats are paid too well, while the common people must struggle along. The government brags about undertakings that must cost a barrel of gold; at the same time economic life is strangled by all sorts of restrictions and crushed by tariffs.

Poor peasant lads are drafted for military service, while the rich man's sons escape. That's Norwegian equality. Have they forgotten the provision of the constitution: The defense of the kingdom is a duty resting upon all. Shall we never remedy such abuses? Will people stand such things forever?

But Guttorm takes it upon himself to reply to these complaints:

I'll admit that in some things you are right; but I remember that there are many things in this world that might be mended. Many burdens have been lightened since Norway gained her independence, many abuses corrected, and many more will be.

Suppose I can live in Wisconsin free from care and anxiety, what good is that if I am not happy there, but long every hour for home? Those who find life in Norway so full of hardships may perhaps discover that life in America is not so much more easy than in the country they left.

Song after song touches upon the powerful economic motives that lie back of the emigration; there are also allusions to broad social issues and to class antagonisms. A poem written in the woods of Wisconsin in 1847 suggests something of this:[11]

[10] *Morgenbladet*, February 27, 1846; and Tormod Knudsen, *Blandede Rimerier*, 46–48 (Skien, 1846). The translation is by Mr. Ruud.

[11] *Nordlyset* (Muskego, Wisconsin), August 19, 1847; reprinted in Holand, *De Norske Settlementers Historie*, 57–58; translated by Ruud, in *Studies and Records*, 2: 4–5.

Farewell, Norway, and God bless thee. Stern and severe wert thou always, but as a mother I honor thee, even though thou skimped my bread. All things vanish. Grief and care sink down upon the heart; still the memory of thee refreshes the soul like the deep sleep of a child.

Other lands offer me independence, and for my labor well-being to my children. These, O Norway, thou didst not give me, for thou art a land of lords and slaves, where the great ones ruled and we obeyed.

Once more, God bless thee; to the day of my death I will pray God to keep thee; for thou wert the keeper of my childhood and the joys of childhood thou gavest me. I will remember thee always, whatever life may bring, and I will pray, " Throw off the chains that embittered my youth for me."

Followers of Marcus Thrane, the labor organizer, were equally vigorous in their criticism.[12]

We common people work under wretched circumstances to win our daily bread, while the great folk live handsomely, for they know how to find the gold. From the busy hand of the working class they receive their steak, larded and hot. They have a monopoly on the labor of Norwegians.

In the same song, Norwegians are urged to emigrate:

Every man with courage in his heart is leaving Norway. America is a glorious country; of that there can be no doubt. True, the Atlantic Ocean is broad, but, my friend, if you can get away, go, for in Norway things are great indeed — but only among the great folk.

The emigrants were frequently taunted with the charge that they were seeking an impossible Eldorado. Occasionally, as in the following song, they denied this:[13]

I do not expect to find gold more easily there than elsewhere. No, I am ready to work in the sweat of my brow. Through effort and industry I shall make for myself a new home.

"You can make a home for yourself here," say many. "Work and save here, where you are, and then you can avoid going there to take a chance in the lottery of luck, to become a foreign slave."

[12] Nils J. Qvarme, " Arbeiderforenings Sang," in *Arbeider-foreningernes Blad,* July 20, 1850; also in P. W. Bergh, ed., *Arbeiderforeningernes Sangbog,* 15–16 (Kristiania, 1850).

[13] K. E., *Emigrantens Farvel til Norge* (Trondhjem, n.d.). A copy of this four-page leaflet is in Videnskabsselskabets Bibliotek, Trondhjem.

"My dear friend, do not talk in this way. I have already tried; through my best years have I labored here; but I am as far from my goal as when I first began, when I viewed so hopefully the prospect of a home."

" Nor does this mean slavery — for America is free. Work is not slavery; and thrift is no lottery. In the free land of the West every man is a free-born citizen."

Aasmund O. Vinje, a poet of the people, himself born of *husmand* folk in upper Telemarken, knew at first hand the problems of the small farmer; on several occasions he was on the point of emigrating himself; and he has expressed the fierce urge that burned within many a young Norwegian: " Gradually as I grew older, I was filled with the desire to leave the *bygd,* to go to America or anywhere else, only not to stay home, where there was nothing for me to do. Away, away, even though it led to the abyss." [14] And in 1866, when he was struggling with the economic difficulties of a poor author, he produced a long poem beginning:[15]

I am going to emigrate. Come along with me; don't sit here at home. Let us turn our backs on all this toil and trouble — a toil, which, indeed, has rich rewards for some, most of all for the philistine, but so little for you and me that we can hardly eke out a living.

Despite every argument against their going, the emigrants went, and though their criticisms were sometimes bitter, they carried in their hearts a deep love for the land of their birth. This affection is a natural theme of many songs, some by emigrants, some by observers in Norway seeking to interpret the emigrant. Among the latter was one who wrote thus of Norway:[16]

From thee every eastern breeze, when its mild breath caresses my cheek, brings me a friendly greeting — and I understand my loss.

---

[14] *Dølen, Eit Vikublad,* January 14, 1866.
[15] *Dølen, Eit Vikublad,* April 22, 1866; and in *A. O. Vinjes Skrifter i Utval,* 3: 185–188 (Kristiania, 1886). The translation is by Mr. Ruud.
[16] Christian Monsen, *Samlede Digte,* 71-74 (Trondhjem, 1854).

An "Evening Prayer on the Atlantic" closes with the words:[17]

Night has fallen; the evening breezes hurry our ship toward a foreign shore. But the ties that bind me to home fire my courage and strengthen my soul. Should all things else perish — fleeting as a shooting star — O God, let not the ties break that bind me to the North.

And an emigrant on the plains of Texas in the fifties sings:[18]

When at the close of my earthly wanderings the twilight of life enfolds me and the angel of death breaks the chains that bind me, my spirit will soar out to my eternally beloved North.

As one reads such verses one remembers the forlorn figure of Beret in Professor Rølvaag's novel of Dakota pioneering and is reminded of the cost of the pioneer's experience. Yet one must be careful not to misinterpret the evidence. Probably the great majority of the emigrants, as the process of transition went its inevitable way, were content with their choice. A western farmer, in a song the form of which reminds one of the cowboy ballads, reviews the story of his experiences in America, the struggles with problems occasioned by forest, farm, language, and social relations in a new environment, and says:[19]

And so, almost unconsciously, we have grown old in the land. And life has treated us right well. Though not every good fortune fell into our hands, yet can we be happy and contented.

Several songs and poems describe the departure of emigrant ships from Norwegian harbors. Thus, from one written in 1861:[20]

[17] Christian Hansen, "Aftenbøn paa Atlanterhavet," in *Morgenbladet*, July 19, 1846; reprinted by Malmin, in *Decorah-Posten*, March 27, 1925; translated by Ruud, in *Studies and Records*, 2:13–14.

[18] J. M. C. W. Wærenskjold, "En Normands Hjemvee," in *Emigranten*, March 19, 1856.

[19] "Korleids dæ gjek," in A. Sollid, *En Amerikatur. Reiseerindringer*, 116–118 (Skien, 1896).

[20] Christian Olsen, *Kvældstunder. Nytaarsgave 1862. Nogle Digte af Rungolf*, 81–85 (Christiania, 1862); originally published in *Morgenbladet*, April 30, 1861;

They go aboard; the old man stands motionless on the shore gazing at the ship, like Mother Norway herself lamenting the going of her children.

. . . .

The winds swell the flapping sails, and the ship glides majestically out to sea. The groves fade away, and the deep valley and the mountain peaks are lost in the mists.

Farewell — the last word of parting. The storms from the North shall shout it, and the little billows gliding softly off-shore shall sing it like a threnody heard in dreams.

And yet, even now, when the last skerry has disappeared, the brothers still stand gazing fixedly at the spot where the last glimpse of the fatherland vanished away.

Numerous special aspects of Norwegian emigration are illustrated in the songs. Before the departure of a gold-hunting expedition in 1850 from Trondhjem for South America and California, its members sang a song of anticipation and farewell:[21]

To the west, where the dazzling sun sinks down to hide behind dark blue waves, a golden cloud drifts away until, hanging over California forests, it catches a reflection that we can glimpse of the riches Heaven gave the western world.

Away, away then, with courage high! For fortune awaits the brave. Even as our bark turns its prow stoutly against the angry, foaming billows, so, with light hearts, we face the dangers that await us, with hope in our souls and trust in God.

. . . .

To thee, beloved land, I bid farewell. Soon I no longer shall view thy beauty nor hear the music of thy waterfalls. Thy snow-capped mountains will fade from sight and slowly thy coast will sink away in the mists like a mother being lowered in the grave. No glimpse then of thy tallest peaks; only a lonely sail on the boundless deep.

One Norwegian who refused to join the gold-seekers explained in verse why he remained at home.[22] He concedes that California is a land of glory:

reprinted by Malmin, in *Decorah-Posten*, March 27, 1925; translated by Ruud, in *Studies and Records*, 2: 16–18.

[21] Monsen, *Samlede Digte*, 346–349. See *ante*, 276.

[22] J. H. Bentzen, "Eldorado," in *Poetiske Smaablomster*, 37–39 (Kristianssand, 1857).

Ah, there the trees bear golden fruits; there sparkling coins issue forth from the mouths of fishes. Stalks of gold spring up from the mold of the fields; and the savannas are crowned with gilded flowers.

He relates that it is not difficult to get supplies in the West:

And if one desires a steak for one's table, one can hurl a lasso and capture a buffalo.

But there are disadvantages:

Of course one's life is often endangered, for one is apt to be scalped by a redskin or, what is scarce better, atrociously carved by a Yankee and plunged into the arms of death by his bowie knife.

After duly considering the matter, he makes his choice:

Love and peace dwell in my heart, and so, enriched by them and by the gold of song, I have found Eldorado in my own home valley.

" On the Return of a Person Who Has Seen the Free States and California " is the imposing title of a poem of 1856 that opens thus:[23]

You ventured far toward the distant west; you went to the Columbian land, where freedom and equality flourish best and coercion is unknown.

One of Norway's famous painters, Tidemand, understood something of the emotion stirred in the hearts of parents by the arrival of an " America letter " from a son. In one of his canvases he has recorded such a moment in the lives of a *bonde* and his wife. This picture occasioned these verses on " The Letter from America ":[24]

But the old father sits wrapped in thought, for the longed-for letter tells nothing of the dreams that ensnared the son, of green fields and shining gold.

A cloud gathers over his brows and, with a deep sigh, he says: " Go not away from the North, you Norwegian farmer. Live thriftily and independently on your ancestral lands; and become at last earth of the earth of your fathers."

[23] Osvald Skov, " Ved en Persons Hjemkomst, der har seet Fristaterne og Kalifornien," in *Nordre Trondhjems Amtstidende*, August 26, 1856.

[24] Conrad N. Schwach, " Brevet fra Amerika," in *Nordlyset* (Trondhjem), December 6, 1847.

Another painting by Tidemand picturing a farewell scene inspired several poems, including one containing these gloomy verses:[25]

A fever sweeps over Norway's mountains into the most distant and hidden valleys. With fearful effect it seizes men and women; it carries people off by the thousands. From home and fireside the younger generation depart — and the aged sorrow in lonely huts.

To the West! To America! Thus comes the mighty call from over the western sea. And in response great throngs set forth to another home — or to an early grave. Has the Fatherland nothing wherewith to feed its own children, since they thus desert it?

Ah, yes! Poor indeed old Norway may be, but it has ever bread to reward industrious toil. And for its mountain homes it has the shelter of freedom. And it has the sweet speech of the motherland. Still, those caught in the toils of the fever must go! Alas, neither wise counsel nor upbraiding is of any avail.

The view of emigration as a devastating epidemic is also reflected in " The Mountain Hut," an anti-emigration play written by Henrik Wergeland on his death bed in 1845.[26] The story, which has its setting in Upper Telemarken, centers about an emigration agent and a little group of peasants. Dreaming of an aroused Norway in which the vigor of its people would give added importance and interest to the national life, Wergeland believed that his country needed to keep its sons and daughters in order to fulfill its destiny. The commerce in which the emigrant ships trafficked was, in his opinion, a commerce of blood, carrying away the country's most precious possessions. In " The Mountain Hut " he introduces a wood-nymph, who sings plaintively of the emigration:

Woe, woe! Once again I am minded of the horrors of the Black Death. Now, as then, the farmsteads lie desolate in the valleys; the hearths are cold; the people have departed.

She turns upon the emigration agent:

[25] " Afskeden," in Andreas Munch, *Nyeste Digte,* 91–92 (Christiania, 1861).
[26] Lassen, ed., *Henrik Wergelands Samlede Skrifter,* 4: 439–469. The translations are by Mr. Ruud.

Curses upon thee, thou serpent, come hither to let the blood of this people. Haste thee to return whence thou came, ere thou art discovered, thou demon, scattering the pestilence abroad.

The poet pictures the enthusiasm of the emigrants after they hear the agent speak of the glories of America. They sing:

Let us away and over the sea; bury our sorrows. Far in the West we will bury the others: cast our sufferings away in the deeps of the forest, a new life to begin. Let us hurry away. Here bread is scarce; in America it falls into one's mouth all covered with sugar. The soil there is rich; and silver and gold jingle in every man's purse. Rather would we die than suffer at home. But nay, in America shall we win a new life! Away, away!

Later, as the emigrants board a waiting ship, a satirical echo of this farewell song is sounded by the sailors:

Away, away! Draw up the ladder-rope! We'll pack you bumpkins like herring in a barrel — 'tis only an interlude twixt barrel and palace, a nice, warm nest with pigs for companions — and perhaps a nice snake will smuggle him in. Your white bread will stick in your throats, and you'll remember with longing your thick, sticky cakes. If only you clodhoppers, when you open your bags, would let loose a good northeast wind!

In another song of the play Wergeland taunts the emigrant:

Many a fool sailed across the sea to America, but came back soon, like a tramp, without a penny in his pocket. For go you east or go you west, a home in Norway is the best of all. There is my God, there is my bride; there will I live to the day of my death.

Not all the songs are satirical, however. There is, for example, the song of Sigrid, — an anticipation of Ibsen's Solveig, — promising to wait faithfully for the return of her emigrant lover:

Here mid these bleak walls, where yet I see him everywhere, here will I live. Here will I cherish my love; here will I pledge each day my faith to my beloved.

Here will I wait for him till I am old and wrinkled: for he will come. The wild winds carried him away; the winds will bring him back.

Here I can see the weathervane from the window, and know how the breeze is blowing. When it comes from the west, then will I weave flowers in my hair; aye, though the locks be silver.

It is interesting to note that Wergeland's famous contemporary, Welhaven, also touched on emigration in his poetry. In 1836 Welhaven got a glimpse at Havre de Grace of the continental emigration that was pouring through that port. In a memorable poem, "The Emigrants," he describes the coming of the Yankee emigrant ship, the throng of poor folk who boarded it, and the melancholy departure.[27] A scene on deck suggests to him the plight of Europe:

On the forecastle sits a mother with a child in her arms; but the babe finds no comfort at her bosom.
For she is like the ancient mother Europe, who whispers that soon the currents of life will be stilled in her breasts.

An interesting development in Norwegian emigration in the forties and the fifties was the departure for America of many young ministers, trained at the University of Christiania. A farewell addressed to one of these "apostles" about to leave Norway in 1851 throws light on the attitude of the Norwegians toward the organization of the religious activities of the immigrants in the West:[28]

Far away, beyond the dark sea waves, is blossoming forth that great land of liberty. There, deep in age-old forests, on green fields, or beside silver-blue waters, many a little Norway is now springing up. For Norwegian brothers — ah, by the thousands — have been fated by the Norns to leave their loved mountains, to depart from ancestral lands in peaceful valleys.

. . . .

And now the great throng, whose departure we have witnessed, who have crossed the sea to the distant strand, look back, with longing and with emotion, to the mother church in the land of their

[27] Johan S. Welhaven, "Emigranterne (Havre de Grace)," in *Den Constitutionelle*, June 18, 1836; and *Samlede Skrifter*, 3: 145–148. The translation is by Mr. Ruud.
[28] "Farvel til Hr. Pastor G. F. Dietrichson, i Anledning hans Afreise til Amerika," in *Stavanger Amstidende og Adresseavis*, April 26, 1851.

youth. For it gathered them in its tender arms; it cradled Norway's sons while they grew strong and great; in that church they dreamed the brightest dreams of their lives and learned the Heavenly precepts of truth and peace.

Over there our brothers sat in the shadow of death; unheard was the pure word of life; but now temples are built there for the worship of God and under their arches abides the Holy Spirit. And we are sending over a pious band of apostles, who, guided by heavenly angels, shall light for our brothers divine beacons pointing the way to our better home.

The return to Norway of a disappointed emigrant is the theme of a long dialect poem, a tale of high hopes blasted, of disillusionment, suffering, losses, and sorrow, culminating in complete discouragement.[29] In this poet's representation of one side — the darkest side — of emigration, the sorrowful recital is concluded with a moral:

And so I have returned to Norway's shores, poorer, alas, than when I left. One first learns to appreciate Norway after one has yielded to the temptation of emigrating to a foreign land.

This narrative in verse was obviously an anti-emigration document. Evidence of the deep concern that the movement prompted in Norway is found in the popularity of songs that had a distinctly anti-emigration tone. Ditmar Meidell's " Oleana," with its rhythm and sharp-pointed satire, came at an opportune psychological moment, made a profound impression, and is still widely known and often quoted and sung.[30]

Other emigrant songs of hostile tone are still sung in Norway. For example, in February, 1929, the present writer met an aged man in Bergen, who sang verses from an old west-coast ballad which describes the spread of " America fever " in the winter, tells of popular anticipations of fortune in America, pictures the departure in the spring from the home communities, and characterizes

---

[29] Nikolai Ramm Østgaard, *Østerdølen hemkømmen fraa Amerika* (Kristiania, 1853).

[30] See *ante,* 303.

the emigrant throng assembled at Bergen.[31]   The vessels
waited in the harbor, according to the ballad:

So we rowed up the bay; and there lay the mighty ships, with
masts hewn of the tallest trees in the forest, — all ready to sail for
America.   It was a wondrous sight to see: the decks swarmed like
an ant heap, kerchiefs and caps of every color — and all were bent
on leaving the country.

Emigrants strolled about the ancient city:

They went knocking about the streets by the hundred; sold their
old clothes and bought new in their place; paraded about in frock
coats like eminent citizens; carried umbrellas and smoked fat cigars.
The girls bought dresses and shawls like young ladies; if our maidens
here at home could have seen them, they would certainly have wished
to forsake their native land.

Then the travelers sailed away to the West, while the
ballad-maker turned homeward, singing as he went:

And, so, as for me, I intend to stay in Norway, even if one cannot get rich there.   I will work and toil for myself and my family, live
and die where my fathers have lived.   I will dig and delve in field and
garden, give thanks to God for his goodness to me, and love and
cherish my native land.

Such are the songs and poems of Norwegian emigration.
In the original many of them have a vigor and a rhythm
that go far toward explaining their longevity.   In general, however, they can lay small claim to our attention
as poetry.   By way of compensation, however, they illumi-
nate and make vivid many aspects of the movement.[32]

[31] The man was Hans T. Reigstad, Hamre, via Bergen.   The full text of the
song, En ny Vise om Udvandringen til Amerika, is in an undated, four-page leaflet,
a copy of which is in Bergens Offentlige Bibliotek.   The translation is by Mr. Ruud.

[32] The texts of some interesting German-Russian emigrant songs are printed in
Viktor Schirmunski, " Das kolonistische Lied in Russland," in Zeitschrift des Vereins
für Volkskunde, vol. 37–38, p. 182–210 (1927–28).   See also Hildegarde Meyer,
Nord-Amerika im Urteil des Deutschen Schrifttums bis zur Mitte des 19. Jahrhunderts
(Hamburg, 1929).   Among the songs printed in this book is one (p. 108) con-
taining these lines:

Rosinen, Mandeln ist man da — wie hier zu Land das Brot.
Denn in dem Land Amerika — hat man garkeine Noth.

XV. CURRENTS AND CROSS CURRENTS OF THE FIFTIES

THE followers of the labor organizer Marcus Thrane evinced so keen an interest in California gold, in Oleana, and generally in emigration that it may be well to examine the Thrane movement, which is one of the chief factors in the unrest characteristic of Norway in the fifties. Its leader, an able man of good family, had traveled on the continent, especially in France and Switzerland, as a young man, and had there become familiar with the ideas of such men as William Weitling, Cabet, Saint-Simon, and Louis Blanc. When the February Revolution generated a new social and political ferment in Europe, Thrane seized the opportunity in Norway to strike out boldly on new lines, to formulate a definite program of humanitarian reform, and to attempt to organize the workers. He was an effective writer and speaker; he had practical organizing ability; and he did not lack the courage to challenge the leaders of conservatism.[1]

Thrane raised the banner of class struggle in 1848 in behalf of two groups, the *husmænd* and the town and country laborers. He saw little prospect of betterment for them in the *bonde* movement, for though the *bønder* had made important gains, these gains were in the interest of their own class, the freeholders, by tradition and practice a rural aristocracy, albeit for the most part small and impecunious holders. As landowners they exercised the

---

[1] The most discriminating account of the Thrane movement is Halvdan Koht, *Marcus Thrane: Til Hundreaarsdagen 14. Oktober 1917* (Kristiania, 1917. 72 p.). In 1914 Professor Koht brought out a preliminary work entitled *Arbeidar-rørsla av 1848 i Noreg* (Oslo, *Norske Folkeskrifter*, no. 60). Other studies are Jacob Friis, *Marcus Thrane* (Christiania, 1917. 104 p.) and O. A. Øverland, *Thraniterbevægelsen* (Kristiania, 1903. 360 p.).

right of suffrage; fighting to free their class from bureaucratic overlordship, they had formed a liberal opposition,
but they were in no sense thoroughgoing liberals — especially the *bønder* of eastern Norway — and on some issues
they were essentially conservative. The salvation of the
husmænd and laborers, Thrane believed, lay in winning
universal manhood suffrage, and thus injecting a third
element, a proletariat, so to speak, into national politics.
The condition of these classes offered a fertile field for
agitation, though neither the country's industrial development nor its stage of political advance held out much
hope of a successful labor movement.

In 1845 the towns had only thirteen per cent of the
total Norwegian population. Of the 162,000 towns-
people, 11,600 were laborers, 6,700 artisans and appren-
tices, and 17,000 servants. The first of these groups,
mainly family heads, represented an element of some fifty
thousand people. Like the *husmænd* the town laborers
were without the suffrage; and their economic condition,
marked by low wages, general poverty, and unsatisfactory
conditions of apprenticeship, was on the whole as unfavorable as that of the rural class. The general situation
of the *husmand* group has been described in the introduc-
tory chapter of this volume. It is clear that agitation
among the *husmænd* promised results; and the advocate
of reform who came forward to organize the agitation
quickly disclosed his skill as a leader.

Thrane was a school-teacher in Lillehammer when the
winds of the February Revolution blew into the North;
in 1848 he was made editor of a newspaper in Drammen,
in which he vigorously voiced his doctrines; ousted from
that position because of his radicalism, he began to organize labor societies, the first of which, in Drammen,
was established on December 27, 1848. In the spring of
1849 he founded *Arbeider-foreningernes Blad* as an organ

of the movement, in which he carried on a sustained attack on the ruling classes and brilliantly voiced the labor demands. After about a year of preliminary work, the organization of labor societies proceeded with startling rapidity: by March, 1850, there were 133, with 11,554 members; and by June the number had increased to 273, with 20,854 members.[2]

Thrane wanted the state to aid the *husmænd* to rise out of their dependent position; in suggesting that it take over all uncultivated tillable lands to sell to workers, especially *husmænd*, and in favoring the establishment of workers' banks he came close to reform ideas that had been urged earlier by Reiersen.[3] But he went much further. As early as November 3, 1849, he issued in the labor paper a general platform, the most significant demands of which were universal manhood suffrage; the improvement of the position of the *husmænd* and the facilitating of their rise to the status of *bønder*; reduction of the tariff on grain; universal military service; a broadening and humanizing of the curriculum of the schools, with history, geography, and civics to supplement the traditional religion, arithmetic, and writing; improvements in civil law, especially with reference to creditors and debtors; and the abolition of trade privileges.[4] It is clear that the program of this farmer-labor leader was that of a humanitarian and liberal fired with the vision of economic and cultural improvement for the common man. That it was considered radical and dangerous seems very strange to the reader of today who does not appreciate the circumstances of its time and setting. Thrane's proposals were substantially embodied in a petition to the government signed by 12,833 persons and presented on

[2] Friis, *Thrane*, 59.
[3] Koht, *Thrane*, 12. See *ante*, p. 157–158.
[4] *Arbeider-foreningernes Blad*, November 3, 1849.

May 19, 1850, and later in a general platform adopted by a convention of labor delegates at Christiania in July of that year. Thrane was also a profound believer in complete religious toleration, and a collision with the clergy brought upon him a charge of blasphemy and a sentence to a half year's imprisonment; but the decision was reversed by a higher court. Meanwhile, in the fall of 1850, it was hoped that labor influence would put into the Storthing some members favorable to the labor program; but though the *bønder* triumphed over the bureaucracy, only one man was elected as a result of labor support — Johan Sverdrup, destined to become one of Norway's greatest parliamentary leaders.[5]

Several interesting books have been written by Norwegian historians on the history of the Thrane movement, but, curiously, they have taken little or no cognizance of its relation to emigration. The records prove a significant connection, however.[6] Soon after establishing *Arbeider-foreningernes Blad*, Thrane published an article on America and emigration in which everyone with small prospects was advised to emigrate and those seeking to discourage or prevent emigration were characterized as enemies of the people. Emigration was justified not alone because of good prospects in the United States and the lack of liberal legislation in Norway, but also from the point of view of the laborers remaining at home. The author of the article believed that a reduction in the number of laborers would have a beneficial effect on wages. Since workers with families ordinarily could not save enough to go, he advised unmarried laborers and especially servants to emigrate.[7] In a later issue it was

<hr/>

[5] Koht, *Thrane*, ch. 4; Friis, *Thrane*, 32–34, 66.

[6] Professor Koht reminds his readers that Thrane went through his intellectual development in a period of unrest, one sign of which was emigration. *Thrane*, 7.

[7] *Arbeider-foreningernes Blad*, May 26, 1849.

even suggested that the state and the communes, considering the burden of poor relief, ought to help people to emigrate.[8] These utterances are typical of the position taken by Thrane. He opened up his pages to article after article giving information for prospective emigrants. In one issue, in a dialogue between two Norwegians, one is made to say: "The difference between Norway and America in short is this: in America one sees the fruits of one's early labor, whereas in Norway the chances are that one will lose ground year by year, as one's family increases and one's powers decline."[9] In the spring of 1850 the paper published a curious proposal for organizing emigration through selling shares for the purchase of an emigrant ship. It was hoped that at least eight thousand shares would be sold at one dollar each; when a sufficient sum was raised to make possible the purchase of a ship, lots would be drawn to determine who among the shareholders should go first; a small fare, less than half the usual rate, would be charged. In effect the scheme was an emigration lottery. Though it does not appear to have been carried out, it is a striking illustration of the labor point of view. In the summer of 1853 a society of prospective artisan emigrants in Christiania worked out plans for chartering a vessel, hoping thereby to get cheaper rates and better accommodations than they could secure by the usual emigrant packets.[10] Another illustration of the labor attitude may be found in the labor songs, among which farewells to Norway, the refrains of which were its unfavorable contrast with

[8] *Arbeider-foreningernes Blad*, September 29, 1849.

[9] *Arbeider-foreningernes Blad*, November 24, 1849.

[10] *Arbeider-foreningernes Blad*, March 16, 1850. Thrane's idea probably goes back to a plan of sixty ship carpenters of Drammen in the fall of 1849 to borrow — from the state — enough money to build an emigrant vessel. In fact Thrane is said to have inspired this plan, which failed, of course, to get any encouragement from the government. *Drammens Adresse*, September 20, 1849. On the Christiania group of 1853 see *Stavanger Amtstidende og Adresseavis*, August 18, 1853.

America, were popular.[11] It is clear that emigration colored the thinking of Thrane and his followers.

As the labor movement progressed Thrane's own position seemed to become somewhat anomalous. On the one side he cautioned moderation to turbulent followers who provoked street demonstrations and seemed to be moving toward revolution. Thrane maintained the right of revolution, but would defer its exercise until every other method had failed. On the other hand he was apparently not ready to knock at the doors of the *bønder,* in whose camp a split was now imminent between the democratic western group and the conservative East. And late in 1850 Thrane withdrew from leadership, though not from the movement. It is possible that he felt, in taking this step, that he would thereby promote self-leadership among the laborers, which in his opinion was desirable. In June, 1851, at a general labor assembly, he again counseled moderation and the use of parliamentary means.

On the whole the movement was moderate in its methods, but the government, long waiting for an opportunity to crush it, moved suddenly in July, 1851. Thrane and other leaders were summarily arrested; an investigating commission was appointed; in all 149 persons were indicted for conspiracy against the safety of the state; less than twenty were acquitted; and the others were sentenced to imprisonment, some for terms as high as fifteen years, Thrane himself for four (not counting a lengthy incarceration pending the verdict). This ruthless treatment of the labor organizers ushered in a severe reaction. The movement collapsed and nothing like it appeared again for thirty years. Thrane himself emigrated to the United States in 1863 and opened a new chapter in his career in the West, active in the interests of the

---

[11] See *ante,* p. 313; P. W. Bergh, *Arbeiderforeningernes Sangbog,* 15, 27, 70.

poor and the downtrodden as an editor and writer. He challenged the Lutheran clergy with something of his old-time vigor; and he interested himself in programs of social justice looking to the amelioration of the condition of workers. Various other members of his group, including the *husmand* Gudbrand Jonsrud, sought refuge in the United States after release from prison.[12]

Ostensibly the Thrane movement failed, but there was success in failure, for it profoundly influenced Norwegian life and thought. Two reforms went through in the very year of its collapse — a *husmand* law which, though conservative, restricted the demands that could be made by the *bønder,* and a reduction in the tariff on grain. Three years later a universal military service law was passed, which removed some of the opportunities for exemption by the privileged classes, though it did not go far enough wholly to satisfy the desires of the country people. The most important political effect of the movement was perhaps its stimulus to a new alignment: the cleavage of the large and small landowners, the latter moving toward an alliance with labor and the creation of a liberal party under Sverdrup, the former toward the conservative fold. The movement for social and political reform went on, though Thrane was cast aside. And the *husmand* class has emancipated itself since the fifties. In 1845 it comprised twenty-six per cent of the country population; in 1875, fifteen per cent; in 1910, four and three-tenths per cent; and in 1920, scarcely three per cent. The tendency is strikingly illustrated by the figures for 1910, which show that only thirty-three per cent of the *husmænd* were under fifty years; forty-four and four-tenths per cent were over sixty; twenty-one and five-tenths per cent over

[12] Koht, *Thrane,* 18–52; Øverland, *Thraniterbevægelsen,* 360; an interesting letter by Johnsrud from Rock County, Wisconsin, written on January 8, 1858, is in *Morgenbladet,* March 9, 1858.

seventy.[13] Not legislation, but economic changes and emigration have been responsible for the elimination of this
important class in the Norwegian population. Touching
on the building of railroads, the development of factories,
emigration, and other changes, Professor Johnson writes,
" This entire development has led youth and labor away
from the country districts to the industries, towns, and
foreign countries; it has depopulated the *husmand*
places. . . ."[14] The Thrane movement heralded the
new day in Norwegian social, economic, and political life;
it profoundly stirred Henrik Ibsen and other literary leaders who soon were to win national and international fame;
and it stimulated the association of the idea of discontent
among laborers with that of emigration.

While the Thrane movement was reverberating in Norway in 1850 popular attention was momentarily diverted
by the activities of a pronounced republican, Harro Paul
Harring, Danish by birth, part Norwegian by blood,
American by adoption, and a cosmopolitan revolutionist
who had been associated with Mazzini and Garibaldi, had
spent five years in the United States as an artist, and had
been driven out of Germany for revolutionary activities
in 1848. Harring put his republican ideas before the
Norwegians in a newspaper, " The Voice of the People,"
which he edited for a short time, and in a play, " The
American Bequest," which developed the theme that all
men are born free and equal. He was an admirer of the
United States, but he condemned emigration, asserting
that every Norwegian should remain and fight for republican freedom in his own country. When the government
summarily deported Harring in the summer of 1850,
Thrane was among those who defended him and protested

[13] Skappel, *Om Husmandsvæsenet i Norge: Dets Oprindelse og Utvikling*, 168,
177, 191.
[14] *Norges Bønder*, 386.

against the arbitrary governmental action, though Thrane did not agree that the republican form of government was enough to satisfy the people.[15]

It was not only *bønder, husmænd,* and laborers who were attracted to the United States. Not a few of the earlier emigrants were from seaport towns, where they had been trained in seamanship. It was natural for individuals with such traditions and experience to seek employment on the Great Lakes or in Atlantic vessels at New York and other ports. The story of the Norwegian sailors on the Great Lakes, whose number greatly increased as Norwegian emigration expanded, has been told in a volume by Dr. Gjerset.[16] Attention must be called here to an aspect of the situation that aroused governmental concern. This was the tendency of Scandinavian sailors, drawn by offers of higher wages in the American merchant marine or by advantages in the American interior, to desert their vessels in New York. From 1846 to 1850, according to a consular report, 502 seamen deserted from 212 Norwegian vessels and 910 from 256 Swedish vessels. Only 25 of the Norwegian and 36 of the Swedish deserters were retaken.[17] The desertions continued on a larger scale in the period that followed. It is estimated that not less than

[15] Harring, *Testamentet fra Amerika* (Christiania, 1850. 156 p.); *Folkets Røst,* May 15, 1850; *Arbeider-foreningernes Blad,* June 8, 1850; the case of the department of justice against Harring is in *Den Norske Rigstidende,* June 1, 1850; and Harring's protest, addressed to "the public opinion of all civilized people," is in *Christiania-Posten,* July 11, 1850. Harring appears to have been an American citizen; in 1853 he drew up a statement of his case for the *New York Herald.* See *Christiania-Posten,* November 19, 1853. Harring was succeeded as editor of *Folkets Røst* by Paul Hjelm Hansen, who later played an important rôle as a western immigrant leader. It should be noted that Ibsen, like Thrane, was among those whose indignation was aroused by the government's action in the Harring case.

[16] Knut Gjerset, *Norwegian Sailors on the Great Lakes: A Chapter in the History of American Inland Transportation* (Northfield, Minnesota, 1928).

[17] A lengthy report by the Norwegian *chargé d'affaires,* Sibbern, "Om den hyppige Rømning af norske Søfolk i Amerika," appears in *Morgenbladet,* September 13, 1852. For later figures see *Lov om utvandring,* 161.

4,050 Norwegian seamen deserted from 1856 to 1865; and after the Civil War the numbers were still higher: 11,200 from 1871 to 1880; and 19,487 for the fifteen-year period from 1876 to 1890 inclusive.

In 1853 the Hudson's Bay Company, seeking trappers and boatmen for work in the northern fur country, advertised in Norwegian newspapers for young men, who would be offered five-year contracts at seventy-five dollars a year; and two years later a similar offer was made. More than fifty Norwegians and some Swedes took service with the company, arriving in 1853, 1854, and 1855. In June of the latter year twenty were in the southern, fifteen in the northern, and twenty-one in the western departments of the company's far-flung domains. In 1858 more than forty Norwegians returned from the company's service, with tales of great hardship and suffering. A newspaper item speaks of many of them as characters well known to the Norwegian police. That they were an uncommonly rough set of men is confirmed by a report by Sir George Simpson, dated at Norway House on June 24, 1858, for he declares the Norwegians a mutinous, quarrelsome, uncontrollable element, unfit for the work for which they were engaged. Eight had spent the preceding winter at Norway House and fourteen had been in the Saskatchewan country. One deserter had gone as far south as Pembina. Not all were villainous: Peter Larsen, for example, was taken into the service of Governor James Douglas, returned to Norway on a short visit in 1859 as a well-to-do man, and hastened back to Victoria to continue in the governor's employ.[18]

[18] *Morgenbladet*, February 25, March 21, 1853, October 21, 1858, August 14, 1859; extracts from Sir George Simpson's report are in *Aftenbladet*, September 9, 1858; a list of the Norwegians in the company's service in June, 1855, is in *Christiania-Posten*, January 11, 1856. See also *Aftenbladet*, May 1, June 27, 1855, September 9 and 11, 1858 (the latter containing extracts from a letter from Norway House), and *Christiania-Posten*, October 21, 1858.

Another emigration cross current of the fifties was engendered by a spirited Mormon proselytism in the Scandinavian countries, with Denmark as a center. Here one of the twelve Mormon apostles, Erastus Snow, and various other emissaries, set up missionary headquarters in 1850, brought out the *Book of Mormon* in a Danish translation, established a bi-monthly organ known as *Skandinaviens Stjerne,* issued numerous tracts, and launched a movement that reached into both Norway and Sweden, won many converts, and stimulated emigration to the Mormon state in the West.[19] It is not to be supposed that there was not sharp opposition in Sweden and Norway to the advance of Mormonism. John E. Forsgren, a Swedish follower of Erastus Snow, was summarily ejected from Sweden shortly after he arrived in that country from the Danish headquarters to act as a Mormon missionary. In Norway the propaganda from Denmark was supplemented by a missionary tour by Bishop Canute Peterson, who had gone to the Fox River settlement in 1837 as Knud Pedersen from Hardanger, had been won over to Mormonism, emigrated to Utah in 1849, and was dispatched to Norway in 1852 for a four-year stay.[20] The appearance of Mormon missionaries in Norway in 1851 caused an enormous amount of public discussion, the central problem being whether or not Mormonism was a Christian sect and hence entitled to toleration under the act of 1845. The question, after various local disputes, was taken up by the church department, which called upon the theological faculty of the university and the bishops of the church for opinions. The faculty declared that

[19] An informing article, "Om Mormonerne i Christiania," by Eilert Sundt, in *Morgenbladet,* March 6 and 7, 1855, lists the Mormon Scandinavian publications and discusses the Mormon doctrines. See also George A. Smith, *The Rise, Progress and Travels of the Church of Jesus Christ of Latter-Day Saints,* 27 (Salt Lake City, 1869).

[20] Anderson, *Norwegian Immigration,* 399–408; *Morgenbladet,* November 26, 1853.

though the Mormons were not Christians in the true meaning of the word, they were in the ordinary historical sense. They were dangerous, since their ideal was to set up a state within a state, yet the law was broad and they were entitled to come under it. Some of the bishops and the department itself took the view that the Mormons could not be regarded as Christians and hence were not entitled to toleration.[21]   In 1853 eleven Mormons were prosecuted and fined.[22]

Notwithstanding this very spirited opposition the Mormons, including Peterson, continued their work with considerable success. In Østerrisør, with a population of two thousand, a hundred Mormons were reported in the spring of 1845. " It is rumored," commented a newspaper, " that some of the sect will emigrate to America this year and it is to be desired that they would all go. . . ." Nevertheless this paper argued against any kind of persecution.[23]   In the fall Peterson, who was said " to be a son of the House of Joseph," declared that four hundred persons had received Mormon baptism in Norway.[24] Fifty-three Norwegians were reported to have left for Great Salt Lake from November, 1854, to April, 1855.[25] By the end of 1858 there were 461 Mormons in Norway and in June, 1859, there were 515. Peterson's wife said later that he brought six hundred Scandinavians with him when he returned in 1856. Perhaps because of the strangeness of the Mormon doctrines and of the Mormon state, the subject received an amount of discussion in Norwegian newspapers and books that seems disproportionate to the head-

21 *Christiania-Posten*, February 12, 1853.

22 *Morgenbladet*, November 7, 1853.

23 *Christiania-Posten*, March 26, 1854.

24 *Christiania-Posten*, November 9, 1854.

25 *Aftenbladet*, September 11, 1855. In the same period 409 Danes, 71 Swedes, 2,919 Englishmen and Scotchmen, and numerous other Mormon immigrants left for the West.

way that the proselytism actually made.   In the early
seventies Peterson made another missionary tour to the
Scandinavian countries and is said to have taken back to
Utah nearly a thousand emigrants.[26]

Apparently few echoes were heard in Norway of a
Moravian communistic experiment initiated among Norwegian immigrants in Wisconsin in 1850.   Moravian influences, reaching out from Count Zinzendorf's colony
in Saxony, touched Norway at an early period, and before
the middle of the eighteenth century Moravian societies
had been established in Christiania, Bergen, and Drammen.
Moravianism never gained much numerical strength in
Norway but it persisted, and in the nineteenth century
furnished some of the impetus to the beginnings of Norwegian missionary activity.   Among the early emigrants
were some Moravians, including a layman, John Olson,
who arrived at Milwaukee in 1846 and three years later
wrote to Moravian leaders in Norway requesting that a
minister be sent to Wisconsin.   A young student, A. M.
Iverson, responded to this call, arrived at Milwaukee in
1849, and was ordained at the Moravian center, Bethlehem,
Pennsylvania, the following year.

In 1850, when the Norwegian Moravians in Milwaukee
were planning to establish a farming settlement on lands
in Wisconsin, they were joined by a somewhat bizarre
figure in the history of immigration.   This was Nils Otto
Tank, scion of a distinguished Norwegian family, enor-

---

[26] *Aftenbladet*, September 21, 1859; Anderson, *Norwegian Immigration*, 403–405.
[Caspar H. Jensenius], *Breve fra Amerika om Mormonernes Religion, Sæder og Vandel*
(Christiania, 1856) contains a letter of disillusionment written at Salt Lake City
on December 31, 1854.   Andreas Mortensen, *Fra mit Besøg blandt Mormonerne*
(Kristiania, 1887) contains much information about the Mormons in Norway.
William A. Linn in his *Story of the Mormons* (New York, 1902) devotes a chapter
to "The Foreign Immigration to Utah," but gives very little information about
the Scandinavians.   The latter, it may be noted, comprised one group in the ill-fated
handcart company of 1856.

mously wealthy, well educated, possessed of a vast library, and fired with the idea of establishing a colony in the West along the lines of Zinzendorf's colony at Herrnhut. Tank had been converted to Moravianism on a journey in Saxony, had married a member of the sect, and had been for some years a missionary at Surinam. On a visit to his home in Norway he had heard of the Moravian immigrants in Wisconsin and decided to cast his lot among them. He purchased 969 acres of land at Green Bay to which the Moravian group, including forty-two adults, removed. The colony, to be known as Ephraim, was to have an academy where immigrants of whatever creed might study theology, science, medicine, or law, and such a school was actually inaugurated in 1851. The colony's lands, augmented by some nine thousand acres that Tank purchased near Green Bay, were divided into small lots; but Iverson apparently feared that Tank, whose father, Carsten Tank, had been one of Norway's great landed proprietors, had in mind the creation of a colony of tenants. He appealed to him to issue land deeds to the colonists as evidence of his disinterested attitude, and when Tank, inspired with the dream of a communistic colony, declined to do this, Iverson sought lands elsewhere, found them in the vicinity of the present village of Ephraim in Door County, and persuaded the colonists in the spring of 1853 to join him there, while Tank himself remained at Green Bay until his death in 1864. The colonists at Ephraim, augmented by new settlers from time to time, became the nucleus of a large and prosperous settlement.[27]

The Mormon and Moravian movements were flurries compared with the advances made in the fifties by the Lutheran orthodoxy in its organization of the religious life

---

[27] H. R. Holand, *De Norske Settlementers Historie*, ch. 25; *Old Peninsula Days*, chs. 10, 11. A good account of the Moravians in Norway is D. Thrap, *Brødremenigheden i Norge* (Christiania, 1908).

of Norwegian settlers in the West. A corps of young men who had received their theological training in Norway went to the United States to further the work launched by Clausen, Dietrichson, and Stub; and the Haugean group under Eielsen and the forces that coalesced in the Augustana Synod made notable progress. The theological struggles in which conservatism triumphed over liberalism in Scandinavian-American Lutheranism have been the subject of numerous published works. Here it will merely be noted that much of the conservative Norwegian-American church leadership was derived from trained state-church ministers who arrived in the fifties. From this group came many of the most influential synod leaders and pastors for more than a generation. To Koshkonong in 1850 went A. C. Preus to replace Dietrichson; before Preus returned to Norway in 1862 he had organized twenty congregations. Nils Brandt went to Pine Lake and other congregations in 1851; H. A. Preus to Spring and Bonnet prairies and Norway Grove and G. F. Dietrichson to Rock Prairie the same year; Jacob Aal Ottesen to Manitowoc in 1852; and U. V. Koren to the Norwegian settlements in northeastern Iowa in 1853. Other accessions included such men as Laurentius Larsen, later president of Luther College, O. F. Duus, J. St. Munch, and C. F. Magelssen. Most of the pioneer pastors served many congregations — one as many as twenty-two, Stub and H. A. Preus fifteen each. By 1860 Eielsen's Synod had five pastors, and the Augustana Synod, eight Norwegian pastors and thirteen Norwegian congregations; while in 1861 the Norwegian Synod had sixty-nine formally accepted congregations and its ministers actually served more than ninety.[28]

[28] Rohne, *Norwegian American Lutheranism up to 1872*, p. 180 and *passim*. On the controversies see Dr. Rohne's book and George M. Stephenson, *The Founding of the Augustana Synod, 1850–1860* (Rock Island, 1927).

One of these ministers, G. F. Dietrichson, advertised his forthcoming departure from Norway in the spring of 1851, announced that the fare on the vessel that he was to take, " The Emigrant," was low, and offered to give information to prospective emigrants.[29]   This was probably an attempt on his part to protect emigrants from the machinations of paid agents and forwarding companies, whose activities furnished another emigration cross current of the fifties in Norway.   In the spring of 1851 William Rischmüller, a general forwarding agent in New York, carried his campaign to Norway, announcing among other things that groups of emigrants could deposit their passage money with the Norwegian-Swedish consul in New York with the stipulation that it would not be collected until the immigrants had reached their destination at Milwaukee or Chicago.   The consul later reported that this agent had never broached such an arrangement to him.[30] In the following spring newspapers reported that skippers and emigration agents had been very active in various mountain districts.[31]   The upward swing of emigration in the fifties stimulated the activities of skippers and shipping companies, and newspapers were filled with their advertisements, one issue in *Morgenbladet* in 1852 announcing as many as ten vessels for America.[32]

Norwegian shippers began to feel the competition of English and German companies for the handling of the emigrant trade.   An attempt to organize it on a large scale was made in 1853 by Morris and Company, a concern with offices in Liverpool and Hamburg and a Norwegian agency at Christiania.   It announced vessels from Liverpool every eight days and promised cheaper and faster transportation

[29] *Stavanger Amtstidende og Adresseavis*, March 11, 1851.

[30] *Christiania-Posten*, April 23, 1851; Sibbern to the department of the interior, July 8, 1851, in R. A., Oslo: Indredept., Journalsager, D, 1851/1350.

[31] *Morgenbladet*, April 6, 1852.

[32] *Morgenbladet*, February 4, 1852.

than the Norwegian skippers in the direct trade could provide. It also advertised for subagents, and late in 1853 it was reported to have a network of runners and agents throughout Norway. A. Sharpe and Company, agents for the Northern Assurance Company, were active in a similar way after 1854.[33] There were complaints from immigrants over conditions on the Liverpool packets and from Norwegians over the exploitation and encouragement of emigration that such companies carried on, but a much greater stir was caused by the arrival in Norway in 1852 and the subsequent activities of Elias Stangeland, agent for the American forwarding company of Maxwell and Patten.

Stangeland, an emigrant from Stavanger *Amt,* had been in the United States four years and for a time had been a school-teacher in Wisconsin. In Norway he traveled about, held meetings, opposed the Oleana colonization scheme, favored the Middle West, especially Wisconsin, and soon found himself the center of a hot controversy that was ushered in by a sharp attack on his activities in the Wisconsin newspaper *Emigranten,* promptly reprinted in Norwegian newspapers. This attack bore the satirical title " On the So-called Interpreters, Who Go Home to Norway to Entice People to Emigrate," and advised emigrants, if they did not want to be cheated, to avoid the employment of such agents. Stangeland promptly accused his anonymous enemy of being himself a runner and declared that it was his own purpose neither to promote emigration nor to make any arrangements with reference to passage nor yet to serve as an interpreter.[34]

[33] *Christiania-Posten,* August 3, 16, 1853, February 4, September 6, 1854; *Stavanger Amtstidende og Adresseavis,* September 29, 1853; *Morgenbladet,* March 13, 23, 1854.

[34] The *Emigranten* article, dated December 26, 1852, is reprinted in *Stavanger Amtstidende og Adresseavis,* February 19, 1853, with Stangeland's reply. On Stangeland's activities see the same paper for February 5, 12, 15, April 5, 21, 28, 1853.

He seems to have given the impression that he had been indorsed by various mid-western ministers, but in the spring
of 1853 G. F. Dietrichson, the two Preuses, and C. L.
Clausen crushingly denied all responsibility for or knowledge of the agent's activities; and later A. C. Preus denounced Stangeland's enterprise as a humbug, explained the
entire system of runners and agents, and advised emigrants
to deal directly with Norwegian ship captains and to let
them arrange for the passage from New York or Quebec to
the interior.[35] Stangeland's influence was further damaged
by bitter complaints received from emigrants whose transportation by Maxwell and Patten he had arranged. The
records do not evidence any fraud on Stangeland's part,
save in implying that he was indorsed by the ministers,
though of course he received commissions. The animus
against him seems to have been in part a result of feeling
against any kind of encouragement or exploitation of Norwegian emigration.[36]

To forward his work in Norway Stangeland prepared
and published in the spring of 1853 an emigrant manual
entitled " Some Guiding Suggestions for Norwegian Emigrants to America." [37] He was very careful to avoid any
direct indorsement of emigration itself, though his comparison of the advantages of Norway and the United States
was artful. After pointing out the difficulties that faced
emigrants, he solemnly advised them to take counsel with

[35] *Christiania-Posten*, July 1, 21, 23, 1853; *Stavanger Amtstidende og Adresseavis*,
September 29, October 4, 1853.

[36] *Stavanger Amtstidende og Adresseavis*, July 4, 1853; and a defense by Stangeland
in the issue for July 11, 1853. Emigration agents have always seemed particularly
obnoxious to Norwegians. Wergeland in one of his plays represented an emigration agent as a pestilence-scattering demon. In 1929-30 the old feeling burst into
flame in connection with the activities in Norway of an American representative
of a Canadian railway.

[37] *Nogle Veiledende Vink for norske Udvandrere til Amerika* (Christiania, 1853.
76 p.). The book was favorably reviewed in various newspapers, e. g., *Christiania-
Posten*, April 7, 1853.

God. If thereupon they were absolutely determined to emigrate, his book was intended to put before them various practical suggestions. On the whole he made out a very good case for the Northwest, condemning Oleana and Canada and questioning Texas. Suggestive of the gradual penetration north and west is his advice to emigrants to spend the first year in Wisconsin or Illinois and then to go to Iowa or Minnesota. The book contains much solid advice on the various practical problems connected with the journey, urges the use of Norwegian vessels to Quebec, and, as may be expected, recommends the Maxwell and Patten forwarding company, which offered to transport emigrants from Quebec to Wisconsin for seven dollars or from New York to the interior for five. Stangeland continued his immigration

Nogle veiledende Vink for norske Udvandrere til Amerika. Af Elias Stangeland.

Christiania. Forlagt og trykt hos Chr. Schibsted. 1853.

REDUCED FACSIMILE OF TITLE-PAGE OF ELIAS STANGELAND'S "SOME GUIDING SUGGESTIONS FOR NORWEGIAN EMIGRANTS TO AMERICA," 1853

work after his return to the United States, and in the spring of 1854 he was appointed as an agent for the state of Wisconsin and stationed at Quebec, a strategic point at which to influence incoming immigrants to go to that state. This appointment was one phase of a vigorous competition by northwestern states and territories to draw to their lands as large a proportion as possible of the potential commonwealth builders thronging at America's doors.[38]

The advertising of the West proceeded vigorously in the fifties. In addition to guides like Stangeland's and the special works occasioned by interest in California and Oleana, various other " America books " were brought out, supplementing those of the thirties and forties. And there were also some novel types of " America advertising." In the summer of 1852, for example, a panorama of the Mississippi River and valley was exhibited for some six weeks in Christiania. Such exhibits, made up of great unwinding rolls of canvas with successions of painted scenes, were the motion pictures of the fifties; and then — as now with the cinema — representations of the wild West were very popular in Europe. Unwound to the accompaniment of a lecture, the one shown in Christiania — it was reported to contain sixty thousand square feet of canvas — pictured America's great river from the Falls of St. Anthony to the Gulf. A newspaper reviewer predicted that it would not be long before those falls would be harnessed, the nucleus of factories and a great city. Thus the future Minneapolis was hailed in Norway before the Norwegian immigrants themselves fully understood the prospects of Minnesota. A. O. Vinje, the well known Norwegian poet, saw the Mississippi panorama and got from it a new understanding of American strenuosity. America, he believed, was destined to conquer the whole world. The pictures impressed him with the tremendous amount of work awaiting the hand of man. " One must go forward, be the consequences what they may "— thus he envisioned the American spirit. Vinje pictured an emigrant mother saying to her children: "Look, this is your heritage. All these prairies are yours, if you can but culti-

---

[38] See the writer's article " The Competition of the Northwestern States for Immigrants," in *Wisconsin Magazine of History*, 3: 3–29 (September, 1919).

vate them. If only the emigration from my narrow home valley will win this inheritance for you, I am willing to pay for the exertion with my life. I gladly dwell in a sod hut that you may build on the same ground a mansion." [39]

" A better lot — that is the alpha and omega of the emigrant ": such was the pithy conclusion of a book entitled " Interesting Reports from North America, Described by a Traveler," published at Arendal in 1852.[40] Not the pioneer West, but New York and the East and the less serious sides of American life were depicted in the volume. A portrayal of American amusements, a description of the celebrated " Five Points " in New York, an account of a dinner with William B. Astor, an essay on American newspapers — these were some of the items in this lively book of travel. Its interest was not lessened by the fact that it was all a plagiarism from an elaborate Danish work by " Axel Felix," or Christian Hansen, who after a few years spent in Norway went to the United States in 1846 and was connected for a time with *Skandinavia,* a newspaper of New York that began publication in 1847. His travel account, entitled " Far from Denmark," is a three-volume work of exceptional interest.[41]

Fredrika Bremer's *Homes of the New World,* which was made available to both Danish and Norwegian readers in a Danish translation of 1855, was undoubtedly an influential and widely read work in all the Scandinavian countries, as it was in England and the United States. The Swedish novelist's prophetic rhapsody after viewing the upper Northwest is famous:

[39] *Christiania-Posten,* July 10, 11, 1852; Vinje's correspondence to *Drammens Tidende,* dated August 14, 1852, is reprinted in his *Skrifter i Samling,* 1: 77–80 (Kristiania, 1916). The 1852 panorama was presented by H. S. Risley.

[40] *Interessante Beretninger om Nordamerika, skildrede af En Reisende* (Arendal, 1852. 59 p.).

[41] " Axel Felix," *Langtfra Danmark: Skizzer og Scener fra de forenede Stater i Nordamerika* (Copenhagen, 1850, 274 p.; 1853, 320 p.; 1855, 368 p.).

What a glorious new Scandinavia might not Minnesota become! Here would the Swede find again his clear, romantic lakes, the plains of Scania rich in corn, and the valleys of Norrland; here would the Norwegian find his rapid rivers, his lofty mountains, for I include the Rocky Mountains and Oregon, in the new kingdom; and both nations their hunting fields and their fisheries. The Danes might here pasture their flocks and herds, and lay out their farms on richer and less misty coasts than those of Denmark. . . . The climate, the situation, the character of the scenery, agrees with our people better than that of any other of the American States, and none of them appear to me to have a greater or more beautiful future before them than Minnesota.

Miss Bremer also gave testimony of the success of the Norwegian pioneers. " About seven hundred Norwegian colonists are settled in this neighborhood, all upon small farms," she wrote of a Wisconsin community. " I asked many, both men and women, whether they were contented; whether they were better off here or in old Norway. Nearly all of them replied, ' *Yes*, we are better off here; we do not work so hard, and it is easier to gain a livelihood.' " [42]

Both in Sweden and in Denmark the early fifties witnessed the publication of various " America books " in addition to Fredrika Bremer's classic Scandinavian description of conditions in the United States. Several books were brought out in Denmark on California and Australia, and general emigrant guides were issued there in 1852 and 1853.[43] And in 1853 two such guides were published in Sweden: C. E. O. Swalander's " Reliable Information Concerning the United States of North America and the Best Way to Emigrate," and Johan Bolin's " Description of the

---

[42] Bremer, *Den nye Verden: Dagbog paa en Reise i Nordamerika* (Copenhagen, 1855). The passages cited are quoted in Babcock, *Scandinavian Element*, 82, 100.

[43] E. g., *Udvandringsbog for Skandinaver: Fører ved Udvandringer til Amerika* (1852); E. Skouboe, *Oplysninger for Udvandrere til Nordamerika* (1853) and *Oplysninger for Udvandrere til Australien* (1853); *Australien og dets Guldegne* (1853); E. Fog, *Reise til Guldminerne: En dansk Haandværkers Breve* (1854); J. Hoppe and A. Erman, *Californien, dets Nutid og Fremtid* (translated by J. C. Schythe, 1850); Rasmus Sørensen, *1ste Brev til mine Venner i Danmark* (1853).

United North American States." [44] The former, by the Swedish emigration commissioner at Göteborg, was an illustrated handbook packed solid with good advice to emigrants. The latter, by a rector in Småland, was also brought out in a Norwegian edition in 1853.[45] It was a useful compilation of geographical and political information systematically arranged and followed by sensible suggestions to emigrants. The author was unaware that Minnesota had obtained territorial status in 1849 and he allotted its lands in part to Wisconsin, in part to Iowa, but he informed his readers that this northern area had

REDUCED FACSIMILE OF TITLE-PAGE OF " AMERICA, OR A DESCRIPTION OF THE 33 UNITED NORTH AMERICAN FREE STATES," 1853

"unbelievably fertile" soil. In 1853 there was also published at Bergen a book entitled " America, or a Description of the 33 United North American Free States "

[44] These two books are ably analyzed by Roy W. Swanson, in " Some Swedish Emigrant Guide Books of the Second Half of the Nineteenth Century," in Swedish Historical Society of America, *Yearbooks*, 11: 105–115 (1926).

[45] *Geographisk-politisk Beskrivelse over de forenede nordamerikanske Stater, i Særdeleshed for Emigranter* (Christiania, 1853. 112 p.).

— a second edition, with a revised title, of " America, Ole Bull, and the New Norway," issued the year before.[46]

None of these works caused so great a stir in Norway as *Uncle Tom's Cabin*, also translated in 1853. The American influence of Harriet Beecher Stowe's novel has been the subject of considerable study by historians of the slavery controversy, but its European influence in molding opinion among the common people has perhaps not received the attention it deserves. If Norwegians in the period when the slavery controversy was approaching its climax came to the United States with sharply defined convictions on the subject, it must not be forgotten that with a natural repugnance for slavery they had also been influenced by the characterizations of the institution that Harriet Beecher Stowe had given the world. Her book seems to have become a best-seller in Norway, both in the original and in the Norwegian edition. The story was reprinted in Norwegian newspapers and was followed in many cases by discussions of slavery, the political party system, and other features of American life.[47]

A missionary journey made by a lay preacher to the Norwegian settlements in the West from 1849 to 1852 resulted in an interesting " America book " published in 1854. The author, Hans Tønnesen Steene, was a man of great piety, whose interest in a journey to the West was aroused while attending a Methodist school in England in 1845. After collecting funds for his trip by public subscription, he set off from Norway via Liverpool in 1849.

---

[46] *Amerika, eller Beskrivelse over de 33 forenede nordamerikanske Fristater. . .* (Bergen, 1853. 168 p.).

[47] Harriet Beecher Stowe, *Onkel Toms Hytte, eller Negerlivet i de Amerikanske Slavestater* (Christiania, 1853. 664 p.); *Christiania-Posten*, December 18, 25, 28, 29, 1852, March 6, 8, 9, 14, 16, 1853; "De politiske Partier i de Forenede Stater," in *Morgenbladet*, May 13, 17, 1853; "Om Slaveriet i de Forenede Stater," by L. K. D. (probably Ludvig K. Daa), in *Christiania-Posten*, July 11, 1853.

He describes a terrible crossing, in which sixteen emigrants died from cholera and he himself was desperately sick. He was glad to see New York: " With what mingled feelings of surprise and joy we saw, for the first time, the wonderful country, which in comparison with our cold North, is a veritable Paradise!" In the West he mingled with many sects, and met Elling Eielsen, of whom he speaks highly, and various other ministers. He gives a detailed account of his travels and experiences and writes with the greatest enthusiasm about the Americans and their institutions. Religious conditions in the United States he found very good — but not among the Norwegians. Of them he writes, " I have never before seen such a bitter and fault-finding spirit as among them." [48]

After 1854 there comes a decline not only in numbers of emigrants but also in the production of " America books." Indeed, if the publication of such books in Norway were charted as one charts fluctuations in emigration one would get somewhat similar rises and depressions. In the period after 1854, however, the earlier books were still available; the stream of " America letters," the reading of which was like taking the economic pulse of the United States, continued; newspapers, also, though with ups and downs of interest, published letters and articles about the West; and emigration propaganda of many types was active. Occasionally there were special investigations, such as that of Dr. Joachim A. Voss, who in 1857 visited the United States to study medical conditions and published a detailed account of his findings after his return to Nor-

[48] Steene, *Beretning om en 3 Aars Reise i Amerika, foretagen i Aarene 1849 til 1851 iblandt de norske Emigranter i de forenede Stater i Nordamerika* (Stavanger, 1854. 32 p.); G. J. Malmin, " A Mission Journey among the Norwegians in America, 1849–1852," in *Lutheran Church Herald*, September 22, 1925; the book is reprinted, with an introduction by Mr. Malmin, in *Teologisk Tidskrift*, 9: 1–34 (October, 1925), together with an account by Steene of a journey to California in 1864.

way.[49] A prolific writer of " America letters " was Frithjof Meidell, a brother of the well-known editor, Ditmar Meidell; he emigrated in 1852 and lived from 1853 or 1854 to 1858 at Springfield, Illinois, and then removed to California; his sprightly travel letters picture mid-western conditions with humor and understanding.[50] The interest of Norwegians in the United States also inspired occasional studies of American history, including in 1860 a book on the discovery of America, and three years later a work on American colonization, based mainly on Bancroft.[51]

[49] " Optegnelser fra en Reise i de Forenede Stater i Nordamerika i Sommeren 1857," in *Norsk Magazin for Lægevidenskaben*, 2d series, vol. 12: 834–854; 13: 169–186, 441–467, 562–600. Also issued separately.

[50] A series of Meidell letters published in *Aftenbladet* from 1855 to 1858 was later reprinted in *Skilling-Magazin*, March 16, 23, 30, April 6, May 11, 1861. This magazine brought out numerous general articles about the United States. Many of Meidell's unpublished manuscript letters from 1854 to 1863 are in the possession of the Historiografisk Samling, Oslo, and transcripts are in the archives of the Norwegian-American Historical Association.

[51] *Beretning om Amerikas Opdagelse af Kristoffer Kolumbus* (Stavanger, 1860. 77 p.); Anton Bang, *Om Bebyggelsen af Nord Amerika. Bearbeidet efter engelske og Amerikanske Forfattere, fornemmelig Bancroft's " History of the United States "* (Christiania, 1863. 352 p.).

XVI. ON THE EVE OF THE CIVIL WAR

NORWEGIAN emigration, according to official statistics, reached a total of 59,700 for the years 1851 to 1865, as compared with 18,200 in the period from 1836 to 1850. The perils of immigration statistics are well illustrated by the fact that although nearly sixty thousand persons are thus on record as having left Norway in this fifteen-year period, — the great bulk of them unquestionably destined for the United States, — American statistics record for the same years the arrival of only 32,424 Norwegians and Swedes together. Since Swedish statistics evidence the departure of 24,276 persons in the period indicated, one gets the impression that though about 84,000 Norwegians and Swedes emigrated, apparently more than fifty thousand of them failed to arrive in the United States. The differences are the more striking when the annual figures are brought into tabular comparison:

EMIGRATION STATISTICS, 1851–1865[1]

	Left Norway	Left Sweden	Departures from Norway and Sweden	Norwegian and Swedish Arrivals in United States
1851	2,640	934	3,574	2,424
1852	4,030	3,031	7,061	4,103
1853	6,050	2,619	8,669	3,364
1854	5,950	3,980	9,930	3,531
1855	1,600	586	2,186	821
1856	3,200	959	4,159	1,157
1857	6,480	1,762	8,242	1,712
1858	2,500	512	3,012	2,430
1859	1,800	208	2,008	1,091

[1] *Tabeller vedkommende Folkemængdens Bevægelse i Aarene 1856–1865*, lxxi (*Norges Officielle Statistik*, 1869, C. no. 1); *Statistical Review of Immigration 1820–1900*, 14–29 (61 Congress, 3 session, *Senate Documents*, vol. 20, doc. 756, serial 5878); and tables in Babcock, *Scandinavian Element*, appendix.

EMIGRATION STATISTICS, 1851–1865 *(cont.)*

	Left Norway	Left Sweden	Departures from Norway and Sweden	Norwegian and Swedish Arrivals in United States
1860	1,900	266	2,166	298
1861	8,900	1,087	9,987	616
1862	5,250	1,206	6,456	892
1863	1,100	1,485	2,585	1,627
1864	4,300	2,461	6,761	2,249
1865	4,000	3,180	7,180	6,109
Totals	59,700	24,276	83,976	32,424

It is interesting to turn from these totals to the American census statistics, which show a gain in the number of Scandinavian-born in the United States from 18,075 in 1850 to 72,582 in 1860 — an absolute increase of 54,507, though in the same ten years the Scandinavian immigration, including 3,749 Danes, amounted to only 24,680, according to United States immigration statistics.[2]

What is the explanation of the wide discrepancy between the European and the American figures? The great majority of the emigrants from 1836 to 1850 followed routes that brought them to New York, Boston, or other American ports either by direct passage or by way of Hamburg, Havre, or Liverpool. A Norwegian statistician has estimated that of the total of 18,200 emigrants in this period, about 12,200 went direct from Norway to America, and of these about 11,960 landed at United States ports and 240 at Quebec.[3] About 6,000 went via the more important European points of departure outside Norway. A marked difference appears from 1851 to 1853, however. Direct shipping from Norway reduces emigration by way of other European countries and

---

[2] The census figures are conveniently assembled in Nelson, *History of the Scandinavians*, 257 (1904 ed.).

[3] A. N. Kiær, in *Tabeller vedkommende Folkemængdens Bevægelse i Aarene 1856–1865*, lxxiii.

Quebec receives a larger proportion of the total Norwegian emigration than New York and other American ports. In this transitional period 7,510 emigrants went direct from Norway to Quebec, 4,550 from Norway to New York and Boston, and 660 by way of Havre, Hamburg, or other ports to New York. From 1854 on the pendulum swings sharply toward Quebec as the initial destination of the emigrants. It is estimated that of 46,900 Norwegian emigrants from 1854 to 1865, all but some 2,800 took the Quebec route — 44,100 direct to Quebec, 520 direct to New York or Boston, and 2,280 via Havre, Hamburg, or other intermediate points to New York.[4] The swing to Canada was due to a trade development that made it possible for shipping companies to reduce passenger fares, but the emigrants were bound, as before, for the American West by way of the Great Lakes, with Milwaukee or Chicago as the goal before dispersing to the settlements. For shipowners the lumber industry at Quebec made possible a very profitable triangular trade: emigrants and ballast from Norway to Quebec; lumber to some British port; and a return from England to the original starting point. The main reason for this rapid development of emigration traffic combined with Canadian and English commerce was the repeal in 1849 of the English navigation laws, making it possible for foreign merchant vessels to engage in unrestricted commerce with the British colonies. As early as 1850 Quebec customs house returns indicate that the Norwegian trade was becoming brisk, for of ninety-six ships listed, forty-four were Norwegian, almost all of which came in under ballast and departed with an " outward cargo " of lumber, for London, Cardiff, Belfast, Hull, Yarmouth, or other British ports.[5]

[4] *Ibid.*, lxxiii.

[5] I. D. Andrews, *Report on the Trade, Commerce, and Resources of the British North American Colonies*, 142–144, 450 (31 Congress, 2 session, *Senate Executive Documents*, no. 23).

The United States government has in the past been very lax in its handling of immigration by way of Canada. Even in the later period, for example, for some years after 1886, no records were kept of entries via Canada, which undoubtedly exceeded a half million by 1893.[6] Records are indeed available for the period from 1850 to 1865, and they show that not less than 102,715 immigrants entered the United States from the British North American possessions; but they do not reveal the European origins of these immigrants.[7] Norwegian emigrants, who are so inadequately represented by American records of arrivals, unquestionably formed a part of this mass of immigrants from Canada. In view of the foregoing facts Norwegian statistics may be considered more reliable than the American for the racial group and period here under consideration. These statistics show that there were three " peaks " from the middle of the century to the early sixties: the first in 1853–54, the second in 1857, and the third in 1861. Sharp declines follow in each case, though in the third the decisive drop comes in the second year after the high point.

The chief factors underlying the stir and bustle of Norwegian emigration in the early fifties have been described in foregoing chapters. It was a period in which Norway grew accustomed to emigrant scenes. The emigrants were thought of as Americans even before they had left their native land. " In these days," ran a newspaper item in 1851, " one continually meets the so-called Americans, that is, *bønder* from Telemarken, who are on their way to the Norwegian colonies in the West." [8] The feelings of the emigrants aroused considerable curiosity. " On their faces," wrote one observer, " one reads neither sorrow nor

---

[6] See the statistics in *Abstracts of Reports of the Immigration Commission,* 1: 88–91.

[7] *Statistical Review of Immigration 1820–1900,* 24–29.

[8] A note from Skien in *Christiania-Posten,* May 8, 1851.

regret, only earnestness and decision. If one asks them if they do not find it hard to leave their home valleys they are likely to reply, ' Oh yes, but we have made up our minds and we will hold to our decision.' " [9] Viewing the manifestations of this spirit, one writer accused his countrymen of stubbornness: " If the Sogning — and this is just as true of other Norwegian *bønder* — once makes a decision, it is rarely possible to shake it, for it seems to me that a special trait in the character of our country people is an unmatched obstinacy and persistence in carrying out plans once made." [10] Whole communities began to have American ties. It is a common saying today that there is not a family in Norway that does not have " American relatives." As early as 1854 it was reported that there were hardly any families in inner Sogn that did not have several members who had emigrated to America. [11]

The *bonde* may have been obstinate in defending his decisions, but he was intelligent in reading the signs of the times. And in 1854, though emigration in that year was comparatively high, the economic winds were veering. By the winter of 1854–55 newspapers, taking stock both of the situation in Norway and of reports from America, correctly predicted a great decline in emigration. Early in 1854 one newspaper writer pointed to the expansion of Norwegian fisheries, lumber, and shipping and characterized the preceding year as good, but found emigration a dark shadow in the picture. Progress in agriculture lagged behind progress in other spheres, he asserted, and he urged the state to take the matter in hand, buy tracts of land, start farms, and then sell them at cost. The burden of his complaint was that something needed to be done about agriculture. [12]

[9] *Christiania-Posten,* May 8, 1851.
[10] *Aftenbladet,* April 3, 1855.
[11] *Christiania-Posten,* September 26, 1854.
[12] *Nordre Trondhjems Amtstidende,* January 10, 1854, quoting *Throndhjems Adresseavis.*

The fifties were in fact a period of vigorous economic improvement in Norway. Turning its back upon its course of *laissez-faire,* the Norwegian government, with a new department of the interior under the able guidance of Frederik Stang, embarked upon important economic reforms. In 1851 the Storthing authorized the construction of the first Norwegian railway, and with the aid of English capital it was completed in 1854. About the same time the state entered upon a broadly conceived program of road-building, which from 1850 to 1900 increased Norway's road mileage from about ten thousand to seventeen thousand. The steamboat and the subsidizing of regular steamboat coastal traffic gave further stimulus to the break-down of the old isolation. The new British commercial policy and the Crimean War opened up a golden period in the history of the rapidly expanding Norwegian merchant marine. The telegraph and a new postal system were introduced and played their parts in knitting the communities of the land together. All this tended to bring the farmer nearer to the towns, — now entering upon a period of new growth, — where he could dispose of his products more easily and at better prices than before and where the product of the factory became more accessible to him than it had been. This implied the beginnings of a shift from the system of household manufacture to the new economy. Coupled with expansion in the iron and lumber industries, it marked, indeed, the beginnings of the economic revolution that has characterized the nineteenth century on both sides of the Atlantic. If this development improved the status of the *bonde,* it also brought new life into the towns. The establishment of Norway's " Hypotekbank " in 1851 and a series of savings banks throughout the country was another sign of the dawn of a new economic era. In effect the government thus established a farm-loan system which enabled the farmer to borrow money at lower rates than those available from private money-lenders. Agricultural education also came to the fore in the fifties. In the earlier part of the nineteenth century Jacob L. B. Sverdrup had established at Sem, near Horton, an agricultural school which for a time received a governmental subvention; some local schools of this type were active in the thirties and forties; and organizations like the Society for Norway's Welfare carried on intelligent programs for the modernizing of Norwegian agriculture. As has been noted in another connection, the director of an agricultural school in 1850 had urged such modernizing of agricultural methods as a means of obviating the need of emigration.[13] Now, in 1854, the government authorized the establishment of a national agricultural school at Aas, in southeastern Norway, and this was opened in 1859, with a model farm attached. Though agricultural education had its ups and downs in the following decade, it played an important rôle in the emancipation of Norwegian farming from mediævalism. But far-reaching agricultural reform, the fashioning of industries, the evolving of means of support for a growing population — these are not achieved in a day or a year.[14]

In the winter and spring of 1855 there was an ominous and reiterated note of warning in the reports that came from the United States. An article from the Swedish *Aftonbladet*, spread broadcast in Norway in February, reported bank failures, a slump in industry, a drop in wages from twenty-five to thirty per cent, the prevalence of unemployment, and the beginnings of a tide of re-migration to Europe. Though it conceded that conditions in the West were better than those in the East, it concluded that

---

[13] See *ante*, p. 261.

[14] *Norway: Official Publication*, 443–444, 470; Gjerset, *History of the Norwegian People*, 2: 515–516; Smitt, *Norges Landbrug i dette Aarhundrede*, *passim*; Bull, *Grunriss av Norges Historie*, 97–99.

no one ought even to think of emigration.[15] From immigrants came similar accounts. A carpenter in New York wrote a detailed letter in February telling of hard conditions and advising against emigration.[16] From the Canadian general agent for immigration came the warning that poverty-stricken immigrants would not be aided by the Canadian government save in cases of illness.[17] Coupled with reports of economic distress were accounts of cholera and malaria in the West. *Morgenbladet,* commenting in the spring on the changed situation, said that not many emigrants were leaving, explained that Canaan was a delusion, and emphatically urged Norwegians to remain at home, where prospects were now improved.[18] And Norwegian emigration in 1855 dropped to approximately one-fourth of what it had been the year before. By August not more than thirteen Norwegian emigrant vessels had arrived at Quebec, as compared with nearly fifty in 1854.[19] Emigration doubled in 1856 and redoubled in 1857, but again came reports of panic and depression in the United States, and despite a similar crisis with resultant hard times in Norway,[20] the trend was sharply downward in 1858. " My inexperienced countrymen are blockheads," wrote an immigrant in the West on December 18, 1857, " if they emigrate to this country at present for the purpose of getting better living conditions; it is a different matter if they come to get experience or to see the world. I came with both purposes, and I believe I shall be successful in the second, but I have deep doubts about the first." He describes the panic in detail: bank failures, collapse of credit,

---

[15] Reprinted in *Lillehammers Tilskuer,* February 6, 1855, and various other Norwegian newspapers.

[16] A letter by Ole Syverson, February 24, 1855, in *Morgenbladet,* April 25, 1855.

[17] *Stavanger Amtstidende og Adresseavis,* January 20, 1855.

[18] *Morgenbladet,* April 9, 1855.

[19] *Aftenbladet,* September 11, 1855.

[20] See, *e. g., Christiania-Posten,* January 17, 1858.

scarcity of money, closing of factories, unemployment, sluggish trade. For immigrants who had land the outlook was serious enough. One farmer was quoted: " I know that the times are desperate and money scarce, but I know also that I have enough food for the winter." For the landless and jobless immigrant, however, the prospect was exceedingly dark.[21]

Only nine of the Norwegian counties were represented in the emigration of the first ten years after 1836, and 63% of the total came from Buskerud and Bratsberg *amter* in south central Norway, while the balance came chiefly from the three western counties of Stavanger, South Bergenhus, and North Bergenhus.[22] In the decade from 1846 to 1855, the south and the southeast contributed 22,875, or 70.9%, the west 9,205, or 28.5%, and the north 190, or 0.6%, to the total of 32,270. The most notable developments in the south and southeast were the penetration of the movement into Kristian *Amt*, the very heart of the south, from which 6,510 individuals emigrated in the decade; the advance into Nedenes and Lister-Mandal at the extreme south, with 2,480 and 770 emigrants respectively; and beginnings from Hedemarken. Buskerud and Bratsberg, with 5,700 and 3,900 emigrants, show that the movement had not waned in the districts which had sent the largest proportion of the earlier emigration. On the west coast the movement was creeping northward. Stavanger had led the western districts in the earlier period, but in the decade from 1846 to 1855, the two counties lying to the north — South and North Bergenhus — had each a larger emigration than Stavanger. The figures for the three, from south to north, were 2,600; 2,700; and

---

[21] *Christiania-Posten*, February 21, 1858. A good account of the effect of the panic in Chicago is in *Nordre Trondhjems Amtstidende*, April 3, 1858.

[22] The Norwegian emigration statistics upon which the following discussion is based are in *Tabeller vedkommende Folkemængdens Bevægelse i Aarene 1856–1865*, lxix–lxxvi, and *Utvandringsstatistikk*, ch. 5 and tables, p. 100 ff.

3,600. Small beginnings had been made still farther north, in Romsdal and in South and North Trondhjem, while the gospel of America had even penetrated to Finmark, far north in the Arctic Circle, which is represented by forty emigrants. By the middle fifties the movement had firm roots in all the more populous southern and western counties. The emigration was preponderantly rural, but it may be noted that Christiania and Bergen contributed respectively 970 and 170 emigrants to the total.

Emigration from 1856 to 1865 was not much greater than in the previous ten years but its sources illustrate the gradual expansion of the movement. Of a total of 39,350, the south and southeast contributed 20,925, the west 15,580, and the north 2,845, the percentages for the respective sections being 53.2, 39.6, and 7.2, as compared with 70.9, 28.5, and 0.6 the previous ten years. In other words emigration both from the west and the north was in the ascendant, and the balance was somewhat more even than it had been. Kristian *Amt* in the southeast and North Bergenhus in the west, with 7,211 and 6,656 emigrants, respectively, had the heaviest drain in actual numbers. They also had the heaviest relative emigration, respectively 6.0 and 7.9 annually per one thousand of population. This means that for these regions emigration already had reached an intensity comparable to that for Norway as a whole in the period from 1876 to 1890. Nearest to them were Bratsberg and Buskerud in the south central region, with respectively 5.8 and 5.5 annually per one thousand of population. The further progress of emigration from the north is shown by the fact that North Trondhjem rises to 1,885 in the ten years from 1856 to 1865, whereas it was only 150 in the previous decade. Nordland appears with 270 emigrants and Finmark, which had 40 in the ten preceding years, now has 690.

Large administrative units are perhaps less revealing than the smaller with reference to emigration changes. The

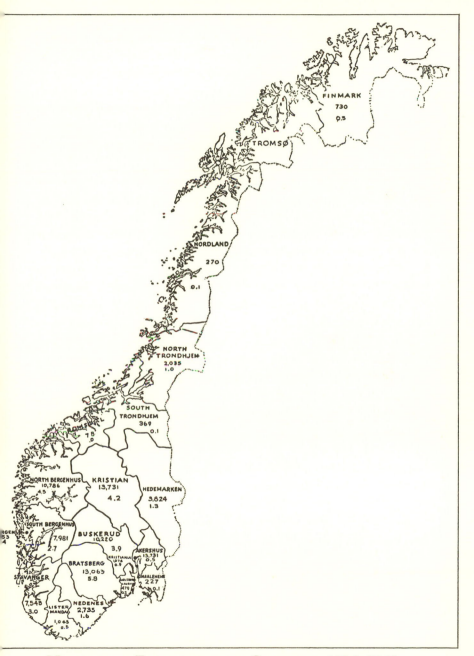

NORWEGIAN EMIGRATION BY COUNTIES, 1836–1865

[Showing total for each *amt* and yearly average per one thousand of population]

Fogderier, for example, throw more light upon the intensity of emigration from local districts than do the *amter.* Thus from 1856 to 1865 Sogn contributed 6,430 emigrants to the total, or an annual average of 17.2 per one thousand inhabitants. This was a higher average by six than Norway attained in the years 1881–85. Valders had 3,144, or 15.6 annually per one thousand inhabitants; Hallingdal 2,248, or 15.2; Hardanger and Voss 2,011, or 9.0; Upper Telemarken 2,143, or 8.4; Numedal and Sandsvær 895, or 6.8; Søndhorland 2,200, or 6.7; Ryfylke 3,112, or 6.6; Lower Telemarken 1,138, or 5.8; Toten 1,377, or 5.8; southern Gudbrandsdalen 1,210, or 4.8; and Størdalen and Værdalen 1,411, or 4.4.

Yet smaller units are the parishes, which enable one to view emigration fluctuations in the localities. In the following table a few interesting cases are selected:

EMIGRATION FROM SELECTED PARISHES, 1856–65

	South Aurdal	North Aurdal	Gausdal	Gran	Ringsaker	Sogndal	Lyster	Nore
1856	11	141	19	16	2	123	138	5
1857	230	99	204	19	34	13	72	102
1858	58	3	30	17	61	4	81	12
1859	4	39	0	15	115	14	13	52
1860	11	8	7	7	114	9	100	23
1861	251	96	63	162	140	95	262	123
1862	32	49	41	138	36	139	248	81
1863	1	6	14	1	2	0	5	7
1864	10	0	10	11	11	38	22	0
1865	25	29	26	23	18	31	5	3
Total	633	470	414	409	533	466	946	408

Very striking is the evidence from these localities of the effect of the panic of 1857 and of the influence that American and Norwegian circumstances had on emigration in the latter half of the period.

Taking the country as a whole the average annual emigration per one thousand of population was 0.5 for the decade 1836–1845, 2.3 for 1846–1855, 2.4 for 1856–1860, and 2.86 for 1861–1865 — a general average for the entire period of 1.8. The annual average for Sweden was 0.63 for 1851–1855, 0.20 for 1856–1860, and 0.63 for 1861–1865; for Germany in the same three periods, 3.60, 1.65, and 1.14; and for Ireland it was 10.69 from 1856 to 1860 and 14.67 for the next five years. While Norway as a whole had an average of 1.8 from 1836 to 1865, Bratsberg (Telemark) stood 5.8, North Bergenhus (Sogn and Fjordane) 4.5, Kristian (Opland) 4.2, Stavanger (Rogaland) 3.0, and South Bergenhus (Hordaland) 2.7. These areas were clearly of outstanding importance. The movement in general was uneven and of course subject to sharp fluctuations, but it was rising gradually in volume and almost the entire country had been brought within its sweep by the sixties.

It is now necessary to examine certain tendencies and developments in the field of Norwegian settlement in the West that are closely interwoven with the emigration movement as a whole. " The rising stream," writes Dr. Babcock, " had, by 1850, worn for itself a clear and definite channel from eastern ports like New York and Boston to such gateways to the Northwest as Chicago and Milwaukee; and through these it continued to flow out over the wilderness of the upper Mississippi Valley extending north of the Missouri and Illinois rivers and west of the Great Lakes. For more than a half century there have been relatively few variations from this course. . . ." [23] The number of Norwegian-born people in the United States increased from 12,678 in 1850 to 43,995 in 1860.[24] By the latter year 18,625 Swedes and 9,962 Danes brought the total number of Scandinavian-born up to 72,582. Thus, though the number of Swedish immigrants was increasing

[23] *Scandinavian Element*, 66.
[24] Nelson, *History of Scandinavians*, 257.

and was destined soon to outrun that of the Norwegian, the latter were still the preponderant factor in the Scandinavian element. Wisconsin led the other states in the number of Norwegian-born: from 8,651 in 1850 the number had increased to 21,442 in 1860. In the latter year Wisconsin had approximately one-half of all the Norwegians in the United States. The settlements in the northeastern part of Iowa continued to grow rapidly after the beginnings made in the late forties and early fifties; by 1860 the state had 5,688 Norwegian-born as compared with 361 in 1850. Norwegian settlement had also worked its way into Minnesota, beginning in 1852 and 1853 in the southern counties of Houston and Fillmore, and by the end of the decade numerous settlements had been formed, chiefly in the south and southeast, and the number of Norwegian-born had been brought up to 8,425. The Norwegian settlers in Illinois had doubled in the decade, but by 1860 Illinois ranked fourth among the states in the number of Norwegian-born, having but 4,891. No other striking developments in settlement had occurred, but it is interesting to observe that by 1860 Norwegians were scattered about, mainly in small numbers, in all the states and territories of the Union save Vermont and Delaware. That the Mormon propaganda in Norway had had small results is evidenced by the fact that in Utah in 1860 there were only 159 Norwegian-born. The number of Norwegians in Missouri had actually declined in the decade, from 155 in 1850 to 146 in 1860; but Kansas in the latter year had 223 Norwegians, recruited in part from the Wisconsin settlements. Michigan had failed to attract the immigrants from the north, for there were only 440 Norwegians in that state as compared with 110 ten years earlier. The situation in the South and on the Pacific Coast has been suggested in previous chapters.[25] A foreshadowing of an

[25] See *ante*, chs. 8 and 12.

important trend was the presence of 129 Norwegians in Dakota, according to the 1860 census. "There are now about 150 Norwegian and Danish families about the town of Vermillion and up the Missouri River," wrote an immigrant in December of that year.[26]

"Between 1849 and 1860," writes Professor Flom in a valuable study of the beginnings of Norwegian settlement in Iowa, "the westward movement of Norwegian immigration was directed especially to northern Iowa and southwestern Minnesota — in Iowa from Allamakee and Clayton counties on the east to Forest City and Lake Mills in Winnebago County on the west."[27]   In this spread of Norwegian immigrants into northern Iowa the old settlements in Wisconsin, as Professor Flom has shown, were usually the parent colonies.   A map of the more important area of Norwegian penetration into the Iowa country reveals a broad band in the four northeastern counties — west from Clayton County, where the pioneers Ole Valle and Ole Tollefson Kittilsland settled in 1846, to Fayette County, and thence north into Winneshiek, swinging in an irregular line eastward through Allamakee County to the Mississippi.[28]   Valle and Kittilsland appear to have been in the forefront of these northern Iowa pioneers, but from 1849 on considerable numbers of Norwegians followed in their trails.   How early Norwegian pioneers first settled in Allamakee County, in the extreme northeastern corner of Iowa, is not certain, but in 1850 an infiltration of Norwegians from Wisconsin moved into this region, finding lands in the vicinity of Paint Creek.   By 1856 there were more than five hundred Norwegians in the county.

[26] A letter by K. P. Rønne, December 7, 1860, in *Emigranten*, February 18, 1861.

[27] "The Coming of the Norwegians to Iowa," in *Iowa Journal of History and Politics*, 3: 375 (July, 1905).

[28] Excellent maps accompany Professor Flom's article, *op. cit.*, 371–372. It should be noted that Valle and Kittilsland had gone to Iowa as early as 1843 to accept government work at Fort Atkinson. Several other Norwegians also took work at that post. Flom, *Norwegian Immigration*, 363.

Immediately west of Allamakee County lay Winneshiek, where in 1850 a colony was started at Washington Prairie by settlers moving north from Wisconsin. Most of these early settlers, according to Professor Flom, were from Voss, Telemarken, Sogn, and Valders, and had left Norway a year or two earlier. The rapid growth of this colony soon spread it out so that it made connections with the settlements to the south and east.[29] The heart of the Winneshiek County settlement — and in a sense of all the Norwegian settlements in northeastern Iowa — was Decorah. Indeed Decorah, for a variety of reasons, became in time one of the important cultural centers for the Norwegians in America. Here was established in 1862 Luther College, still one of the strongest Norwegian Lutheran colleges in the United States. Here were issued publications in Norwegian that were widely read on both sides of the Atlantic. Perhaps no Norwegian magazine published in this country has attained a higher literary and cultural excellence than *Symra*, issued at Decorah. As late as 1930

[29] Flom, in *Iowa Journal of History and Politics*, 3: 375–383. An interesting picture of the processes of migration is given by Abraham Jacobson in his reminiscences of settlement in Winneshiek County in 1850. His parents started out from the Muskego colony in Racine County, together with several other families, with Coon Prairie in Vernon County, Wisconsin, as their intended destination. The leader of the party, one Nels Johnson, had "a large military wagon drawn by six oxen." Jacobson writes that "On the outside was placed, lengthwise of the wagon box, several joints of stovepipe, so the outfit with a little stretch of imagination looked like a man of war." The caravan included "vehicles of all sizes and shapes, from truck wagons, the wheels [of which] were made of solid sections of oak logs, down to our own cart on two wheels." In the Koshkonong settlement large additions were made to the party, so that it numbered more than a hundred people. At Prairie du Chien the group divided, half going to Vernon County, Wisconsin, the other half, attracted by reports received from an Iowa settler, going west of the river to Winneshiek County. "The journey had taken five weeks, counting from the time of starting," writes Jacobson. "Those who had room enough slept under the wagon covers. The others slept on the bare ground under the wagons." Jacobson's reminiscences appear in Edwin C. Bailey, *Past and Present of Winneshiek County, Iowa*, 1: 217 ff. (Chicago, 1913). An interesting sketch of Jacobson's career is given by Clara Jacobson in her article "A Pioneer Pastor Who Knew Lincoln," in *Scandinavia* (Grand Forks, North Dakota), 1: 38–39 (March, 1924).

one of the most ably edited and influential Norwegian newspapers in America was *Decorah-Posten*. Here, too, in recent years has been built up, in connection with Luther College, a museum that includes among its purposes that of preserving log cabins and other buildings of the pioneer period and of reconstructing the material conditions of the life lived by the pioneers. For those who are interested in what Professor Dixon R. Fox has termed " civilization in transit," a center such as Decorah offers unusual opportunities for analysis.

Religious ties, according to a student of American immigration, have often determined the location of immigrant settlements; " and those church statesmen who had at heart the future of their faith used this sentiment for the benefit of both the settler and his organization." [30] A colonizer of this type was the Danish pioneer minister, C. L. Clausen, whose earlier activities were mainly among Norwegian immigrants. The Rock Prairie settlement in Wisconsin, where Clausen was pastor, attracted numerous new immigrants after its lands were largely occupied. In the late forties the Norwegian jurist, Ole Munch Ræder, visited Clausen in Wisconsin and wrote of him:[31]

For the time being he is busy writing a book on America, which, to judge by a few portions of it that he read to me, will not merely discuss the merits of Wisconsin as an immigrant residence but will give a comprehensive survey of the history and the political institutions of the entire country. As he has spent several years in America, has been both pastor and farmer in several places, under conditions which made it imperative for him to familiarize himself with all that pertains to the lot of the immigrant and since he is as trustworthy as he is capable and enterprising, his book will undoubtedly be a great help to Scandinavian immigrants in the future.

If Clausen completed this book, it at any rate seems never to have seen the light of publication. Meanwhile, how-

---

[30] Marcus L. Hansen, in *American Historical Review*, 32: 506 (April, 1927).
[31] *America in the Forties*, 136.

ever, he interested himself in helping the land seekers from Norway who were swarming into the West. Early in 1850 he appealed to the governor of Minnesota Territory, Alexander Ramsey, for information about the domain which he governed.[32] " A large number of Emigrants who came in last season," he explained, " are now staying over the winter around here in the settlement, purposing to look out in the spring for public lands to settle upon, but as they are alike unacquainted with the country and the language here, it is to be feared that many of them may be misled to their serious disadvantage, if left entirely to themselves, or, which is often worse, to the guidance of interested speculators." In the interests of these people Clausen desired information, especially about the region in the vicinity of Lake Pepin and of the St. Croix. " Those Norwegians, in whose behalf I now principally write," he continued, " are generally poor, but sober, hardy and industrious farmers and mechanics; but I have received letters from Norway & Denmark, informing me that several men with considerable capital, wish to go over here, if I can lead them to places where they can invest their capital profitably, in improving water powers, erecting mills and other machineries, and building towns, etc. . . ." Clausen stated that if the governor's reply were favorable, he proposed to make a journey to Minnesota to examine the region for himself. The next summer he set off for the Minnesota country, his travels taking him to such places as St. Paul, St. Cloud, and St. Anthony Falls, up the Minnesota River, and to the vicinity of St. Croix Lake, where on the Wisconsin side, in the neighborhood of Rush River, he found land that seemed satisfactory to him. His reports upon his return to Rock Prairie aroused the interest

---

[32] Clausen to Ramsey, January 22, 1850, in the Ramsey Papers, Minnesota Historical Society, St. Paul. The writer is indebted to Mr. Martin Odland for calling his attention to this interesting letter.

of a handful of Norwegians, who went north and formed the nucleus of a colony that later grew to large proportions in St. Croix and Pierce counties, Wisconsin. For the majority of the newcomers in southern Wisconsin, however, these lands seemed too far north.[33]

In the summer of 1852 Clausen with two companions explored the rich farming area along the Iowa-Minnesota boundary and took out a claim in Mitchell County, the second county beyond Winneshiek in Iowa's northern tier, which he thought admirably suited for a Norwegian colony. He returned to Rock Prairie and published in *Emigranten* an account of his trip, describing the land on Big Cedar River as fertile prairie, with woods along the stream, and numerous other advantages.[34] Only some four or five claims had been taken and for a distance of thirty miles in Iowa and Minnesota the land was open and available. In the spring of 1853 a caravan of some forty canvas-covered wagons drawn by oxen conveyed about forty families to the colony, which was named St. Ansgar. About three hundred head of cattle were driven with the caravan, for Clausen believed that cattle-raising would prove the most profitable industry. " The journey lasted three weeks," writes a woman who was a member of the party, " and most of us walked on foot the whole way, driving the cattle. I can remember that I carried children across creeks and rivers, where we had to ford the streams. No settlers were found in Mitchell County when we came there, but at Osage some had raised tall poles with names on, to indicate that they claimed the land. . . . Our first house was a small log cabin thatched with sod. . . .

---

[33] A master's thesis entitled " Claus L. Clausen, Pioneer Pastor and Settlement Promoter, 1843–1868," by Margrethe Jorgensen, presented at the University of Minnesota in 1930, contains much new material on its subject. A copy is in the possession of the Minnesota Historical Society.

[34] *Emigranten*, October 1, 1852, reprinted in Holand, *De Norske Settlementers Historie*, 398–401.

Rev. Clausen helped those who were sick, as far as he was able. . . . The greatest hospitality was practiced, and we loved each other as if we were all brothers and sisters." [35] Clausen was the active leader in the enterprise; arranged for the building of a mill, a church, a post office, and cabins; opened a school in his own cabin; inaugurated regular church services two weeks after arrival; and took a leading part in the business affairs of the colony. He continued to promote interest among the people of the older Wisconsin settlements in the new area which he had helped to open. A hundred families arrived in 1854 and numerous accessions occurred in the following years. From St. Ansgar, from the settlements in the two northeastern Iowa counties, and from Wisconsin in general settlers filtered and then streamed into the southern counties of Minnesota.[36]

" I believe the entire population of Wisconsin is on the way to the west now," wrote the wife of a pioneer Iowa pastor one spring day in 1854. " Yesterday a young man stopped here with greetings from Pastor Preus. On his way he had passed more than three hundred wagons of Norwegians, most of whom were going to Minnesota, some to Pastor Clausen's. There is no land to be had for them here now. Those who are thus traveling are either new-comers who have spent the winter in Wisconsin or else people who have sold their small farms to older Norwegians and are now going to regions where they can easily get much land at low prices. Many are leaving the congregations of pastors Preus, Stub, and others." [37] Those who followed the rough overland trails in wagons, covered and uncovered, were supplemented by immigrants who came

[35] Quoted by Gjerset and Hektoen, in *Studies and Records*, 1: 11.

[36] On Clausen as a colonizer see R. Andersen, *Pastor Claus Laurits Clausen*, 129 ff. (New York, 1921); and Holand, *op. cit.*, chs. 46–50.

[37] *Fra Pioneertiden. Uddrag af Fru Elisabeth Korens Dagbog og Breve fra Fem-tiaarene*, 168.

north on Mississippi steamboats. An Iowa traveler of the middle fifties has left an interesting description of a party of Norwegians seen on the wharf in Lansing, a river town in Allamakee County. " The first sight that greeted my eye," he wrote, after going ashore from the " Golden Era," a popular boat of the time, " was between three and four hundred hardy Norwegians, with their goods and chattels piled up on the wharf, awaiting a conveyance to the country. As near as I could understand them, a large colony have purchased (through their agent) a tract of land a few miles west, and they were then on their way to their new home. They were in good health and excellent spirits, and had not lost one of their number since leaving Norway." The Iowa traveler understood that the party was made up of potential builders of commonwealth, but he may have been somewhat naïve in crediting its members with wealth. " From the fact that these immigrants came over in a steamship," he added, " as well as from the appearance of a small, well-guarded iron chest in their possession, it may be inferred they are wealthy and industrious people, who will be a great accession to this portion of the State." [38]

While immigrant settlers thus were streaming into northeastern Iowa, a thrust was made to the northeast from the old Fox River colony in Illinois that resulted in the building up of an important colony in central Iowa, centering in Story County. The coming of the Norwegians to that county, writes a local historian, " was not a straggling movement, nor one in which a number of individuals of family relationship or previous personal association joined their efforts, but it was a matter of deliberate colonization." [39] The Illinois colony continued to be a magnet for immigrants from western Norway,

[38] Nathan H. Parker, *The Iowa Handbook for 1856*, 113 (Boston, 1856).
[39] William O. Payne, *History of Story County, Iowa*, 1: 23 (Chicago, 1911).

owing to the strong representation of that element in the early migration to Illinois, but since the land in this region was largely occupied, the newcomers were naturally much interested in reports of settlement opportunities to the west and north. In 1854 a considerable group of immigrants sent a scouting party of four men — Osmund Sheldal, Ole Flatland, Ole Apland, and Osmund Johnson — to investigate prospects in Iowa. When this committee returned it had selected good land in Story County. A full report of its observations and conclusions was presented in a formal meeting, and plans were made for an exodus to Iowa. Before the departure of the main group in the spring of 1855, its members formed a Lutheran congregation, selecting a minister, a sexton, and a school-teacher. Their expectations with regard to the outcome of the project are perhaps intimated in the adoption of the name " Palestine " for the congregation. In May, 1855, this congregation, comprising 106 persons, set off from the Fox River country on its overland trek with ox-teams and wagons, and a month later it reached its destination, forming the so-called southern settlement in Story County. It is interesting to note that shortly after these church people, with their pastor, set out for the Iowa Palestine, the Haugeans in the Fox River settlement, who had had little to do with this move, dispatched an investigating committee of their own to the same general region. The eight men comprising this committee chose lands some twenty-five miles to the north of the Palestine congregation. Two of the Haugeans appear to have settled in this tract in 1855, but the main Haugean body went north from Illinois in 1856, in a caravan of twenty-four wagons. The Story County enterprises are of special interest as illustrating not only planned colonization, with investigators reconnoitering the ground in advance, but the organization of settlement on religious lines, with a marked cleavage between two groups.[40]   The colonists, moreover, seem to have been predominantly of western Norwegian origin.   It is obvious that the planting of these central Iowa settlements can only be understood in the light of religious and provincial forces that have old-world backgrounds, in coalescence with economic and other motives that influenced the pioneer land seekers.

In pushing into Minnesota in the fifties the Norwegians participated in and contributed to one of the remarkable settlement stampedes of American history.   The Indian treaties of 1851 opened up the greater part of Minnesota west of the Mississippi south of the Sioux-Chippewa line — a region of prairie and woodland, gemmed with lakes, patterned with streams, certain, as Fredrika Bremer had foretold, to appeal to the imaginations of Norwegians, Swedes, and Danes.   The westward movement, favored by the opening of the gates to this rich land; by the advance of railroads to the Mississippi at Rock Island in 1854, to East Dubuque in 1855, to Prairie du Chien in 1857, and to La Crosse in 1858; by the overflow of settlers from older regions in the Middle West; and by the vigorous propaganda for settlers carried on by official and unofficial agencies, touched Minnesota as with a magic wand, transformed the territory into a state, and increased the population from less than 5,000 people in 1849 to more than 172,000 in 1860.   Native American stock, representing New England, New York, and the Middle West, was the chief factor in this characteristically new-world boom, but immigrants also played their part.   Thus the Scandinavian-born increased from 12 in 1850 to nearly 12,000 ten years later (with Norwegians comprising two-thirds of this total), and the number of German-born from 147 to 18,400.

[40] The best account of the Story County settlements is that given in Holand, *De Norske Settlementers Historie*, ch. 54.

North of the Iowa settlements lay the southern tier of Minnesota counties — Houston, Fillmore, Mower, Freeborn, Faribault, and the rest. It was entirely natural for the Iowa centers of Norwegian settlement to be bases for northward extensions; but many of the Norwegian beginnings in Minnesota represented direct lines from the older Wisconsin and Illinois colonies, supplemented by arriving immigrants; and many land hunters passed by the first tier of Minnesota counties to establish settlements farther north. One interesting aspect of the processes of Norwegian settlement in the West is the close family connections that the new settlements have with the earlier Norwegian immigration through secondary or tertiary migrations. Clausen's St. Ansgar colony, for example, contributed to the Norwegian settlement of Mower, Freeborn, and Faribault counties in 1853, 1854, and succeeding years, but the process was supplemented by parties from the parent colony of Rock Prairie and from other noted Wisconsin colonies, including Koshkonong. Houston and Fillmore counties received swarms of Norwegians from the near-by Iowa settlements and from Rock Prairie, Koshkonong, Muskego, and elsewhere to the southeast, with the process beginning in 1851 and 1852. It may be noted incidentally that the converging of different lines in this region resulted in the building up of a very compact settlement. The Houston County center, Spring Grove, for example, was almost a solid Norwegian-American town and has retained this character, with the modifications of time and the transition to the second and third generations, down to the present. To the west, Fillmore County counted among its accessions of 1853 not a few settlers from the first Norwegian colony in the West, that in Illinois, among whom was such a prominent pioneer as Hans Valder, who had come to America on " Enigheden " in 1837. A prominent Goodhue County pioneer was Halvor P. Haugan, who had

followed Ansten Nattestad from Numedal to Jefferson
Prairie in 1839. To Goodhue County, which was also a
favorite center for early Swedish settlement, — with Vasa
as the nucleus, — came a party of Norwegian pioneers by
covered wagon from the Washington Prairie settlement in
Iowa in 1855, making Wanamingo their destination. It
was natural for Norwegian settlement to expand into Rice
County from Goodhue. Settlers had come from Dane
County, Wisconsin, to Waseca County in 1855, and they
were augmented the next year by a Rock Prairie contingent, which arrived with twelve span of oxen and eighty
head of cattle. "My father and I and Ole Thoresen,"
wrote Magnus W. Samson from Christiania, Dakota
County, in 1859, "were the first settlers in this colony."
They came in the spring of 1854 from Koshkonong, where
they had lived for eight years; for five before that they had
resided in the Fox River colony. In 1855 a caravan of nine
covered wagons came to Dakota County from Muskego;
and there were also accessions from other Wisconsin communities.[41]

These more or less typical items might be supplemented
with numerous details from Nicollet County, beginning
in 1853 or 1854; from Carver — an early Swedish center
— where Norwegians arrived as early as 1852 and 1855, in
the latter year including the family of Ole Paulson, who
later fought in the Sioux War and thereafter became a
noted pioneer minister; from Meeker, to which Rock
Prairie colonists of Hallingdal origin found their way in
1856; from Kandiyohi, where Lars Endreson Rosseland and
his wife Guri Rosseland — the latter destined to become
the outstanding Norwegian heroine of the Sioux Outbreak
— arrived in 1857; and from numerous other Minnesota
counties. Though natural highways of travel and the circumstances of the time doubtless made Minnesota an in-

[41] *Emigranten*, March 14, 1859.

evitable Mecca for great numbers of immigrants, decisions
were frequently the result of careful consideration of the
comparative advantages of different states. For example,
a Fillmore County settler wrote in 1859 that he made his
choice after comparing all the information he could get
about Kansas, Nebraska, and Minnesota.[42] The lines from
the older settlements were supplemented by lines from
Europe by way of Quebec and the usual routes to the
West; for the immigrants were interested in Minnesota,
where towns and farming communities were springing into
existence in a fashion so extraordinary. In immigrant
letters one catches glimpses of such communities before
they fairly emerged from the embryonic stage. Thus a
letter from Blue Earth County in 1856 describes a group
of settlers residing temporarily in the covered wagons that
had conveyed them to Minnesota.[43]

Echoes of the swarming of Norwegians into Minnesota
in the fifties were heard in Norway not only through
" America letters " but also through public reports, especially of missionary journeys by pioneer preachers interested in church organization. For example, H. A. Stub,
of " Coon Prairie P. O., Bad-Ax County," Wisconsin, in

[42] *Emigranten,* March 14, 1859.

[43] *Emigranten,* October 31, 1856. A master's thesis entitled " Pioneer Norwegian
Settlement in Minnesota (to 1876) " has recently been completed (1930) at the
University of Minnesota by Mr. Carlton Qualey. It is to be hoped that this
excellent treatise may lead toward an adequate comprehensive historical study of the
Norwegian element in Minnesota. Considerable information about the early Minne-
sota settlements is in Holand, *De Norske Settlementers Historie,* and some interesting
items are included in J. S. Johnson, *Minnesota: En Kortfattet Historie av Nord-
mændenes Bebyggelse av Staten,* 41 ff. (St. Paul, 1914). Valuable work on the
history of the Norwegian settlements in the United States is being done by Mr. Carl
G. O. Hansen, in a series of articles entitled " Glimt fra Livet i det norske
Amerika," published in the *Minneapolis Tidende,* of which he is the editor.
Beginning with the weekly issue for November 13, 1930, special attention is devoted
by Mr. Hansen to the settlements in Minnesota, especially in Goodhue County.
An article by Theodore L. Nydahl, published in *Studies and Records,* 5: 50–60, tells
interestingly about " Social and Economic Aspects of Pioneering as Illustrated in
Goodhue County, Minnesota."

1857 explained to Norwegians the need of a minister in Goodhue County, where he said there were from two to three hundred Norwegian families. He was compelled to admit that the settlers had proved themselves " smart "— an admission that, coming from a clergyman, had an unfamiliar sound to Norwegian ears. " They have chosen a very favorable spot for settlement," he said. " They are almost all old farmers who have sold their property in the older settlements, partly in Wisconsin and partly in Illinois, and have come to this blossoming territory with not inconsiderable sums of money; for this reason most of them, in the short time they have been here, have made much progress. The new settlement bears marked signs of the prosperity of the farmers." Though doubtless without conscious purpose in the matter, Stub was doing more than advertising the need of a minister; he was advertising Minnesota as a home for immigrant settlers.[44] And in the spring of 1858 Laurentius Larsen, pastor at the Rush River settlement in Pierce County, Wisconsin, made an extended missionary journey in Minnesota, visiting settlers and organizing congregations. His report was published not only in Wisconsin but also in the capital of Norway. He had previously organized a congregation at Stillwater; he now added one at St. Paul; at Carver he found thirty to forty Norwegian families and four or five times as many Swedes, but he did not attempt to organize a congregation since the Swedish minister stationed at that place regarded him as an un-Christian trouble-maker; he then went to St. Peter, where he held a church service; in Nicollet and Sibley counties he found a settlement of about fifty families and organized a congregation; in Steele and Waseca he visited a settlement of about sixty Norwegian families and suggested the possibility of a congregational

[44] The report appeared on the first page of *Morgenbladet*, June 4, 1857.

union either with Olmsted County settlers or with a settlement of some forty families living west of Wilton. Goodhue County seems to have impressed him as the most robust of the Norwegian settlements in Minnesota. Here he held six services in six different places; and he expressed the opinion that about two hundred families would join a congregation.[45] " Never have I preached to such large audiences as here in Goodhue," he wrote in a second report stressing the need for ministers in the West.[46] A minister in 1859 after a somewhat similar missionary journey wrote that he had visited regions, especially in Meeker and Monongalia counties, the beauty and attractiveness of which surpassed anything he had ever seen, north or south.[47] Thus the ministers preached the gospel of Minnesota.

So on the eve of the Civil War the Norwegian immigration, which had begun not forty years before with a handful of immigrants settling on the New York frontier, had swept westward to the spacious valley of the Mississippi and was striking deep roots in several states beyond the river. Here in the American hinterland immigrant pioneers of many nationalities, side by side with native Americans, wrestled with the wilderness. The day of the trapper and trader, drawn into the West by the lure of adventure and profit, was passing, and the day of the new West, of the farmer and of the city-builder, was dawning. The immigrants on the agricultural frontier of the Middle West, joining in the establishment and building up of new communities, played a part in one of the most significant of American transitions even while they were coping with

---

[45] *Christiania-Posten*, September 22, 1858, reprinted from *Emigranten*.

[46] *Christiania-Posten*, September 27, 1858.

[47] A. E. Fredrichson, " Beretning om en Reise gjennem en stor Deel af de Miterste og Vestlige af Minnesota og flere norsk-evang.-luth. Menigheders Oprettelse," in *Emigranten*, October 10, 17, 24, November 7, 1859.

the problems of their own adjustment to the new and ever-altering environment. Among the elements that figured in the peopling and in the development of America's inland empire were the Norwegians. By the eve of the Civil War they had identified themselves with the Northwest. This region, in the era of growth and expansion that followed the war, was sought by thousands upon thousands of northern immigrants who followed the trails of the early pioneers. And on this region the Norwegians have perhaps left some of the deepest imprints of their nationality.

APPENDIX

"SLOOP FOLK" PROBLEMS

1. THE PEERSON LETTER OF 1824

Considerable attention is devoted in chapter 2 of this book to a letter written by Thormod Madland at Stavanger on June 28, 1825, to Mauris Halvarsen of Østrimdal, Birkremsogn, Norway. Its importance lies in the fact that it contains a copy of a letter written by " Kleng Pedersen "— Cleng Peerson — from New York on December 20, 1824. The document was first used by the writer in an article on " Cleng Peerson and Norwegian Immigration," in the *Mississippi Valley Historical Review* for March, 1921. In *Skandinaven* (Chicago), March 21, 1924, Professor R. B. Anderson questioned the genuineness of the letter. A reply by the present writer was published in the same paper for July 11 and 12, 1924, and reprinted in the semi-weekly edition for July 16. Mr. Anderson later reprinted his article as a part of his book *Cleng Peerson og Sluppen Restaurationen*, 57–60. As the document is a significant one, it seems desirable to publish here its text and a literal English translation.

THORMOD MADLAND TO MAURIS HALVARSEN, June 28, 1825 [1]

[Minnesota Historical Society Mss.— A. L. S.]

Til kiere ven Maauris H: S. og hans kone S:A:D:

Kopia af et brev som K: Pedersen haver skrevet til sine Slegtninger og Venner, hvad han har udrettet for os efter sin til bagekomst til americha, og lyder som følger

Nevÿrk[2] den 20.de *December* 1824.

KIÆRE FADER, BRODER, SØSTER, SVAAGER OG VENNER. Ieg lader Eder vide at ieg er lykkelig og vel kommen til *americha;* Efter 6 Ugers

---

[1] The transcription was made with the aid of Mrs. Gudrun Natrud of Oslo, a scholar familiar with manuscripts and archives of the period, and it was collated with Dr. Fr. Scheel, state archivist, Statsarkiv, Oslo.

[2] All the words here italicized are written in roman letters in the manuscript; the rest of the document is in Gothic script.

Reise vare vi i *Nevÿrk,* hvor ieg fandt alle mine Venner vel med helsen
og anamede mig meget ømmeligen; vi stansede der 5.dage; saa toge
vi *Dampmaskinen William Pen,* til Alboni, som er 150 miile det er 30.
Norske miile det kostede 2. daler for hver af os, ogsaa fik vi fri kost,
hvor vi Reiste i 24 timer, siden til *Trøÿ,* Siden væstover i gienem den
store Canal 200.mile til Salina³ saltværk, hvor det kostede os intet
uden arbeide, siden tog vi en anden baad, for resten til mine Venner
i *Faningtaun,* hvor ieg forlod min kamrat, og til Geneve til Lands
hvor *Landsherren* bor, for at kiøbe Land for mig og til Eder, som før
er omtalt, *Landesherren* er meget vinskebeligen og haver lovet saa
megen Understøttelse som mueligt; vi haver akoderet om 6. Støker
Land, som ieg haver udvalt, og skal staa for os til høsten. Ieg haver
allerede et Huus i byggning 12. alen lang og 10 allen bred, hvilket
ieg haaber at faa færdig til *Nytaars* dag, siden Vente vi Vinter for et
par *maaneder,* hvilket er got for at kiøre fra skovene, Da ieg var i
Raadkirster kiøbte ieg en Ovn for 20. daler med alt behør, saasom
Pande, grÿde til kiedet, bagerovn med mere; saa vi behøver ingen
Skorsten. — Ieg haver bygget dette Huus paa de andre stykker til eder
som ieg venter at komme; men til Vaaren om Herren vil Ieg lever, vil
ieg bygge paa met Eget støkke; Ieg haver 5. ac[i ?]kers af *Land* hvilket
er 330 pr. arec[i], at have Rede til Vaaren at saa og Plante; Ieg haver
en Koe i *Faningtun* koster 10 daler, og nogle Faar, Ieg haver meldet
Priserne paa alle ting i *Knud Eies* brev. Ieg er meget bekymret i mit
sind angaanden Eders komme til *Americha* Naar ieg tænkker paa min
søster og andre mine Venner, O. hvor ieg Ønsker den tid var over, og
hvor glad ieg vilde blive veddet bud at de komme til *Nevÿrk* at ieg
kunde omf[a]vne Eder der; Ieg frÿgter ikke i kan Reise igienem
Canalen meget mageligt og for got kiøb, Vennerne i *Masedon* haver
lovet og sagt min Søster med de flere skal blive hos dem til vi faar
bygget Huuse for dennem; See her er mange som kiøbe *Land* her om-
kring; her er mange opdyrkede stykker at lodbrüge for os; det vil
snart blive fuldt her om kring og det nærmeste *Canalen.*— Ieg maa
overgive alt til Forsynet, — det hand vilde i og giøre; I maae ikke lade
Eder af skrække med snak; Ieg haver fundet Forsynets Hielp, Naar ieg
allene bliver ved i Haabet det alt vi kan. Ieg har fortalt eder alting
munteligen; og ieg vil ved blive mine løfter; skriv mig alene til i tide,
saa vil ieg giøre mit beste. Ieg talte med mange i *Nevyork* om

³ In the manuscript the letter *n* is inserted under the final *ia* of " Salia."

Fartøyet at selge i vil visseligen faa selget et lidet Fartøy, men et stort er i mod *Lands* loves tilladelse, Giører der for hvad i finde for godt, Unge mennisker kan lættelig komme over til *London* og der fra til *Nevÿörk* for 30. daler,— mine Venner i Nevÿörk har lovet at giøre alt hvad muelig er, selge Fartøyet saa got som mueligt. Der i mod, der som i kunde kiøbe Eders Penge op i Iern, fra Svrig, og fragte et fartøÿ, det vil giøre det same. Ieg haaber i vil skrive mig brev til naar i ere færdige og Underrete mig om eders forehavende; for alting handler broderligen med hverandre, Værer ingen noget skyldige uden at Elske hverandre; det opfylder; lader os betragte os selv, saadane som vi Virkelig ere usselhed og afmagt, da vil vi see at vi altid trænger til Hielp og Frelse fra Almagtens Hand, saa vil vi adlyde hans kald og paa mendelser. — Ieg er ved en god Helsen til denne tid, og min kamrat, *Andrias Stangelan;* Helser alle Vener der, min Fader, og Søskend, Venner og alle andre bekiente der; Ieg ven og tiener til Døden.

KLENG PEDERSEN

Dette haver ieg skrevet til eder at i kunde have et got haab om vor Reisses udfald, saa sandt som Herren hielper os væl og løkkelig over, thi ieg kiender eders vælmente og Øme Hierte for os, de er saa god og lader *Lars G. Torllef Ma*: m: fl: høre det.
Stavanger den 28: *Juni* 1825

THORMOD MADLAND.

Til
   MAURIS HALVARSEN
      Østrimdal i Bierkim sog.
   THORMOD MADLAND TO MAURIS HALVARSEN, June 28, 1825
      [*English translation*]

   To my dear friend Maauris H. S. and his wife S. A. D.
A copy of a letter written by K. Pederson to his relatives and friends, [telling] what he has accomplished for us since his return to America, and running as follows:

NEW YORK, December 20, 1824

DEAR FATHER, BROTHER, SISTER, BROTHER-IN-LAW,[4] AND FRIENDS:—
   I let you know that I have arrived in America happy and well. After a journey of six weeks we reached New York, where I found all my

---

[4] Cornelius Nelson Hersdal, one of the "sloop folk," was married to Peerson's sister, Kari Peerson Hesthammer. The present writer, in the *Mississippi Valley Historical Review*, 7: 310 n., mistakenly states that Lars Larsen was Peerson's

friends in good health and they received me very affectionately. We remained there five days; then we took the steamboat " William Penn " for Albany, which is 150 miles, that is 30 Norwegian miles,[5] it cost two dollars for each of us and we also received free board, where we arrived in 24 hours. Later we went to Troy, and then westward through the great canal 200 miles to Salina Salt Works, paying our way by working; thereafter we took another boat and went the rest of the way to my friends in Faningtown [*Farmington*],[6] where I left my comrade. I then went overland to Geneva, where the land commissioner lives, to buy land for myself and for you, as previously discussed. The land commissioner is very friendly, and has promised to give us as much aid as possible. We reached an agreement in regard to six pieces of land which I have selected, and shall be held for us until next fall. I already have a house in process of building, 12 ells long and 10 ells wide,[7] which I hope to complete by New Year's day. We then expect winter for a couple of months which will be a good time to haul wood from the forests. When I was in Rochester I bought a stove for 20 dollars with full equipment such as pans, pots for meat, a baking oven, and other things; so we shall not need any fireplace. I have built this house on the land selected for you whose arrival I am waiting, but in the spring, if the Lord permits me to live, I shall build on my own land. I have 5 acres of land, which is 330 per *arec*[*i*],[8] to have ready in the spring to sow and plant. I have a cow in Faningtun [*Farmington*] which cost me ten dollars, and a few sheep. I have reported the prices of all things in Knud Eie's letter. I am very much concerned in my mind about your coming to America. When I think of my sister and of other friends of mine, oh, how I wish that that time were over, and how glad I would be to receive word that you were coming to New York that I might greet you there. I have no doubt that you will be able to journey

brother-in-law. Larsen married Martha Georgiana Peerson, but she was not a sister of Cleng Peerson. The writer is indebted to Mr. Cadbury for calling attention to this error. *Studies and Records*, 1: 92.

[5] Peerson makes an error in this estimate, for a Norwegian mile is equivalent to seven English miles.

[6] *Cf. ante*, ch. 2, n. 42.

[7] An ell is two feet.

[8] This phrase is not clear to the translator. It may mean " which costs $3.30 per acre."

through the canal very comfortably and at a cheap rate. The Friends in Masedon [Macedon] have promised and said that my sister and the others shall stay with them until we get houses built for them. Well, many persons are buying land in this vicinity; there are many cultivated pieces of land here that we may work on share. It will soon be filled up around here and especially nearest the canal. I must leave everything to Providence; what He wills, you also do. You must not let yourselves be frightened away by talk. I have found the help of Providence as long as I have kept steadfast in hope; that is all we can do. I have told you everything orally, and I will stand by my promises. Only write me in time, then I will do my best. I talked with many persons in New York about selling the vessel. You will certainly be able to sell a small vessel, but a large one is against the permission of the law.[9] Therefore do whatever seems best to you. Young persons can easily get over to London and from there to New York for thirty dollars. My friends in New York have promised to do all that is possible to sell the vessel as advantageously as possible. On the other hand, if you could put your money in iron from Sweden and hire a vessel, that would come to the same thing. I hope you will write me a letter as soon as you are ready and let me know about your intentions. Above all, deal with one another in a brotherly spirit. In no wise fail to love one another. Fulfill that. Let us see ourselves as we really are, wretched and feeble, Then we shall understand that we always need help and salvation from the hand of the Almighty, then we will heed His call and admonitions. Up to the present time I have been in good health, also my comrade Andrias Stangelan. Greet all friends there, my father, Søskend,[10] friends, and all other acquaintances there. Your friend and servant unto death,

KLENG PEDERSEN

I have written this for you in order that you may have a good hope as to the result of our journey, as truly as the Lord will help us to cross well and happily over, for I know the kindness and tenderness of your hearts for us, be so good as to let Lars G., Tollef Ma., and others hear this.

THORMOD MADLAND

STAVANGER, June 28, 1825.

ØSTRIMDAL, BIRKREM PARISH

[9] This remark by Peerson may explain why the "sloop folk" purchased so small a vessel for their voyage.

[10] This word means brother and sister, or brothers and sisters.

For several reasons Professor Anderson doubted the genuineness of this letter. It clashes with the traditional view that Cleng Peerson, who had spent the period from 1821 to 1824 in America and then gone back to Norway, returned to America in 1825. It fixes the date of his return as 1824, not 1825. It indicates that Andrew Stangeland accompanied Peerson to America in 1824, and this seems to clash with the view that Stangeland came to America in 1825 on the "Restauration." Furthermore, Professor Anderson questions how this letter happened to turn up when it did, asks where the original Peerson letter of 1824 now is, and states that the descendants of Madland know nothing about this document from 1825. He also declares that Peerson was little given to writing, perhaps could not write. Finally, he questions the genuineness of the letter because it records Peerson as apparently arranging for the purchase of land in Ontario County, New York, whereas it is well known that most of the immigrants who came on the "Restauration" went, not to Ontario County, but to Orleans County.

Professor Anderson based his judgment on internal evidence alone and wrote his article without having examined the original. It is proper to explain how the letter came into the possession of the Minnesota Historical Society and to consider the problem of its genuineness first on the basis of external criticism. The letter was turned over to the writer by Mr. Alfred Adsem of Minneapolis, who knew of the writer's interest in Norwegian immigration. Mr. Adsem received it from a relative of his, Mr. Martin Mauritzon of Chicago. Mr. Mauritzon, in a letter of May 18, 1924, to Mr. Adsem explains the document's origin.

MARTIN MAURITZON TO ALFRED ADSEM, May 18, 1924

[Ms. in possession of T. C. Blegen; translated from the Norwegian.]

CHICAGO, May 18, 1924

TO MR. ALFRED ADSEM:—

I received a letter from you a few days ago in which you ask me, or rather Mr. Theodore C. Blegen asks me, how I came into possession of the letter which Thormod Madland wrote to my grandfather, Mauritz Halvorsen, Østrimdal, Birkremsogn.[11] You may write to him and tell him that my father, Aadne Mauritzen, had the letter in his possession together with a number of other old letters, including one dating from the war with England in 1807, which I now have. I can remember these letters from the time when I was quite young — five or six years old — and since then they have been preserved along with other old books and documents. It was not the value of the letter which accounts for its being saved. Nobody cared about it, and many a time I have had it in my hands and have been on the point of burning it up. It was kept in an attic together with some other old stuff. After having been at sea for a number of years I went to America in 1881, to Chicago, and have lived there ever since except for a period of six years spent at home in Stavanger. At that time I ran across this letter. I had heard much about how the history of the Norwegian settlers was going to be written and that Cleng Pedersen's name was connected with it. Therefore I took care of the letter and when I returned to Chicago in 1900 I took it with me. Mr. Alfred Adsem came to Chicago on a visit and I let him see this letter and asked him if it could be of any use for the history of the Norwegian settlers. Mr. Adsem said he would investigate. Several years later he wrote to me and asked me to send him the letter and this was done. This is all I can tell about the history and ownership of the letter. When you meet Mr. Blegen you may read this letter to him. If he wishes me to, I can make out an affidavit that all is true which I have written.

Your friend,
MARTIN MAURITZON

1418 N. Kedzie Avenue, Chicago

With reference to the external characteristics of the letter, Dr. Grace L. Nute, curator of manuscripts, Minne-

---

[11] Mrs. Natrud examined the Norwegian census records for me to ascertain whether or not there was a Mauritz Halvorsen of Østrimdal. The census for 1801 records the family of "Hadvar" Mouritzen, one of whose sons was Mouritz Halvardsen, then nineteen years of age. Mrs. Natrud has also found records of a "Tollof Mouritzen Malmey" and a "Lars Hadvarsen Grytteland" in that neighborhood, who may have been the individuals referred to at the end of Thormod Madland's postscript.

sota Historical Society, has given the writer the following opinion:

As an attempt has been made to prove that the copy of Cleng
Peerson's letter in the possession of the Minnesota Historical Society
is not genuine, i.e., that the document is not a genuine copy made in
1825 of a letter written by Cleng Peerson in 1824 — I wish to state
that all external evidence goes to show that the document must have
been written at approximately the date claimed for it. It would be
almost impossible to reproduce so exactly the peculiar texture of paper
of that date; the rusty tint of the ink and the frayed edges and breaks
in the material characteristic of documents of such age; not to mention the faded and yellowed aspect of the paper. After one has handled
many manuscripts, one comes to know, almost by sense of touch, the
age of a document. In this case, I should say, if no clue as to date
other than the " feel " of the paper could be found, that the manuscript
is about one hundred years old.

To this opinion the writer can add that the script and
language of the letter are characteristic of the twenties.
Norwegian archivists who examined the document found
no reason to question its genuineness.

One point in Professor Anderson's criticism is unquestionably true — his claim that Peerson was " little given
to writing." In 1851, twenty-seven years after the time
of the letter under discussion, a brief statement by Peerson, then living in Texas, as printed in various Norwegian
newspapers, was signed " Cleng Pedersen — med paahold-
en Pen." [12] This would make it appear that Peerson could
not write, since he required the services of someone else
in writing a statement and signing his name. It is con-
ceivable that in 1851 — Peerson was then sixty-eight years
of age — age or sickness or both may have made it necessary for him to get help in penning a letter, even though
he had been able to write earlier, but, in the absence of

[12] *Morgenbladet*, June 18, 1852; the item is reprinted from another source by
Malmin in *Decorah-Posten*, February 6, 1925.

proof of such circumstances, the phrase certainly casts doubt on Peerson's ability to write. The fact remains, however, that Peerson was indisputably the author of several letters, whether he wrote them with his own hand or had them written for him by someone else. Thus in the issue of *Democraten* (Racine, Wisconsin), for September 7, 1850, there is printed a long letter by him, dated at Norway, La Salle County, Illinois, on August 20, 1850. No qualifying phrase appears under his name, and the editor, Knud Langeland, prints the document with the statement, in matter-of-fact tone, that he has received a letter from his old friend Peerson which will interest the readers of the newspaper.

Another letter by Peerson, dated at Bergen on April 28, 1843, was published in Norway, in *Bergens Stiftstidende*, for April 30, 1843.[13] There is no qualifying phrase under the signature in this case. This letter introduces another complication, however. In it Peerson, then in Norway, defends himself against the " charge " that he is an emigration agent. To prove that he is not engaged in stirring up people to emigrate he explains that he had not brought letters from immigrants with him to Norway and he further asserts that his own correspondence home has been limited to one letter after his first emigration twenty-two years earlier. It is possible that despite its emphasis upon " first emigration," this is an allusion to the very letter here under discussion. Peerson is recalling in the forties an event that happened in the twenties. He remembered that he had written one letter in the early period. The Madland transcript makes it conjecturable that the letter that he was recalling was in fact the letter of 1824. In any case, it is clear that one cannot reject the letter of

[13] The letter is reprinted by A. Ragnv. Brækhus, " Cleng Peersons Norgesbesøk i 1843," in *Nordmands-forbundet*, 18: 230–231 (April, 1925).

1824 because of the supposition that Peerson could not write.[14]

The letter indicates that Peerson returned to America in 1824. He had been in America three years, from 1821 to 1824. Obviously he must have made only a comparatively short visit to Norway in 1824 before hurrying back to America to arrange for the purchase of land for the prospective emigrants. Ole Rynning in his *True Account of America*, published in 1838, states that Peerson made *en Snartour* to Norway in 1824.[15] The dictionary translation of *Snartour* is a " flying visit." A newspaper article published in Stavanger early in 1843, — at a time when Peerson was again back in Norway, — referring to Peerson's visit to Norway in 1824 says that he *foer tilbage samme Aar* to America, that is, " hurried back the same year." [16] These items would appear to confirm the evidence in the letter. It remains to point out that no contemporary evidence has been found to show that Peerson remained in Norway until 1825. Various writers have tried to explain why, if Peerson was in Norway when the

[14] Mr. Cadbury, discussing this point in *Studies and Records*, 1: 91–92, accepts the letter as genuine, but suggests that in writing the letter of 1824 and those of 1843 and 1850, Peerson had the help of more literate Norwegians notwithstanding the fact that in these three cases the phrase *med paaholden Pen* is not used.

[15] " I 1824 var han en Snartour tilbage til Norge, og ved hans Beretninger om Amerika vaktes hos Flere Lysten at reise didhen." *Rynning's True Account of America*, 34.

[16] " Efter hvad Kleng Pedersen Hesthammer, der reiste over til Amerika 1821, kom tilbage i 1824, og var den Første, som underrettede Folket her om Forholdene der, foer tilbage samme Aar, og efter 19 Aars Ophold der kom her tilbage i afvigte Høst, og flere Breve fra en Deel af dem berette, befinde de sig vel og have rundelig Udkomme." *Stavanger Amtstidende og Adresseavis*, January 8, 1843. The value of this evidence is lessened by the fact that the writer of the article, hazy as to when the " sloopers " left for America, suggests the year 1824. It is to be noted, however, that the reference to Peerson is couched in unusually emphatic and specific terms. In conjunction with the question here at issue, the mere fact that such a reference occurred at all in the early records must be considered a confirmation of the genuineness of the Madland letter.

" Restauration " sailed in 1825, he did not accompany the sloop party. It has been well known that when the sloop arrived at New York, Peerson was there to meet it. The Madland letter seems to furnish the explanation of this.

Apropos of the suggestion that the descendants of Madland know nothing about the letter, it may be said that a grandson of Halvarsen, to whom Madland wrote the letter, not only knew about it but also had it in his possession. What became of the original Peerson letter is not known. It was not addressed to Madland and it is reasonable to suppose that it was merely lent to him for the purpose of making a copy. Madland copied it a few days before he sailed for America as a member of the " sloop party." It was natural of him to wish to let his friends know about the prospects in America.

Another of Professor Anderson's counts against the letter is that it states that Peerson went to Geneva, Ontario County, New York, to make land purchases for himself and his friends in Norway. This item, however, is only another confirmation of its genuineness. The agent of the Pultney Land Office at Geneva was Joseph Fellows.[17] This office controlled lands both in Ontario County and in Orleans County. The " sloop folk," as is well known, took land in Orleans County. Moreover, Joseph Fellows met the party in New York when it arrived in 1825, and he sold to its members their land in Orleans County; on both of these interesting points Mr. Anderson himself is our authority.[18] The Peerson letter of 1824 appears to supply the reason for Fellows' contact with the sloopers. Peerson does not state definitely the location of the land that he selected; the present writer at first suspected that it was in Ontario County, perhaps near Farmington. But it is to be noted that Peerson went to Rochester to buy a stove.

[17] See *ante*, ch. 2, n. 43.
[18] Anderson, *Norwegian Immigration*, 64, 77.

If Rochester was a natural trading center for him, it is reasonable to suppose that his land was in the region tributary to that town. Consequently the letter is susceptible of the interpretation that the pieces of land selected by Peerson were in the Kendall settlement, near Rochester, to which the " sloop folk " actually went. When the " sloop folk " arrived in 1825, newspapers announced that their destination was Ontario County — but they went to Orleans County. Was this announcement a mistake resulting from the fact that Fellows' land office was in Ontario County?

The letter indicates that Andrew Stangeland went to America with Peerson in 1824. Professor Anderson states emphatically that Stangeland came on the sloop in 1825. On this point the genuineness of the letter has received interesting support since Professor Anderson published his article in 1924. When Dr. O. N. Norlie was preparing his *History of the Norwegian People in America* for the Norwegian-American Centennial of 1925 he communicated with Mr. B. F. Stangeland, a son of the supposed " slooper." Dr. Norlie writes (p. 123) : " B. F. Stangeland says that his father, Andrew Stangeland, came over before the sloop, and did not, as far as he knows, return to Norway and come back on the sloop." It is hardly credible that such a family tradition could be in existence if Stangeland really had come on the sloop. This bit of information, taken in conjunction with other items, appears to be a striking confirmation of the genuineness of the document under discussion. The ordinary rôles in historical procedure are here reversed, for a stray bit of family tradition confirms the accuracy of contemporaneous documentary evidence.

The Madland letter is unquestionably genuine. It makes a valuable contribution to our understanding of the migration of 1825 and thus to the history of Norwegian immigration to the United States.

2. WHEN DID "RESTAURATIONEN" SAIL FROM STAVANGER?

The traditional date of the sailing of "Restaurationen" from Stavanger in 1825 is July 4, but *Den Norske Rigstidende* for July 25, 1825, contains an item dated at Stavanger on July 7 which states that the emigrants left "Iforgaars," that is, the day before yesterday, or July 5. *Cf.* on this item and its significance Malmin, in *Decorah-Posten*, November 21, 1924, and an exchange of opinion between Malmin and Anderson, *ibid.*, November 28, December 12, 19, 1924. One or two small items may be added to the discussion of this nice question. Simon Pedersen Lihme, one of the sloop's passengers, was present as late as Monday, July 4, 1825, at a hearing before the Stavanger *Bytingsret*, where certain financial matters were disposed of and he received official permission to emigrate. The record does not indicate at what hour of the day the council met, but the item at any rate makes it probable that the "Restauration" did not sail on the morning of that day. S. A., Bergen: Stavanger byfogeds bytingsprotokoll C no. 33, 1821–1826, fol. 270b. In Stavanger the present writer learned of an interesting family tradition. Mrs. Serine Bjørnsen of that city, a granddaughter of the sloopers Thormod and Sigrid Madland, says that Madland started with six children: Serine, Gurine, Rakel, Marta, Kristine, and Jens. The last three became seasick and earnestly requested to be returned to Stavanger. They prevailed upon their parents, and the "Restauration" returned to "Dusevigen" and landed them. One of the three, Marta, later married in Stavanger and became the mother of the present Mrs. Bjørnsen, now in her nineties. Mrs. Bjørnsen's daughter, Marie Halvorsen of Stavanger, reports the story in a letter to the writer dated March 28, 1929. This tradition, which tempts one to suggest that the sloop started on the fourth, perhaps late in the day, but returned and took its final departure on the fifth, is not confirmed by the health record dated July 4, 1825, and signed by Løwold at the Stavanger *Raadstue,* for the latter gives the number of passengers as 45 and of the crew as 7. If the tradition were based on fact one would expect to find the number of passengers recorded as 48. The Løwold document is printed in *Norges-posten* for October 8, 1925. This health record shows that the sloop was officially " cleared " on July 4 for sailing, but this release may have come late in the day, and the sloop may not have departed until the next morning. The passengers may all have gone on board on the fourth, thus fixing that date in their minds as the date of their farewell to Stavanger. This is of course conjecture. Meanwhile the contemporary record of the date of departure must take precedence over the traditional date. Such revisions of tradition are common. This very voyage of the " Restauration " affords, in fact, another striking illustration. Anderson, following an unusually explicit tradition, says that the sloopers arrived in Funchal on Thursday, July 28, and left Sunday, July 31. *Norwegian Immigration,* 59. The item is the more striking because July 28 did indeed fall on a Thursday in 1825. The truth of the matter, however, proved by contemporary records, is that the " Restauration " arrived at the Madeira port on August 1 and sailed on August 7. See *ante,* ch. 2, n. 67. The case gains in comparative interest when it is noted that the Swedish-Norwegian consul at Madeira officially cleared the sloop's papers for sailing on August 6, the day before its departure.

A word may well be added here about the name of the sloop. It was built at Hardanger in 1801 and was probably known first as the " Emanuel " and then as " Haabet." After being rebuilt and enlarged in 1820, it was dubbed the " Restauration." This name is probably derived from this " restoration " of 1820 and is without deep symbolical significance. See Scheel, in *Nordmandsforbundet*, 16: 325–326.

3.   THE PASSENGERS ON " RESTAURATIONEN "

Unfortunately no contemporary list of the passengers on the sloop " Restaurationen " of 1825 has been found. The official manifest made for the New York Customs House may have been sent to the department of the treasury at Washington, but that department's records prior to 1830 have been destroyed by fire. Anderson, in *Norwegian Immigration*, 91–93, has drawn up a traditional list of the 53 persons on board the sloop when it reached New York, but documentary evidence makes necessary some changes. The present writer tentatively offers the present revised list: Lars Larsen, wife, and child; Daniel Stenson Rossadal, wife, and five children; Cornelius Nelson Hersdal, wife, and four children; Johannes Stene, wife, and child; Oyen Thompson, wife, and three children; Simon Pedersen Lihme, wife, and three children; Thormod Madland, wife, and three children; Torwad Holde and wife; Henry Christopherson Hervig and wife; Nels Nelson Hersdal and wife; Lars Olsen Helland; Peder Eriksen Meeland; Johannes Jacobsen Soledal; Gudmund Danielsen Haugaas; Jacob Anderson Slogvig; Sara Larsen; Ole Johnson (Eie); George Johnson; Thorstein Olson Bjaadland; Andrew Dahl; Halvor Iverson; Nels Thompson; and Ole Olsen Hetletvedt.

Andrew Stangeland (no. 51 in Anderson's list) went to America in 1824. *Cf.* the letter published in the present Appendix, no. 1, and Stangeland family tradition noted in Norlie, *Norwegian People in America*, 123. Knud Anderson Slogvig (no. 39 in Anderson) emigrated in 1830, as is proved by a parish record in S. A., Bergen: Kirkebøker, Skjold, 5 (1815–1830), folio 94, no. 12. There is of course a possibility that he went on the sloop, returned to Norway, and re-emigrated in 1830. It should be noted that Rynning refers to him as " one of the first emigrants," but he gives no suggestion that Slogvig's visit to Norway in 1835 was not his first return. *Rynning's True Account of America*, 74. The evidence of a grandson of Johannes Stene, reported by Norlie, *op. cit.*, 123, indicates that Johannes Stene and wife were accompanied by only one child, whereas in Anderson's list two children are allotted to them. The contemporary list of the " Restauration " crew (see *ante*, ch. 2, n. 47) adds the name of Johannes Jacobsen Soledal; and the report of Bishop Munch dated August 27, 1825, adds Torwad Holde and wife. R. A., Oslo: Kirkedept., 3die Aflevering, 27. Cadbury, in *Studies and Records*, 1: 63, suggests reducing the number of Simon Pedersen Lihme's children from three to one, but the source which he cites does not appear to support the suggested change. The Munch report of August 27, 1825, refers to " Simon Lihme with wife and children " as being among the emigrants.

INDEX

INDEX

For the convenience of users the characters *æ* and *ø*, which occur frequently in names cited, are alphabeted respectively as *ae* and *o*.